SOCIALIST BANKING AND MONETARY CONTROL: THE EXPERIENCE OF POLAND

Soviet and East European Studies

Editorial Board

The National Association for Soviet and East European Studies exists for the purpose of promoting study and research on the social sciences as they relate to the Soviet Union and the countries of Eastern Europe. The Monograph Series is intended to promote the publication of works presenting substantial and original research in the economics, politics, sociology and modern history of the USSR and Eastern Europe.

SOCIALIST BANKING AND MONETARY CONTROL

THE EXPERIENCE OF POLAND

T. M. PODOLSKI

CAMBRIDGE

AT THE UNIVERSITY PRESS

1973

Published by the Syndics of the Cambridge University Press
Bentley House, 200 Euston Road, London NW1 2DB
American Branch: 32 East 57th Street, New York, N.Y.10022

© Cambridge University Press 1972

Library of Congress Catalogue Card Number: 72–76088

ISBN: 0 521 08598 5

Printed in Great Britain by
William Clowes & Sons Limited, London, Colchester and Beccles

Contents

Preface

So far the subjects of banking, credit and monetary control in socialist (here meaning Soviet-type socialist) economies, though not completely neglected,[1] have not been popular among Western scholars. Certainly there have been few attempts at a comprehensive presentation of the subjects, which is surprising in view of the fact that since the mid-fifties the role of banking and of bank finance and control in socialist economies has been considerably increased by successive economic reforms, and that in the sixties there was a remarkable surge of interest in and controversy about banking and monetary policy in Western economics. It is thus hoped that this book helps to fill a gap in Soviet studies and at the same time that it will be of comparative interest to economists, in particular those specialising in monetary economics.

It is now generally recognised that there is a close relationship in capitalist economies between economic development (development of 'real infrastructure') and financial development (development of 'financial superstructure'), though the direction of causation between the two is a matter of dispute. In socialist planning the structure and activity of financial institutions, which are almost exclusively banks, are deliberately adapted to changing methods and policies of national economic management. The purpose of this book is to describe systematically this process of adaptation, using as the chief example the Polish economy, on which the author has been fortunate enough to have gathered a substantial amount of statistical data, enabling him to identify and appraise different approaches to banking, finance and monetary control. As far as Polish banking and credit are concerned, the book presents a comprehensive analysis of their development since the war.

Throughout the book attempts are made at international comparisons. Soviet experience in particular is relevant. However, attempts

[1] A number of works are mentioned in Part I of the book.

are also made at comparisons with Western economies, especially
in the realm of monetary control (defined in chapter 1). Thus, although the study is not claimed to be fully comparative, the author
has endeavoured to pinpoint some similarities and striking differences
between Western and socialist banking, credit and monetary policy.

Attention is focused mainly on the banking structure, the scope
of credit finance and monetary control. However, to appreciate the
role of these in a changing approach to national economic planning
and development it is necessary to relate them to the overall political
and economic situation at a particular time, and especially to such
matters as devolution of decision taking, the autonomy of enterprises
and budgetary and other sources of non-bank finance. Care has thus
been taken to present matters of specific interest in their broader
setting, so that a reader not acquainted with the general economics
of socialist countries may get a reasonably full appreciation of the
subject without having to refer elsewhere for additional information.

The structure of the book needs a brief explanation. Part I may
appear somewhat odd, as its three chapters deal with diverse matters
ranging from aspects of Western monetary theory to the development
of the Soviet banking and monetary system. They do, however,
present methodological, definitional and background matters utilised
in the rest of the book. Chapter 1 should prove useful mainly as a
background for some comparative (East–West) sections of the book
(especially in chapter 8). Chapters 2 and 3 are helpful mainly in
understanding the development of the Polish credit system.

Chapter 1 contains a miscellany of information, including the
definition of monetary control as understood in this study. It also
gives a brief account of the main issues in Western monetary controversy upon which comments are made, in the light of socialist
monetary experience, later in the book. This should enable Sovieto-
logists who are not economists to obtain a superficial awareness of
disputed questions in Western monetary economics. Special treatment is given to the 'real bills' theory which, as the book attempts to
show, has considerable application to Soviet-type banking and credit.

Chapter 2 is of key importance. It reviews and analyses the development of Soviet banking and principles of monetary control. These
principles were, at any rate up to the late fifties, accepted by all
Soviet bloc economies (including Poland after 1948) as the principles
of socialist monetary management. Thus the chapter deals with the
origins of socialist banking and monetary control, which must be

understood to appreciate fully their implementation and performance in the Polish economy.

Chapter 3 describes the role of banking and credit in pre-war Poland, a neglected but interesting subject worthy of a more probing treatment, but here presented merely as a sketch, useful to the understanding of post-war developments, particularly during the 'Polish road to socialism' of 1945–9 (discussed in chapter 4).

Part II of the book deals with banking and monetary control in centralised planning. Chapter 4 gives an account of an interesting experiment with an eclectic financial system, combining elements of pre-war Polish and Soviet financial systems with some original Polish solutions. The system was quickly replaced by the Soviet 'model' in the reforms of 1948–50 described in chapter 5. Chapter 6 is devoted to an appraisal of the efficacy of Soviet-type monetary control, using the example of Poland.

Part III covers developments after 1955. This was a period of frequent changes, which invariably involved financial adjustments imposing new tasks and new banking practices upon the banks. Chapters are divided on the basis of the successive financial changes which were thought necessary to carry out the policy of economic decentralisation. In chapters 7 to 9 interest centres on changes in the principles and techniques of monetary control, though other aspects of banking, including credit finance of investment, are not neglected. The main reason for this is that up to the mid-sixties, the period covered by the two chapters, the banking system was the main supplier of short-term credit. The role of what in the West would be the capital market was performed mainly by the budget. After the reforms of 1965–6 (chapter 10) there were no substantial changes in monetary policy and attention turns mainly to the finance of investment, which was to play a key role in the transition from 'extensive' to 'intensive' economic development. Chapter 11, dealing with the latest (1969–70) reforms, is almost entirely devoted to changes in banking and the attempt to use predominantly bank, instead of budgetary, finance of capital investment.

The most important function of socialist banking and credit is to finance and control enterprises in the socialised sector (viz. the predominant sector) of the economy, and it is this which receives most attention. However, as there has been a growing tendency to expand the finance of private ventures (instalment trading, private housing, private agriculture), a brief review of credit finance in the private sector of the economy is given in Appendix A. Other appendices contain mainly statistical tables. Tables whose numbers are prefixed with a capital letter (e.g. Table A1) refer to tables found in Appendices (e.g. Appendix A) at the back of the book. A list of abbreviations used follows the preface.

The book draws heavily upon a Ph.D. thesis presented at Birmingham University in December 1970. It was completed under the supervision of Prof. R. W. Davies, the Director of the Centre for Russian and East European Studies, for whose guidance and criticisms, always constructive and inspiring, I am very grateful.

To the National Bank of Poland I owe an immense debt for supplying me with most valuable material, both unpublished and published.

My final expression of gratitude goes to my wife, who encouraged my work not least by patiently typing its numerous drafts.

Abbreviations

For abbreviations of titles of periodicals and other publications see Selected Bibliography. (s) signifies that an abbreviation refers to the Soviet economy, (P) to the Polish economy.

AB	Agricultural Bank (P)
BCT	Bank of Craft and Trade (P)
BLC	Bank for Long-Term Credit (s)
BMS	Bureaux of Mutual Settlements (s and P)
CC	Central Committee (s and P)
CEC	Central Executive Committee (s)
CM	Council of Ministers (s and P)
CPC	Council of People's Commissars (s)
CPO	Central Planning Office (P)
CSB	Common Savings Bank (P)
DF	Development Fund (P)
DLC	Department of Long-Term Credit (s)
ECCM	Economic Committee of the Council of Ministers (P)
IB	Investment Bank (P)
IFA	Investment fund of association (P)
IRF	Investment and repairs fund (P)
MB	Municipal Bank (P)
MIT	Ministry of Industry and Trade (P)
NBP	National Bank of Poland (P)
NEB	National Economic Bank (P)
NEP	New Economic Policy (s)
PC	Planning Commission (P)
PCNL	Polish Committee for National Liberation (P)
RCBs	Rural Co-operative Banks (P)
SAB	State Agricultural Bank (P)
SCEP	State Commission for Economic Planning (P)
SLCs	Savings and Loans Co-operatives (P)
SYP	Six Year Plan (P)
TB	Trade Bank (P)
TYP	Three Year Plan (P)
UWCB	Union of Workers' Co-operatives Bank (P)
bil	billion (1000 mil.)

The transliteration of Russian words follows the system proposed under the British Standard 2979C:1959.

PART I

Background information

1

Monetary control: meaning, problems of comparative treatment, some relevant Western concepts

Some difficulties of comparative treatment of monetary control

It is not possible in a single book to present all aspects of money and banking in a reasonably advanced economy. This study thus focuses on certain important aspects of socialist money and banking. As until recently the socialist banking systems were essentially short-term credit suppliers, much attention is given to problems of monetary control. Throughout the book the treatment of monetary control (based on short-term credit) is separate from credit finance and control of investment. It may be useful at the outset to make clear what is understood by monetary control and what aspects of money receive less attention.

The same basic problem of national economic management faces both Western and socialist economies. It is the selection of priorities from among a multitude of possible economic objectives and the consequent adoption of policies designed to apportion scarce means to achieve them. Economic calculations of one kind or another must be made in the solution of this problem. Money as a standard of measurement is used in both types of economies, but the measurement of values for purposes of decision taking is different. It is not so much money but prices which reflect value, especially in a market economy. Money is merely the 'third commodity' (due often to its general acceptability as a means of exchange), which serves as a common denominator reducing heterogeneous commodities to uniformly denominated units, thus facilitating economic calculations. But, to explain why differing amounts of, for instance, apples and bread, pig iron and tractors, effort of miners and teachers, are exchanged per unit of money, one would have to examine forces going well beyond the subject of money, however defined. Furthermore, decision taking by the entrepreneur (who may be a 'firm' or a 'central planner') may well depend not merely on the availability of money, or a system of relative prices and its reliability for purposes of resource allocation, but also on such factors as accounting systems, conventions used in costing, and non-economic considerations based on political or ideological convictions. Thus in a money economy, regardless of whether it is socialist or capitalist, almost every economic act is in some way connected with money. Such vital economic activities as price formation and entrepreneurial decision taking in particular may be regarded as constituting a part of monetary management. Here, however, money would be only one among many factors, and in many cases it is its technical aspects (as unit of measurement, means of exchange, store of value) which would be relevant.

Issues of the definition of money, of its technical functions, of price formation and of decision-taking processes are not the prime objects of this study, though they are not irrelevant and do receive some consideration. One of its essential objects is to investigate the use made of some monetary variables, mainly bank credit and interest rates, in socialist national economic management. Thus, in terms of institutions, the study concentrates mainly on the relationships between the banking sector and other institutions in a socialist economy, chiefly enterprises. The view is taken that an analysis of the relationships which subsist in socialist planning between banks, as institutions charged with the task of manipulating monetary variables, and enterprises, as units which are the ultimate allocators of resources, not only allows us to make propositions about the efficacy of monetary control, but also throws some light on the nature of money and the way in which it fulfils its various technical functions. The study is, therefore, in no way intended to present a fully comprehensive account of money in a socialist economy; it is only intended to elaborate in detail one of its aspects, that connected with monetary control. Its other aspects are investigated only in so far as they are relevant to the main theme of monetary control as defined above.

An attempt is also made to compare socialist monetary control with that in Western economies, especially the UK. This, in conjunction with the fact that it was thought wise to consider socialist monetary control in various settings at different points in history, produces serious difficulties of presentation.

Money in the context of monetary control has been among the most controversial subjects in economics. One of its difficulties is that whereas economics, and in particular Western economics, has sought to discover some generally applicable principles of money and monetary control, financial markets, which in relatively developed economies generate claims considered to constitute money supply, are continuously changing. Just as no two economies are the same, no two financial markets are the same and it may well be that, though we may expect some common regularities to occur in diverse economies,[1] we may not have a generally applicable theory of money and monetary control. Their nature would differ with such underlying factors as the nature of the economic system and the level and the policy of economic development. In view of this it has been decided to present the subject of socialist banking and monetary control in historical perspective, by analysing its general strategy, its tactics and its efficacy in various stages of economic development. An additional reason for this approach is that political and administrative factors play an important part in socialist monetary management. Government decisions are often of greater importance in socialist management than the observed propensities or regularities of social and economic behaviour which form the basis of Western economic theorising. It is interesting to observe how government decisions have affected, or have been affected by, monetary considerations over a period of time.

An attempt has been made to anchor the analysis of socialist monetary control and institutions to well known propositions found in Western monetary economics. It is hoped that this adds to the clarity of analysis, makes it more palatable to Western economists and shows that, in spite of considerable differences in the economic systems, some Western concepts may be usefully deployed in analysing socialist money and banking. Indeed, particular attention is paid to those elements which occur in both socialist and Western monetary control.

This type of comparative treatment, however, is difficult not simply because we are dealing with different economic systems, but also because of differences in economic theorising and because there are no universally accepted views on the nature of money and

---

[1] In an interesting study (*Financial Structure and Development*, Yale, 1969) R. W. Goldsmith discovered a number of 'regularities' in the financial development of various countries. The study is, however, confined mainly to non-communist economies, and the author doubts whether the study enables us to formulate a truly general theory of financial development.

monetary policy in the West, in spite of a great upsurge in research, discussion and enquiry (Radcliffe Committee in the UK, Commission on Money and Credit in the USA, Royal Commission on Banking and Finance in Canada) on the workings of monetary systems in the late fifties and in the sixties. The Western economist has been keenly interested in the theoretical foundations of monetary control, whereas the East European economist has tended to give priority to the explanation of some officially accepted principles of monetary control and to the implementation of these in national economic administration. Indeed a hint of the theoretical basis of Soviet-type monetary management has been given by Western economists writing on Soviet monetary affairs.

A superficial review of the theoretical foundations of Western monetary control

Before elaborating the last proposition it may be useful to take as a starting point the Western monetary theories to which references are made in the text. For our purposes the state of Western monetary debate may be summarised, indulging quite obviously in gross oversimplification, by reference to three broad groups of theories: (A) those based on the concept of exogenous money supply, (B) those treating money supply as an endogenous variable and (C) those postulating the need to control the total flow of credit, rather than some strictly defined stock of money.

(A) Much monetary theorising in the West has been concerned not with the technical functions of money mentioned earlier, but with the search for a monetary variable M, over which monetary authorities have full control, enabling them to affect the level of aggregate demand. The most generally accepted theories, including the Keynesian and quantity theories, take the view that 'money matters', money (viz. variable M) being currency and bank deposits. The key propositions of such theories are that money supply is an exogenous variable and that the money demand function (whether in terms of a relatively simple Keynesian liquidity preference schedule or a more complex function regarding money as one of a number of ways of holding wealth) is stable, enabling us to predict the effects of changes in money supply. The most debatable issues in these theories concern the explanation of the way in which changes in money variables affect real variables. For instance, the mechanism which translates monetary changes into real changes is clearly specified in Keynesian models, but has some serious weaknesses (e.g. the simplicity of the liquidity preference, the interest elasticity of investment demand); quantity theorists, relying mainly on observation (and testing based on regression and correlation techniques), propose causation going from the variable M to real variables, without convincingly explaining the mechanics of causation. Though the nature of the transmission mechanism of causation from M to real variables has by no means been resolved, the views discussed here have provided the theoretical foundations of monetary policy in many western countries, including the UK.

(*B*) There have, however, always been economists who disputed the exogenous nature of money supply, and its power to affect real variables, claiming that money adjusts to the requirements of the economy. They deny the validity of monetary causes of economic disturbances and the potency of monetary control over aggregate spending. Such views may broadly be identified with the nineteenth-century Banking School of monetary theory, whose present-day supporters may be said to be J. R. Hicks and N. Kaldor.[1] More is said about this approach to monetary economics later, as it has some relevance to monetary control in socialist economies.

(*C*) The third group of monetary theories is really a variation of the preceding one. The great difficulty of defining money (variable M) is strongly emphasised. It is held that, of the large number of claims existing in an economy, it is difficult to single out those which may indisputably be defined as money. Furthermore, control of M as defined above makes little or no impact on aggregate demand, because control over bank credit is easily offset by a net (viz. over and above savings flowing into financial institutions) expansion of credit from other sources (non-bank intermediaries, trade credit). Thus monetary policy based on the control of money supply is frustrated by a compensatory creation of claims which are good substitutes for money conventionally defined. The policy prescription based on such theories, which in England may be identified with the Radcliffe Committee and R. S. Sayers,[2] is that monetary

---

[1] J. R. Hicks, *Critical Essays in Monetary Theory* (Oxford, 1967) esp. chs. 1–3; N. Kaldor, 'The new monetarism', *Lloyds Bank Review*, no. 97, July 1970.

[2] *Committee on the Working of the Monetary System* (HMSO: London, 1969); R. S. Sayers, 'Monetary thought and monetary policy in England', *Economic Journal*, December 1960.

authorities must control the total flow of credit ('general liquidity') rather than merely a narrowly defined stock of money.

Though, as stated above, there is no universally accepted monetary theory, monetary authorities in the West appear to have been impressed by the views outlined in (*A*) and to some extent by those in (*C*). This does not mean to say that the authorities have piecemeal accepted a specific theory in formulating their policies. They have, however, endeavoured to control money supply and interest rates in order, with the aid of other instruments of control (e.g. fiscal policy), to affect the level of employment, growth, price stability and the balance of payments. The Governor of the Bank of England recently stated:

The conduct of monetary policy is never a simple matter. Our understanding of the links between the financial world on the one hand and the real world of output and spending on the other is far from perfect. There is a wide divergence of view about how effective monetary policy is in influencing spending and through what particular channels it should primarily aim to operate.[1]

Monetary control has thus been a method of controlling the level of aggregate demand – a macroeconomic tool of national economic management.

In contrast, monetary control in Soviet-type economies is primarily a microeconomic control – control by banks over the activity of individual firms. Each firm must bank with only one bank (usually a branch of the central bank), which settles its debts, in which cash reserves are kept, and which is the exclusive source of credit.

The importance of bank credit

An important element common to Western and socialist monetary control is the role played by bank credit. In the West control of money supply has become essentially the control of the total volume of bank deposits. This the authorities try to achieve by affecting the demand for bank credit (e.g. by acting on the rates of interest paid by borrowers), and/or by acting on the liquidity of commercial banks, and/or by imposition of direct restrictions on advances. Where (as in the UK) monetary control has been extended to other financial intermediaries, continuous monetary control (e.g. based on a fixed

[1] 'Monetary management in the U.K.', *BEQB*, vol. 11, no. 1 (1971) p. 37.

minimum reserve ratio) tends to apply only to commercial banks; other financial institutions are intermittently 'requested' to adjust their lending. Thus, in spite of attempts to extend monetary control to other institutions, attention is still focused on banks.[1]

Two points may be stressed. First, currency issues, as opposed to issues of credit, are of secondary importance in peacetime monetary control both in the West and in socialist economies. They are quantitatively less important and frequently are governed by technical (e.g. seasonal) considerations. Furthermore in both types of economies the currency in circulation is a declining proportion of other financial claims. In short, currency is merely 'the small change' of the financial systems.

However, the illustration of this is not a straightforward matter. Table 1 gives some indicators, though these are by no means strictly comparable. In Western economies, especially, the definition of money supply is a major problem, which cannot be elaborated here. As stated earlier it is debatable whether some claims of the many have the unique characteristics of 'moneyness' and can therefore be indisputably classed as money supply. The table thus uses three officially published concepts of money supply in the UK, of which $M2$ and $M3$ would probably be closer to the 'money supply' used in the columns referring to Poland. Although $M3$ is sometimes known as the 'broad definition' of money it does in fact omit liabilities of many financial institutions in the UK. If this definition were broadened to include some of these, namely building societies, trustee savings banks (special investment departments) and finance houses, then the ratio of currency to that total would be 10.8% for the end of 1969; the inclusion of insurance (life) companies would further lower this ratio to 7.4%.

Thus the salient feature of both Western and socialist monetary control is the attempt to achieve certain objectives by manipulating credit conditions.[2] Indeed, in socialist literature, the terms 'monetary policy' or 'monetary control' are used comparatively rarely, preference being given to the term 'credit control'.

[1] At the time of writing measures have been announced changing the techniques of monetary control in the UK. See *BEQB*, vol. 11, no. 2 (1971) pp. 189–94, 'Reserve Ratios and Special Deposits, *Bank of England*, Sept. 1971.

[2] It may be noted that the Canadian Royal Commission on Banking and Finance (reporting in 1964) in evaluating the efficacy of monetary policy specifically analysed the effect of 'credit conditions' on aggregate expenditure (see esp. ch. 24).

Table 1

Currency in circulation in relation to other bank liabilities in the UK and Poland 1963–9

(*percentages based on data of balances outstanding at the end of the year*)

	UK			Poland	
	Currency with the public as % of[1]:			Currency with the public as % of 'money supply'[2]	Preceding column + cash balances in socialised enterprises as % of 'money supply'[2]
Year	$M_1(1)$	$M_2(1)$	$M_3(1)$		
1963	31.7	21.4	19.9	13.8	14.4
1964	33.6	22.3	20.6	13.8	14.6
1965	34.9	22.6	20.6	13.4	14.1
1966	35.4	22.5	20.2	13.0	13.6
1967	34.4	21.8	19.1	12.3	13.0
1968	33.7	21.1	18.1	–	12.6
1969	35.5	22.0	18.5	–	11.2

Notes:

[1] M_1–M_3 are series of money supply officially published in the UK. M_1 includes notes and coin + current deposit bank accounts of private sector residents denominated in sterling. M_2 is M_1 + sterling deposit accounts of private sector residents + deposits of discount houses. M_3 consists of notes and coin outside banks + all resident deposits with UK banking sector in sterling or foreign currency. For explanations see: A note on definitions of money supply, *Economic Trends* no. 202 (Aug. 1970) p. xi.

[2] Here measured as total balance sheet liabilities of the banking system. For more details see table B1b.

Sources: *Economic Trends*, p. xiv. GUS – *RSF 1945–1967*, p. 232; NBP – *Information Bulletin 1970*, p. 42.

Secondly, in a socialist economy banks, whose functions are strictly defined, comprise the whole system of financial institutions. In contrast, in a Western economy banks, whose legal status and definition in economic terms often present difficulties, are merely one of a number of financial intermediaries comprising the financial sector. In the UK at the end of 1969 the deposits of the UK deposit banks, which the monetary authorities have regarded as especially important for purposes of monetary control, were 75% of the deposits in the remainder of the 'banking sector' – national giro, accepting houses, overseas banks, discount markets[1] – and 48.1% of the assets

[1] *BEQB* vol. 11, no. 2 (1971) p. 242.

held by some non-bank financial intermediaries: insurance (life) companies, building societies, trustee savings banks (special investments department) and finance houses.[1]

Bearing in mind the above differences, concentration on the control of the supply and cost of bank credit allows us to investigate the most essential aspect of monetary control and achieve some comparability between monetary control in the West and in socialist planning. In the West special attention is paid to bank credit because bank deposits are considered to be the larger part of money supply, because monetary authorities tended to lean towards theories proposing causation between money supply and other variables (e.g. national income level), because deposit banks are among the largest financial institutions and because they were thought to be able to 'create' credit (and hence to create money).[2] In soviet-type economies control of the supply and the cost of credit is considered to be the most appropriate form of bank control, though, as will be seen later, it is not the only form. Socialist banks also exercise forms of control (e.g. over wage funds of enterprises) which are completely alien to Western banking systems. One further difficulty occurs in a socialist system, namely the growing tendency to use credit for financing investment. The term monetary (or credit) control is reserved for control via the supply and/or cost of short-term credit, making it roughly comparable with the Western practice. Credit finance of investment in a socialist economy is really a counterpart of the Western finance of investment via various instruments customarily traded in stock exchanges. Thus bank finance (and control) of investment is treated separately from monetary control throughout the book.

To sum up, the controversial nature of money and monetary control and the specificity of Western and socialist monetary systems necessitate a loose definition of monetary control in terms of attempts to achieve certain objectives by using monetary means, in particular bank credit supply and/or interest rates. Whenever comparisons between Western and socialist economies are made it is necessary to

[1] Without insurance (life) companies the ratio is 100.1%, 'The Financial Institutions', *BEQB*, vol. 10, no. 4 (1970) p. 425; vol. 11, no. 1 (1971) pp. 54–64.
[2] It must be mentioned that, especially in the last decade in the UK, the rate of growth of deposit banks has been relatively slower than that of other financial intermediaries. Moreover, it is now believed that multiple credit creation is not a unique characteristic of deposit banks.

bear in mind the basic differences between the economies and especially the fact that, whatever the ultimate objectives of monetary policies may be, control over bank credit in the West is a macroeconomic method of control, viz. operating primarily on the level of aggregate demand, whereas control over bank credit in socialist economies is a microeconomic control calculated to check or influence the business behaviour of individual enterprises.

The 'real bills' theory of banking

It has become commonplace in Western literature on Soviet-type money and banking to refer to the influence of the 'real bills' theory on Soviet monetary thought and management, particularly up to the mid-1950s.[1] Though few specific details on the subject are given, one infers that Western writers disapproved of the credit system based on such theoretical premises, whether in Soviet or Western conditions. The following points emerge from their rather scanty observations on the subject: (*a*) the 'real bills' theory influenced Soviet and East European economists, (*b*) the acceptance of the theory, which has been discarded in the West, indicated a lack of sophistication in monetary thought in the East, (*c*) its acceptance resulted in liberal credit policies encouraging inflation. Because the author takes issue with the above view, because the 'real bills' theory is today rarely considered in Western economics in the form in which it is relevant to us and because it is convenient to borrow some terms from its jargon and employ them in analysing socialist credit principles, a brief account of the theory may be useful.

Monetary theories, and especially policy prescriptions based upon them, rarely make sense unless they are discussed in their historical

---

[1] F. D. Holzman, *Soviet Taxation* (Cambridge Mass., 1955) pp. 27 and 49. D. R. Hodgman, 'Soviet Monetary Controls Through the Banking System' in G. Grossman (Ed.) *Value and Plan* (Berkeley, 1960) p. 109. Holzman's comment on Hodgman's article, *Ibid.*, pp. 127 and 129. G. Garvy, 'The Role of the State Bank in Soviet Planning' in J. Degras (Ed.) *Soviet Planning* (Oxford, 1964) p. 48; *Money Banking and Credit in Eastern Europe* (Federal Reserve Bank of New York, 1966) p. 68. J. M. Montias, 'Bank Lending and Fiscal Policy in Eastern Europe' in G. Grossman (Ed.) *Money and Plan* (Berkeley, 1968) p. 56. In the above studies reference is often made to R. P. Powell's unpublished study on Soviet Monetary Policy (1952) which apparently criticised Soviet acceptance of the 'real bills' theory on the grounds that it allowed excessive credit expansion, rendering monetary policy ineffective against inflation.

setting and in relation to the objectives of monetary authorities and the structure and practices of the banking mechanism to which they refer. The 'real bills' theory has a long history, during which it was expounded in different economic contexts.[1]

The first concise formulation of the theory was by Adam Smith, who, it must be remembered, postulated it in the environment of small competing firms, of small-scale unit banking engaged mainly in discounting bills, in the absence of central banking as understood today, and above all in an environment of currencies convertible into gold and of expanding international trade.[2] Smith made two main points: (a) credit against real bills, by which he meant bills drawn for values (goods) received, allowed firms to dispense with cash reserves[3] and (b) 'The whole paper money of every kind...never can exceed the value of the gold and silver...which...would circulate there, if there was no paper money.'[4] He argued that any excessive paper money would be returned to banks and exchanged for gold and silver, which could then possibly be sold abroad.

Smith's views on banking led to a crude formulation of the 'real bills' theory, namely that as long as banks advanced money against bills financing working capital of industry and trade, notes could not be over-issued causing inflationary pressure. In this crude form the theory was used by the Bank of England directors to justify the actions of the bank (which included an increase in note issue) during the French wars, when currency convertibility into gold was suspended.

The theory was later developed by disciples of the Banking School in the monetary controversy surrounding the Bank Charter Act of 1844. Broadly speaking the Banking School agreed with their opponents (the Currency School) that bank notes should be convertible into gold, but refused to accept the proposition that an automatic control of note issue by the inflow our outflow of gold amounted to a

---

[1] Reference to it may be found especially in L. W. Mints, *A History of Banking Theory* (Chicago, 1945); F. W. Fetter, *'Development of British Monetary Orthodoxy 1797–1875* (Cambridge, Mass., 1965).

[2] A. Smith, *The Wealth of Nations* (1776), (London, 1965) pp. 250–94.

[3] 'When a bank discounts to a merchant a real bill of exchange drawn by a real creditor upon a real debtor, and which, as soon as it becomes due, is really paid by that debtor, it only advances to him a part of the value which he would otherwise be obliged to keep by him unemployed and in ready money for answering occasional demands.' *Ibid.* p. 269.

[4] *Ibid.* p. 265.

monetary strategy ensuring a crisis-free economic development. They refused to believe that phenomena such as inflation and falling exchange rates could be explained in purely monetary terms, suggesting that the supply of 'circulating medium' tended to adjust itself to demand and that note issue especially was governed by the 'needs of business'. In particular they developed the Smithian idea that excessive note issue automatically returned to the banking system. This was the essence of the 'law of reflux' which stated that, as long as banks were ready to convert notes into gold, over-issue and the consequent pressure on the price level would not occur.[1] The 'real bills' doctrine was now formulated in broader terms, laying down that banks should lend to satisfy genuine 'needs of business' and should avoid speculative lending. In this less specific form it had a significant impact on American monetary thought.

It may be interesting to note that though the 'real bills' theory originated in Britain it is rarely considered in modern British books on banking. American books on the other hand rarely omit a reference to 'real bills' doctrine (or its synonym 'the commercial loan' theory), though few of them approve of its principles. This is not surprising, as the doctrine had some impact on the US monetary policy before the second world war. In the past the Americans tended to blame banks for business depressions and looked for a formula for an 'elastic currency' capable of rising when demand for it increased.[2] Here the 'real bills' doctrine offered a solution. The 1864 National Bank Act was to some extent inspired by the theory. More important, its tenets were accepted in the 1913 Federal Reserve Act which created the Federal Reserve System (FRS). Indeed L. Currie claimed that 'The theory of banking underlying the Federal Reserve Act is that the primary function of banks is that of meeting the short-term borrowing needs of "legitimate" business.'[3] The culminating point in the influence of the doctrine on American credit policy came in the 1920s, when little reliance could be put on the automatic adjustment mechanism operating under the pre-war gold standard

[1] It may be noted that Marx approved of the 'law of reflux': 'The quantity of circulating notes is regulated by the turnover requirements, and every superfluous note wends its way back immediately to the issuer.' *Capital*, vol. 3 (1894) (Moscow, 1962) p. 512. Marxian views that changes in the price level are a cause rather than the effect of changes in money supply are also consistent with the tenets of the Banking School.

[2] P. B. Trescott, *Financing American Enterprise* (New York, 1963) pp. 152–6.

[3] *The Supply and Control of Money in the United States (1934)* (New York, 1968) p. 38.

because of war disruptions and post-war tendencies towards protection in international trade.[1] FRS concentrated mainly on supplying credit for seasonal needs and emergencies and not on control over the supply of money as understood today. Credit creation satisfying the 'needs of business' (mainly loans against self-liquidating securities such as 'real bills') was not thought to be inflationary, whereas speculative loans and credit created on the basis of government securities were deemed inflationary. In the Tenth Annual Report (1923) the Federal Reserve Board stated that 'The FRS is a system of productive credit. It is not a system of credit for either investment or speculative purposes. Credit in the service of agriculture, industry and trade may be described comprehensively as credit for productive use.'[2] It was on the basis of this report that D. H. Robertson formulated the term 'the Principle of Productive Credit'[3] which is quoted in Holzman's book.[4] It must be mentioned that the 'real bills' doctrine lurking behind this principle became the so-called *qualitative tests* of credit issue; the Federal Reserve authorities were also to apply *quantitative tests*, where credit supply was also to be justified by 'a commensurate increase in the Nation's aggregate productivity'.[5] The concepts just described are, of course, a part of the theories classified under (B) on page 7.

The 'real bills' theory was attacked almost from the very beginning of its existence. Its original Smithian formulation was rejected in a well-reasoned essay of H. Thornton who, though approving of the idea of lending against real bills as a principle of sound banking, thought that lending on good security by individual banks might not necessarily result in developments advantageous from the national point of view.[6] He feared (as indeed did Smith himself) that banks might sometimes unwittingly discount 'fictitious' bills; he was uneasy about the fact that the amount of trade bills in circulation was 'greater than the amount of all the bank notes of every kind' and about the fact that the amount of bills 'may be multiplied to an

---

[1] For a full discussion see E. R. Wicker, *Federal Reserve Monetary Policy 1917–1933* (New York, 1966) ch. 7. For a survey of banking literature on the 'real bills' doctrine in the USA after 1913 see Mints, ch. 13.

[2] *Tenth Annual Report of the Federal Reserve Board*, 1924, p. 33.

[3] 'Theories of Banking Policy' (1928), *Essays in Money and Interest* (Manchester, 1966) pp. 24 and 36–8.

[4] Holzman, pp. 27 and 49.

[5] *Tenth Annual Report*, p. 33.

[6] H. Thornton, *Paper Credit of Great Britain* (1802) (London, 1962) esp. chs. 8–11.

extremely great extent'.[1] Thornton clearly perceived the problem, later echoed by others, that the term 'needs of business' does not signify anything specific or quantifiable from the point of view of credit expansion. In addition he thought that the issue of credit by the Bank of England should also be related to an external criterion, notably to the movement of exchange rates. Later the theory was rejected in the famous Bullion Committee report of 1810 and finally the passing of the Bank Charter Act of 1844 symbolised the preference in Britain for central banking based on rigid rules, relating the issue of notes to specie flow, rather than for a discretionary policy trying to adapt lending to legitimate 'business needs'. The revival of interest in the 'real bills' doctrine in the twenties and thirties of the twentieth century was mainly caused by the quest for an appropriate monetary policy for the FRS. The System's adherence to the 'principle of productive credit' was attacked especially by D. H. Robertson in Britain[2] and in the USA by a number of writers[3] including L. Currie.

It is important to note that both Robertson and Currie were looking for a stabilisation policy in conditions when the gold standard could no longer be relied upon to provide a guide to central banking behaviour. They were not primarily interested in sound lending or in the liquidity aspects of the distribution of bank assets, but in a national monetary policy designed to stabilise the trade cycle. Banking policies based on the 'real bills' doctrine were thought to be too passive, and hence inadequate for purposes of stabilisation. Currie, a predecessor of the present monetarist school of K. Brunner and M. Friedman, maintained that movements of commercial loans were unsuitable as indicators of a community's requirements for money, because commercial loans rose in the upswing and declined in the downswing of the trade cycle. 'Hence a strict application of the "needs of business" criterion would involve an expansion of money during the upswing and a contraction during the downswing of the cycle.'[4] This would accentuate the trade cycle. Thus Currie advocated

[1] H. Thornton, *Paper Credit of Great Britain* (1802) (London, 1962) pp. 94 and 253.
[2] Robertson, pp. 36–8. See also *Banking Policy and the Price Level* (London, 1926) esp. chs. 3–6. *Money* (1922) (Cambridge, 1946) ch. 5. Robertson's works are quoted in support of rejection of the 'real bills' doctrine in the West by Holzman (p. 27) though perhaps a more convincing attack was launched by L. Currie with Robertson's warm approval (see review of Currie's book in *Economic Journal*, March 1935, p. 128).
[3] See Mints, ch. 13.
[4] Currie, p. 42.

the abandonment of the 'commercial loan theory' of banking and the adoption of 'monetary theory of banking', viz. monetary policy specifically designed to iron out economic fluctuations.

Indeed, as already mentioned, monetary policy in the West, especially since the early 1950s, has been anticyclical, often described as 'leaning against the wind'. Monetary stringency has been applied during periods of inflation and monetary ease during periods of recession or stagnation. The theoretical foundations of such an approach lay in theories classified under A or to some extent C (see pp. 6–7).

To conclude, the 'real bills' theory has been discarded[1] in the West mainly because it failed to give a specific criterion for purposes of monetary policy. Legitimate 'needs of business', even when narrowly defined in terms of 'real bills', could not be translated into a reasonably specific target variable at which monetary authorities could aim. By presuming a passive adjustment of money supply to business needs, it denied the usefulness of monetary policy as an instrument of macroeconomic control and indeed was thought to encourage fluctuations. In developed Western economies the last point was crucial. Though, as stated earlier, views on the efficacy of monetary control varied, monetary policy has been a principal method of national economic management used to end inflation and alleviate balance of payments and currency crises.

The Soviet monetary management discussed in chapter 2 clearly exhibits some elements of the 'real bills' doctrine. It may however be noted that no specific references to it are made in East European literature. It is difficult therefore to say whether the Soviet authorities took any notice of the Western debate on the doctrine when laying down the principles of socialist banking and credit. The similarities between the doctrine and the principles may be coincidental, not necessarily implying an influence of Western economic thought. It is also doubtful whether there exists a clear 'Marxist transliteration of the real bills doctrine'.[2]

---

[1] Strictly speaking the 'real bills' doctrine has been discarded in the West in the form in which it has been defined in this chapter. Elements of the doctrine still survive, though they appear in the more sophisticated setting of the contemporary debate on the question 'Does money matter?', in particular in the context of the controversy on the endogeneity or exogeneity of money supply. Those who oppose the 'new monetarism' associated with Friedman often stress the endogenous nature of money supply.

[2] As proposed by Garvy in Degras, *Soviet Planning*, p. 48.

Marx's pronouncements on monetary matters[1] were, in the main, critical of capitalist theories. It is true that he leaned strongly to the Banking School view in his review of the mid-nineteenth century British monetary debate and opposed the Quantity theory principles inherent in the Currency School. Believing that 'the quantity of means of circulation' was a dependent variable (dependent on e.g. the price level), Marx may be classified as an adherent of the 'real bills' theory. On the other hand, from his pronouncements on money it is impossible to sift out constructive proposals which might be applicable to the monetary management of a socialist economy. It is also relevant to observe that Marx was mainly concerned with the technical functions of money in an economy on a gold standard. Strangely, although in the *Contribution to the Critique of Political Economy* he realised that 'credit money' belongs to a higher stage of production (and so presumably would apply to a socialist economy) and 'conforms to very different laws',[2] he devoted himself entirely to a discussion of the gold standard. It is doubtful whether he offered any guidance in the shaping of the Soviet monetary system.

Lenin, who exerted some practical influence in this respect, was not concerned with monetary principles, but mainly with the acquisition of the existing banking system from capitalists and its utilisation by the socialist authorities for purposes of 'control' – the accounting sort of control rather than monetary control as understood in the West.

[1] Mainly in vols. 1 and 3 of *Capital*; also in *A Contribution to the Critique of Political Economy* (1859) (London, 1971).

[2] See e.g. pp. 64 and 116.

2

The origins of socialist banking and monetary control

Soviet banking and credit before the financial reforms of the 1930s

This chapter deals mainly with the development of Soviet banking and credit principles and control. It is a brief review showing the evolution of the monetary system which in the late forties and early fifties was adopted piecemeal by Soviet satellite economies, and represents only a background study undertaken because of its bearing on Polish banking, finance and monetary control, which are subjected to a more rigorous investigation.

There was considerable doctrinal and political pressure in the Soviet Union to nationalise the banking system. Marx and Engels included 'Centralisation of credit in the hands of the state, by means of a national bank with state capital and an exclusive monopoly' in their programme of communist revolution.[1] Lenin was impressed with the influence which banks exercised over the economic and political activity of developed countries in the late nineteenth and early twentieth centuries.[2] Thus in 1917 he was a very keen advocate of the nationalisation of banks and their amalgamation into a single state controlled bank.[3] He considered the acquisition of control over banks to be an essential move by the revolutionaries in their bid for power, but the revolutionary authorities had no concrete plans

[1] *Manifesto of the Communist Party* (1848) (Progress Publishers: Moscow, no date given) p. 80.

[2] V. I. Lenin, *Imperialism, the Highest Stage of Capitalism* (1916) 11th impression, (Foreign Language Publishing House, Moscow, no date given).

[3] V. I. Lenin, 'The Impending Catastrophe and How to Combat It', Sept. 1917 in *Questions of the Socialist Organisation of the Economy* (Progress Publishers: Moscow, no date given) pp. 17–23. The nationalisation and unification of the banking system were also proposed by Lenin in 'Theses on Banking Policy', *Collected Works*, vol. 27 (Progress Publishers) pp. 222–3 and in the 'April Theses', *Collected Works*, vol. 27, pp. 318–19.

for the operation of banks under their control.[1] The processes of nationalisation of banks and their subsequent amalgamation were represented by Lenin in very naive terms. 'No special machinery, no special preparatory measures on the part of the state would be required, for this is a measure that can be effected by one single decree, at a "single stroke"...*All* that is required is to *unify accountancy*...But there is not the slightest technical difficulty in the way of the amalgamation of the banks.'[2]

In practice considerable difficulties were encountered in the acquisition of control over banks and especially in managing them. The State Bank (Gosbank) was taken over by the revolutionary authorities a few days after the October Revolution. Workers' control was imposed on other banks. The staff of the banks, however, did not co-operate with the authorities and, as a result, the pressure to nationalise the banking system increased.[3] Nationalisation was decreed on 27 December 1917; at the same time it was decided to merge all the banks into a single People's Bank (Narodnyi Bank). The process of nationalisation was completed by December 1918, but the unified banking system which emerged never functioned as a co-ordinated unit. Indeed, until the introduction of the New Economic Policy (NEP) in 1921, the Soviet government failed to put into operation any effective policy for the stabilisation of currency and the development of a banking apparatus. Inflation, which was an important economic problem then as it had been before the revolution, was allowed to accelerate and led to a complete loss of confidence in the currency in the period of War Communism. By the end of the civil war the monetary system of the economy had ceased to exist.[4] The People's Bank was abolished in 1920 and its offices were used merely for making budgetary allocations and for keeping accounts.

The evolution of the Soviet credit system may be said to have started with the introduction of the NEP in March 1921. The NEP's basic aim was economic recovery; market forces were thought to offer the necessary incentives to raise production quickly and to integrate the economies of town and country. The direct allocation

[1] V. V. Ikonnikov (Ed.), *Denezhnoe Obrashchenie i Kredit SSSR* (1952) p. 126.

[2] Lenin, *The Impending Catastrophe*, pp. 19–20.

[3] Ikonnikov, pp. 122–7.

[4] A. Z. Arnold, *Banks, Credit and Money in Soviet Russia* (New York, 1937) especially ch. 5.

of resources practised before 1921 was to be superseded by distribution through the market, and the expansion of trade became the authorities' key short-term economic objective.

Following the introduction of the NEP factories were generally amalgamated into trusts and the term 'enterprise' in industry referred, as a rule, to trusts rather than to single factories. A resolution of the Central Executive Committee (CEC) and the Council of People's Commissars (CPC) passed on 10 April 1923, laid down that state industrial enterprises must act on the principles of 'commercial accounting' and aim at making a profit.[1] The term 'commercial accounting' (*kommercheskii raschet*) was used to emphasise that enterprises were to be guided by market considerations in making decisions. They were 'to learn to trade' so as to make a profit and, in order to be able to do this, they were given considerable financial and trading autonomy.

To attain the NEP's immediate aim of reviving market forces it was necessary to create a new monetary system conducive to the expansion of trade. The main monetary problem became the establishment of a new currency which would command public confidence. Such a new currency emerged, after a period of currency reform (1922–4), in the shape of the *chervonets* which became the main legal tender of the economy after March 1924.[2]

The return to a money economy necessitated the re-establishment of a banking system. The State Bank was created in October 1921 and commenced its operations a month later. Its short-term objective was to help the recovery of the economy by encouraging trade. The bank alone, however, could not satisfy the demand for banking services and so, shortly after its establishment, other banks were created to specialise in financing the development of different branches of the economy. These banks became known as 'specialised banks' (*spetsial'nye banki*).

Initially the impact of the new banking system was small. Rapidly depreciating currency made banking difficult. The currency reform, however, restored confidence in money and encouraged the development of banking. At the beginning of the NEP relatively little attention was paid to the problems of organisation of banking and credit.

---

[1] 'On industrial state enterprises acting on principles of commercial accounting (on trusts).' *SUiR*, 29 (1923) Art. 336.

[2] Arnold, p. 215. On currency reforms see also Ikonnikov, ch. 5; Ya. A. Kronrod, *Den'gi v Sotsialisticheskom Obshchestve*, 2nd Ed. (1960) pp. 37–59.

The possibility of using banks to control the activities of their customers was realised, but the questions of the structure of banking and of banking practice appropriate to a socialist economy were overshadowed by the urgent need to stabilise the country's currency and to create financial conditions conducive to economic reconstruction.

When the banking system was revived in the early years of the NEP the State Bank was intended to be the central bank, though it was not clear what precisely were to be the central banking functions in the new system. The bank was responsible for carrying out some central bank functions, such as the issue of legal tender (after 1922) and rediscounting bills of other banks. In addition, however, it performed functions similar to those of other banks – for example it granted both short and long-term credit to trusts and syndicates. Other banks were intended to specialise in granting both short and long-term credit to a particular branch of the economy or a particular region of the country (mainly by discounting bills or promissory notes). In general there was little co-ordination and no definite division of function between banks.[1]

By 1926 the first stage of the NEP was over. In December 1925 the 14th Party Congress marked the beginning of the second stage, which was a transition to the process of 'socialist industrialisation of the economy'. Discrimination against the private sector in favour of the state sector was intensified. Priority was given to the development of industry, particularly heavy industry. Industry was to expand in a planned way, which meant that industrial production was increasingly subjected to planning and was less and less governed by the profit motive, as it had existed in the first phase of the NEP. Competition between enterprises was to be entirely superseded by the planning of their production.

Competition in industry was gradually reduced after 1922 and a measure of planning resulted from the operations of syndicates which, in the late 1920s, monopolised trade in a number of major industries and assumed an important role in planning industrial production. Apart from engaging in trading activities the syndicates began to

[1] The first move to regulate the activity of the banks came in June 1924 when the State Bank set up a Banking Committee (Komitet po Delam Bankov) to co-ordinate the activities of credit institutions, but the commission was ineffective. Arnold, pp. 266–7; A. Gusakov, V. Labazov, M. Sveshnikov, *Denezhnoe Obrashchenie i Kredit SSSR* (1960) p. 100.

take decisions concerning output and capital investment, often duplicating the work of the Chief Administrations (*glavnye upravleniya*) of the Supreme Council of National Economy, which were, *de jure*, responsible for planning industrial development. This system of industrial organisation continued up to the reform of 5 December 1929 which is discussed later.

The changes in economic policy initiated in 1926 had an impact on the organisation of banking and credit. The tenets of the early period of the NEP and the lack of a clear division of function between banks led to bank competition. After 1926 there was a shift of emphasis in banking from the problems of currency and of financing economic revival to the problems of planned distribution of credit. The existing banking structure and practices and in particular the competition between banks, including rivalry between the State Bank and specialised banks, were criticised on the grounds that the existence of competition indicated the existence of too many banks and was 'unhealthy' in a socialist planned economy. In their endeavour to attract customers the banks were often accused of taking part in a 'chase for clients'; to attract customers, especially those likely to have constantly increasing cash reserves (social insurance, the textile syndicate, trade unions),[1] banks offered competitive increases in deposit rates and sometimes gave credit too easily.

Much criticism was levelled at increasing overlapping in the work of banks (usually called 'parallelism' by Soviet writers).[2] The tendency towards universal banks encouraged enterprises to use the services of more than one bank, undermining the possibility of effective control over the activity of enterprises. As stated before, all banks granted short and long-term credit. Though more than half of the total short-term credit was granted by the State Bank, there was no definite division of function in this respect in the banking system. The purposes of short and long-term credit were not specified. Enterprises sometimes financed permanent capital expenditure from both long and short-term credit; it was not unusual for an enterprise to finance working capital from long-term credit.[3]

Important changes in banking and credit were introduced following the decree of 15 June 1927 'On the principles of the credit

[1] Ya. Rubinstein, *Ocherki Razvitiya Sovietskogo Kredita* (1958) p. 32.
[2] For example all enterprises could obtain credit in municipal banks; agricultural banks credited trading and industrial enterprises. Ikonnikov, p. 198.
[3] Gusakov, p. 104.

system',[1] which accepted both the principle of centralised, planned distribution of credit in the economy and the dominant role, in this respect, of the State Bank. The spheres of activity of each bank were outlined so as to eliminate the possibility of bank competition. This led to the delimitation of clientele between banks, so that enterprises could obtain credit from only one bank. Thus the 1927 reform introduced an important banking principle of 'one client – one bank'.[2] It represented the first move towards Soviet-type monetary control – control firmly based on the relationship of the enterprise with one exclusive supplier of short-term credit. Following the reform the issue of short-term credit began to be concentrated in the State Bank[3] and long-term credit in specialised banks.[4]

The 1927 reform represented only a step towards the planned distribution of credit. It concentrated on the determination of the relationship between the banks and the division of function between them. Two fundamental problems still remained to be solved, namely the method or technique of crediting consistent with the planned distribution of credit and the determination of the relationship between banks and their customers, which was vital to 'control by the rouble'. Solutions to these problems are discussed in the next section.

Financial reforms of the 1930s

(a) Towards a division of function between the banking system and the budget

In 1926, after the decision to proceed with rapid industrialisation had been taken, the authorities faced the complex issue of the capital accumulation needed to accomplish their programme. This involved some basic questions, namely how to raise investment funds, how

[1] Passed by the CEC and the CPC, SZ 35 (1927) Art. 364.
[2] Kronrod, p. 82. The principle was not immediately implemented. Some large industrial enterprises continued to obtain credit from both the State Bank and other banks (see Ikonnikov, p. 199; Z. V. Atlas, *Denezhnoe Obrashchenie i Kredit SSSR* (1957) p. 81.
[3] Percentage ratios of short-term credit granted by the State Bank to the total short-term credit of the banking system differ in various Soviet sources. Rubinstein, p. 39, gives them for October 1st of each year as: 1923, 68.5; 1924, 57.0; 1925, 57.9; 1926, 57.3; 1927, 59.3; 1928, 71.2; 1929, 76.8. Ikonnikov, p. 200: 1929, 81.6; Gusakov, p. 111: 1926, 56.4; 1929 (July 1st), 73.0.
[4] Ikonnikov, pp. 180–90 and 202–8.

to distribute them and what methods to adopt to encourage their rational utilisation.

The state of the economy restricted the choice of solutions. Voluntary private savings were too small to be relied on as an adequate source of investment finance and the possibility of foreign aid or loans was remote. The most likely sources of capital accumulation were the savings of enterprises. As far as the mechanism of accumulation was concerned, the Soviet capital and money markets were not sufficiently developed to mobilise the funds required for the ambitious programme of speedy industrialisation. The budget and the state banking system were thus the most likely instruments for the accumulation and redistribution of the surpluses of enterprises. Enterprises could also plough their profits straight back into production. At first the extent to which they were to be permitted to refinance from profits was not clear.[1] Equally the role of the budget and of the banking system in capital accumulation were not clearly defined until after 1930. In the late 1920s the budget was continually growing in importance. Its contribution towards financing capital accumulation is, however, difficult to estimate precisely, because of the relationship of the budget to the banking system. The latter relied heavily, in the NEP period, on the funds of the People's Commissariat of Finance.[2] As already observed, investment could be financed by both short and long-term credit granted by banks, and in some cases from budgetary allocations. After the reform of 1927 there was an increasing tendency to use specialised banks as a channel for distributing budgetary resources for investment purposes.

It may be interesting to trace here the development of the Industrial Bank (Prombank) which supplied credit to industry. Established in October 1922, it concentrated up to 1924 on granting short-term credit. After 1924 its long-term credit expanded rapidly, although short-term credit still predominated. With the general emphasis on faster capital investment, it was decided on 17 May 1926 to organise a special department within the bank to be known as the Department of Long-term Credit (DLC), designed to extend credit (from one to ten years) to industrial enterprises. Originally the DLC was to raise funds from the profits of enterprises and of the

[1] R. W. Davies, *The Development of the Soviet Budgetary System* (Cambridge, 1958) pp. 147–52 and 195.
[2] S. S. Katzenellenbaum, *Russian Currency and Banking 1914–1924* (London, 1925) pp. 168 and 172–5; Arnold, pp. 251–3.

Industrial Bank. The considerable growth of the DLC started only after a decree of 14 July 1927 'On the system of finance of long-term credit in industry', which provided that budget finance of fixed investment in industry was to take place exclusively through DLC. The Industrial Bank was to be responsible for granting credit, controlling the utilisation of credit, securing the repayment of principal and ensuring that interest was paid. Granting of credit was to proceed in accordance with financial plans worked out by the Supreme Council of National Economy and approved by the Council of Labour and Defence. On 14 February 1928, the Industrial Bank was reorganised and officially renamed the Bank of Long-Term Credit of Industry and Electrification (Bank Dologosrochnogo Kreditovania Promyshlennosti i Elektrokhozyaistva; BLC). Some of its short-term credit balances were transferred to the State Bank, while some long-term credit balances were transferred to the bank from the State Bank. It also took over the long-term credit activity of the Bank for Electrification (Elektrobank), which was liquidated and whose short-term credit business was taken over by the State Bank. The BLC was now engaged specifically in the distribution of long-term industrial credit.[1]

The methods and institutions of capital accumulation existing in the late 1920s were put to the test by the policy of accelerating the pace of industrialisation embodied in the first Five Year Plan, 1928–9 to 1932–3, which aimed at a level of investment expenditure equal to $2\frac{1}{2}$ times that attained in the previous five years. This substantial rise was to be achieved on the assumption of a rapid rise in the labour productivity of enterprises, leading to a fall in costs and a rise in investible profits. No radical changes in the financial system were contemplated.[2] Credit institutions were naturally expected to play an important part in financing the plan. The State Bank was to expand short-term credit by attracting new deposits, by cash issues and by increasing its capital. Specialised banks were to expand long-term credit partly from increases in deposits and bank profits and partly from budgetary allocations.

In the first two years of the plan, however, labour productivity failed to increase as rapidly as expected and costs of production rose

---

[1] Whereas the total long-term finance granted to industry by the DLC in 1926 amounted to about 28.1 million roubles, the total long-term credit granted to industry by the BLC amounted to 1766.1 million roubles in 1929. Ikonnikov, p. 203.

[2] Davies, p. 195.

sharply. The serious inflationary situation which resulted forced the authorities to take steps to improve the efficiency of enterprises. To this end on 5 December 1929 the CC of the Communist Party passed a resolution entitled 'On the reorganisation of the administration of industry,[1] making the individual factory the basic production unit in industry. Factories were to operate on the basis of 'economic accounting' (*khozraschet*) and were to take 'complete responsibility for the fulfilment of their programme'. Chief Administrations (see p. 23) were abolished, as were the syndicates, whose functions were transferred to the newly formed combinations (*ob'edineniya*) which were in general horizontal integrations of factories. After the reform the term 'enterprise' referred, as a rule, to single factories on economic accounting.

The problem of financial organisation of the economy was brought to the forefront by the decision to raise the efficiency of enterprises through strict, centralised, financial control over their activities. Criticisms of the existing financial system, made even before the first Five Year Plan, were now highlighted by the difficulties encountered in plan fulfilment, producing a climate of opinion conducive to fundamental financial reconstruction. The reforms which followed had two main aims: first to create a completely new method of capital accumulation appropriate to a system of centralised planning[2], and second to devise a financial system which would ensure that enterprises used their resources rationally and in accordance with their plans.

The answer to the first aim of the reform was largely provided by the budgetary reforms of 1930–1 which in essence established a new system of raising revenue based on turnover tax and deductions from profits. Budgetary expenditure was to be more systematic and more effective control was to be exercised over it.[3] Fixed capital investment was to be financed largely from the budget, so that after 1930 the budget emerged as the central fund for collecting and distributing investible funds in the economy.[4] At the same time the banking and

[1] *Direktivy PKSS i Sovetskogo Pravitelstva po Khoziyaisvennym Voprosam* (1957) pp. 126–33.
[2] The budgetary system which operated in the NEP period had many of the pre-1914 war budget elements and was very complicated, especially on the revenue side (see Davies, pp. 64–5, 190–204).
[3] For more details see Davies, chs. 8 and 9.
[4] Between 1931 and 1935 about 80% of capital investment expenditure came from the budget. Arnold, p. 451.

credit systems were reshaped so as to provide a system of finance complementary to and co-ordinated with the budget.

(b) Towards bank monopoly of credit

Even before the NEP it was realised that banks, as credit suppliers and as institutions likely to be in frequent contact with their custo- mers, could have considerable influence on the activity of enter- prises. The problem was not how to devise a monetary system whereby, as happens in the West, credit conditions would influence the level of aggregate expenditure by enterprises, but how to organise the relationships between banks and enterprises so that credit was distributed in accordance with plans and so that the banks' potential influence over enterprises could be used by the planning authorities to provide effective 'control by the rouble'. The solution to the problem was not immediately obvious. The 1927 banking reforms dealt mainly with relations between banks. It was now necessary to revise relations between banks and enterprises and to devise financial practices conducive to 'control by the rouble'.

As already mentioned, bank credit consisted largely of discounts of bills of exchange.[1] Banks were widely used in settling bills – the usual practice being for a holder of a bill about to mature to pay it into his bank, which then sent it to the drawee's bank for payment.[2]

Attempts to reconcile the practice of bill finance with the aim of planned credit distribution during the NEP revealed the first sign of the Soviet authorities' faith in the prescriptions of the 'real bills' theory. It was difficult for banks to control the supply of credit in the economy, because they could not control the drawing and issue of discountable paper by enterprises. Banks granted credit only indirectly, in the sense that credit was originally given by the seller to the buyer who accepted a bill. When the seller discounted the bill with a bank, the bank in effect granted credit indirectly to the buyer. Thus the flow of bank credit depended largely on the avail- ability of commercial paper in the portfolios of enterprises. This

[1] The percentage of bill discounts in the total credit and discount operations was 36.1 on 1 Oct. 1923, 50.3 on 1 Oct. 1924, 52 on 1 Oct. 1925 and 56.4 on 1 Oct. 1926. Z. V. Atlas, pp. 74–5; Ikonnikov, p. 178. It was thought that the volume of discounts declined after 1 Oct. 1927. This view may have been due to a change in bank accounting, rather than to a real tendency to dispense with bills. Arnold, p. 345.

[2] Ikonnikov, pp. 210–11.

method of crediting made it difficult for the banks to make certain that the purpose for which credit was given was consistent with plans or regulations. A major aspect of the problem was that bank discounts were not always made on 'real' viz. trade bills. There was, for example, a practice of issuing 'advance bills' (*avansovye vekselya*), whereby the acceptance of a bill took place before delivery of goods. In this way purchasing enterprises actually financed production. An effect of this was to increase the liquidity of the economy without increasing the supply of goods on the market. After the volume of advanced bills reached significant proportions[1] their use in the socialised sector of the economy was forbidden by a resolution of the CPC 'On the issue of bills and the prohibition of advance payments in the socialised sector of the national economy', passed on 18 November 1929.[2]

There were also 'financial bills' (*finansovye vekselya*), which were mere promises to pay at a future date made in order to obtain bank credit. They were thus not 'real' trade bills but an unsound security, which Smith and Thornton (see p. 15) called 'fictitious' or 'accommodation' bills. Lending on non-real bills was generally considered inflationary and was the chief factor which militated against the abolition of all bill finance in the socialised sector. It may also be mentioned that when, at the time of issue of the 1928–9 control figures, attempts were made at credit planning, the broad principle adopted was 'credit follows goods; no plan, no credit'.[3] The idea that money flows must always follow real (goods) flows was firmly reflected in later credit reforms and inspired the formulation of the Soviet 'law of money circulation', often quoted in Soviet textbooks, insisting on the proportionality between the stock of money (*denezhnaya massa*) and the stock of goods (*tovarnaya massa*).[4]

Apart from the above mentioned objections, finance by bills was also criticised for being expensive and for unnecessarily complicating accounting operations.[5] Finally, there were doctrinaire objections: discounting of bills was considered to be a capitalist method of finance not appropriate to a socialist system.

---

[1] Z. V. Atlas, *Denezhnoe Obrashchenie i Kredit SSSR* (1947 ed.) p. 94 estimated that in 1929 'advance bills' and post-dated bills issued as a guarantee on agreements reached between enterprises were 20% of the total issue of bills in industry and about 40% of the total bills issued in some regions.

[2] *SZ* 72 (1929) Art. 694.   [3] Rubinstein, p. 35.

[4] See e.g. Z. V. Atlas, pp. 158–63.   [5] Z. V. Atlas, pp. 95–6.

In June 1929 a commission of the State Bank recommended that commercial credit, including bill finance, should stop and that banks should be the only source of credit.[1] The recommendation was accepted and implemented in the bank reform of 30 January 1930 which is discussed below.

However, the elimination of bill finance was not sufficient to ensure direct control by banks over the activity of all production units. There were some factories which never received credit directly from banks. In some industries (for example textile and metal industries) syndicates obtained credit from banks (through discounts) and then redistributed it (e.g. against bills) to their members.[2] In this way syndicates acting as middlemen between banks and enterprises performed the vital role of allocating the credit originally granted by banks. Finally, the existence of an alternative source of credit in the form of trade credit (viz. book credit granted by the seller to the buyer) offered a possibility of getting external finance outside the banking system.

Another important step towards reshaping the credit system was the above-mentioned industrial reform of December 1929, which implied that all enterprises on economic accounting would now come into direct contact with their banks. Fundamental changes in the country's monetary system were, however, carried out in the early 1930s. The first of these was the resolution 'On the credit reform' passed on 30 January 1930 by the CEC and CPC.[3] Its main aim was to establish a planned system of credit and financial control over plan fulfilment by enterprises. It consolidated some principles accepted earlier and added some new elements, of which the most important was the abolition of commercial credit. This meant that any form of credit by enterprises (trade credit or bill credit) in the socialised sector was made illegal. Existing trade credit balances were transferred to the State Bank and future settlements between enterprises were to be through the banking system. Each enterprise was to receive credit directly from its bank in accordance with credit plans prepared by its superior body (trust or combination). Direct crediting was to make it possible for banks to check the purpose for which

---

[1] For more details see Arnold, pp. 346–9.
[2] For more information see Z. V. Atlas (1947 ed.) p. 198; V. M. Batyrev, M. M. Usoskin, *Kratkosrochnyi Kredit i Organizatsiya Denezhnogo Obrashcheniya v SSSR* (1952), pp. 38–40.
[3] *SZ* 8 (1930) Art. 98.

credit was granted. The resolution also encouraged the process of concentration of short-term credit in the State Bank which, it may be recalled, had already started in 1927. As a result, on 1 January 1931, the State Bank was responsible for 93% of all short-term credit granted in the economy.[1] Thus the 1930 reform was a major move towards the realisation of a long standing Soviet ideal of a single powerful bank serving at the book-keeping and clearing centre of the entire economy.[2]

(c) The system of automatic crediting

The reform, however, was soon strongly criticised.[3] Three main interconnected shortcomings emerged in the course of the implementation of the reform: (a) the use of a single current account (kontokorrent) for all forms of banking operations, (b) mechanical settlements of accounts by the State Bank (avtomatism raschotov), (c) the practice of mechanical or automatic crediting.

After the abolition of bill finance, enterprises used banks to carry out settlements of debts arising out of current transactions. These settlements were organised in the following way: the supplier on delivering goods sent his invoice (schot-faktura) to the bank, which then credited him with the full value of the invoice, regardless of whether the buyer was satisfied that the delivery had been made in accordance with his order, regardless of the correctness of the invoice and regardless of whether the buyer could pay the bill. If the buyer could not settle, he automatically received an overdraft. Consequently automatic settlements led to automatic crediting.

The State Bank was not ready to undertake the numerous operations connected with settlements and was overwhelmed by the work.[4] This contributed to a general relaxation of discipline in crediting.

From April 1929 each enterprise was to keep its cash reserves in only one bank; this requirement was a natural consequence of the principle of 'one client – one bank' mentioned earlier. After the 1930

[1] Z. V. Atlas, p. 99.
[2] It is interesting to note that the Soviet authorities resisted proposals (see e.g. G. Nagler, 'Rekonstruktsiya Kredita i Kreditnoi Sistemy, Vestnik Finansov 1 (1930)) to set up a single bank for both short and long-term credit.
[3] Details of theoretical discussions on the 1930 act and of difficulties in its implementation are given in Arnold, pp. 354–63.
[4] Arnold, pp. 356–7.

credit reform all monetary resources of enterprises were kept in a single current account so that there was no distinction between borrowed money and 'own funds' (*sobstvennye sredstva*), making financial analysis of enterprises difficult. Banks granted credit as long as they were satisfied that their clients were obliged to fulfil their planned targets (*kreditovanie pod plan*), but without checking that credit was really necessary, that plans were in fact being correctly fulfilled and that the clients' management was generally sound. It may be said that the monetary system followed an absurd interpretation of the 'real bills' doctrine, whereby banks passively extended finance for 'business needs' as stated by enterprises, which endeavoured, often regardless of costs, to achieve their ambitious planned targets. Clearly, in this situation, banks did not, and indeed could not, assess the creditworthiness of their customers; there were no effective means of financial analysis of enterprises and no clear criteria for granting or refusing credit.

The 1930 reform therefore did not succeed in introducing an effective 'control by the rouble'. On the contrary, it led to practices inconsistent with it and conflicting with the principles of economic accounting. Automatic crediting moreover did nothing to discourage inflation, which at the time had become the most pressing short-term economic problem. This does not mean that credit expansion was a cause of the inflationary impetus,[1] nor that credit stringency could, without changes in other spheres of national economic management, curb inflation. It is shown later that in a Soviet-type economy monetary restrictions cannot be relied on to eliminate excess spending. Unquestioning extension of credit by banks, however, did little to encourage enterprises to improve their financial management.

(d) The emergence of socialist principles of monetary control

New measures were undertaken to rectify the shortcomings in banking practice which followed the credit reform. First, on 14 January 1931, steps were taken to eliminate the automatic settlements

---

[1] As has been suggested by some Western writers. L. E. Hubbard, *Soviet Money and Finance* (London, 1936) pp. 239–44, for instance, regarded credit expansion before 1931 as a contributory cause of inflation, not seriously considering the view that currency and credit expansion could well have been an effect of inflation.

practised after the 1930 reform. These are described later. On 20 March 1931, the CPC passed a resolution[1] containing the following points. It criticised automatic crediting on the strength of the plan (*pod plan*) and called for its cessation.[2] It emphasised that the State Bank should exercise control over plan fulfilment by enterprises and endeavour to improve their economic accounting. The basis of business relations between enterprises was to be the agreement (or contract), whose terms were to be strictly observed.[3] Credit was to be given only for temporary, e.g. seasonal, needs and it was to be granted for a specific period and for a specific purpose. The completion of legislation concerning this aspect of the credit system came in a resolution of the Council of Labour and Defence passed on 23 July 1931, entitled 'On the working capital of state combinations, trusts and other economic organisations.'[4] It introduced a number of very important changes concerning the management and finance of working capital. Deploring the absence of distinction between 'own' financial resources and borrowed financial resources, it laid down that a minimum of working capital, viz. some minimum value of current assets (specified as stocks of raw materials, fuel, semi-finished products, work–in–progress, etc.) must be covered by own funds. This marked the first step towards the institution of the 'normative' (see pp. 41–2) of working capital which is further discussed later. All cash reserves were to be kept in a current account and separate credit accounts were to be opened. Thus the single *conto corrento* was abolished and strict separation of own resources (kept in a current or settlement account) from borrowed funds (kept in loan accounts) was introduced. Short-term credit, entered in the loan accounts, was to finance only temporary 'above-normative' (*sverkhnormativnye*) working capital needs and was to be issued for a specified purpose consistent with the plans of the enterprise requesting credit.

[1] 'On changes in the system of crediting and on the strengthening of the credit operations and on safeguarding economic accounting in all economic organs.' *SZ* 18 (1931) Art. 166.

[2] After 1931 credit was to be given only if it was consistent with planned targets and the recipient was actually correctly fulfilling its plans (*kreditovanie v meru fakticheskogo vypolnieniya plana*).

[3] The importance of contracts was stressed again on 12 April 1931, in Directives of the CC of the Party 'On corrections of credit reform and campaign to enter into contracts' (Direktivy KPSS, pp. 269–72).

[4] *SZ* 46 (1931) Art. 316.

After the July reform, credit was said to have acquired the main characteristics of socialist credit, which are analysed separately. On 21 October 1931, the government issued an appeal 'On the new measures to inculcate economic accounting' which summarised the main provisions relating to finance of enterprises, stating that

> By granting the combinations, trusts and enterprises own working capital, by granting bank credit only for strictly determined needs of production and distribution and solely on the basis of repayment within a specified period, a further step forward is being taken to strengthen economic accounting and improve the discipline of agreements and the process of plan fulfilment. In order to exercise active control by the rouble over economic organs the bank has a new instrument, namely credit, for strictly specified needs of the economy and a strictly determined period of time.[1]

Thus after the amendments to the 1930 credit reform, credit was to be given only for legitimate 'business needs' and the principles of short-term credit, which are further analysed in the last section of this chapter, strictly defined these needs. The principles also changed 'the automatic credit' policy into a policy which, it will be contended later, was a stringent credit policy.

Fundamental changes in the credit system in the early 1930s ended with reforms of investment finance. A resolution of the CEC and the CPC of the USSR passed on 5 May 1932, concluded the division of function between banks envisaged in the 1927 reform.[2] Specialised banks were reorganised into four investment banks: The Industrial Bank, the Agricultural Bank (Sel'khozbank), the Co-operative Bank (Vsekobank) and the Municipal Bank (Tsekombank).[3] The resolution thus provided for important changes in the structure of banking as well as in the function of banks. It did not, however, amount to a drastic reform, but was a culmination of trends clearly visible, especially in the late 1920s and in the period of the credit reform. The centralised banking structure which emerged in 1932 was a result of a process of concentration in earlier years. The growth of the Industrial Bank has already been mentioned. Although before

[1] *SZ* 64 (1931) Art. 419.
[2] 'On the organisation of special banks of long-term investment.' *SZ* 31 (1932) Art. 191.
[3] The Industrial, Agricultural and Municipal banks were abolished in 1959 and their activities were taken over by the State Bank and the newly created Investment Bank (Stroibank).

1932 there were networks of agricultural, municipal and co-operative banks, their activity was increasingly directed by their respective central banks[1] and the State Bank.

The investment banks were to serve as a channel through which all investment expenditure in the economy was to flow in accordance with the plans. Their primary function was to redistribute budgetary resources for capital construction and to control the utilisation of all funds dispensed by them.[2] Up to 1934 the investment banks distributed capital resources by means of long-term credit[3] and grants. There was an increasing tendency to use the latter for financing investment and, on 9 March 1934, the CEC and the CPC resolved that all funds distributed by the banks were to be in the form of non-returnable grants.[4] All the outstanding capital debts of enterprises were annulled. The banks became in effect an integrated part of the budget and it is indeed doubtful whether the term 'bank' was appropriate to these institutions. 'Despite their designation as banks, it is, in fact, difficult to think of them as such. Inasmuch as their chief function at the present time is the *exercise of control* over the expenditure of funds by their "clientele", they are in reality control departments of the Commissariat of Finance.'[5]

(e) Bank control through settlements

During the period of the NEP enterprises were in general free to choose their methods of settling debts and to manage their cash resources. The most popular means of settlement were bills of exchange which, as observed earlier, played an important part in the

[1] The central bank of the agricultural credit institutions was the Central Agricultural Bank of the USSR (established in 1924, reorganised in 1930 into the Agricultural–Co-operative–Collective Bank of the USSR). The Central Municipal Bank and All Russian Co-operative Bank were central banks of municipal and co-operative credit institutions respectively.

[2] The banks were not certain how to interpret the function of control imposed on them. To clarify this a decree was passed on 27 April 1933, 'On the system of control exercised by the banks of long-term credit over the finance of investment.' For more details see Arnold, pp. 457–60; Ikonnikov, p. 411.

[3] They were also authorised to grant short-term credit, but only to enterprises in the building industry.

[4] 'On the non-returnable finance of capital construction of state enterprise in industry, transport and communications.' *SZ* 15 (1934) Art. 105.

[5] Arnold, p. 517.

credit system of the economy. One of the aims of the Soviet authorities in the late 1920s was to establish a system of supervision over the management of cash and the settlement of debts by enterprises.

On 3 April 1929 the CEC and CPC passed a law requiring all state and co-operative enterprises to deposit all money except sums needed to cover current transactions in the institution from which each enterprise obtained credit.[1] It has already been mentioned how, following the abolition of the bill of exchange, settlements between enterprises were to be carried out through the banks (in most cases the State Bank). This meant that settlements were to be carried out by accounting transfers between current accounts of enterprises kept in and administered by banks. For this reason they became known as 'cashless settlements' (*beznalichnye raschety*).

To eliminate the automatic settling which developed after the 1930 credit reform (see p. 31), the CPC passed a resolution on 14 January 1931, 'On measures necessary to improve the implementation of the credit reform',[2] which introduced a new principle, namely that of 'acceptance' (*aktsept scheta*).[3] The buyer was to settle his bill for the delivery of goods from his own funds, but before doing so he was to be given an opportunity to refuse to accept it if he was not satisfied with the delivery. Up to 1936 the buyer was to communicate his acceptance in writing within three days of the receipt of the bill. This was called positive acceptance (*polozhitelnyi aktsept*). In 1936 a tacit acceptance (*otritsatelnyi aktsept*) was introduced; the invoice was deemed to have been accepted if, in the period allowed for acceptance, the buyer did not refuse to accept. The acceptance method became the most common method of settlements.[4] Up to 1935 'the acceptance' of invoices was organised in such a way that the seller sent the invoice directly to the buyer and a copy to the buyer's bank. The movement of documents between the buyer and the seller

---

[1] 'On the need to deposit all cash resources of state enterprises and co-operative organisations.' *SZ* 25 (1929) Art. 215.

[2] *SZ* 4 (1931) Art. 52.

[3] The January 1931 reform also established two other methods of settlement, namely the '*akkreditiv*' and 'special accounts' (*osobye scheta*). For details see Batyrev and Usoskin, pp. 128–30; Ikonnikov, pp. 379–81; *Gosudarstvennyi Bank SSSR* (1957) pp. 103–4.

[4] On 20 March 1931 the acceptance method was declared the most appropriate method of settlement. In 1940, of all cashless settlements carried out by the State Bank 88.7% were by acceptance. Gosudarstvennyi Bank SSSR, p. 103; Gusakov *et al.* p. 193 give a corresponding figure of 77.9%. Ikonnikov, p. 371 states that 81.0% of all cash settlements made in 1940 were by the acceptance method.

by-passed the seller's bank so that it could not in any way supervise the seller in drawing up the invoice. The resolution of 8 June 1935, passed by the CPC introduced the *inkasso raschotnykh dokumentov* method of settlements,[1] whereby the seller on completion of the order sent the invoice to his own bank. The bank, having checked the invoice, sent its copies to the buyer and his bank, demanding payment. It is interesting to note that the *inkasso* method was practised in the early 1920s with bills of exchange. As mentioned on page 28, when bills were about to mature, the holder placed them in his bank which then sent them to the drawee's bank for payment.

Settlements by the acceptance method involved a lapse of time between the presentation of the invoice by the seller to the buyer and its ultimate payment. In order not to leave the seller short of funds to continue his production, a new form of short-term credit was instituted by the resolution of 14 January 1931, known as 'credit for sums in transit' (*kredit na summy v puti*).[2] It was to be granted to the value of the goods delivered and repaid at the end of the period prescribed for the completion of the settlement.

(f) Bank control through wage payments

The question of wage payments is very complex and is beyond the scope of this study. On the other hand the control of wage payments became a key function of Soviet banks and had significant macro-economic implications. Cash in the Soviet system was injected into the economy largely through wage payments. The planning of cash flow, therefore, involved the planning of wages. On the basis of the national economic plan the wage fund necessary to fulfil the plan was estimated. To avoid monetary disequilibria (mainly inflationary pressure leading to rises in prices or shortages of consumers' goods) the planners endeavoured to ensure that the wage fund generated over a planning period was equated with the value of consumers' products supplied on the market. It may be said, therefore, that an important task of a Soviet-type incomes policy was to ensure that

---

[1] 'On changes in the technique of settlements arising from trade between enterprises in different towns.' *SZ* 33 (1935) Art. 287. A bibliography on the acceptance method: Ikonnikov, pp. 375–9; Z. V. Atlas, pp. 271–6; Batyrev, pp. 123–8.

[2] Later also known as credit on documents in transit (*kredit pod raschotnye dokumenty v puti*).

planned wage payments were not exceeded unless productivity rose correspondingly.

Experiments to control wage payments started in the early thirties, but bank control of wage payments may be said to have started in 1939. To fulfil its plans each enterprise was allocated a wage fund. On 15 August 1939 the CPC passed a resolution 'On the method of control of payments from wage funds of industrial enterprises',[1] introducing the important principle of bank control of wages. The payment of wages could take place only with the knowledge of the bank advancing cash for that purpose. Before allowing payments the bank was to make certain that the enterprise paid wages in the course of the correct fulfilment of its production plan and not merely in agreement with its planned wage fund. It was thought that this method of wage payments would allow banks to control the management of wage funds by enterprises, and would encourage enterprises to use their wage funds rationally.

Changes in Soviet banking and credit after the 1930s were not of fundamental importance. The reforms of the late 1920s and 1930s established principles which governed the Soviet monetary system in subsequent years and, as will be shown later, were copied by Poland after the second world war. It may be noted that, although they contained certain *a priori* elements (for example Lenin's idea of a single bank as the accounting and control centre) and were perhaps in keeping with the socio-political doctrine of 'democratic centralism', these principles had a considerable empirical content and were largely a product of evolution.

An analysis of the main principles of Soviet banking and monetary control

(a) *Enterprises on economic accounting*

The preceding sections were mainly concerned with the development of Soviet credit institutions and principles. These, together with other elements of economic management, were, after the late forties, recognised by most East European countries as constituting the socialist economic system and adopted outright. Their performance in practice is tested later, mainly with respect to the experience

[1] *SZ* 49 (1939) Art. 396.

of Poland. It may, at this stage, be useful to adopt an analytical approach in order to summarise and elucidate them together with some other concepts used in subsequent chapters.

As already stated, socialist monetary control is a microeconomic type of control whose understanding necessitates a study of the relationships between enterprises and their banks. Aggregate expenditure is determined directly by national economic plans.

The immediate objective of socialist enterprises is the fulfilment of their plans. In the long run the management of enterprises is based on economic accounting, whose precise definition is difficult to frame. Sometimes it describes the philosophical basis of the operation of the socialist enterprise, and sometimes its constitutional rights and obligations. The most usual approach is to suggest that economic accounting embraces a number of important characteristics of the socialist enterprise. The enterprise is a legal person; the status, which for a firm in a capitalist country has important property implications, has very little meaning from the point of view of ownership in a Soviet-type economy, as all enterprises are publicly owned. They do, however, like their capitalist counterparts, have rights and obligations distinct from those of other legal persons. They can, for example, enter into contracts in their own names. From the economic viewpoint, or, more strictly, from the point of view of business management, socialist enterprises are autonomous in a qualified sense. They are equipped with the means of production (fixed and circulating capital) for which the management of an enterprise is responsible. Their production is determined by a national plan, but they are encouraged to undertake independent decisions in order to carry out their planned tasks efficiently, that is, they are said to have 'operative autonomy' in plan fulfilment. On the other hand they are fully responsible for their activities and are expected to manage resources so as to be able to cover their current expenditure from their current income.[1] The above characteristics are usually included in the concept, although the emphasis placed on them varies in different contexts to suit the purposes of particular writers.[2]

---

[1] This aspect is emphasised by V. Diachenko, 'Khozraschet Kak Sotsialisticheskii Metod Khozyaistvovaniya', *Voprosy Ekonomiki*, 2 (1951) p. 13.

[2] Parfanyak thus summarised the basic principles of economic accounting: 'Granting by the state to industrial enterprises their fixed and working capital; allowing them an operative economic autonomy, imposing on the heads of enterprises the responsibility for the fulfilment of planned tasks and for a thrifty and rational utilisation of state

It may be considered that economic accounting is a substitute for some elements of a market mechanism. First, it stresses the necessity of estimating the costs incurred and revenues realised exclusively by the enterprise, in order to assess profitability or efficiency. Secondly, it stresses the need for incentives to production, which in a market economy are embodied in the profit motive. Enterprises are encouraged to maximise the difference between revenues and costs by seeking methods of fulfilment of output targets at lowest cost or maximum saving. This incentive effect is frequently linked with the autonomy of the enterprise and the operation of the 'law of value'. [1]

In conclusion it must be emphasised that economic accounting is not a simple technical concept, but a controversial economic problem. What emerges from the discussions of it in East European literature is a general agreement that the socialist enterprise, to function efficiently, must (*a*) possess 'operative autonomy' in its production, (*b*) be able to estimate its costs rationally (indeed the term *khozrashet* is sometimes translated as 'cost accounting') and (*c*) be given incentives to minimise its costs. To furnish enterprises with the above characteristics the government gives them certain rights and imposes on them certain obligations. The important issue is whether in fact the rights and obligations of enterprises are, at any point of time, such as to endow them with these characteristics.

(*b*) Credit and the finance of capital

One aspect of economic accounting is that enterprises are furnished with the necessary capital to enable them to fulfil their obligations. A strict distinction was made between fixed and working capital of enterprises, in relation both to planning methods and to finance. Fixed capital investment was financed in accordance with investment plans by non-returnable interest-free budget grants distributed by specialised investment banks. As far as working capital was concerned the broad principle applied was that the total financial resources of an enterprise must be strictly related to the current assets needed to

property; accurate accounting of social labour expended on production (cost calculation); covering of all cost from own income and the creation of planned accumulation; encouragement of material interest in the results of work and of economic initiative by the management of enterprises and by all workers in economising and revealing reserves of production; state and social control over the fulfilment of planned tasks.' P. Parfanyak, *Voprosy Bankovskogo Kontrolya Rublem v Promyshlennosti* (1954) pp. 4–5.

[1] Diachenko, p. 12; Kronrod, p. 166.

fulfil its planned production targets. In this respect there are interesting similarities and differences between socialist and capitalist firms. Both in the capitalist economies (due to the profit motive) and the Soviet-type economies (in keeping with economic accounting) firms try to decrease the length of the operating cycle,[1] in order to reduce their working capital to a minimum. However, in socialist economies working capital loses an important aspect attached to it in the West – that connected with business solvency. Thus Western firms, in estimating their working capital requirements, must also take care not to impose undue risks on their owners. The absence of solvency risks reduces the planning of working capital in socialist countries to technical considerations.[2] Whether this simplification justifies the contention that it is possible to estimate accurately certain working capital needs – which is implicit in financing of working capital in socialist countries – is a debatable point.

To estimate their working capital requirements over a period, socialist enterprises were to work out 'norms' for various current assets. Not all current assets were 'normed', a distinction being made between those subject to norms, such as stocks and work–in–progress, and those not subject to norms, usually only cash and trade debtors. Only current assets subject to norms were taken into account in working out the 'normative' of working capital, which represented the amount of working capital constantly needed to carry on production. The remainder of the assets subject to norms, called 'above-normative' requirements, represented working capital needed temporarily.[3]

---

[1] That is, the period necessary to turn raw materials, etc. into goods, which must be sold to purchase further raw materials to start another production cycle.

[2] The absence of the risk of insolvency in managing socialist enterprises does not imply the absence of uncertainty concerning future development.

[3] In the West the term 'working capital' usually refers to net working capital, viz. the difference between current assets and current liabilities. In socialist economies the expression 'working capital' usually refers to what in Western countries would be called 'gross working capital', viz. the sum total of current assets. In financing working capital in socialist countries, however, some current liabilities are taken into account. At any time an enterprise may have certain outstanding obligations – e.g. unpaid wages, or debts to other enterprises arising from delayed settlements. The minimum level below which the sum of these liabilities does not fall is known as 'constant liabilities'. The correct volume of own funds which an enterprise should possess is equal to the normative of working capital less constant liabilities. On the concept of the normative see, e.g. Z. V. Atlas, pp. 297–8 or a Polish work: Z. Fedorowicz, *Finanse w Gospodarce Socjalistycznej* (1962) pp. 199–200.

The normative was calculated by working out the minimum needs for particular current assets over a period and then adding these minima. As a general rule, enterprises financed the normative from 'own funds', but when these were not sufficient, or if increases in the normative could not be covered from profits, they received a budget subsidy to cover the deficiency. Equally, when own funds were in excess of the normative the surplus was paid into the budget.

Above-normative requirements were, as a rule, financed by short-term credit. The concept of the normative implied that enterprises whose production was subject to seasonal fluctuations had to resort to credit and hence subject themselves to bank control. It was thought that this arrangement would give the bank an opportunity to notice mismanagement in enterprises manifested by either a shortage or an excess of working capital. Enterprises with non-seasonal production did not escape bank control, as only a part of their normative was covered by own funds, the remainder being financed from credit known as 'normative credit'. The term 'credit' applied here is misleading, for it was not expected to be repaid. It was usually granted to the co-operative sector, trade and heavy industry.[1]

Thus credit provided by the central bank financed only temporary working capital requirements, which was consistent with the 'real bills' theory. The significant difference here was that the enterprise was not to have all its financial needs met from the budget or own funds, but had to resort to credit in the course of its production, in order to give its bank an opportunity to exercise control by credit.

It may be noted that in both Soviet and Polish literature it was often claimed that there was some 'objective necessity' or 'indispensability' of credit in a socialist economy. Credit, it was suggested, was necessary in a community which used money. Ikonnikov, for instance, maintained that 'credit and banks will exist as long as there

[1] It originated in the Soviet Union in the 1930s. When credit granted for seasonal needs only was hampering the increase in the turnover of trading enterprises, the CPC passed, on 16 August 1933, a resolution 'On the method of crediting trade organisations' (*SZ* 55 (1933) Art. 326) permitting 'crediting on the turnover of goods' (*kreditovanie po tovaroborotu*). In the late 1930s it was noticed that enterprises in some sections of heavy industry not subject to seasonal fluctuations did not have to resort to credit, escaping 'the control by the rouble' of the State Bank. A decision was made to credit a part of their constant requirement of working capital. First experiments on this form of credit, known as credit 'on the turnover of expenditure' (*po oborotu zatrat*), were made in 1939 in machine building enterprises (see Z. V. Atlas, pp. 322–3). Subsequently credit 'on the turnover' became more widespread.

exists commodity production with its "monetary economy", as long as accounts and control in the process of production and distribution of national product are made in monetary form'.[1] He further stressed, as did some other authors, that the need for credit arose from two forms of ownership and production, namely state and co-operative. Kronrod, on the other hand, accentuated the lack of uniformity in production processes (seasonal and other fluctuations in production and distribution creating the need for credit), and the need for credit to bridge the gap between production and sales.[2]

The arguments on the indispensability of credit in a socialist economy were not convincing. Bearing in mind that priority was given to planning in physical terms and that production decisions were made by a central planning body, it may be argued that credit in the state sector could well be dispensed with. All state enterprises could, for example, be financed wholly from the budget. They could escape the need to obtain credit in cases of fluctuations in production and distribution by carrying adequate cash reserves. Furthermore, the existence of a co-operative sector gives no convincing reason for the existence of credit within the state sector. The co-operative sector could obtain credit from a central co-operative bank. The Soviet authorities simply found credit to be a useful institution in the planning mechanism. The retention of money necessitated the retention of banks to administer the economy's mechanism of payments. Banks were in addition utilised to perform other functions, which are discussed below.

(c) Bank control and other forms of 'controls'

A socialist enterprise is subjected to a complex system of incentives and disincentives, of which financial stimuli and penalties (elaborated below) are a part, and to various forms of 'control'. The term 'control' appears in a variety of contexts in East European literature and its meaning is not always the same, often becoming clear only after a careful examination of the relationships between the controlling body and the controlled, and of the methods of control used. It is beyond the scope of this study to analyse all the different meanings or shades

---

[1] Ikonnikov, p. 57.

[2] Kronrod, pp. 305–7. In this context we refer to Kronrod's discussion on indispensability of credit in socialist planning. Kronrod's main contribution in the field of Soviet monetary economics lies in his macroeconomic view of credit. Broadly, his thesis is that credit is a way of issuing money – every new issue of credit amounts to an issue of money.

of meaning of the term. However, an attempt is made to clarify concepts such as 'financial control', 'control by money' and 'bank control', which are directly relevant to the study.

Socialist enterprises were subjected to five forms of external 'control' (viz. 'control' by outside institutions).[1] First there was what might be called political 'control' (often called state control in East European books). Theoretically, supreme political organs were empowered to 'control' (in the sense of checking on the legality of operations of enterprises) other bodies, though this was usually done by the specialised Ministry of State Control. On the local level, local government organs could intervene in the affairs of enterprises.

Second, enterprises could be subjected to 'social control', whose form was not very specific. In theory, individuals and many social organisations could intervene in the affairs of enterprises, but usually interventions were confined to trade union organisations or local Party cells, the control by the latter being often very important, as enterprises could not undertake vital decisions without their prior approval. Here again 'control' referred in general to various forms of interventions, whose object was to check on the observance of laws and regulations by enterprises and to prevent fraudulent or unfair acts by managements.

The third form of control was ministerial control, frequently called 'internal control' in the sense that it was organised within an economic ministry of which an enterprise was a part. As far as the enterprise was concerned it might, however, be regarded as external control exercised by special auditors and inspectors of the respective ministries, making certain that the enterprise fulfilled its obligations correctly.

Another form of control distinguished in Soviet-type economies was 'mutual control'. Trade between socialist enterprises was to proceed on the basis of contracts or agreements into which enterprises had to enter. The contracts set out terms and conditions of business, including terms of settlement by which enterprises were obliged to abide. This was considered to be yet another manifestation of economic accounting. However, enterprises were not free to enter into any kind of contract they wished. Contracts had to be consistent

---

[1] These may be studied in conjunction with a chart in Appendix C which refers to Poland only, although in general it would also apply to the respective institutions in the USSR and other East European countries.

with the plans of the parties to them and were indeed considered to be the last phase of planning. It was the duty of each party to the contract to see to it that the other party fulfilled its contractual obligations and legal action could be taken over breaches of contracts. In this way the parties were said to carry out 'mutual control' over their activity. Banks had a responsibility to reinforce this mutual control by making certain that enterprises settled in accordance with their agreements and by taking action against enterprises failing to carry out their obligations.[1]

Finally there was 'financial control', which again cannot be clearly defined. Sometimes the term was used in a narrow sense to mean a form of administrative 'control' by a special control apparatus of the Ministry of Finance, confined mainly to checking documents and accounts, making inspections or requesting information. The term was also used in a wider sense to embrace various forms of financial 'control' including the 'control by money', or more exactly in the Soviet context, 'control by the rouble' (*kontrol' rublem*), which acquired a specific meaning at the time (late twenties and early thirties) of the shaping of the Soviet planning system and indeed is usually considered in the context of planning as an inseparable part of the planning mechanism.[2]

Control by money was exercised in conjunction with monetary flows generated in the process of production and distribution. The broad economic foundations of control by money are to be found in the circular flow of income. The adoption of money as a medium of distribution of national income implied that the real income flow would have its counterpart in the flow of money. Thus an analysis of money flows might be useful in the study of business management, and the control of money flows (on the part of the budget and the banking system) might have a direct effect on business management. Indeed in East European literature, it was often emphasised that, unlike in a capitalist economy, money in a socialist economy was used to exercise control. It was suggested that the way in which money performed its functions (usually listed as: means of exchange, means of payment, measure of value, means of accumulation and savings)

---

[1] See, e.g. Parfanyak, p. 7.

[2] After the second world war all East European countries introduced control by money: in Poland – *kontrola poprzez złotówkę* (or *za pomocą złotówki*), in Hungry – *kontrol lewom*, in Czechoslovakia – *kontrola koronou*, in East Germany – *Kontrolle durch die Mark*, etc.

in socialist planning enabled the authorities to exercise control by money.[1]

Control by money could be exercised through the budgetary system of payments and through banking operations.[2] Budgetary control was said to be exercised through a careful economic analysis of management in enterprises before making budgetary allocations, especially in financing a deficiency of own working capital or deficits (viz. 'planned deficits' caused by the working of the price system). In financing investment, control was carried out by investment banks which were to make certain that expenditure took place in accordance with investment plans and that money was being advanced to construction enterprises only in the course of proper fulfilment of investment plans. On the revenue side, the collection of the turnover tax gave the budgetary authorities an insight into the fulfilment of production and sales plans, and the collection of payments from profits enabled an analysis of the profitability of enterprises and the fulfilment of their plans for lowering the costs of production. Many budgetary transactions involving cash transfers, such as tax collection or the distribution of working capital subsidies, were carried out by the departments of budget servicing of the central bank. On the basis of this activity the departments compiled quarterly reports concerning the enterprises they serviced.

The most important form of control by money was bank control. The term 'control' used in the context of banking again did not always convey the same meaning. Earlier in this chapter it was noticed that Lenin, who was very impressed with the power of banks in developed, capitalist countries, in the early years of Soviet rule often advocated control or regulation of economic life through the

[1] Kronrod, pp. 185 and 276. On the subject see also: Z. V. Atlas (1947) pp. 38–9; Ikonnikov, pp. 28–32; A. V. Bachurin (Ed.), *Finansy i Kredit SSSR*, 2nd ed. (1958) pp. 11–16.

[2] 'Control by money' was sometimes given a wider meaning not confined solely to monetary flows associated with either the budget or the banking system. These quotations may serve as an example: 'In its function as a means of exchange, money allows the buyer to exercise control by the rouble over the quality and assortment of goods produced and sold. Control by the rouble on the part of customers helps to improve the work of trading organisations and industrial enterprises and contributes to increasing efficiency of Soviet trade.' A. V. Bachurin (Ed.), p. 12. 'Control by the rouble is performed as much by customers who have the right to refuse payment for poor quality products and to refuse to pay excessive prices as by railways who impose fines for tardy loading and unloading of carriages etc.' (*Teoria i Praktika Khoziaistvennogo Raschota*, p. 128).

banking system. Yet he never actually specified any details concerning the relationship between banks and enterprises; rather he wanted to take over the banking system in order to finance development in a direction which suited the purposes of the Soviet government. It was also thought that the nationalisation of banks would lead to control of a more precise political nature. As Atlas put it: 'The nationalisation of banks made possible the establishment of control over money incomes of capitalists.'[1] Only after the Soviet credit reforms of the thirties did the expression bank control begin to acquire a more uniform meaning which is explained below.

It has been observed that enterprises had to use their banks for keeping cash reserves and for making payments. Finance of working capital was so organised that enterprises were forced to obtain bank credit. Indeed, the view is taken in this study (compare p. 43) that the main reason for retaining the institution of credit was to use it as a method of monetary control over enterprises. The bank was thus in a position to scrutinise the financial flows of its customers and to detect their business mismanagements. Moreover, as East European writers often stressed, enterprises came into daily contact with their banks and hence control by them, as opposed to budget control and other forms of 'control', which were intermittent, was the only continuous and systematic control.[2]

Before describing the various methods by which it was exercised, an attempt is made to analyse the objective of bank control over enterprises. Two types of control may be distinguished.[3] The first is connected with planning in a broad sense and we shall refer to it as 'planning control'. The opinion and approval of banks were to be sought on the financial plans of enterprises. The most important role of the bank, however, was to exercise control over plan fulfilment by enterprises and, as has already been seen, the credit system had been organised so as to enable them to do that. Banks were not only to detect failures or mistakes in plan fulfilment; they were to endeavour to rectify or eliminate them. Thus the essence of 'planning

[1] Z. V. Atlas (1947) p. 125.

[2] See e.g. Z. V. Atlas, p. 259; Batyrev and Usoskin, p. 84; A. Tymowski, 'Znaczenie Kontroli Bankowej w Gospodarce Socjalistycznej, *ŻG* 24 (1951) p. 1317.

[3] In socialist texts three aspects of bank control are usually distinguished: (*a*) preliminary control (opinions on and the acceptance of financial plans, the analysis of the normative), (*b*) current control (control over the process of plan fulfilment, the elimination of shortcomings), (*c*) subsequent control (the analysis of financial results of enterprises). See e.g. Z. V. Atlas, p. 346.

control' was to contrast the actual position of an enterprise with that which had been prescribed for it by its plans, coupled with the *duty to take remedial steps in case of a discrepancy*.

The second type of bank control was much less precise and much broader. Banks were not simply passively to exercise control over plan fulfilment, but were to be actively concerned with the improvement of the management of enterprises, so as to achieve higher productivity. They were to make sure that enterprises used their wage funds efficiently and maintained good 'financial discipline', which included prompt settlement of obligations to other enterprises, credit institutions, the budget and employees. This type of control we shall call 'management control'. In spite of the fact that its scope and methods were not clearly defined, in particular *vis-à-vis* the managerial functions of directors of enterprises, 'management control' by banks received much emphasis.[1]

The wide scope of management control was often explained by suggesting that banks in a socialist economy acted on behalf of the government to safeguard the efficient use of public property. Shenger summarised this viewpoint by saying that 'in relation to an enterprise on economic accounting the bank appears as a representative of the state and it can, and indeed is obliged to, control the activity of the enterprise, demanding a proper utilisation of state resources.'[2]

Distinction is made in this study between 'bank control' and 'control by credit' (viz. monetary control), the former being a general expression embracing not only control by credit, but also control of wage payments and control through settlements. Before analysing separately the term 'control by credit' the other two forms of bank control are briefly summarised.

Control over payments from the wage funds of individual enterprises was a very important part of bank control. As already stated (pp. 37–8), it had important macroeconomic significance, because through it the authorities endeavoured to operate an incomes policy designed to prevent increases in purchasing power unaccompanied by rises in productivity. A detailed treatment of the control of wage payments cannot be undertaken in this study, but before leaving the subject it may be observed that no banking system outside Soviet-type economies performed a similar function. The control of wage payments, more than any other form of bank control, indi-

---

[1] See e.g. Parfanyak, pp. 123–4.

[2] V. E. Shenger, *Ocherki Sovetskogo Kredita* (1961) p. 18.

cated that in such economies the banking system was used chiefly as a convenient instrument of control. It may be noted that there was no direct link between wage control and control by credit. For instance, unjustified overpayment of wages could not be advanced by banks as a reason for not granting credit on some specific stocks held by the enterprise. A system of sanctions, different from credit sanctions, applied when wage bills were overdrawn.

There was some overlapping between bank control by settlements and control by credit, as settlements involved the granting of credit (*inkasso credit*). Nevertheless, the distinction is useful in analysing bank control. Each enterprise could have only one current or settlement account in the appropriate bank (usually the central bank), from which payments were made. It could obtain credit only from the same bank, separate credit accounts being opened for that purpose.

In their current account enterprises were required to keep all their cash reserves, except a small float. This facilitated control over the total supply of credit by centralising all monetary resources in the banking system (mainly in one bank), making them available for credit purposes. It also had an important meaning from the point of view of bank control over enterprises. If cash resources were left in the hands of the enterprise then it would be difficult to detect unauthorised or 'illegal' payments. Settlements were to be in the main cashless, viz. carried out by bank transfers following the settlement of invoices. Once an invoice was accepted by the buyer its payment was carried out by the banking system.

It may be noted that cashless settlements are common to East European and Western economies, especially those with a well-developed banking habit, where most business debts are settled by cheques cleared through the banking system. Whereas Western banks merely supply payments services, passively executing the instructions of their clients, socialist banks had to make certain that settlements were not mere transfers of sums passively carried out by them in the process of bank clearing. They were supposed to scrutinise all debts carefully, in order to establish whether they arose from business transactions consistent with the planned targets of enterprises and with various regulations. It is this control motive which prevented a widespread use of cheques as a medium of money transfers in socialist economies, perpetuating the system of clearing invoices which was administratively more cumbersome and less economic. Banks were also to make certain that enterprises followed a prescribed order of payments when they were short of funds.

Apart from exercising control through wage payments, settlements and credit, banks had wide powers of direct intervention in business affairs. For example, they could request information in the form of detailed reports on financial matters, in addition to documents which were to be produced as a matter of routine in the course of extending credit or making settlements. Furthermore, banks could carry out inspections of enterprises, either to check that information given in documents was in fact correct or to discover reasons for excessive indebtedness or other financial difficulties. It was not clear to what extent the banks were in theory to exercise these forms of direct intervention. Equally it was not clear whether banks were to intervene in all cases of mismanagement of enterprises of which they were aware, or only those directly related to credit or payments operations.[1]

(d) The main principles of socialist monetary control

The terms describing various forms of bank control have so far been direct translations of Soviet terms. 'Control by credit' is also a Soviet term, meaning influencing the behaviour of enterprises through the supply and/or cost of credit. This, as has been proposed in the first chapter, is the essence of 'monetary control', which is an expression commonly used in the West but not in East Europe. Thus the terms 'monetary control' and 'credit control' may be used interchangeably, but preference is given in subsequent sections to the former.

Control by credit in East European literature was often regarded as the most appropriate as well as the most important form of bank control. This is perhaps partly because credit activity is a traditional banking function in any economic system and partly because socialist credit was thought to have acquired, by complying with certain principles, excellent control capabilities. After the amendments to the 1930 credit reforms socialist credit was to: (a) be granted

---

[1] In 1930 a view was expressed in the Soviet Union that control by banks must only be exercised in conjunction with various banking functions (credit, settlements). F. Radetskii, 'Bankovskii Kontrol' i Ego Zadachi v Protsesie Rekonstruktsii Kredita', *Vestnik Finansov* 2 (1930) p. 24 et seq.; Ya Rubinstein, p. 8, expressed a similar view more recently.

for a definite period, (*b*) be returnable, (*c*) be granted for a specific purpose, (*d*) be secured, (*e*) be granted in a planned way.[1]

The first two characteristics may be treated together. Credits had to be repaid in a stipulated time, determined by the duration of seasonal or temporary needs or, in the case of credit on documents in transit, by the time necessary to finalise settlements of debts between enterprises. As in the course of production resources were generated or 'freed', credits were repaid, so that an enterprise did not have excessive credit at any stage of production.[2] Failure to repay credit was taken as indicative of mismanagement.

Credit could only be claimed for a specific purpose. If an enterprise required a sum of credit X, it could not make a general application for that sum, but had to make separate applications for specified purposes. The sum of credit claimed in these applications might well add up to X. The characteristic of 'specific purpose' was rather narrowly interpreted. To make certain that credit was indeed granted for a legitimate purpose, a detailed classification of credit by purpose became binding on both banks and enterprises. Each type of credit was kept in a separate account. It was not sufficient for an applicant to request credit to solve some difficulty peculiar to his enterprise – credit could only be demanded for a purpose strictly defined by the instructions of the bank.

Credit was said to be secured by the fact that it was issued for a specific purpose and was therefore linked with some material value. In general, enterprises were expected to possess stocks which they wanted to finance from credit and which were regarded as the main security of loan repayment. Indeed, after 1956 in Poland this mode of crediting was generally called the 'refund method of credit' (*refund-acyjny sposób kredytowania*), as credit merely refunded expenditure which must already have been incurred by enterprises in acquiring stocks. It was believed that this method would not only secure credit repayment (after stocks were utilised in production), but would also prevent inflationary financing, as it was thought that

---

[1] The respective Russian terms are: (*a*) *srochnost'* (*b*) *vozvratnost'*, (*c*) *tselovoe napravlenie*, (*d*) *obespechennost'*, (*e*) *planovost'*. A bibliography of characteristics of socialist credit: Z. V. Atlas (1947) pp. 293–8; Z. V. Atlas (1957) pp. 299–304; For Polish texts see M. L. Kostowski, 'Zasady Systemu Kredytowego', *ŻG* 2 (1951) pp. 78–80; Z. Karpiński and J. Lindner, *Organizacja Bankowości w Polsce Ludowej* (1954) pp. 78–81; M. Kucharski, *Kredyt Krótkoterminowy i Planowanie Kredytowe* (1955) pp. 182–5.

[2] This is reminiscent of 'the law of reflux' (see p. 14) proposed by the Banking School in Britain.

3

credit not so secured would encourage wasteful expenditure by enterprises. Banks were also to make certain that the credit was actually required for a special purpose and that it was rationally used. To ascertain the existence of a security, banks were to carry out 'preliminary checks' before payment and then 'subsequent checks' on the efficient use of loans granted until full repayment. Credit connected with settlements (viz. on documents in transit) was secured by documents on goods involved in settlements. This particular principle of insisting on a good self-liquidating credit security very strongly reflected the 'real bills' doctrine.

Furthermore, banks were to ensure that credit was granted not only in the framework of the bank's credit plan (viz. within limits set for various types of credit) and in accordance with planned targets or credit limits set for an enterprise (viz. 'on the strength of the plan'), but also that it was actually required by enterprises whilst *correctly fulfilling their production plans*. Thus, essentially, credit was to finance not merely the planned but the actual needs consistent with the attainment of planned production targets. Provided that the above condition were observed banks had little discretion in crediting.

The bank could not refuse credit to clients complying with the said principles, but had to refuse credit in cases of non-compliance which suggested the existence of some shortcomings in plan fulfilment or management in general. As already noted, banks had the duty to try to rectify such shortcomings. The principal economic sanction used by banks was credit restriction. Banks could threaten to cut the supply of credit, decrease or even cease lending altogether, until a shortcoming in the enterprise's management was rectified. It was generally assumed that a shortage of credit would coerce enterprises to better management. Thus, a vital aspect of socialist bank control was what might be called 'coercive credit control'.

It must be added that much more emphasis was put on sanctions based on the supply of credit than on the cost of credit. Although overdue credit was automatically burdened with a penal rate of interest and lip service was paid to the salutary effect of higher interest charges on enterprises,[1] interest as a weapon of control was neglected. Interest rates on credit were at one stage regarded chiefly

[1] It was thought, for example, that a penal rate on overdue credit would encourage quicker repayment of credit by causing a rise in costs, thus endangering the fulfilment of the plan for lowering production costs.

as a price of banking services.[1] The authorities moreover aimed at low interest charges, thinking that this would encourage banks to increase their efficiency and would also be conducive to lowering the costs of production of enterprises. Rates of interest were rarely altered, banks having no discretionary power to change them.

As has been rightly observed by some Western economists (see p. 12), the system of Soviet monetary control incorporated the prescriptions of the 'real bills' theory. It is difficult, however, to see why they did not approve of this. It must be remembered that the Soviet monetary system functioned in conditions which have never been experienced by Western countries which discarded the doctrine. First, it functioned in a closed economy. Soviet international trade did take place but its volume declined after 1930.[2] It was conducted mainly on the basis of bilateral agreements. Currency, though it had a gold parity, was not freely convertible. Internal prices were completely divorced from world prices. Monetary policy was thus freed from external criteria and from motives which have always played an important role in Western industrial development.

Secondly, aggregate expenditure was controlled directly by the national plan. The unified financial plan, incorporating the budget, the credit and the cash plans, was based on the national plan. The possession of money, or the ability to raise money, did not necessarily enable enterprises to undertake expenditure. Monetary authorities could not take measures (e.g. changes in the supply of money) designed specifically to change aggregate spending. The financial plan may be said to provide *quantitative tests* for the monetary authorities (compare p. 15).

Thirdly, the credit system consisted mainly of a single short-term credit bank.[3] In extending credit the bank was not constrained by any specific currency and deposit rules: issue was not dependent on

[1] Ikonnikov, p. 77.

[2] Between 1930 and 1938 the volume of international trade (measured by the sum of exports and imports at current prices at exchange rates of January 1961) fell by 71.1%. The fall in exports was 71.7% (for details see: Ministerstvo Vneshnei Torgovli SSSR – *Vneshnaya Torgovlya SSSR* (1967) p. 9). Between 1928 and 1940 national income increased by more than five times and industrial output by more than six times. Tsentralnoe Statisticheskoe Upravlenie (TsSU) – *Strana Sovietov za 50 let* (1967) p. 29. After the war international trade began to grow, see e.g. TsSU –*Narodnoe Khoziyaistvo SSSR (NKh) v 1967* (1968) p. 764.

[3] In 1932 the State Bank issued 97.8% of all short-term credit and in 1940 98.7%, Vorob'ev, *Denezhnoe Obrashchenie i Kredit SSSR* (1965) p. 92.

gold or minimum reserve (or liquidity) ratios, such as apply in Western banking.[1] There was thus a need for some specific criteria for granting credit. These criteria were stated in terms of the credit principles discussed above,[2] which may be said to have provided the *qualitative tests* for extending credit (compare p. 15).

Fourthly, the credit principles specifically defined the legitimate 'business needs', thus eliminating the vagueness of the 'principle of productive credit' applicable to Western banking (see pp. 15–16). It must be emphasised that the business needs were defined precisely and that the key criteria for their assessment were the planned targets of enterprises and their correct fulfilment.

The above propositions go a long way towards removing the major objections to the 'real bills' theory discussed in chapter 1. Furthermore, the simplicity of the credit system as compared with Western credit systems and the limited objectives of monetary policy help to explain the lack of sophistication of East European monetary thought. Other factors which may account for this simplicity are the rather thin heritage of Marxism and Leninism in monetary matters and the fact that, at least before the mid-1950s, the chief object of monetary theorists was to explain and justify the existing monetary principles.

According to some Western writers the Soviet monetary system, resting on the premises of the 'real bills' doctrine, resulted in a liberal credit expansion which contributed to, or at least was permissive of, inflation. Holzman, for instance, believed that 'the principle of productive credit' resulted in a 'financial slack' conducive to inflation, whose main cause lay in excess demand planning.[3] In a different context he concluded that 'Soviet planning is believed to

---

[1] Almost all assets of socialist banks are credit to the economy. No specific ratio of one type of credit to total deposits ever operated. The main liabilities of the banking system consist of current accounts, other accounts, budgetary deposits, currency and, in recent times, savings accounts. Again no specific ratios were prescribed. Variations in the structure of liabilities in the Polish banking system may be seen in tables B1a and B1b.

[2] Discussing the principles Garvy remarked: 'The textbooks of communist countries, in extolling the virtues of these principles, never inform their readers that, except for the first, they happen to be identical with the "real bills" (self-liquidating loan) doctrine generally discarded in the West.' (*Money, Banking and Credit*, p. 68).

[3] It is not clear whether Holzman associated inflation with the 'real bills' theory on theoretical or empirical grounds. He wrote: 'The Soviets put their faith in the "principle of productive credit", expecting Bank policies based on this principle to bring them financial stability. They did not realise that considerable slack was necessary for economic planning, as they practised it. If the principle of productive credit had not already existed and had not inadvertently provided them with financial slack, no doubt

have been basically responsible for the Soviet inflation of the inter-war period though it was, no doubt, aided and abetted by the pursuance of an inflationary credit policy.'[1]

An analysis of socialist credit principles and the conditions in which they were to be applied does not suggest that the credit policy was liberal. On the contrary credit conditions became quite stringent.

It will indeed be argued that the credit principles and policy which, as stated earlier, emerged as a reaction to the 'credit automatism' of 1930, were in practice not liberal but stringent.[2] They could neither have been a contributory factor to inflation nor an effective anti-inflationary weapon. Furthermore, though few theoretical objections can be raised against the adoption in Soviet-type planning of a monetary system based on the 'real bills' doctrine, it will be shown that the monetary authorities, in implementing stringent monetary control, were not strictly consistent with the doctrine.

In conclusion it must again be stressed that monetary control in the sense in which it was discussed above was a feature peculiar to Soviet-type banking systems. As mentioned in chapter 1, in the West monetary control is a macroeconomic tool of national economic management, and the relations between banks and their customers receive relatively little attention and are regarded as simply technical aspects of banking. It is, on the other hand, possible to consider the existence in the West of control by credit in a microeconomic sense.

In making advances, banks must naturally evaluate the credit-worthiness of firms by looking into their business affairs. This is done not in order to exert pressure on firms to improve their management, but primarily to ensure the repayment of loans granted to them. In this way firms assessed as bad risks are not likely to receive credit, whereas firms which are thought to have good business prospects are more likely to get credit.

It may be said that such behaviour amounts to a form of control by banks over credit applicants. As profit-making organisations and in the interest of their shareholders, banks must discriminate in

the Soviets would have had to invent it.' *Soviet Taxation*, p. 49. Earlier (pp. 27–8) the author spoke of the inflationary nature of Soviet short-term credit programme and 'excess bank credit' before the 1950s.

[1] Holzman, *Financing Soviet Economic Development*; in *Capital Formation and Economic Growth* (Princeton, 1955) p. 264. In a comment on the above, Powell attributed the relative stability of post-war development mainly to financial management (pp. 274–82).

[2] Which does not mean that they were effective.

granting credit between good risks and bad risks. Consequently, before it receives credit, a firm may have to satisfy the bank as to its business efficiency. The impact of banks on firms depends largely on the financial system of an economy. In well-developed financial systems, where banks are only one of a number of specialised financial intermediaries, the influence of banks may be small, due to a large number of alternative sources of finance. The ability to get trade credit may further weaken the influence of banks. The nature of banks may also be important. Specialised banks, such as the British commercial banks, typically granting short and medium-term credit, are likely to have less influence over firms than universal banks (e.g. Grossbanken in Germany), which combine the function of the British commercial and merchant banks, supplying firms with working capital and helping them to acquire permanent capital. Furthermore, bank influence on firms may be diminished by the practice of self-finance. When firms can satisfy a large part of their demand for funds by ploughing back profits, credit may become a relatively less important source of finance. Hence the influence of banks on firms may be small.

Thus, in general, in distributing their resources, Western banks are governed primarily by the profit motive. However, in recent years lending has also been affected by central bank requests or directives to commercial banks and other financial intermediaries. These direct non-market weapons of credit control have been increasingly used to supplement traditional instruments, such as open-market operations and the rediscount rate. However, even if monetary authorities resort to non-market controls, they do so in order to affect the level of total bank deposits or the level of advances or a particular type of advances, but not in order to intervene in the relations between banks and their specific customers or to interfere with the activities of particular firms.[1] In short, direct controls simply impose limitations within which banks may freely pursue

---

[1] In England, for example, the Bank of England must not use direct controls to interfere with the relations of the commercial banker and his customer. Clause 4 section 3 of the Bank of England Act 1946 provides that 'The Bank of England, if they think it necessary in the public interest, may request information from and make recommendations to bankers, and may, if so authorised by the Treasury, issue directives to any banker for the purpose of securing that effect is given to any such requests or recommendations. Provided that: (a) no such request or recommendation shall be made with respect to the affairs of any particular customer of a banker', *Halsbury's Statutes of England*, 2nd ed. (1948) p. 278.

their activities with a view to making a profit. In socialist planning bank intervention in the management of enterprises is the very essence of bank control.

We may reflect that bank control over firms in the West, weak as it may be in practice, is based mainly on the possibility of refusal of credit to a firm which a bank may assess as a bad risk. In a socialist economy enterprises were entitled to credit within planned limits and, as a rule, banks could not refuse to grant credit. Credit refusal could, however, be a sanction against an enterprise which had mismanaged its affairs. In the West, private enterprise and the operation of market forces make such control superfluous; in the East it is conditioned by the system of planning adopted.

3

Banking and credit in Poland before 1939

Introduction: Polish etatism

The Polish economic system between the two world wars was often described at the time as etatism, to signify a high degree of state intervention in the economic activity of the country. State intervention was either based on public ownership or exercised through fiscal and monetary policies.

After the first world war the state acquired property in a number of ways: by taking over property as a result of the recovery of territories from the partitioning powers, by establishing new enterprises or expanding existing ones, by granting financial help to private firms in difficulties and then by taking them over when they failed to repay their credits. It is generally asserted that the state owned a large part of the total wealth of the country, although exact estimates of state property were difficult, partly because of the occasional lack of official evidence of state ownership, as the state sometimes established or took over enterprises without promulgating special laws, and partly because state participation took a variety of organisational forms. Furthermore, over the period 1918–39 both the share of state ownership in the country's wealth and state intervention, whose forms are described below, increased. Zweig observed that 'The etatism deeply rooted in Polish soil grew like a tree with great and wide spreading branches. It had manifold sources, some inherited, some new, but every period of the short Twenty Years contributed to its development.'[1]

In trying to explain the reasons for the growing state activity, Górecki, the chairman of the National Economic Bank, stressed the historical evolution of Polish etatism, emphasising that, in the period of the country's partition, public authorities were the most active element in promoting economic growth. He also pointed out

[1] F. Zweig, *Poland Between Two Wars* (London, 1944) p. 106.

58

that, after the war, Poland inclined towards what was a general tendency at the time: protectionism and 'state nationalism'.[1] In the 1920s there was a rising demand for large scale capital to integrate the economies of regions previously administered by different partitioning powers. In other words, it was necessary to develop the infrastructure of a single economy. Private enterprise could not provide the necessary funds; it was weakened by inflation in the 1920s, during which period the state significantly increased its ownership, or participation in the ownership, of industrial firms, which otherwise would have had to cease production.

The main reason for the more rapid development of etatism in the 1930s was the weakness of Polish capitalism, coupled with the desire of the state to develop the economy in order to provide more employment and greater military strength. Voluntary accumulation of capital in the private sector of the economy was too small to serve as a basis for economic development. Indeed Kwiatkowski, the Minister of the Treasury and the Vice-Premier, in a speech to the Sejm delivered in 1937, stressed that one of the causes of etatism in Poland was 'the weak economic dynamics of the Polish society'.[2] The middle class possessed too little funds to generate economic development. The market for industrial products was, due both to the low income of the population (especially of the peasantry) and to high unemployment, too small to secure the yield on investment necessary to attract large scale capital. In such a situation, particularly after the need to strengthen defence became pressing in the late 1930s, state initiative in stimulating and guiding economic development became vitally necessary. This in fact did take place. Zweig remarked that after 1936 Poland tended increasingly towards a type of state-planned economy designed to industrialise the country and to develop its defence potential.[3]

Banking and credit before 1939

The pre-1939 banking system was largely a product of financial reforms carried out in 1924 by W. Grabski, who became Premier

[1] R. Górecki, *The Activity of the National Bank of Poland*, (Warsaw, 1928) p. 8; *Rola Banku Gospodarstwa Krajowego* (1928) pp. 14–23.

[2] E. Kwiatkowski, *Obraz Gospodarstwa Polski w Roku 1937* (1937).

[3] F. Zweig, 'Nowe Drogi Przemysłu Polskiego', *Ekonomista Polski* (London) 3 (1943) p. 41.

and Minister of the Treasury in December 1923. One of the key reforms was the currency reform[1] and the establishment of the central bank – the Bank of Poland (Bank Polski). The bank was created as a Joint Stock Company with share capital of 100 million złoty, 'in order to maintain the stability of the currency, to regulate the money circulation and credit'.[2] Its immediate task was to administer the newly created currency – the złoty.

At first the state holding of shares in the Bank of Poland was negligible. In 1927, however, the state purchased the Second Issue, amounting to 50 million złoty nominal value. The shares carried no voting rights and the dividend on them was limited to 10%. They were repurchased from the state in 1936.

Although the central bank was not owned by the state, it was not completely free from state supervision. The Chairman of the bank was appointed by the President of the Republic on the recommendation of the Council of Ministers. He could not, however, be a member of the Sejm or the Senate. He had the right of suspensory veto in respect of decisions of the Bank Council, if the decisions were contary to the laws of the land or the public interest. After the veto the ultimate decision rested with the State Treasury. The statute also empowered the Minister of the Treasury to appoint a Bank Commissioner, who was a member of the Bank Council and was permitted to attend meetings of the Board of Directors in an advisory capacity. Through the commissioner, the state was to exercise continuous supervision over the activity of the bank.

In practice the bank co-operated closely with the state in carrying out the government's economic policy. Perhaps the only major exception to this was the conflict between the government and the bank in 1925, on the question of the policy for stabilising the złoty. International confidence in the złoty declined in 1925, but Grabski was determined to maintain its fixed rate of exchange at all costs. In November of that year the bank refused to give further support to the złoty by running down its reserves of gold and foreign currencies. The refusal proved to be the immediate cause of Grabski's resigna-

[1] The old Polish mark was replaced by the new legal tender, the złoty, at the rate of 1 złoty = 1,800,000 marks = 1 Swiss gold franc. The exchange rate against the US dollar was 5.18 zł. For more information see F. Młynarski, *The Genoa Resolutions and the Currency Reform In Poland* (Warsaw, 1925).
[2] Quoted from the Statute of the Bank of Poland, published in C. H. Kisch and W. A. Elkin, *Central Banks* (London, 1932) p. 371.

tion.[1] Thus the crisis had a unique ending – the Premier was ultimately defeated by the banking institution whose establishment he
himself had inspired. The 1925 conflict between the government
and the bank was, however, exceptional. Co-operation between
them proceeded smoothly in general and was especially pronounced
in the 1930s, when the bank served as an important source of finance
for the Treasury and distributed credit in accordance with the
government's policy.

Up to 1936 the bank concentrated its activity exclusively on short-
term credit, the bulk of which was extended by discounting or rediscounting bills (see table 2a). It was, as far as other banks were
concerned, the lender of last resort, and a great proportion of its
discounts were discounts of bills presented by other financial
institutions (see table 2b). From 1936 the bank began to extend
credit for investment purposes as well, but this activity remained a
small part of its business.[2] The amount of credit granted by the bank,
compared with the credit activity of other credit institutions, is given
in table 3.[3] The table provides only a very rough comparison between
the credit institutions listed, largely because, due to the lack of
appropriate data, long-term credit of a number of institutions is not
given. From descriptive accounts of these institutions it appears that
their long-term credit activity was much less significant than their
short-term credit activity. Nevertheless the absence of data for long-
term credit in some cases prevents a strict comparison between the
institutions.

As shown in table 3, the most important commercial banks in
Poland were two state owned banks: the National Economic Bank
(Bank Gospodarstwa Krajowego) and the State Agricultural Bank
(Państwowy Bank Rolny). The National Economic Bank (NEB) was
created in 1924 by merging a bank which had been important during
the Austrian partition of Poland – the Polish National Bank (Polski
Bank Krajowy) – with the State Bank for Reconstruction (Pań-
stwowy Bank Odbudowy) and the Credit Institute of the Cities of
Małopolska (Zakład Kredytowy Miast Małopolski). The bank was a

[1] Z. Karpiński, *Bank Polski* (1958) pp. 26–8.   [2] *Ibid.* p. 184.
[3] The data on the Bank of Poland's credit in table 3 excludes discounting of foreign bills
and the debt of the Treasury (both given in table 2a). The table lists only the most
important credit institutions – it omits minor institutions. There were for instance 975
Rural Loans and Savings banks, but they were not very important. In 1937 their share
in the total short-term credit of the banking system was only 0.8% (GUS *Mały
Rocznik Statystyczny 1938*, p. 201).

Table 2a

Credit activity of the Bank of Poland 1935–8

(Balances at the end of the year : million złoty)

Year	Total	Domestic bills	Foreign bills	Treasury bills	Loans on collateral	Treasury debt
1935	959.1	689.1	2.9	67.6	109.5	90.0
1936	947.9	681.3	2.3	66.9	107.4	90.0
1937	790.8	660.9	2.3	23.3	24.3	80.0
1938	1072.0	830.8	2.2	81.9	112.1	45.0

Sources: *Annual Report of the Bank of Poland for the Year Ending December 31st, 1937*, p. 28. *Annual Report of the Bank of Poland for the Year Ending December 31st, 1938*, p. 27.

Table 2b

Domestic bills discounted by the Bank of Poland 1936–7

(Balances at the end of the year)

Bills presented by	1936		1937	
	mil. zł.	%	mil. zł.	%
Credit institutions	615.6	90	606.0	92
Industry	39.7 ⎫		37.0 ⎫	
Agriculture	4.8 ⎪	10	4.1 ⎪	8
Trade	17.8 ⎬		11.0 ⎬	
Miscellaneous	3.4 ⎭		2.8 ⎭	
Total	681.3	100	660.9	100

Source: *Annual Report of the Bank of Poland for the Year Ending December 31st, 1937*, p. 27.

universal type of bank, combining the usual banking functions, such as the accumulation of deposits, money transfers, short-term and long-term credit, with such activities as issues of securities, participations and mergers. It also received from the state deposits destined to be distributed in the form of credit in accordance with government policy.[1] Of its numerous functions two must be emphasised.

[1] The volume of Treasury deposits in the bank varied according to the way in which the government chose to finance expenditure. In the late 1930s there was a preference for financing building from new bond issues rather than by bank credit. Thus Treasury deposits as a ratio of total deposits with the bank fell from 64.3% in 1935 to 52.8% in 1936 and 40.0% in 1937 – see *The Report of Directors for 1937*, p. 20.

Table 3

Principal credit institutions 1935–8

(*Balances at the end of the year*)

Credit institutions	No. of banks in 1938	Credit in mil. zł.[1]			
		1935	1936	1937	1938
Bank of Poland[2]	1	866	856	708	1,025
State banks	3	1,891	1,985	2,092	2,220
NEB	1	1,119	1,184	1,231	1,387
short-term		239	270	370	333
long-term		181	147	173	191
Treasury[3]		699	767	688	863
State Ag. Bank	1	739	763	813	787
short-term		108	111	147	111
Treasury[3]		631	652	666	676
Postal Savings Bank	1	33	38	48	46
Municipal banks and mun. savings banks[4]	357	678	644	653	701
Co-operative banks [4,5]	5,607	451	364	409	435
Private banks[4,6]	58	665	633	664	724
Grand total	6,026	4,551	4,482	4,526	5,105

Notes:

[1] Cash credit.

[2] Short-term credit including discounts.

[3] Long-term credit from Treasury funds administered by the bank.

[4] Short-term credits.

[5] Ten co-operative banks plus 5,597 loans and savings co-operatives.

[6] Twenty-six joint stock banks, twenty-eight large banking houses and four branches of foreign banks.

Sources: *Bank Gospodarstwa Krajowego. Report of Directors for the Financial Year 1938*, p. 19; Ministry of Information, *Concise Statistical Year Book of Poland 1939–1941*, p. 93; W. Jaworski, *Obieg Pieniężny i Kredyt w Gospodarce Socjalistycznej* (1963) p. 27.

The bank played a key role in the state financial apparatus. It co-operated with the Treasury, managed state funds and administered Treasury allocations made for specific purposes such as house-building, or to encourage exports. It was also the main instrument used by the state in taking over private firms which failed to

Table 4a

Credit granted by NEB for public purposes 1935–8

(*Balances at the end of the year*)

Year	Total mil. zł.	Source of credit		Credit for public purposes		Credit for private purposes	
		General banking section	Treasury funds[1]	mil. zł.	%	mil. zł.	%
1935	1,169	470	699	694	59	475	41
1936	1,210	443	767	750	62	460	38
1937	1,232	544	688	741	60	491	40
1938	1,424	561	863	918	64	506	36

Note:

[1] Long-term credit operations conducted jointly by the Bank and the Treasury and administered on Treasury accounts.

Source: *Bank Gospodarstwa Krajowego. Report of Directors for the Financial Year 1938*, p. 25.

meet their debts. Such enterprises were grouped in the bank's consortium (Koncern Banku Gospodarstwa Krajowego). The finance of expenditure for public purposes, for example expenditure by public institutions or expenditure generally entailed in the pursuit of specific government policy, was the primary function of the bank. Table 4a shows that in 1938 64% of the credit granted by the bank was granted for public purposes. More specifically, the most important customers of the bank were state institutions and enterprises. In 1938 they received 46% of the total credit extended by the bank (see table 4b); local authorities received 8%.

Secondly, the bank was a chief source of long-term credit for investment purposes. Indeed it was mainly a long-term credit bank – in the late 1930s over 70% of its credit was long-term (see tables 3 and 4c). The bank was, moreover, actively concerned in promotional activity in the economy and engaged in new issues. It was the most important supplier of what, in Polish terminology, was called 'issue credit' (*kredyt emisyjny*).[1] This, as Górecki explained, was long-term credit secured by mortgages on the basis of which the bank issued

[1] In contrast, the other type of credit, with which we have been concerned so far, was called 'cash credit' (*kredyt gotówkowy*).

Table 4b

Credit granted by the NEB to state institutions and firms and to local governments 1936–8
(*Percentage of total credit granted by the Bank*)

Year	State institutions and firms	Local governments	Total
1936	36.2	8.5	44.7
1937	38.4	8.5	46.9
1938	46.2	8.0	54.2

Sources: *Bank Gospodarstwa Krajowego. Reports of Directors: for the Financial Year 1936*, p. 25; *for the Financial Year 1937*, p. 25; *for the Financial Year 1938*, p. 35.

Table 4c

Short and long-term credit of the National Economic Bank 1935–8
(*Balances at the end of the year*)

Year	Total	Short-term credit[1]		Long-term credit	
		mil. zł.	% of total	mil. zł.	% of total
1935	1,169	289	25	880	75
1936	1,210	297	25	913	75
1937	1,232	372	30	860	70
1938	1,424	370	26	1,054	74

Note:
[1] Excluding rediscount operations.
Source: *Bank Gospodarstwa Krajowego. Report of Directors for the Financial Year 1938*, p. 34.

bonds, placing them on home or foreign capital markets.[1] Table 5 shows that in the late 1930s issue credit was a substantial part (about 40%) of the bank's lending activity. All private institutions granting this type of credit, of which three Credit Societies (Ziemskie Towarzystwa Kredytowe) in Warsaw, Poznań and Lwów were the most important,[2] granted less issue credit than the bank. Its share of

[1] R. Górecki, *Poland and Her Economic Development* (London, 1935) p. 52.
[2] R. Górecki, *Gospodarczy Dorobek Polski w Latach 1918–1938* (Polish Army Abroad: London, 1946) p. 132.

Table 5

Issue credit and cash credit of the National Economic Bank 1935–8

(*Balances at the end of the year*)

Year	Total mil. zł.	Issue credit		Cash credit	
		mil. zł.	%	mil. zł.	%
1935	1,962	793	40	1,169	60
1936	2,134	924	43	1,210	57
1937	2,138	906	42	1,232	58
1938	2,360	936	40	1,424	60

Source: *Bank Gospodarstwa Krajowego. Report of Directors for the Financial Year 1938*, pp. 19, 24.

Table 6

Issue credit granted by institutions of long-term finance 1938

(*Balances at the end of the year*)

	in mil. zł.	% of total
National Economic Bank	936	47
State Agricultural Bank	209	10
Private Credit Institutions	867	43
Total	2,012	100

Source: R. Górecki, *Gospodarczy Dorobek Polski w Latach 1918–1938*, p. 132.

total issue credit was 47% in 1938 (see table 6). The bank also played an important part in the finance of investment programmes coming into operation after 1936, which will be discussed later.

The NEB, through its diverse functions, closely resembled the universal 'industrial banks', modelled perhaps on the French Credit Mobilier, which played such an important part in the industrial development of some continental European countries, Germany in particular. Indeed an eminent historian, appreciating their role in development, thought of such banks as 'perhaps the greatest organisational innovation in the economic history of the century'.[1] The

[1] A. Gerschenkron, *Europe in the Russian Mirror* (Cambridge, 1970) p. 102.

Table 7

Credit activity of the State Agricultural Bank 1935–8

(*Balances at the end of the year : million złoty*)

Year	Short-term credit	Long-term loans from government funds administered by the bank
1935	108.2	630.8
1936	111.5	652.5
1937	146.7	665.7
1938	1115.	675.9

Source: *Bank Gospodarstwa Krajowego. Report of Directors for the Financial Year 1938*, p. 19.

NEB, however, differed from many of its Western counterparts in that it was publicly owned.

Another state owned bank of key importance in the economy was the State Agricultural Bank (Państwowy Bank Rolny). This bank was established in 1919, but did not begin its operations until 1924. Its main function was to finance state agricultural reform and generally to promote agricultural development and trade in agricultural commodities. Most of the credit granted by the bank was long-term, financed jointly by the bank and the Treasury (see table 7).

Apart from the above mentioned banks, the state owned the Postal Savings Bank (Pocztowa Kasa Oszczędności). The direct credit activity of this bank was very small (see table 3). Its main functions were money transfers and the accumulation of savings in the community, which it transferred to NEB, the State Agricultural Bank and other credit institutions. In this way it contributed to the supply of long-term finance in the economy. In 1933 the government secured the establishment of the Acceptance Bank (Bank Akceptacyjny), which was a joint stock bank instituted to help farmers financially by prolonging the repayment of their debt to other financial institutions and by reducing interest rates on their loans.[1] The state also held a financial interest in some private joint stock banks.[2]

[1] R. Górecki, *Gospodarczy...*, p. 127.

[2] For example: Union of Workers' Co-operatives Bank (Bank Związku Spółek Zarobkowych) and Polish Industrial Bank (Polski Bank Przemysłowy).

Table 8

Short-term credit granted by various types of
financial institutions 1937–8

(*Balances at the end of the year: million zloty*)

	No. of banks	1937	1938
Bank of Poland	1	708	1,025
State banks[1]	3	566	491
Municipal banks and municipal savings banks	357	653	701
Co-operative banks	5,607	409	435
Joint stock banks and banking houses	58	664	724
Total	6,026	3,000	3,376

Note:
[1] Viz. NEB, State Agricultural Bank and Postal Savings Bank.
Source: As in table 3.

In addition to the banks already mentioned, the banking system in Poland in the inter-war period consisted of two municipal banks and a large number of municipal savings banks, co-operative banks, rural credit and savings banks and private joint stock banks (see tables 3 and 8). All these institutions were on a small scale compared with the state banks and in general they specialised in short-term credit activity. Perhaps the most important were the private joint stock banks. Their credit activity was almost entirely concentrated on short-term finance. According to the data in table 8 in the years 1937 and 1938 their share in total short-term credit was 22.1% and 21.5% respectively.

The dominant institutions in the Polish banking system before 1939 were thus the state banks. The reasons for the rise of state banking relative to other banking largely coincided with the reasons for the development of Polish etatism. Capitalism in Poland had not reached a developed stage. Private banks were weak. Their small scale did not inspire sufficient confidence in them to develop the banking habit in the community. In the early 1930s private banking was further weakened by the flight of foreign short-term capital following the international monetary crisis of 1931. This weakness of private banking, coupled with great demand for capital and the desire of the state to develop the economy and reduce unemployment, was mainly responsible for the creation of strong state banks, whose functions were not only to supply industrial finance, but also to foster industrial initiative and enterprise.[1]

Credit policy

The banking system represented an important instrument of economic control in the hands of the state. In exercising this control the state did not utilise the traditional means of monetary policy, such as rediscount rates or open market operations. The money market was not sufficiently developed to permit effective use of such techniques. Market forces did exercise an influence on the credit market, but they were not of fundamental importance. In 1937 for example, when, with rising confidence in the economy, banks began to attract more deposits and found that as a result their liquidity was rising, rates of interest were decreased.[2] Although the decline of interest rates was considered to be an incentive to the expansion of private investment, interest rates were not generally relied on as a method of controlling the demand for credit.

Basically, the state used the credit system as a mechanism for credit rationing.[3] This was especially true of state owned banks, whose lending resources included a substantial volume of budgetary funds. The cash reserves of the budget were held by the state banks. The Treasury sometimes gave special allocations to the banks to raise their lending potential.[4] It created a wide variety of funds, such as the State Building Fund (Państwowy Fundusz Budowlany), which financed specific types of expenditure and were administered by the state banks. Commenting on this multitude of funds, Tennenbaum suggested that there was a belief that most types of expenditure could be financed by credit. The creation of funds reflected the desire to

---

[1] It may be noted that a deliberate development of financial structure as part of a growth strategy is today often advocated for underdeveloped economies. See e.g. E. Nevin, *Capital Funds in Undeveloped Countries* (London, 1961); U. S. Hicks, *Development Finance* (Oxford, 1965) ch. 3.

[2] *Sprawozdanie Banku Polskiego 1937* (1938) p. 18.

[3] Górecki, *Gospodarczy...*, p. 38; M. Drozdowski, *Polityka Gospodarcza Rządu Polskiego 1936-39* (1963) pp. 252-6 and 270.

[4] H. Tennenbaum, *Struktura Gospodarstwa Polskiego*, vol. 2, *Kredyt* (1935) pp. 26-41.

plan credit. There seemed to be as many funds as there were purposes for credit. Financing by credit was thus, in general, a very popular form of state finance. Tennenbaum noticed that 'The Polish state delights in issuing credit'.[1]

Credit was directed by the state in accordance with its policy objectives. The creditworthiness of recipients and their ability to meet a required rate of interest were often of secondary importance in distributing it. Broadly speaking, between 1932 and 1936 credit policy was 'defensive' – designed to help industrial and agricultural firms avoid liquidation in order to save the jobs of their employees. After 1935 it became 'offensive' – calculated to stimulate economic development generally.[2]

In 1936 etatism in Poland entered into a new phase, when the government undertook a programme of economic development. In the spring of 1936 representatives of the government, of various sections of the economy and of trade unions held a conference following the deliberations of which the government produced the first investment plan for the years 1936 to 1939. The first variant of the plan, providing for investment valued at 1650–1800 million złoty, was extended in 1937 to a total of 1800–2400 million złoty. Development was to be concentrated in central Poland, in the Central Industrial Region. Priority was given to defence, transport and communication, heavy industry and electrification. The second variant of the 1936–9 plan was fulfilled before time. Encouraged by this, at the end of 1938 Kwiatkowski, the chief architect of Polish pre-war planning, presented to the Sejm a draft of a long-term investment plan (15 years up to 1954), divided into five three-year plans. By then investment planning appeared to have become an accepted way of national economic management.

Polish pre-war planning had some interesting features. It was in no way modelled on Soviet planning. There were no central government institutions in Poland specifically designed to work out plans and supervise their implementation. Planning was confined mainly to investment planning, carried out chiefly in the Planning Bureau of the Treasury. In March 1938, however, the Bureau of Coordination of Planning and of Propaganda was established to coordinate the investment projects of various ministries and to engage in propaganda supporting government investment policy.

[1] H. Tennenbaum, *Struktura Gospodarstwa Polskiego*, vol. 2, *Kredyt* (1935) p. 147.
[2] Karpiński, pp. 160–81.

In the realm of finance, it is interesting to observe that the role of the state budget in the finance of investment plans was important but declining. In the budget years 1936-7, 1937-8 and 1938-9 the contribution of the state budget to the finance of the investment plans was 47%, 34% and 31% respectively, whereas funds raised through the banking system (including the NEB and the Postal Savings Bank) and from state enterprises independent of the budget amounted respectively to 46%, 61% and 64% of total investment expenditure. The remainder of the funds came mainly from the budget of Silesia and from the national insurance.[1] The above figures show a growing tendency for the government to cover investment expenditure from non-budgetary sources. This can be explained first of all by the balanced budget policy pursued by Kwiatkowski and secondly by the desire on the part of the government to avoid control by the Sejm, which was entailed in all budgetary expenditure.

The banking system closely co-operated with the government in implementing investment plans. As mentioned earlier, from 1936 onwards even the central bank began to make a direct contribution to the finance of investment. Of all the banks however, the most important part in this respect was played by NEB.

The Polish banking system played a key role in pre-war planning. Indeed the character of the system largely dictated the type of planning adopted. The dominance of state banks in the capital market of the country allowed the government to direct non-budgetary financial resources to be used consistently with government economic policy. Thus on the whole before 1939 the Polish banking system had a considerable tradition and experience of co-operation with the state and represented a key instrument through which the government exercised its economic policy.

[1] Drozdowski, p. 137, table 26 and pp. 251-2.

PART II

Banking and monetary control in centralised
socialist planning

4

Banking and monetary policy in Poland before the financial reforms of 1948–50

Introduction: the Polish road to socialism

After the second world war the government of Poland was faced with the problems of general economic revival and of economic integration caused by post-war territorial changes. Against this background it set about constructing a new economic system based on socialist principles. The authorities had to decide on the form of socialist society appropriate to Poland and on the strategy necessary to realise it.

Until 1948 it was evident that the architects of the Polish socialist system did not intend to adopt outright the 'Soviet model' of a socialist economy. Although it was not clear what precisely would be the ultimate shape of socialist society aimed at, it was clear that the Poles meant to attain it in an evolutionary way, which would give scope for original solutions to various organisational problems. Dietrych, the Vice-Minister of the State Treasury and the future Chairman of the Central Planning Office (Centralny Urząd Planowania – CPO) and Minister of Finance wrote in 1947, 'under the influence of the impact of customs, views, historical forces, certain social rigidities and sometimes even prejudices, Poland is creating a specific type of economy which more and more often is given the name of the Polish economic model'.[1] He further suggested that 'Soviet experience in particular is to us of primary importance. However, because an economy of the Polish type is an economy *sui generis* it follows that the problems and solutions engendered in planning must be the products of native economic thought.'[2]

The main economic characteristics of the 'Polish model' were: a mixed economy, the autonomy of various sectors, and state control

[1] T. Dietrych, *Elementy Polityki Finansowej Polski Współczesnej* (1947) p. 5.
[2] *Ibid.* p. 6. A similar idea was expressed by M. R. Wyczałkowski, 'Polityka Pieniężna i Kontrola Finansowa w Gospodarce Planowej', *WNBP* 3 (1946) p. 25.

75

over the whole of the economy through national economic plans.[1] There were to be three sectors, the basis for the division being the ownership of property: the state sector, the co-operative sector and the private sector. A similar division had existed in Poland before the war.

After the act of nationalisation of basic industries[2] the state sector emerged as the dominant economic sector particularly as regards industry. In 1946 the approximate contribution to total industrial production was 76% by state enterprises, 4% by co-operatives and 20% by private firms.[3] In agriculture and trade, however, private and co-operative sectors predominated over the state sector (see table 17 in chapter 5).

The nationalisation of the main industries was not a drastic reform. As the liberation of the country proceeded, provisional governments – first the Polish Committee of National Liberation (Polski Komitet Wyzwolenia Narodowego; PCNL) and then the Provisional Government (Rząd Tymczasowy), formed in July 1944 and January 1945 respectively – extended their administration over many enterprises with little opposition. Many firms were already state-owned before the war; all property belonging to the German occupier was placed under the government's administration; that of absent owners (who were either foreign, living abroad, missing or dead) also came under the administration of the government. Factories, whose production was often revived spontaneously by their former employees, found themselves increasingly administered by the Ministry of Industry (Resort Przemysłu), formed in December 1944. The expansion of state control over factories continued in 1945 and by the time the law of nationalisation was passed the state in effect controlled the country's industry. Bobrowski, the Chairman of the CPO, reminisced that 'at the time of the passing of the law, all nationalised enterprises without exception were under *de facto* state administration (some for a number of months); moreover, there already existed a skeleton of central and intermediate institutions designed to control these enter-

[1] For more details and an assessment of the political situation at the time see T. P. Alton, *Polish Postwar Economy* (New York, 1955) esp. pp. 108–11; M. K. Dziewanowski, *The Communist Party of Poland* (Harvard, 1959) pp. 196–222 (mainly political background); J. M. Montias, *Central Planning in Poland* (Yale, 1962) ch. 2, esp. pp. 51–6.

[2] Law of 3 January 1946 'On taking into public ownership the basic branches of the national economy.' *DURP* 3 (1946) item 17.

[3] B. Minc, *O Planie Trzyletnim* (1948) p. 158.

prises. The law, therefore, concluded rather than opened the process of nationalisation.'[1]

The co-operative and private sectors were to be allowed to coexist alongside the state sector. It was considered sufficient for successful economic planning to nationalise only key sections of the economy.[2] Enterprises which were not nationalised were to remain 'inviolable private property'.[3] Gomułka, General Secretary of the Polish Workers' Party, suggested that 'wholesale nationalisation of industry and trade would mean pouring out the baby with the bathwater... In our economic system we have also provided for the private sector. This provision is valid for today and for the future. We have retained in our hands all the links of political power and the basic economic links.'[4]

Each sector of the economy was to be autonomous in the sense of being allowed to pursue methods of economic development appropriate to it, but only within the framework of national economic plans embracing the activity of all sectors. Indeed the state was to use the national plan as the main weapon of control over the co-operative and private sectors, whose existence was not felt to endanger the ability of the state to control the economy as a whole effectively.

Attempts at economic planning were made soon after the cessation of hostilities. Early in 1945 the Provisional Government established the Economic Committee of the Council of Ministers (Komitet Ekonomiczny Rady Ministrow; ECCM) to deal with economic matters. On 10 November 1945 the CPO was created to become the central organ of economic planning. It produced its first national economic plan – the Three Year Plan (TYP) 1947–9 – a year after its establishment.

It must be emphasised that the concept of 'the Polish road to socialism' was very widely accepted before 1948 by the socialist authorities. It was even supported by the so called Muscovites of the Polish Workers' Party, though this might have been tactical rather than sincere support, calculated not to arouse opposition at a time

---

[1] C. Bobrowski, 'Początki Planowania w Polsce Ludowej', *GP* 11 (1966) p. 5.
[2] M. Orłowski, 'Gospodarka Planowa a Sektor Prywatno-Gospodarczy', *WNBP* 11 (1946); T. Dietrych, *Zasady Systemu Finansowego Polski Ludowej* (1947) p. 24.
[3] By the law of 3 January 1946 'On the establishment of new enterprises and the support of private initiative in industry and trade.' *DURP* 3 (1946) item 18.
[4] W. Gomułka, 'Od Frontu Jednolitego ku Jedności Ograniczonej', *ND* 3 (1947) p. 20.

when the party was trying to consolidate its power.[1] The idea that the tri-sectoral structure was to remain a stable structure was equally generally acceptable, but the relative development of various sectors was subject to controversy, particularly as regards the role of the private sector. Some advocated its decline in favour of the state sector. In practice, in spite of the formal acceptance of its existence in the 'Polish model', the private sector was never given an adequate basis for expansion.

Another interesting feature of the Polish road to socialism was the government's policy in respect of consumption. Its basic aim was to increase the living standard of the community, and raising the level of consumption became the key objective of the TYP.[2] Production of capital goods was not neglected: in 1946 the ratio of production of capital goods to total industrial output was 55%, rising to 59% in 1949.[3] However, in expanding investment the stress was mainly on those projects which would contribute to a rapid rise in the production of consumers' goods.[4]

State enterprises before 1950

Until April 1950, the date on which Poland accepted 'economic accounting' as the method of management of enterprises, the status and the management of enterprises were gradually changing. It must be stressed that at that time the term 'enterprise' referred in general to industrial combinations (*koncerny*), usually embracing several factories or plants and resembling Soviet trusts in the NEP period. Before 1950 economic accounting, as interpreted in Soviet economic

[1] Perhaps the chief political feature of the Polish road to socialism was the multiparty system. Between 1944 and 1948 the Polish Workers' Party, which enjoyed the support of the Soviet Union, successfully campaigned for hegomony over other parties. The party itself, however, was divided into informal factions: the Muscovite group and the Native group. See Dziewanowski, pp. 190–3 and 199–203; R. Hiscocks, *Bridge for the Abyss?* (London, 1963) pp. 111–13.

[2] The plan aimed at raising the average standard of living above the pre-war standard. B. Minc, p. 32.

[3] *The Fulfilment of the Three Year Plan of Economic Reconstruction in Poland* (Warsaw, 1950) p. 21.

[4] Discussing planning in Poland, Czechoslovakia and Hungary, S. E. Harris (*Economic Planning*, New York, 1949, p. 433) observed that 'Unlike the aim of the various five year plans in the USSR, a rise in consumption standards seems to be not only an ultimate, but also a proximate objective. Investment is justifiable only insofar as it will yield more consumption goods and reasonably soon.'

practice, was not considered to offer an appropriate basis for the management of state enterprises in Poland. Attempts were made to formulate principles of management without copying Soviet methods.

Immediately after the war state enterprises enjoyed considerable autonomy and their production was not subjected to any rigid form of planning. Having paid the required tax, they retained their profits and as long as they had funds they could, as a rule, pursue their own sales and purchases policy. There were no general regulations concerning the manner of settling debts between enterprises and a variety of methods was used. Beginning in 1946 the activity of enterprises gradually became subject to a growing volume of government regulations, which mostly concerned the finance of fixed and working capital and whose observance by enterprises was often supervised by banks.[1]

On 3 January 1947 an attempt was made to define the principles of the operation of state enterprises in a decree 'On the formation of state enterprises', which stated that 'Enterprises function on commercial principles on the basis of financial and economic plans formulated in a manner prescribed by the statutory law.[2] The decree gave state enterprises wide powers to manage their working capital, and to purchase and sell fixed assets unless specifically forbidden to do so by law. The autonomy granted to enterprises was to encourage their initiative in lowering the costs of production and increasing profitability, and to improve the quality of output. The management of enterprises was similar to that in the USSR in the NEP period. The emphasis was on the 'commercial' basis of their operations – in general they were to aim at the attainment of maximum profit. As will become apparent from the subsequent sections of this chapter, the financial system was organised so as to enable enterprises to make profits and to retain a substantial part of them.

The currency reform and the emergence of a new network of financial institutions

(a) New legal tender

After the socialist authorities gained political power they immediately set out to symbolise their sovereignty by issuing a new currency.

---

[1] They are discussed in detail later.

[2] *DURP* 8 (1947) item 42.

Their first aim in the realm of finance became the solution of the complex currency problems so as to provide the economy with a single, stable legal tender. This became the immediate task of the National Bank of Poland (Narodowy Bank Polski – NBP) which was established by a decree of the PCNL passed on 15 January 1945.[1] The bank, whose general function was 'to regulate currency and credit', began to operate in February 1945 from headquarters in Kraków.[2] In theory, this was a completely new bank; in practice, it replaced the Bank of Poland (whose headquarters were moved to London in 1939), which was formally put into liquidation, but the bulk of whose staff was transferred to the NBP. In 1945, 66% of the NBP's staff were former Bank of Poland employees and 11% were staff from other pre-war banks.[3]

Immediately after the retreat of German forces from the territories which were to become post-war Poland, four different currencies were in circulation: the złoty issued by the Bank of Issue which had been created under German occupation, the German mark used in the territories claimed during the war by the Third Reich, the rouble brought in by the Soviet forces, and the new złoty of NBP. The last mentioned notes, though bearing the name of NBP, were issued before the bank was actually set up.[4] A number of decrees were passed setting out the conditions of conversion of the other currencies into NBP notes.[5] The złoty became Poland's sole legal

[1] 'On the National Bank of Poland.' *DURP* 4 (1945) item 14.
[2] The headquarters were transferred to Łódź in March 1945 and then to Warsaw at the end of 1946.
[3] L. Laskowski, 'Zagadnienie Kadr w Pietnastoletnim Rozwoju NBP', *WNBP* 6 (1960) p. 269.
[4] The notes were printed in Moscow in August 1944 with the permission of PCNL. By the end of 1944 their value was about 8.5 mil. zł. Some of the notes were allocated to the Soviet armed forces but most were given to the Polish Communist authorities in Lublin. After the establishment of NBP new notes were printed in Poland. See Z. Landau, 'Banki i Kredyt Polski Ludowej w Roku 1944', *WNBP* 10 (1964) p. 344; Z. Karpiński, 'Organizacja Systemu Pieniężnego w Latach 1945–1950', *WNBP* 1 (1965) pp. 2–3.
[5] The main decrees comprising the currency reform of 1945 were (*a*) Decree of 6 January 1945 'On the surrender and exchange of the bank notes of the Bank of Issue of Poland' *DURP* 1 (1945) item 2, modified by a decree of 5 February 1945, *DURP* 5 (1945) item 18. (*b*) Decree of 13 January 1945 'On the withdrawal from circulation on the territory of Poland of the currency of the USSR.' *DURP* 2 (1945) item 5. (*c*) Decree of 5 February 1945 'On the surrender and exchange of German marks on the territories of the Republic of Poland, freed from occupation after 6 January 1945. *DURP* 5 (1945) item 17, modified by an Order of the Treasury of 28 February 1945, *DURP* 11 (1945) item 61.

tender and from February 1945 was *de facto* issued and administered by the bank.

As a result of monetary changes some purchasing power was transferred from the population to the country's monetary authorities. With the conversion of the Bank of Issue złoty and the German mark into the new currency, maximum limits were imposed on the quantities that a single person could convert. For example, in exchanging the Bank of Issue złoty for the NBP złoty the exchange rate was one for one, subject to an upper limit of 500 per head. The Bank of Issue złoty ceased to be legal tender and convertible into the new notes on 28 February 1945. Karpiński estimated that of ten billion złoty in circulation at the time only four billion were converted into the new currency so that the total purchasing power in terms of the old złoty declined by six billion.[1] This margin enabled the government to finance some of its expenditure from issues of new money through the credit system. Currency in circulation rose from 8,726 mil. zł. on 30 April 1945 to 60,066 mil. zł. at the end of 1946. Currency formed a large part of total bank liabilities in 1945–6, its ratio to liabilities at the end of these years being 69.2% and 50.9% respectively, falling gradually to 14.5% in 1950.[2] In other words, the currency reform furnished the economy with a new legal tender and at the same time provided the government with an interest-free loan from the community.[3] It was claimed that because of the reform the increased issue of currency by the NBP was not inflationary.[4]

(b) Credit institutions

The establishment of a single, relatively stable currency laid the foundation for the revival of an effective banking system. The NBP functioned as the central bank of issue and at first its banking activities corresponded with those of the Bank of Poland before the war.

[1] Karpiński, p. 3.

[2] GUS – *RSF 1945–1967*, p. 231. For more details of the liabilities of the banking system see tables B1a and B1b.

[3] For more details on currency changes see K. Sztajer, 'Z Polskich Zagadnień Walutowych Okresu Odbudowy Gospodarczej 1944–1949', *Finanse* 5 (1957); Z. Karpiński, 'Zmiany Ustroju Pieniężnego w Polsce w Okresie Między Rokiem 1918 a 1950', *WNBP* 12 (1958); Organizacja, pp. 2–3; M. Kucharski, *Pieniądz Dochód Proporcje Wzrostu* (1964) pp. 243–59; 'Z. Landau, *Polityka Finansowa PKWN* (1965).

[4] Kucharski, *Pieniądz...*, pp. 251–6. Between 1945 and 1946 the so called 'free market prices' remained steady.

Until 1946 its credit operations were largely confined to refinancing credit of other banks, mainly by rediscounting bills. By 1945 the bank refinanced 84.5% of all credit granted by banks.[1] The main condition of rediscounting facilities at the bank was that banks should inform the NBP of their credit activities. In this way the NBP and the State Treasury, to which it was subordinated, could exercise their influence over banks and shape the country's credit policy.

The other banks revived gradually after the retreat of the German forces of occupation. Some branches of pre-war state and co-operative banks, mainly in the regions of Lublin, Rzeszów and Białystok, restarted banking operations as early as 1944,[2] but most branches were reactivated in the first half of 1945.

Early post-war banking had two interesting features. First, the reconstruction of state, municipal and co-operative banks took place without the promulgation of any new acts or decrees. The pre-war bank statutes gave the Treasury sufficient power of control over the banks to dispense with additional legislation. In February 1945 an appeal was launched urging pre-war staff to rejoin their banks. The re-opening of branches largely depended on the initiative of staff who responded to the appeal. In general bank employees were anxious to return to their old occupations and did not refuse to co-operate with the authorities. At a conference of the NBP's senior staff held in November 1947, both the bank's Chairman and the Minister of the Treasury praised the personnel for their work and co-operation in the shaping of the new credit system.[3] Staff initiative was vital in restarting the operations of pre-war state, municipal and co-operative banks. Private banks, however, did not as a rule manage to secure permission (*koncesje*) from the Treasury to re-open and in effect ceased to exist without formal nationalisation or liquidation. In

---

[1] Kucharski, *Kredyt...*, p. 150. Of all the bank's credit outstanding at the end of 1945, 82.3% was refinance credit, GUS – *RSF 1945–1967*, p. 232. By the end of 1945 the banks rediscounted 58% of their total credit with NBP; K. Niemski, Banki, *FPL 1944–1960* (1964) p. 464. For details on rediscounts by each bank see W. Jaworski, *Zarys Rozwoju Systemu Kredytowego w Polsce Ludowej* (1958) p. 90.

[2] The role of banks in 1944 was not important. Their activity was directed by the Ministry of the National Economy and Finance of PCNL which, as a rule, extended credit directly to enterprises. Banks gave some credit but their main function was the distribution of budgetary allocations. See Landau, *Banki...*, pp. 348–9.

[3] M. L. Kostowski, 'NBP w Latach Organizacji Systemu Bankowego', *WNBP* 1 (1965) p. 8. In this respect the situation in Poland differed significantly from that in the Soviet Union in 1917–18 (see p. 20).

addition many small institutions, such as the Rural Loans and Savings Banks (see p. 61 and table 9), were not revived.

Secondly, the adaptation of banking to the requirements of the new regime followed the general strategy of the Polish road to socialism. Pre-war financial institutions were not indiscriminately abolished or remoulded in the Soviet image. Many of them were revived in their pre-war form and initially were allowed to continue their pre-war practices. From February 1945 onwards the State Treasury and the NBP began increasingly to exercise supervision over the activities of banks. In August 1945 a conference of senior bank officials, organised by the Treasury, outlined the scope of activity of various credit institutions. Different sectors of the economy were to be served by different banks. The NEB was to finance state industrial and commercial enterprises, enterprises administered at the time by the state, and urban construction. The State Agricultural Bank (SAB) was to finance the agricultural reform and credit for state and private farms and other agricultural units. It was to co-operate with rural Savings and Loans Co-operatives (Spółdzielnie Oszczędnościowo–Pożyczkowe, SLCs). As before the war, a distinction was preserved between the state economy and the municipal economy, which embraced the activities of local governments in municipalities. Financing the municipal economy became the function of two municipal banks: the Polish Municipal Bank in Warsaw (Polski Bank Komunalny) and the Municipal Credit Bank (Komunalny Bank Kredytowy) in Poznań. These two banks were later to be merged into the Municipal Bank (Bank Komunalny) and, in addition to the functions mentioned above, acted as the central bank of Municipal Savings Banks (Komunalne Kasy Oszczędności).[1]

In the co-operative sector the 'Społem' Bank (Bank Społem) was to finance the urban co-operative economy, whereas the Central Bank of Rural Co-operatives (Centralna Kasa Spółek Rolniczych) was to finance rural co-operative enterprises.

The private sector was to be serviced by two joint stock banks, which were the largest of the pre-war private banks. The state held a substantial part of their share capital. Large private industrial and commercial firms were to be credited by the Trade Bank of Warsaw (Bank Handlowy w Warszawie, TB); medium and small scale firms were to receive credit from the Union of Workers' Co-operatives Bank (Bank Związku Spółek Zarobkowych, UWCB).

[1] See *DURP* 12 (1946) item 77. In actual fact the merger did not take place until 1949.

4

Table 9

Principal financial institutions in 1938 and 1946

	1938		1946	
Institution	Banks	Branches	Banks	Branches
National Bank of Poland[1]	1	49	1	77
National Economic Bank	1	19	1	24
State Agricultural Bank	1	14	1	22
Municipal banks	4	–	2	4
Municipal savings banks	353	115	266	111
Co-operative Bank[2]	1	9	2	195
Savings and Loans Co-ops.	5,597	–	1,180[3]	–
Postal Savings Bank	1	9	1	16
Joint stock banks	30	93	2	44
Banking houses	28	–	–	–
Credit societies	18	–	–	–
Rural Loans and Savings Bks.	975	–	–	–

Notes:
[1] Bank of Poland in 1938.
[2] The union of Co-operative banks.
[3] Merged into a single Co-operative Bank in July 1946.
Sources: Ministry of Information, *Concise Statistical Year Book of Poland 1939–1941*, p. 93; GUS – *RS 1949*, p. 166; *Bank Gospodarstwa Krajowego. Report of Directors for the Financial Year 1938*, p. 3.

Thus each economic sector had banks financing its economy. In some cases, however, banks retained their pre-war specialisation by industry. This was especially true of the SAB which financed agriculture in general regardless of the sector. The credit system which emerged in 1945 therefore reflected both the tri-sectoral approach to economic development and the pre-war heritage.

The banking system was less complex and more concentrated after the war than before the war (see table 9). Indeed table 10 shows that in 1946 and 1947 the NBP, the NEB, the SAB, and the Co-operative Bank granted over 94% of all bank credit, the NBP and the NEB granting about two thirds of the total. Such a high degree of concentration increased the usefulness of the credit system for purposes of economic control.

After 1945 a number of changes in credit activity and credit techniques did occur, to meet the requirements of the emerging

Table 10

Credit by the principal credit institutions 1945–7
(*Balances at the end of the year*)

	1945		1946		1947	
	mil. zł.	%	mil. zł.	%	mil. zł.	%
State Banks:						
NBP[1]	821	7.7	17,498	22.4	59,032	25.8
NEB	5,416	50.6	33,860	43.4	102,941	45.0
SAB	1,293	12.1	10,350	13.2	24,480	10.7
Co-operative Banks:						
The Co-op Bank	2,127	19.9	11,763	15.1	29,117	12.7
SLCs	88	0.8	554	0.7	1,693	0.7
Municipal Banks:						
Municipal banks	214	2.0	764	1.0	2,232	1.0
Municipal Savings banks	343	3.2	1,851	2.4	5,521	2.4
Joint Stock Banks:						
Trade Bank	242	2.3	791	1.0	1,639	0.7
UWCB	168	1.6	677	0.9	2,117	0.9
Total	10,712	100.0	78,108	100.0	228,772	100.0

Note:
[1] Direct credit (viz. credit excluding refinance of banks).
Sources: GUS – *RS 1947*, p. 123; *Rocznik Polityczny i Gospodarczy 1948*, p. 672.

social and economic order. Up to 1949 these changes, which will be discussed later, occurred without major institutional reforms. Banks were adapting themselves, as they had done before the war, to the changing environment. One institutional change worth mentioning was the fusion in 1946 of the two co-operative banks referred to earlier into a single Co-operative Bank (Bank Gospodarstwa Spółdzielczego).[1] The financial reform of 21 August 1947, which is fully discussed later, outlined the financial apparatus envisaged for the future. The NBP, the central institution of the apparatus, was to finance state enterprises (except in the building industry) either directly or indirectly by refinancing the credit of other banks. The remainder of the system consisted of seven 'central credit institutions': (*a*) the NEB, to give mainly medium and long-term credit to state

[1] Resolution of the CM passed on 28 February 1946 *MP* 49 (1946) item 95. Decrees: *DURP* 18 (1946) item 120, 29 (1946) item 191.

enterprises, (*b*) the SAB, to finance production and sales of agri-cultural products, (*c*) the Postal Savings Bank, to accumulate savings and issue bonds, (*d*) the Co-operative Bank, to supply working and fixed capital to co-operative enterprises, (*e*) the Municipal Bank, to finance mainly investment in the municipal economy, (*f*) the TB to finance larger private firms, (*g*) the UWCB, to finance smaller private firms. The last two banks were also to finance some co-operative enterprises.

Thus the law of August 1947 merely confirmed the existing struc-ture of the credit system, in which banks specialised mainly by the sector which they were to service. This structure survived until the latter part of 1948, when a more fundamental banking reform was undertaken.[1] It took place at a time when significant political and economic reorganisation was beginning. As it happened, this reform merely initiated structural changes in banking which were superseded in the early 1950s and it is therefore treated as a prelude to those changes discussed in the next chapter.

Sources of finance

(*a*) Budget finance

Finance after the war was in a state of continuous change, due partly to organisational changes and partly to economic development and policy. The purpose of this section is to show the main sources of finance; other sections deal in detail with the principles of bank finance and control.

One important source of finance was the state budget. The post-war budgetary system functioned on basically pre-war principles. Indeed until 1950 there was no legislation introducing any funda-mental alteration in the system. The changes which occurred in the state budget up to 1950 reflected general economic and social changes in the country.[2] There was a substantial rise in the total level of budgetary revenue and expenditure (see table 11), due largely to the economic revival of the late 1940s. The chief source of revenue was

---

[1] 'On the bank reform.' *DURP* 52 (1948) item 412.

[2] For more details on the budgetary system before 1950 see Z. Pirożyński, E. Winter, *Budżet Państwowy Polski Ludowej* (1961) ch. 2; A. Komar, *Struktura Budżetu P.R.L.* (1966), ch. 2.

Table 11

Budgetary expenditure 1947–9

	1947		1948		1949	
	mil. zł.	%	mil. zł.	%	mil. zł.	%
Administration[1]	182,091	85.1	358,893	87.1	296,912	45.5
Enterprises[2]	4,528	2.2	3,641	0.9	2,848	0.4
Funds[3]	–	–	–	–	22,278	3.4
Investment[4]	27,244	12.7	49,413	12.0	330,855	50.7
Total	213,863	100.0	411,947	100.0	652,893	100.0

Notes:

[1] Current expenditure on state administration, but in 1948 included expenditure on working capital grants to state enterprises. This explains the sudden rise in administrative expenditure.

[2] Current expenditure of enterprises settling directly with the budget, for example State Railways, State Road Transport, The Post Office.

[3] For example State Land Fund, Labour Fund (fundusz pracy).

[4] Includes investment expenditure not included in the investment plan.

Source: GUS – *RSF 1945–67*, p. 42.

payments from the socialised sector, which rose with the development of that sector. Revenue from the private sector was less important. Its rate of growth declined, especially after discrimination against the sector was intensified in 1948.

Table 11 shows that the largest item of expenditure was spending on current state administration. However, in 1948 'administration' included the finance of working capital of enterprises[1] (in spite of the fact that there was a separate group of expenditures entitled 'enterprises and establishment', where one might expect this type of expenditure to be found). The budget was not, however, the major source of funds for working capital, which was financed mainly by enterprises' own funds. It must be pointed out that, unlike fixed capital investment for which planning started in 1946, until 1948 working capital was not planned and a variety of sources – own funds, the budget, commercial credit (bills of exchange, other credit by suppliers) and short-term bank credit – were used in different proportions depending on the industry. No definite trend in its finance emerged until after the introduction in 1947 of the normative of working capital, which is explained later.

[1] Budget grants financing the 'normatives' of working capital which are discussed later.

According to data given by Pirożyński, in 1947 24% and in 1948 31% of budgetary expenditure was spent on the national economy (e.g. industry, agriculture, transport).[1] Thus the budget, as before the war, mainly financed current expenditure on state administration, but expenditure on the national economy was rising. Until 1949 only about 12% of budgetary expenditure was on investment (see table 11). Though this was a sizeable contribution to the supply of investible funds in the economy, the key role in this respect was played by the banking system. The 1949 change in the structure of budgetary expenditure, which affected investment, is discussed later.

Up to 1950, besides the state budget and the banking system, there were other financial systems, such as the budgets of local authorities and the national insurance, which functioned independently of the state budget.[2] Though up to 1950 they continued to function autonomously, these 'budgets' were by 1949 linked to the state budget in the sense that their surplus was paid into the budget.

(b) Credit and the finance of investment

Shortly after the war bank credit became the principal source of finance in the economy. For many enterprises it was the only external source of funds. Chiefly for this reason its growth (see table 12) was dynamic.[3] All banks except the NBP (which gave only short-term credit) granted both short and long-term credit. Short-term credit as a rule financed working capital, whereas medium or long-term credit financed investment expenditure.[4]

From the moment of its revival the banking system became an important source of investment funds. It was observed earlier that the budget supplied investment finance – in 1948 12% of budgetary

[1] Z. Pirożyński, 'Założenia i Rozwój Budżetu Państwowego', in *FPL 1944–1960*, p. 115. The data included investment expenditure (given in table 11).

[2] Pirożyński (p. 113) estimated that in the years 1947–9 the expenditure of local authority budgets was, in bil. zł., 76, 152, 27 and the national insurance spent 27, 70 and 169 bil. zł. respectively. These totals may be compared with the total for the state budgetary expenditure given in table 11.

[3] In Tables 1–11 data on credit are in pre-1950 currency. The currency reform of 1950 decreased values in the ratio of 3:100. Figures in table 12 onwards are in the post-1950 currency. All data based on sources published after 1950 are in the new currency.

[4] Banks did not at that time pursue an independent credit policy. They followed government recommendations, giving priority to enterprises capable of restarting production immediately without major capital repairs, enterprises producing means of production and consumers' goods for which there was a primary demand, and transport enterprises.

Table 12

Credit granted by the banking system 1945–9

(*Balances at the end of the year*)

Year	Type of credit	Credit structure		Index: previous year = 100
		mil. zł.[1]	%	
1945	Total	336.0	100	
	Short-term	316.0	94	
	Medium-term	20.0	6	
1946	Total	2,343.2	100	697
	Short-term	1,556.2	66	492
	Medium-term	787.0	34	3,935
1947	Total	6,863.2	100	293
	Short-term	4,270.1	62	274
	Medium-term	2,593.1	38	329
1948	Total	13,847.6	100	202
	Short-term	7,482.0	54	175
	Medium-term	6,365.6	46	246
1949	Total	35,308.9	100	255
	Short-term	16,614.3	47	222
	Medium-term	18,694.6	53	294

Note:

[1] Absolute values in 1950 currency.

Sources: GUS – *RS 1950*, p. 99; *RSF 1945–1967*, p. 230.

expenditure was on investment (see table 11) – but until 1949 budgetary finance was of secondary importance. Table 13 shows that credit was the largest and (until 1949) an increasingly important source of funds for state investment plans. The government was anxious to plan investment expenditure as early as possible, the first investment plan coming into operation in 1946. Banks in this respect were not only the key supplier of finance, but also served as the most important instrument through which the state executed its investment policy. It may be recalled that before the war the banking system, and in particular the state banks, played a key role in investment finance (see pp. 64–71).

Immediately after the war banks concentrated on the issue of short-term credit, which was often sufficient to enable many industrial enterprises to commence production. Until the end of 1945 it was granted to finance working capital as well as investment, which at that time consisted mainly of the most urgent capital repairs whose completion permitted enterprises to restart or expand production.

Table 13

Sources of finance of investment carried out in the framework of investment plans 1946–8
(*Percentages of total investment expenditure*)

Sources of funds	1946	1947	1948
1 Bank credit	58.9	61.6	72.2
2 Bugdetary grants	32.0	23.8	25.4
3 Own funds	9.1	14.6	2.4
	100.0	100.0	100.0

Note:

J. Boguszewski and Z. Fedorowicz in *Finanse Polski Ludowej 1945–1960*, p. 281, using Ministry of Finance data, show slightly different figures. The figures corresponding to line 1 of the table are 58.7%, 64.1% and 72.4% respectively.

Source: GUS – *RS 1950*, p. 95.

Such investment yielded quick returns, enabling enterprises to repay their debts in a short period of time. After that year enterprises could accumulate funds from other sources including profit. The chief external source of investment funds became medium and long-term credit. In January 1946 the granting of short-term credit for investment purposes was forbidden.[1] Short-term credit was to finance working capital only and was often called 'circulating' or 'turnover' credit (*kredyt obrotowy*). The shortage of investment funds, however, and the fact that credit for investment purposes was generally granted in accordance with investment plans, drove many enterprises to finance some of their investment expenditure by short-term credit, in spite of the prohibition of such practices.[2] From 1946 until 1949, banks granted medium-term credit known also as investment credit (*kredyt inwestycyjny*), of up to four years, to finance new investment and capital repairs.[3] After 1945 this credit

[1] At the same time enterprises were forbidden to finance their investment from their working capital funds. These changes were introduced by an order of the Ministry of Industry 'On investment and capital repairs' issued on 6 January 1946. See J. Szczepański, *Finansowanie Srodków Obrotowych* (1965) p. 119.

[2] J. Boguszewski and Z. Fedorowicz, Finansowanie Inwestycji i Kapitalnych Remontów in *FPL 1944–1960*, p. 283.

[3] *Ibid*, p. 279. W. Iwanicki, 'Wykonanie Finansowe Państwowych Planów Inwestycyjnych', *SPB* 3 (1948) p. 205, informs that medium-term credit was typically given for three years at 6.5% interest.

Table 14

Credit granted by National Economic Bank 1946–8
(*Balances at the end of the year*)

| Year | Total credit mil. zł. | Medium-term credit | | |
		Total mil. zł.	% of total	% of all credit[1]
1946	1,015.8	685.6	67.5	87.1
1947	3,088.2	2,207.1	71.5	85.1
1948	6,441.3	5,260.8	81.7	82.6

Note:
[1] Percentage of all medium-term credit of the banking system, shown in table 12.
Source: GUS – *RS 1950*, p. 99.

expanded quickly (see table 12), its rate of growth being higher than that of short-term credit. Table 12 shows that in the 1940s the finance of investment through medium-term credit was becoming an increasingly important function of the banking system – the ratio of investment credit to total credit rising from 34% in 1946 to 46% in 1948.

Throughout the period the most important bank in this respect was the NEB, although its importance was declining gradually (see table 14). The bank was a specialised investment institution for state industry, transport and communications and building. In 1947 59.0% of its total investment credit was granted to state industry and this represented 96.8% of all medium-term credit granted to industry by the banking system. For industry, transport and communications and building the respective figures were 97.3% and 94.0%.[1] The bank also credited the investment of state trading enterprises.

As a general rule, medium-term credit was to be repaid from the depreciation funds which enterprises were obliged to establish from 1946 onwards.[2] Sometimes the period of repayment of credit was continually postponed and in some cases enterprises could be released from repayment altogether. Thus some credit amounted to *de facto*

[1] GUS – *Statistical Year Book of Poland 1948*, p. 145.
[2] J. Boguszewski i Z. Fedorowicz, p. 282; B. Blass i M. Weralski, 'Rozwój Systemu Finansowania Przedsiębiorstw Państwowych' in *FPL 1944–1960*, p. 158.

grants, but no data are available to evaluate the size of this 'non-returnable credit'.

General principles of credit finance

It has been observed in the previous section that the banking system played an important role in financing economic development. The principles and methods of bank finance underwent a swift process of evolution, the starting point being the pre-war practices which were revived after the war and then gradually modified or superseded by new practices. A comprehensive system of financial principles appropriate for the 'Polish economic model' emerged by the end of 1947. Although in its evolution Soviet principles of finance were not mechanically copied, the influence of Soviet experience could be observed in a number of instances noted below.

The main aim of the authorities in constructing the financial system was to achieve a planned distribution of funds and to enable banks to exercise financial control over credit recipients. First the general principles of bank finance are outlined. The question of control is then discussed separately.

Immediately after the war banks followed the pre-war practice of granting credit mainly by discounting bills. Table 15 shows that in 1945 over 79% of credit granted by banks (except the NBP, whose credit activity consisted largely of rediscounting bills presented by other banks) was in the form of discounts. The bill therefore was an important method of settling debts and was the basis of bank credit.

The importance of bills did not continue for long. As early as 1946 the bill began to be superseded by other forms of settlement and credit. Following the act of nationalisation, state enterprises were encouraged to pay their debts without resorting to drawing bills and to obtain credit 'directly' viz. without discounting, but on the basis of an agreement between banks and enterprises. Investment credit, whose expansion was particularly fast, was financed mainly by term loans after 1945. Consequently, as may be seen from table 15, there was a significant drop in the amount of credit extended through discounting bills. Their issue in the state sector did not, however, become illegal until 20 May 1947, when a resolution 'On settlements of accounts for deliveries and services' of the ECCM specifically forbade enterprises to extend trade credit to one another and to

Table 15

Types of credit extended by the banking system 1945–7
(*ExcludingNBP balances at the end of the year*)

Year	Total mil. zł.	Bills discounted		Credit on current account		Fixed-term loans	
		mil. zł.	%	mil. zł.	%	mil. zł.	%
1945	296.8	235.0	79.2	41.3	13.9	20.5	6.9
1946	1,818.3	568.8	31.3	388.4	21.4	861.1	47.3
1947	5,092.2	502.6	9.9	1,859.5	36.5	2,730.1	53.6

Source: GUS – *Statistical Year Book of Poland 1948*, p. 145. Values in 1950 currency. The data in the source were converted from pre-1950 currency.

draw bills of exchange.[1] Thus in 1947 commercial credit was abolished as far as state enterprises were concerned and bank credit became the only credit available to them. In the Soviet Union such a provision came into force in 1930 (see p. 30).

There was little controversy, at least in economic publications, about the elimination of the bill. The case against its use was similar to that advanced in the Soviet Union in the 1929–30 period. It was generally agreed that bill financing was incompatible with the desire to control the total credit supply effectively and to establish bank control over the activity of enterprises. One objection to bill finance often emphasised was, as it had been in the Soviet Union (see p. 29), that a large proportion of bills were not trade bills but 'finance bills' (*weksle finansowe*), viz. promissory notes issued specifically to obtain bank credit, whose discounting was considered inflationary.[2] Thus the influence of the 'real bills' theory could be detected.

After this law was passed credit granted by discounting bills fell sharply, accounting for only 9.9% of credit in 1947 (see table 15). The bill continued to be used in the non-state sectors, mainly in the private sector. With the fall in the discounts of bills, rediscounts by the NBP declined in step, but the bank did not lose control over the activities of other banks. The loss of control associated with diminished rediscounting was balanced by the acquisition of statutory

[1] The resolution was not published, but is mentioned in for example Kucharski *Kredyt...*, p. 139; Kostowski, pp. 7–8.

[2] Kostowski, p. 7, estimated that trade bills (viz. 'real bills') in industry accounted for only between 17% to 35% of bills issued.

powers of control over other banks, so that the bank never lost its character as the central bank.

Apart from the use of bills other aspects of bank – enterprise relations were undergoing changes. Soon after the war Poland began to adopt methods of settlement of debts which were very similar to those introduced in the Soviet Union in the early 1930s. In 1945 the Ministry of Industry (the only economic ministry at the time) issued instructions[1] to some state enterprises and institutions subordinated to it, asking them to open 'discount accounts' (*rachunki żyrowe*) with NBP or bank accounts with an appropriate specialised bank, and to carry out all their financial operations exclusively from these accounts, keeping their cash surplus in the bank. The above regulations, it must be remembered, were not general, referring only to institutions designated by the Ministry of Industry.

A decree of the CM 'On the duty of participation in cashless turnover', passed on 3 February 1947, for the first time laid down the legal requirements in connection with settlements.[2] It imposed on all state enterprises the duty to have an account in only one bank, thus accepting the principle of 'one client – one bank' introduced in the Soviet Union in 1927 (see p. 24). Enterprises were to deposit in the bank all money except a petty cash float, paying accounts by bank transfers as opposed to cash (with the exception of small debts). The 1947 law is regarded as the beginning of 'cashless settlements' in Poland.

The principle of 'one client – one bank' also applied to credit. It became known as 'the principle of credit exclusiveness' (*zasada wyłączności kredytowej*), requiring enterprises to obtain their short-term credit only from the banks which carried out their settlements. Attempts were made to implement the principle in 1946, but it was only after the decree of 3 February 1947 that it was widely observed by state enterprises.

The law of 20 May 1947, which has already been mentioned in connection with the abolition of bill credit, made further important provisions concerning settlements, by making the invoice drawn up after the fulfilment of an order the basic document used in settlements. Invoices were to be settled through the banking system, mainly by the *inkaso* method – similar to the *inkasso* method first

---

[1] *Okólnik*, Nr. 122. Ministra Przemysłu, 1 June 1945.
[2] *DURP* 16 (1947) item 61. The new legislation was to become operative three months after the issue of the decree.

introduced in the USSR in 1935. Thus the seller, having carried out his order, had to produce an invoice and send it to his bank (this was the *inkaso*). The bank then presented the invoice to the buyer for acceptance. The buyer had five days in which he could either accept or refuse to accept it.[1] If he did not refuse to accept the invoice in the stipulated time, the bank, assuming tacit acceptance, paid the invoice from the buyer's current account. The above provisions were not strictly obeyed by enterprises and the authorities did not enforce them rigorously.

Shortly after the war attempts were made to ensure that the distribution of credit by banks proceeded in a planned way. It was noted earlier that investment planning started in 1946. Investment plans were the basic guide to the distribution of medium-term credit which, as observed before, was the chief source of investment finance. The planning of working capital did not start until later, so that initially there was the problem of estimating how much working capital was needed by enterprises to fulfil their planned tasks. Until that problem was solved there was no clear criterion for deciding how much short-term credit was required to finance the working capital of enterprises. The solution was sought in the Soviet concept of the normative of working capital (see pp. 41–2). The first attempt to apply the normative was made on 5 November 1946, when the ECCM passed a resolution requiring state enterprises in industry and trade to determine their normatives,[2] but in practice the resolution had no significant immediate impact.

The most important and the most comprehensive piece of financial legislation in the period of the Polish road to socialism was embodied in the resolution of the CM 'On the principles of the financial system' passed on 21 August 1947.[3] Before discussing its provisions it must be stressed that the law referred to state enterprises, which at that time were usually multi-factory units subordinated to the Ministry of Industry and Trade (MIT) the only ministry managing state industry and trade.

The law stated that 'The finance of investment in enterprises must be strictly separated from the finance of current production'.

---

[1] The buyer could only refuse to accept if the goods delivered were not those which had been ordered or were of poor quality.

[2] The resolution: 'On the normatives of working capital' is appended to T. Dietrych, *Zasady Systemy Finansowego Polski Ludowej.*

[3] *MP* 120 (1947) item 762. First mentioned on p. 85.

Working capital was to be financed by 'own funds' or by bank credit. Financing investment from funds designed to finance working capital was prohibited. Enterprises were asked to determine, under bank supervision, their normatives of working capital, which played a key role in finance after 1947. The 1947 law established a system of equalisation accounts. In the realm of working capital finance these were known as 'working capital equalisation accounts'. The general principle governing the finance of the normative was that the normative must be financed by own funds. All discrepancies between the normative and the funds in the possession of enterprises were financed via the equalisation accounts.

Working capital equalisation accounts (wcea) were set up in 'associations' of enterprises (*zjednoczenia*), in 'central administrations' (*centralne zarządy*), to which the associations were subordinated, and in the MIT. If an enterprise accumulated own funds in excess of its normative requirements, the surplus was paid into the association's wcea. If on the other hand the enterprise possessed less own funds than the normative requirements, then the deficit was covered from the account. Associations settled their surplus or deficit with the wcea of central administrations, which in turn settled their discrepancies with the wcea of the MIT. Finally the ministry settled its surplus or deficit with the budget or paid the surplus into its investment account at the NEB. Increases in normatives were as a rule to be financed from profits, but if profits were not high enough they could be financed from equalisation accounts. All equalisation accounts were administered by the NBP. In the Soviet Union enterprises (viz. single factories) settled their deficits or surplus of working capital directly with the budget.

The main motive behind the organisation of the financial system in 1947 was to enable all enterprises to fulfil their planned tasks and at the same time make a profit. This was consistent with the view that enterprises should function on a 'commercial basis' (see p. 79). Consequently the price system adopted in effect guaranteed enterprises a profit. Enterprises did not sell their produce directly to their customers but to 'sales centres' (*centrale zbytu*). Each enterprise's selling price, known as an 'accounting price' (*cena rozliczeniowa*), covered the enterprise's planned costs and planned profit. Thus, assuming that the enterprise fulfilled its plans, it was guaranteed a profit. Sales centres sold their products at 'effective prices'. Accounting sales prices incorporated purchase cost, the centre's costs of distribution, a turnover tax[1] and a profit margin. These prices were uniform for a particular commodity and the discrepancies which inevitably occurred between the two prices were settled through 'equalisation accounts of price differences' (eapd). If effective prices were higher than accounting prices the surplus was paid into the eapd of the association of enterprises. Deficits arising when effective prices were lower than accounting prices were settled by payments from the account. Eapd's existed in associations of enterprises, central administrations and the MIT and were all administered by the NBP.

Investment after 1947 was financed from bank credit (which has already been discussed) and depreciation. Having covered the cost of capital repairs from their depreciation funds, enterprises transferred the remainder of the funds to their investment accounts, usually at the NEB. Funds on the investment account were used to repay investment credit and to finance new investment. Funds over and above investment requirements of enterprises were transferred from their investment accounts to the investment accounts of associations, which covered shortages of investment funds of enterprises. Again investment accounts existed at the association, central administration and MIT level and were administered by the NEB.

The 1947 financial reform laid down that planned profits of state enterprises were to be divided in the following way: 10% was to be left as a bonus for the staff of enterprises, 10% was to be paid into the budget as profits tax and 80% remained for purposes of working capital finance. It is interesting to note that before 1949 enterprises retained a relatively substantial part of their financial accumulation.[2] In 1947 enterprises subordinated to MIT retained 41% of their accumulation (the rest was paid into the budget and equalisation accounts).[3]

To conclude, the most interesting feature of the pre-1949 financial organisation was the key role played by the banking system. Banks

[1] The turnover tax at that time was not the important source of budgetary revenue which it became after 1950. It was fixed at a uniform rate for all enterprises in a particular industry. It was not used as a 'regulator of profitability' of enterprises, but was simply a means of collecting revenue. Profitability was largely a function of differences between accounting prices and effective prices.

[2] The term 'financial accumulation' is a translation of the Polish '*akumulacja finansowa*', which is the difference between the value of sales and the costs of production.

[3] Pirożyński and Winter, p. 37. The respective figure for 1949 was 29%.

financed not only working capital requirements but also investment; they administered the equalisation accounts of enterprises. They were therefore responsible for ensuring that the flow of funds into enterprises was consistent with the planned tasks facing the enterprises. At the same time, the only direct contact between enterprises and the state budget was through tax payments. Matters such as investment allocations or coverage of deficits of working capital in the state sector were settled not between the budget and individual enterprises (as was the case in the Soviet economic practice) but between the budget and the MIT which represented the whole state industrial sector of the economy.[1]

Thus the general approach to problems of financial management at the time combined the retention of some traditional, pre-war features (e.g. the important role of the banking system and credit finance of investment) with modifications or reforms, some of which were inspired by Soviet experience (e.g. the adoption of the normative), while others represented the product of original thought (e.g. the equalisation accounts system). Commenting on the financial legislation of 21 August 1947, Blass remarked 'The principles which have been enacted are strictly related to our organisational model and their confrontation with the principles of financial systems of other countries (the USSR, Czechoslovakia, Yugoslavia) reveals the originality of the basic ideas.'[2]

From administrative to monetary control

Soon after the war it was generally accepted that banks must exercise control over state enterprises and other credit recipients. It was widely appreciated that pre-war banks exercised some control over their customers in the process of granting credit. However, it was also believed that in the new socialist system bank control was to be more intensive, exercised not merely from the point of view of safeguarding bank interests or even broad national interests, but also from the point of view of the efficiency of enterprises. Banks were to look upon state enterprises from the viewpoint of their owner, for in

[1] For more information on the financial system of 1947–8, see B. Blass, 'Nowy System Finansowy', GP 21 (23) (1947) 'Rozwój Systemu Finansowego Przedsiębiorstw Państwowych w P.R.L.', Finanse 9 (1961); Blass and Weralski, pp. 255–61.

[2] B. Blass, 'Zasady Systemu Finansowego', WNBP 10 (1947) p. 30.

the new system they 'assume the duties of the previous owner of the enterprise'.[1] Potentially, the banks were the only existing institutions capable of exerting a continuous influence over enterprises. As mentioned in previous sections, up to 1949 they were the major source of finance for enterprises and this alone gave them considerable scope for influencing the activities of their clients.

Although the proposition that banks must exercise control over enterprises was beyond dispute, it was not clear how this new function was to be discharged. In keeping with the concept of the Polish road to socialism, attempts were made to evolve a Polish system of bank control. It was believed that 'There is no universal golden rule for exercising control based on some design or scheme.'[2] Views expressed in early publications (1946–7) on bank control were interesting, even if they were not completely clear. Some attempts were made to distinguish between the macroeconomic and microeconomic aspects of control. The general objective of control was sometimes described as 'Co-ordination of the flow of money with the flow of goods and services on the market.'[3] In issuing credit, banks were to take into account the overall economic situation. This aspect, implying the macroeconomic function of bank control, was not unfortunately debated in greater detail and was not emphasised as much as the microeconomic aspect of bank control.

As far as enterprises were concerned, banks were not to be mere watchdogs over their activity. Orłowski suggested that

we are not basically concerned with the detection of excesses... Furthermore, in exercising bank control over individual establishments we are not concerned with the immediate elimination of shortages and shortcomings which may have been noticed, or with teaching the employees the necessity of different behaviour. The control as such has nothing in common with the work of an instructor. The banker who controls industry cannot, and has no time to, correct, instruct or teach the personnel of an establishment subjected to control.[4]

It was on the whole agreed that banks must gather facts about the work of enterprises, analyse them and supply their findings to the

[1] Dietrych, *Zasady...*, p. 22.

[2] T. Dietrych, 'Elementy Polityki Finansowej Polski Współczesnej', *WNBP* 10 (1946) p. 35.

[3] *Ibid.* p. 35. M. Orłowski, 'Bank i Kontrola Finansowa', *WNBP* 5 (1946) p. 33.

[4] Orłowski, *Bank...*, pp. 32–3.

enterprises and to their superior bodies, such as the State Treasury or the CPO. Indeed this view of banks as a centre of research into the economy of enterprises was frequently stressed.[1]

Although all banks were charged with the duty of exercising control over their customers, the role of the NBP and the NEB in this respect was of outstanding importance. The former in particular quickly began to acquire the character of the key control institution of state enterprises. From 1946 its role in the credit system began to change. Its position as the central bank of the credit system was not challenged, but it ceased to act entirely as 'the bankers' bank' and started to extend credit directly to enterprises. As stated before, on 3 January 1946 the country's main industries were formally nationalised. On 8 February 1946 the ECCM resolved that the state enterprises sub-ordinated to the Central Administrations of the coal, iron and steel and textile industries should receive short-term credit directly from the NBP.[2] It must be remembered that the bank, or strictly speaking the Bank of Poland, did grant credit (but in small quantities) directly to enterprises before the war (part of 'loans against collateral' in table 2a). In this sense the 1946 change was not revolutionary. However, credit given directly to enterprises by NBP grew and ultimately this form of credit became typical of the NBP finance.[3] As may be seen from table 16, in 1945 its quantity was small (17.7% of total credit) though not insignificant (it was granted for example to enterprises in whose vicinity there were no branches of appropriate specialised banks), but in 1946 it rose sharply, and in 1950 amounted to 72% of the total credit of the bank.

The law of 8 February 1946 started another important trend in banking, notably towards the NBP's near-monopoly of direct short-term credit, which, as is shown later, was eventually attained in the early 1950s. From 1945 to 1946 the share of the NBP in the total

---

[1] See Orłowski, Bank..., Dietrych, 'Elementy..., WNBP 10 (1946); F. Czernichowski, 'Zadania Banków na Tle Zasad Systemu Finansowego', WNBP 12 (1947) p. 12 and in SPB, December 1947, p. 926.

[2] The resolution 'On financial control of industry' was not published. See e.g. Kucharski, Kredyt..., p. 122; Kostowski, p. 6.

[3] Direct credit was issued by the State Bank in the USSR (see p. 30). M. Orłowski, Reforma Bankowości Polskiej (Toruń, 1949) p. 152 noticed that there was also a precedent for this in Polish banking. The Bank of Poland set up in the Kingdom of Poland after the Congress of Vienna in 1815 granted both short-term and investment credit directly to firms. Quoted in J. and Z. Jaśkiewicz, Polski System Finansów Publicznych (1966) pp. 127–8.

Table 16

Expansion of direct credit of the NBP 1945–50
(*Percentages of total credit granted by the NBP*)

	1945	1946	1947	1948	1949	1950
Direct credit	17.7	31.7	40.8	36.6	60.8	72.0
Refinancing	82.3	68.3	59.2	63.4	39.2	28.0
Total	100.0	100.0	100.0	100.0	100.0	100.0

Source: GUS – *RSF 1945–67*, p. 232.

short-term credit of the system rose from 7% to 34% and in 1949 it was 54.9%.[1]

The expansion of direct crediting by the NBP and the concentration of short-term credit in the bank indicated the bank's growing involvement in control over enterprises. The February law for the first time imposed on the NBP a specific duty to control the activities of enterprises in the coal, iron and steel and textile industries. The form which this control was to assume was to be discussed between the Ministry of Industry, the CPO and the councils of enterprises (*rady zakładowe*). The control envisaged by the resolution had two interesting features. First, bank control was to apply to all enterprises in the above-mentioned industries, including those not requiring credit. From this point of view the law had a revolutionary character. The NBP, whose activity had hitherto been confined to implementing the country's monetary policy through refinancing (usually by rediscounting) the commitments of other banks, was now directly to control state enterprises, irrespective of whether they required credit or not. Secondly, and this partly follows from the first point, control was to take the form of a direct involvement of the bank with the management of enterprises. In exercising control the bank was to see that enterprises used the most economic methods of production. However, the form which bank control was to take and the nature of bank involvement with the management of enterprises were not specified. It was not therefore clear whether banks were to be partners in the management of enterprises, or whether they were to act in an advisory or in a supervisory capacity. What was beyond doubt was that they were to exercise some control over the management of state enterprises. The 1946 resolution stated that 'Control shall embrace the current review of economic activity, in particular

[1] GUS – *RS* 1950, p. 90. The figure for 1945 only was taken from Kucharski, p. 173.

in respect of financial management and the management of stocks, a periodic verification of fixed assets and of current activity as reflected in periodic and annual reports, an analysis of the above reports and the correct assessment of costs of production.'[1]

At that stage production plans for enterprises were not yet fully elaborated and so less attention was paid to control over plan fulfilment. The exception here was the control over the fulfilment of investment plans introduced in 1946 and, as noted earlier, financed mainly by medium-term credit. Before advancing credit, banks (mainly the NEB) were to make certain that it was granted for purposes consistent with investment plans and that it was rationally used by enterprises.

Initially control by credit, as opposed to more administrative forms of bank control, received relatively little attention. This must not be taken as meaning that monetary control was deemed inappropriate to the 'Polish model' of socialism. Banks, and in particular the NBP, were asked to exercise 'management control' (see p. 48) by direct co-operation, rather than control solely in the process of crediting; first because credit policy was not yet elaborated, in the sense that banks were not always certain as to the purpose for which short-term credit was to be extended,[2] and secondly because of the scarcity of managerial staff in enterprises. In these circumstances bank control was used as part of the centralised management of enterprises. Examining the preference for 'supervisory' control over monetary control, Kucharski suggested that

This can largely be explained by the fact that in the first period of the organisation of socialised enterprises the need for a wide control of their activity arose above all from a generally low quality of managerial apparatus and from the failure to observe financial discipline. Financial mismanagement, which frequently occurred at that time in enterprises, resulted from the emphasis on the quantitative and technical side of production and the neglect, or at least undervaluation, of costs, savings, profitability and the rate of turnover of working capital. This reflected insufficient appreciation of the role of finance in economic planning.[3]

Thus economic conditions made expedient bank control which was not based on credit.

Banks exercised control with the help of two accounts. The first

[1] Quoted in Kostowski, p. 6.
[2] Enterprises were equally uncertain as to the purpose for which they could claim credit.
[3] Kucharski, *Kredyt...*, p. 123.

was a 'preliminary estimate' (*preliminarz finansowy*) of the income and expenditure of an enterprise for a period of time (usually a quarter). All payments actually made by the enterprise had to have bank approval and were recorded on a special 'control sheet' (*arkusz kontrolny*), which was often the only comprehensive account of the expenditure of enterprises. Comparisons of the entries on the control sheet with the preliminary estimates were often used by banks as a basis for the assessment of efficiency of enterprises and for granting credit. Thus the use of the two documents enabled banks continually to control enterprises, irrespective of whether they required credit or not.

After 1946 more attention was increasingly paid to bank control over the fulfilment of planned tasks by enterprises. Such control became necessary after the TYP began to be implemented. The law of 21 August 1947 specified the following objects of control: (*a*) strict fulfilment of current financial plans, (*b*) the observance of the principles of thrifty and rational financial economy, and (*c*) the observance of the principles of monetary and credit policy. According to the law bank control was to consist of: (*a*) giving opinions on financial plans and the normatives of working capital, (*b*) estimating credit requirements, (*c*) seeing that production was carried out as planned, (*d*) the study of methods of sales and purchases from the financial point of view, and (*e*) the supervision of costing and of general management. More details concerning the methods of control were given after the act of August 1947 by an Official Instruction, issued in September 1947,[1] which distinguished 'preliminary control' consisting of such activities as the sanctioning of the preliminary estimates, 'current control' consisting of control over current expenditure of enterprises and the use of the control sheet, and 'subsequent control' consisting largely of analysis of accounts and reports of enterprises. These terms were used in Soviet financial terminology (see p. 47).

After 1946 bank control in the process of issuing credit also received more attention than before. The NBP, having been allotted the task of working out credit methods appropriate to a socialist economy, worked out the main types of credit available to enterprises. The basic short-term credit was the 'normal credit' (*kredyt normalny*).[2] To determine their demand for this credit, enterprises, with the help of their banks, evaluated the financial requirements to fulfil their

---

[1] 'Control and direct crediting of industry'. Kostowski, p. 8.

[2] Also called 'normative credit' (*kredyt normatywny*) in those cases where enterprises managed to work out their normatives of working capital.

production targets. The credit covered the difference between these requirements and the funds in the possession of enterprises. To calculate their financial requirements enterprises had to estimate their 'turnover cycle' viz. the period from the start of expenditure on production to the time of receiving revenue from the sale of production. The NBP issued general instructions to be followed by state enterprises in making the above assessments.

Enterprises could also receive other forms of credit. 'Transitional credit' (*kredyt przejściowy*) financed shortages of working capital which might have arisen when plans were not fulfilled, for instance because of bottlenecks in supplies or in sales; 'special credit' (*kredyt specjalny*) financed temporary needs, such as seasonal stock accumulation. In addition, separate credit financed imports and exports. Normal, transitional and special were the main credits extended up to 1949. Their ratio to total short-term credit in 1948 was 73%.[1]

Although crediting of enterprises proceeded in a more orderly way after 1946, until 1948 bank control continued to be administrative, based on checks of entries on the control sheet and direct supervision of management in enterprises.[2] As such control proved cumbersome and expensive it was decided to simplify it by improving the accounting of enterprises and by developing their internal financial control. Enterprises were to exercise 'self-control' (*samokontrola*), by maintaining their own control sheets and checking that entries on them corresponded to the items on the preliminary estimates sheet. Bank assessment of the work of enterprises was to be based on periodic analyses of accounts submitted by enterprises.[3] Banks also endeavoured to establish a continuous control linked to the credit process. Thus they were to withdraw from direct participation in the financial management of enterprises and to attempt monetary control. Consequently they ceased to give their 'opinion' on such matters as financial plans and ceased to participate in the evaluation of the normatives of working capital.

For reasons which should become apparent later it is more convenient to discuss the methods of the new monetary control adopted in the 'Polish model' of socialism in the next chapter.

[1] W. Jaworski, *Obieg Pieniężny i Kredyt* (1963) pp. 196–7.

[2] Banks were, moreover, reluctant to restrict credit in this period, for reasons discussed later in connection with 'credit liberalism'.

[3] J. Hermanowicz, 'Uwagi o Kontroli Finansowej Przedsiębiorstw Państwowych', *WNBP* 1 (1949).

5

The financial reforms of 1948–50 and the emergence of a centralised financial system

Introduction: the end of the Polish road to socialism

In the years 1948 to 1950 the economy of the country underwent a drastic change. The Polish road to socialism was abandoned and the speedy adoption of a highly centralised economic system, copied from the Soviet Union, began, mainly for political and doctrinal rather than economic reasons.[1] As the world political situation was growing tense, the Soviet Union decided to strengthen its domination of Eastern Europe by creating a monolithic bloc of Soviet countries. Those, especially Gomułka, who defended the Polish road to socialism were accused of 'right-wing tendencies' and ultimately purged. At the plenary session of the CC of the Polish Workers' Party, held between 31 August and 3 September 1948, Gomułka's thinking was described as being characterised by 'unconquerable national parochialisms, national narrow-mindedness which diminishes his political vision and the understanding of the role of the USSR'.[2] The new political party – the Polish United Workers' Party – created in 1949 and completely subservient to the USSR agreed that 'All tendencies, aiming at the weakening of collaboration with the Soviet Union undermine both the basis of the People's democracy in Poland and the independence of our country.'[3] The official party view, the only view which was tolerated and publicised,

---

[1] For background information see: Alton, pp. 112–16; Dziewanowski, pp. 225–35; Montias, pp. 54–7. The political nature of changes at the time comes out vividly in a number of speeches made during the Eighth Plenary Session of the CC of the Polish United Workers' Party, published in *Nowe Drogi* 10 (1956). O. Lange (*Some Problems Relating to the Polish Road to Socialism*, Warsaw 1957, pp. 10–17) pointed out that the adoption of the Soviet model in Eastern Europe took place in spite of significant differences between the countries.

[2] *ND* 11 (1948) pp. 26–7. See also B. Bierut's speech, *ND* 11 (1948) pp. 9–39; Dziewanowski, ch. 11.

[3] *ND* 1 (1949) p. 11.

was that only the Soviet interpretation of socialism was correct and that the Soviet 'model' was the only possible model for a socialist economy.

Little has been published on the economic debate of 1948 and 1949. The events which followed, however, made it plain that the supporters of the tri-sectoral economic system of 1948, proposing a 'cautious approach' to planning, made no impression on the party. The advocates of rapid industrial expansion based on the development of the state sector received all the publicity.[1]

From 1949 onwards Poland began the rapid adoption of a Soviet type planning apparatus.[2] A new hierarchy of planning institutions was created in a law of 10 February 1949 'On the change of organisation of the main institutions of the national economy.'[3] The supreme economic authority became the ECCM. The CPO was abolished and the nerve centre of the planning mechanism became the State Commission for Economic Planning (Państwowa Komisja Planowania Gospodarczego, SCEP), which had very wide powers. Broadly speaking, the Commission was responsible for working out economic plans based on general directives of the Economic Committee. On the basis of these plans, the economic ministries[4] completed detailed planned targets for enterprises subordinated to them. Thus the most important decisions concerning the management of enterprises were imposed 'from above', leaving little scope for initiative at the enterprise level. The fulfilment of physical targets determined by the plan was of paramount importance. The system of wage and bonus payments was based on it.

The economic policy adopted after 1948 was similar to that followed by the USSR. The idea of the mixed economy was abandoned in favour of 'building the bases of socialism' in the Soviet style. This meant a speedier process of socialisation and a rapid development of industry.

As may be seen from table 17, the process of socialisation in Poland continued steadily from the end of the war. In industry the socialised sector was predominant throughout. The elimination of private enterprise occurred mainly in the fields of handicrafts, trade (especially retail) and agriculture, although agriculture remained funda-

---

[1] See e.g. *Plan Sześcioletni* (1951) (Collection of Speeches).
[2] Minc et al. (Ed.) *Zarys Rozwoju Metodologii Planowania w Polsce Ludowej 1944–1954* (1956).   [3] *DURP* 7 (1949) item 43.
[4] MIT was abolished and new ministries for each important industry were established.

Table 17
The growth of the socialised sector 1946–50

Approximate % share of socialised sector in:	1946	1947	1948	1949	1950	
national income	45	50	58	64	70	76 in 1952
industrial production	86	90	92	95	–	99 in 1951
agricultural production	2	–	–	–	–	12 in 1951
wholesale trade turnover	80	–	–	98	–	100 in 1953
retain trade turnover	22	30	–	56	80	94 in 1951
investment expenditure	55	58	66	83	90	97 in 1951[1]

Note:

[1] Figures according to GUS – *RS 1956*, p. 221 are: 83 in 1950, 91 in 1951, 93 in 1952, 96 in 1953, 97 in 1954, 97 in 1955.
Sources: H. Minc, 'Zadania Gospodarcze na 1951 Rok', *ND* 1 (1951) pp. 51–2; *WykonanieNarodowych Planów Gospodarczych 1948–1952* (1952) (Planning Commission communiques) p. 10; O. Lange, 'Rozwój Gospodarczy Polski Ludowej w Latach 1945–54', *Ekonomista* 3 (1954) esp. pp. 10–13; GUS – *RS 1964*, p. 77.

mentally based on private peasant holdings. In trade, private enterprise, taking advantage of irrational pricing policies, made easy profits. This alarmed the authorities who, instead of improving pricing, decided in the middle of 1947 to launch a campaign ('the struggle for trade') against private trading, which continued in later years (see table 17).

Discriminatory (often fiscal) measures against the private sector, initiated in the late 1940s, had immediate as well as delayed effects. Investment in the private sector, taking 1949 as the base year, was still 96 in 1950. But in 1951 it fell to 36 and in 1952 and 1953 it settled at a level of 43.[1] Between 1947 and 1949 the contribution of the socialised sector to the national income rose from 50% to 64%; between 1949 and 1951 from 64% to 72%; and between 1951 and 1953 from 72% to 76%.[2]

The policy of rapid industrialisation was embodied in the Six Year Plan of Economic Development and the Building of Bases of Socialism 1949–55, involving an increase in the rate of investment expenditure (especially of investment in heavy industry) and a substantial

[1] It picked up in 1954 to 59 and in 1955 was 93. A. Szerwentke, 'Wykonanie 6-letniego Planu Inwestycji', *GP* 1 (1957) p. 15.
[2] O. Lange, 'Rozwój Gospodarczy Polski Ludowej w Latach 1945–1954', *Ekonomista* 3 (1954) p. 13.

rise in industrial production. The TYP which preceded the Six Year Plan (SYP) was drafted on the assumption that the rate of growth of industrial production must fall with economic development over time. Thus it provided for an overall rise in industrial production of 140%, but with a falling rate of growth of 50% in 1947, 26.1% in 1948 and 21.7% in 1949.[1] The relatively cautious attitude to growth was now abandoned but not, one must assume, without a struggle in the Party. In December 1948 the planners were directed to aim at a level of industrial production in 1955 of 85–95% more than in 1949. In a speech delivered to the Party's CC in July 1950 H. Minc, the chief architect of the post-1949 development, announced a revised project, according to which industrial production in 1955 was to surpass the 1949 level by 158%.[2] The new version of the plan was produced without consultation with enterprises and their associations. It was the product of central planning organs and it is believed that pressure from Moscow was a major force in increasing planned targets.[3] Thus the revised version of the SYP represented a decidedly more ambitious, but at the same time more arbitrary scheme of economic development. Total investment in 1955 was to be 3.5 times greater than investment in 1949, priority being given to investment in industry, especially heavy industry.[4]

The plan for 1950 was very ambitious, aiming at rises of 22% in industrial production, 36% in net investment, between 8% and 10% in private consumption and 16% in national income.[5] Some indices of the process of industrialisation are given in table 18.

These changes were accompanied by a fundamental reconstruction of the financial system. Budgetary and banking reforms are described in separate sections; currency changes can be described here only very briefly. The price reform of 17 April 1950 abolished accounting prices (see pp. 96–7) based on the production costs of individual

[1] Minc, *O Planie Trzyletnim*, p. 44. The TYP was successfully completed, being regularly overfulfilled: in 1947 by 5%; in 1948 by 14% and in 1949 by 12%. See *Plan Sześcioletni* (1951) p. 24. The average annual rate of growth of industrial production in 1947–9 was app. 30%. See Lange, *Rozwój*..., p. 15.

[2] *Plan Sześcioletni* pp. 24–6.

[3] See a pronouncement at the VIII Plenary Session of the Party's CC in 1956, *ND* 10 (1956) p. 70. Also Dziewanowski, pp. 226–7.

[4] B. Minc, 'Sześcioletni Plan Rozwoju Gospodarczego i Budowy Podstaw Socjalizmu w Polsce', *ND* 4 (1950) p. 11.

[5] E. Szyr, 'Niektóre Zagadnienia Walki o Realizację Planu Gospodarczego na 1950 Rok', *ND* 2 (1950) p. 160.

Table 18

Some indicators of industrialisation 1947–53

(*At 1961 prices*)

	1947	1948	1949	1950	1951	1952	1953
Indices 1950 = 100 :							
National income	57	–	87	100	108	114	126
Industrial production	47	64	78	100	122	145	170
Total investment	51	62	72	100	112	133	154
Industrial investment	26	38	61	100	130	171	198
Percentage share of :							
Investment in national							
income	16	–	16	21	21	23	28
Industrial investment							
in total investment	20	23	32	38	44	48	48
(socialised sector only)	(34)	(35)	(38)	(42)	(45)	(50)	(50)
Agricultural investment[1]							
in total investment	30	26	17	13	8	9	9
(socialised sector only)	(16)	(13)	(11)	(9)	(7)	(7)	(7)

Note :
[1] Including forestry.
Sources: GUS–*RS 1964*, pp. 67, 77; *RS 1968*, p. 77; *RSIiST 1946–1966*, pp. 1, 5, 24–5, 28.

enterprises, introducing from 1 January 1951 uniform 'sale prices' for all producers, consisting of three elements: the planned average costs of an industry plus a planned profit plus turnover tax. The new pricing system had some serious anomalies. Production costs, for instance, on which prices were based, did not include capital costs, as fixed capital was financed by interest free budgetary subsidies (this will be explained), and no charge was made for ground rent.[1] Furthermore, the adoption of average cost pricing resulted in many deficit enterprises,[2] whose planned costs were higher than the average for their industry.

On 28 October 1950 the authorities carried out a currency reform[3] aimed at stabilising the currency to enable rational economic management. The NBP notes were exchanged for the new złoty at a rate of

[1] The only charge on capital was depreciation which in practice was low, as the capital was usually undervalued. This was part of the Soviet approach to economic development – low prices for capital goods were considered to stimulate investment.

[2] Also in some surplus enterprises.

[3] *DURP* 50 (1950) item 459.

100 to 1; prices and wages were in general recalculated in a ratio of 100 to 3. Thus the reform not only created new legal tender but also reduced the purchasing power in the economy, in particular of those who held their wealth in the form of cash (mainly traders forced out of business by the process of socialisation).

Changes in the status of enterprises

On 17 April 1950 the CM passed a law basing enterprises on economic accounting as interpreted in the USSR.[1] The law divided state enterprises broadly into two groups: (a) budget enterprises and (b) enterprises on economic accounting. The former were enterprises whose expenditure was independent of their income, consisting of institutions of control, supervision or co-ordination. The latter were production enterprises, subdivided in turn into enterprises on 'full economic accounting' and those on 'internal economic accounting'. The enterprises on internal economic accounting were largely plants belonging to multiple firms whose separation was not feasible. Some of these were to function on 'full economic accounting', others were to operate on 'limited internal economic accounting', having limited autonomy as compared with enterprises on full economic accounting (they had fewer rights). The main rights and privileges of enterprises on full economic accounting included 'full operative autonomy' in fulfilling planned tasks and the capacity to enter into contracts with other enterprises and organisations.

The law made all enterprises responsible for fulfilling their own plans and specified some important aspects of their financial management. It outlined their pricing system, their taxation, the way in which profits were to be divided and the method of financing working capital and capital repairs. A decree 'On state enterprises', passed on 26 October 1950 by the CM emphasised that 'State enterprises are created to fulfil tasks set by national economic plans', confirming that enterprises were to function on the basis of economic accounting.[2]

After 1950 enterprises were administrative units designed to fulfil detailed plans handed down by superior authorities. Indeed some wondered whether the term 'enterprise' was appropriate, as in fact

[1] 'On the principles of financial organisation and financial system of state enterprises embraced by the central budget.' *DURP* 55 (1950) item 630.
[2] *DURP* 49 (1950) item 439.

they were merely 'establishments of work'. Their autonomy in making decisions concerning output or capital expansion was negligible. Little finance was left at their disposal; in 1950 industrial enterprises retained 6.3% of financial accumulation, the rest being absorbed by the budget (compare p. 97). The figures for 1951–3 were 1.4%, 2.0% and 1.2% respectively.[1] In view of this 'own funds' became practically a euphemism for budgetary allocations.

The above mentioned laws referred to enterprises in the sense of single factories or workshops and no longer to multi-factory units. The implementation of the laws involved what in Polish literature is usually called 'decentralisation of enterprises', ordered by the ECCM on 12 May 1950.[2] Multi-factory units were divided into single factories on economic accounting. From 1950 onwards the term 'enterprise' referred to single-plant units directly subordinate to their respective economic ministries.

Budgetary reforms

(a) The finance of investment

It was noted earlier that until 1949 bank credit was the main source of investment finance. On 11 December 1948 the CM introduced a 'principle of uniformity' in financing investment, by laying down that the investment of state enterprises was to be financed by budgetary grants only and not by both grants and long-term credit. More specifically from 1 January 1949 the whole investment of state enterprises and institutions (for example banks, social and professional organisations, insurance institutions) was to be financed from non-returnable budget allocations and the existing debts of enterprises to banks were to be written off.[3] Bank credit continued to finance the investment of firms in the co-operative sector and of local government

---

[1] Szczepański, p. 134.

[2] *Biuletyn PKPG* 12 (1950) item 145. The Committee resolved that 'the basic economic unit in the key industry should be a single-plant enterprise operating in the framework of the national economic plan and based on economic accounting.' Szyrocki, *Samofinansowanie Przedsiębiorstw* (1967) p. 56.

[3] Also investment in the economy was to proceed strictly in accordance with the investment plan, so that investment finance granted to an enterprise was entirely unconnected with its capacity to accumulate investible funds. Even a very small investment project had to have the approval of the central authorities. When enterprises managed to accumulate funds which were not envisaged by the investment plan, sometimes called

Table 19

Sources of finance of investment carried out in the framework of investment plans 1948-9

(*Percentages of investment expenditure*)

Sources of funds	1948	1949
Bank credit	72.2	16.4
Budget grants	25.4	79.5
Own funds	2.4	4.1

Source: As in table 13.

enterprises. Consequently, as shown in table 19, there was a drastic fall in the finance of investment by banks[1] and a sharp rise in budgetary finance.[2] This explains the change in the structure of budgetary expenditure in 1949 shown in table 11 (p. 87), where it can be seen that budgetary expenditure on investment was 12.0% of total budget expenditure in 1948 and 50.7% in 1949. This reform increased the importance of the budget in the economy, but did not basically alter the budgetary system.

(b) The reform of 1950

Preliminary steps towards a fundamental budgetary reform were taken early in 1950. The autonomous local government system was incorporated into the central government system, thus abolishing 'the dual authority in regions' and turning hitherto autonomous

'non-limited funds' (e.g. from gifts, insurance indemnities), they could be invested only after inclusion in the investment plan and with the prior consent of the SCEP. After 1951 there appeared a tendency towards greater flexibility in undertaking 'non-limited investments'. This is discussed in chapter 7.

[1] There was also a drastic change in the structure of liabilities of banks. The ratio of investment accounts to total liabilities dropped from nearly 35% to nearly 5% (see table B1a).

[2] There appears to be an inconsistency in the figures for bank credit in 1949 given both in the *Statistical Year Books* and in the annual report of NBP for 1949. Long-term credit is shown to have increased in spite of the fact that it ceased to finance investment. The Bank's officials kindly explained to the author that the apparent discrepancy arose largely because of misuse of the word 'credit'. Non-returnable grants distributed by banks were often called 'credit'. For more details see T. M. Podolski, 'The Role of Bank Credit in Financing State Enterprises in a Socialist Economy', unpublished thesis (Birmingham University, 1970) p. 85.

local councils into 'the regional organs of the unified state authority'.[1] A law of 7 March 1950 replaced the State Treasury by the Ministry of Finance, which was equipped with substantially wider powers 'To fulfil the great tasks of the SYP and to carry out a fundamental reform of national finance, to create a unified state budget based on socialist principles, to increase financial control and define its scope and form.'[2]

The actual budget reform took place on 17 April 1950, when the CM passed a resolution 'On the preliminary directives concerning the principles of the state budget for 1951'.[3] The new budgetary system was to follow Lenin's concept of 'democratic centralism', the budget becoming 'the basic financial plan of accumulation and distribution of funds necessary to finance the economy, the social and cultural needs of the people, the strengthening of state defence, the maintenance of state administration and the administration of justice.' The first new budget incorporating these aims was worked out for 1951. It was based on the national economic plan and embraced the following 'budgets', which up to then had been separate; (a) the state budget, (b) the budgets of local government, (c) the national insurance, (d) the social fund of state enterprises, (e) the system of equalisation accounts. The 1951 budget was thus the first Soviet-type unified budget adopted in Poland.

After 1950 a large part of budgetary expenditure was devoted to financing the national economy (see table 20).[4] Following the incorporation of equalisation accounts into the budget, changes in normatives of working capital were settled with the budget. More specifically, a surplus of normative working capital was paid into the budget and shortages or increases of normatives were financed by budget grants. The budget also became the most important source of investment expenditure. As already stated, changes involving a switch from credit to budget finance of investment were made in 1949. In 1953 90% of total investment expenditure was financed from the state budget.[5]

[1] Pirożyński and Winter, p. 41.
[2] 'On the transformation of the office of State Treasury into the Ministry of Finance.' *DURP* 10 (1950) item 101.
[3] *MP* 55 (1950) item 631. It was passed at the same time as the law setting up enterprises on economic accounting.
[4] Table 20 is not comparable with table 11 because of changes in the scope and statistics of the budget after 1950.
[5] Z. Pirożyński, 'Budżet Państwa Podstawowym Planem Finansowym PRL', *Finanse* 4 (1954) p. 8. The figure for 1954 was 88%.

Table 20

Budgetary expenditure 1951–5
(a, bil. złoty; b, percentages)

	1951		1952		1953		1954		1955	
	a	b	a	b	a	b	a	b	a	b
Total	51.6	100	61.3	100	96.3	100	116.5	100	123.2	100
On national economy	22.8	44	30.0	49	52.9	55	68.7	59	70.0	57
On fixed investment	19.4	38	21.1	34	28.1	29	29.1	25	30.9	25

Source: GUS – *RS 1960* p. 415.

As in the Soviet Union, the key source of budgetary revenue became the turnover tax, which, as previously noted, was a component of sale prices. In practice turnover tax was paid mainly by the producers of consumer goods. As compared with the turnover tax levied before 1951 (see p. 97), it was a completely different tax. Its rates were differentiated for different commodities, because it was to be a 'regulator of planned profitability'.[1]

Two further effects of budgetary changes on the management of enterprises must be mentioned. The division of profit of enterprises enacted in 1947 was replaced by a division similar to that operated in the Soviet Union. Profits tax gave way to payments from profits into the budget, which were not to be less less than 10% of profits. Some profit was to be used to supplement 'own working capital' and a small payment (1 to 4%) was to be made to a newly created 'factory fund' (*fundusz zakładowy*), to be distributed at the discretion of enterprises.[2]

As already stated, average cost pricing led to many enterprises

---

[1] The expression 'regulator of profitability' was used in two technical senses. First, the rate of the tax determined the revenue (indicating in a Soviet type economy, the availability of investible funds) expected from the production of a product on which the tax was levied. Secondly, the accumulation (see p. 97) of enterprises consisted mainly of profit and the turnover tax. In this way the differentiated turnover tax was indeed a regulator of the accumulation of the enterprises which paid it.

[2] The fund was created by a law of 4 February 1950 'On the factory fund.' *DURP* 6 (1950) item 53. (A similar fund, called 'the director's fund' was set up in the USSR in 1936 and renamed 'the enterprise fund' in 1955.) In practice after 1950 only very small sums were left at the disposal of enterprises.

having a planned deficit or surplus. These were to be settled by a system of equalisation payments organised within an industrial ministry. The old system of equalisation accounts (see pp. 96–7), operated for the MIT by the NBP was discontinued. However, industries failed to elaborate an effective internal mechanism of equalisation payments and in practice deficits of enterprises resulting from the price system were compensated for directly by budgetary subsidies. In this way the change in pricing involved a further decrease in the importance of the banking system in favour of the budget.

Changes in the structure and functions of banks

(a) Reforms of the banking system

On 25 October 1948 the CM passed a decree 'On the bank reform',[1] laying down that the banking system was to consist of three main types of institutions: (a) the NBP, (b) the Investment Bank (Bank Inwestycyjny; IB) and (c) specialised banks. The NBP was to be the bank of issue and short-term credit. It was to conduct all the cash transactions of the state budget and to be responsible for planning the activity within its scope. IB, which took over the activities of the NEB and was manned mainly by its staff, was to accumulate investible funds and to carry out the financial control of investment.[2] The main specialised banks were: the Agricultural Bank (replacing SAB), the Bank of Craft and Trade (Bank Rzemiosła i Handlu; BCT), the Municipal Bank (Bank Komunalny) and the Common Savings Bank (Powszechna Kasa Oszczędności). The Co-operative Bank ceased to exist.

The Agricultural Bank (AB) was to finance fixed and working capital in agriculture and in addition to supervise the activities of Rural Co-operative Banks (Gminne Kasy Spółdzielcze), which replaced the SLCs.[3] It was also to credit some rural co-operative

---

[1] *DURP* 52 (1948) item 412. It was supplemented by two decrees passed on 28 October 1948, dealing with the liquidation of credit institutions embraced by the reform: *DURP* 52 (1948) item 410; *DURP* 52 (1948) item 411. The reform was ultimately codified on 4 February 1951, *DURP* 36 (1951) item 279.

[2] It also took over some of the activities of the Co-operative Bank in the field of investment.

[3] The retention of small scale co-operative banking was a feature distinguishing the Polish banking system from most other East European systems. Co-operative banking was abolished in Czechoslovakia, Hungary, Rumania and Bulgaria.

5

enterprises previously financed by the Co-operative Bank. The BCT which took over the assets and liabilities of UWCB and part of the assets and liabilities of the Co-operative Bank, the TB and the Municipal Savings Banks, was to finance working capital of small scale industry, crafts and trade in co-operative and private sectors. It was to advance credit for investment purposes as directed by the IB and to supervise the activities of Municipal Credit Co-operatives. The Municipal Bank (MB) which was created by a merger of the two existing municipal banks (completed in 1949), was to supply credit for fixed and working capital to municipal undertakings. The Common Savings Bank took over the functions of the Post Office Savings Bank. The TB was to be renamed the Foreign Trade Bank (Bank Handlu Zagranicznego) and to finance trade with capitalist countries. The bank, which has been in existence since 1870, has never actually adopted the proposed name.

The 1948 reform aimed at the creation of two central institutions of credit: the NBP to distribute short-term credit directly or indirectly through other banks, and the IB, to distribute investment credit directly or indirectly through other banks. Thus state enterprises were to obtain credit from the NBP to finance their working capital, while financing their fixed capital by advances from the IB. State control over banks, exercised by the State Treasury, was to increase. In fact Polish authors often described the reform as the nationalisation of the banking system. Such a description is misleading. It was perhaps used more to emphasise the ideological content of contemporary changes, rather than convey the true nature of the reform. The law merely accelerated the processes already visible before that date. The basic skeleton of the traditional banking system was still preserved, but the co-operative and private sectors lost their separate credit institutions, their credit coming mainly from the BCT. The reform however marked the beginning of the transition from the Polish 'model' to the Soviet 'model' of banking.

Processes of centralisation and socialisation after 1948 led to further changes in the structure of credit institutions. Considerably less credit was given to agriculture, especially to privately owned farms, and to the private non-agricultural sector.[1] Co-operative and

[1] A detailed analysis of credit to the private sector is not available. Kucharski, *Kredyt...*, p. 134, estimated that during 1947 credit to the sector was rising (esp. for small-scale industry and trade), in 1948 it became static and in 1949 fell drastically, to a third of the

municipal firms were made to function on lines similar to state enterprises and hence it was thought unnecessary to retain for them credit institutions different from those financing state enterprises. It was thus decided to abolish the BCT. Particularly after 1950 the NBP began to take over the bank's activities, but the Minister of Finance could not abolish a state bank until the law of 22 March 1951 'On the change in the provisions of the bank reform', which gave him wide powers of intervention in the banking system, including the power to liquidate state banks and to order a bank to carry out tasks not envisaged in the bank's charter.[1] The law made the changes in the banking system in the early 1950s possible. The BCT was abolished and its functions taken over mainly by the NBP and to a lesser extent by the IB, the AB and the MB. The last mentioned, however, was abolished on 1 January 1952, its short-term credit activities being taken over by NBP and its investment finance by the IB.

Although the AB was not abolished, the scope of its activity was gradually diminishing. First, in 1951, the bank lost its function of financing agricultural industry (mainly fish and fruit processing); in 1952 it ceased to finance a number of co-operative agricultural enterprises; but the final and most serious blow came in 1953, when it lost the function of financing enterprises subordinated to the Ministry of Agriculture and the Ministry of Forestry, which included the state farms. Furthermore, it ceased entirely to finance co-operative firms and to supervise the activities of Rural Co-operative Banks (RCBs), which remained the only co-operative credit institutions in existence after 1952; their supervision was transferred to the NBP. The AB's short-term credit activities were taken over by the NBP and its investment financing by the IB. Thus by 1953 the AB had become relatively unimportant – it financed investment of some agricultural enterprises and serviced the activity of enterprises carrying out investment in agriculture. Of the total investment finance distributed by banks in 1953, only 7.5% was distributed by the bank (see table 21).

credit granted in 1948. W. Jaworski ('System Kredytowy w 15-leciu Polski Ludowej', *Finanse* 7, 1959, p. 43) gave data suggesting a continuously falling ratio of credit to the private sector to total credit: 8.0% in 1946 (4.7% for agriculture), 5.9% (2.8%) in 1947, 4.5% (2.7%) in 1948. Some problems of credit to the private sector are elaborated in Appendix A.

[1] *DURP* 18 (1951) item 143.

Table 21

Payments made by the banks for investment purposes
1950-3

(*In percentages*)

	1950	1951	1952	1953
Investment Bank	81.7	85.5	90.8	92.5
Agricultural Bank	11.4	8.7	9.2	7.5
Municipal Bank	6.9	5.8	–	–
Total	100.0	100.0	100.0	100.0

Source: J. Trendota, 'Zagadnienia Banków Finansujących Inwestycje na Obecnym Etapie', *Finanse* 6 (1953) p. 18.

With the liquidation of the BCT and the MB, the IB ceased to be
the central investment bank supervising the investment crediting
of the specialised banks. Like the AB, it became simply a specialised
bank financing investment. In consequence of the 1948–53 banking
and budgetary changes the IB in reality lost its character as a bank,
becoming the chief institution for distributing investment funds (see
table 21). The bulk of these were budgetary grants, so that during the
period of the SYP the bank became an executive organ of investment
finance and financial control by the Ministry of Finance.[1] Its own
contribution to the formulation of investment plans was negligible.

Thus, after these reforms, there were two distinct flows of funds –
one financing working capital, serviced and controlled mainly by the
NBP (discussed further in the next subsection) and the other financing investment, serviced and controlled by budgetary institutions,
mainly the IB. An appendix at the end of this chapter summarises
the main changes in financial institutions between 1939 and 1953.

(b) The mono-bank credit system

The banking system which emerged in Poland after the changes of
the early 1950s is often called in East European literature the 'mono-
banking system'. In this subsection, largely with the help of statistics,
an attempt is made to summarise the impact of the reforms on the

[1] In essence by 1953 specialised banks in Poland carried out similar functions to specialised
Soviet Banks. (see pp. 34–5).

Table 22a

Changes in the relative importance of credit institutions 1950–5
(*Credit balances at the end of the year*)

	1950		1955		
	mil. zł.	%	mil. zł.	%	Branches in 1955
NBP[1]	19,418	64.9	59,686	88.9	435[3]
IB	2,673	8.9	3,580	5.3	41
AB	7,479	25.0	3,124	4.7	276[4]
RCBs[2]	351	1.2	719	1.1	291[5]
Total	29,921	100.0	67,109	100.0	

Notes:
[1] Excluding refinancing of other banks.
[2] viz. Rural Co-operative Banks which after 1948 replaced the SLCs.
[3] Including 17 regional headquarters, one in each voivodship.
[4] Branches and offices attached to the NBP.
[5] The number of co-operative banks.
Source: GUS – *RS 1957*, p. 302; GUS – *RSF 1945–67*, p. 234.

credit system and to define more precisely the main characteristics of the mono-banking system in Poland.

Table 22a, showing the relative size in terms of credit granted of various credit institutions, suggests that the banking system was not, strictly speaking, a mono-bank. It was, however, very centralised by 1955, with only four types of institutions, of which the NBP granted 89% of the total credit extended by the whole system. Thus, the bank had a near-monopoly of credit. The evolution of this situation is illustrated by tables 22b and 23.

The credit granted by banks was mainly direct credit (see pp. 100–1), as it was felt that only this type of credit allowed banks to exercise effective control over enterprises. The NBP did refinance other banks, but in the main its credit too was given directly to enterprises.[1] Direct crediting is a salient feature distinguishing Soviet-type central banks from their Western counterparts. Thus, whereas the Western central bank acts mainly as the 'bankers' bank',

[1] Refinance by NBP amounted in 1950 to 2.5% of all credit and to 28% of credit granted by NBP. The figures for 1955 were 0.6% and 6.0% respectively (see table 16 and GUS – *RSF 1945–1967*, p. 234).

Table 22b

Bank credit 1950-5

(*Balances at the end of the year: a, mil. zl.; b, % of total*)

Year	Total a	NBP[1] a	b	To socialised sector a	b	Short-term[2] a	b
1950	29,921	19,418	64.9	29,240	97.7	28,506	95.3
1951	37,205	24,764	66.6	36,398	97.8	34,871	93.7
1952	47,596	36,447	76.6	46,377	97.4	44,964	94.5
1953	62,867	54,583	86.8	61,098	97.2	59,573	91.6
1954	66,401	57,133	86.0	64,205	96.7	62,515	94.1
1955	67,109	59,686	88.9	64,652	96.2	62,981	93.8

Notes:
[1] Excluding refinancing of other banks.
[2] Credit for working capital excluding credit to private industry and trade, some of which may have been short-term, and excluding instalment purchase credit.
Source: GUS – *RSF 1945–1967*, pp. 230–4.

it may be said that a socialist central bank is essentially 'the enterprises' bank'.[1]

Table 22b shows that credit was given mainly to the socialised sector; the private sector and individuals received on the average less than 3% of the total credit, in spite of the fact that agriculture remained based on private farming. The table also shows that the credit system was basically a short-term system, financing working capital. Investment credit was granted mainly to the co-operative and private sectors.

Looking at credit finance in the socialised sector (table 22c), it can be seen that the monopoly position of the NBP in that sector was even stronger than it was in the economy as a whole (compare with table 22b), and that the share of short-term credit in the total was higher than that shown in table 22b.

[1] The notable exception here is the National Bank of Yugoslavia, which was a 'monobank' organised on basically Soviet principles up to 1955, but which then started to change, abandoning direct credit relations in the early sixties and after the 1965–6 reforms resembling a Western more than a Soviet-type central bank. See J. J. Hauvonen, 'Postwar Developments in Money and Banking in Yugoslavia', *IMF Staff Papers*, vol. XVII, no. 3, 1970.

Table 22c

Credit extended to the socialised sector 1950–5

(*Balances at the end of the year: a, mil. zł.; b, % of total*)

Year	Total a	Credit by NBP a	b	Short-term credit a	b
1950	29,240	19,418	66.4	28,155	96.3
1951	36,398	24,764	68.0	34,402	94.5
1952	46,377	36,081	77.0	44,508	96.0
1953	61,098	53,765	88.0	59,052	96.7
1954	64,205	56,214	87.6	61,926	96.5
1955	64,652	58,902	91.1	62,317	96.4

Source: GUS – *RSF 1945–1967*, pp. 230, 234.

Table 23

Credit by NBP to the socialised enterprises 1950–5
(*Balances at the end of the year*)

Year	Total[1] mil. zł.	Short-term credit mil. zł.	% of total	% of s-t credit[2]	Investment credit mil. zł.	% of total
1950	19,418	19,347	99.6	68.7	71	0.4
1951	24,764	24,363	98.4	70.8	401	1.6
1952	36,081	35,973	99.7	80.8	108	0.3
1953	53,765	53,591	99.7	90.8	174	0.3
1954	56,214	56,103	99.8	90.6	111	0.2
1955	58,902	58,799	99.8	94.4[3]	103	0.2

Notes:
[1] Excluding refinancing of other banks.
[2] Percentage of short-term credit given in column 5 of table 22c.
[3] The highest ratio in the bank's history was 95.2%; in 1956.
Source: GUS – *RSF 1945–60*, pp. 230, 234.

Table 23 gives more details about the NBP, showing that it did not issue short-term credit exclusively. No details are given in Polish literature on the type of investment credit extended by the bank, but most of it was likely to be 'credit to be refunded from the investment plan', viz. granted to bridge the gap between the start of capital projects and the issue of budgetary funds for their finance. The total investment credit was, however, very small. The table also shows the monopoly position of the bank in short-term credit to the socialised sector.

(c) The wider scope of bank control

Tables 22–3 emphasise the dominance of the NBP in the credit system. However, as mentioned earlier, credit became a less important source of funds, compared with budgetary finance. It was now used mainly to finance above-normative working capital of enterprises; investment and changes in the normative of working capital were financed by the budget. What the tables do not reflect is the fact that the key function of the NBP became the control of enterprises, closely modelled on the control system in the USSR (see chapter 2).

The bank acquired new techniques of control and the scope of control was widened. It was to be exercised by granting credit (this is discussed separately later), by supervising wage payments and by carrying out settlements.

Between 1945 and 1949 banks were not involved in the process of wage payments. Problems of remuneration, especially up to 1947, were generally to be solved by enterprises themselves, and there was no question at that time of planning wage payments. Priority was given to solving the problems of determination of wage rates for different jobs and of methods of payment. Also the planning of wages was made difficult by rationing and the fact that a large proportion of remuneration was usually paid in kind. In 1946 only 42.7% of an average real wage was paid in money; at the end of 1948 the proportion was 81.0%.[1] The planning of the wage fund started in 1949, following a reform of wage payments and the abolition of rationing in January of that year. On 21 June 1949 the CM gave banks the responsibility for control of wage payments, which was organised in the same way as in the Soviet Union (see chapter 2). The banks were to ensure that withdrawals for wages requested by enterprises were within the limits of the wage funds allocated to the enterprises and earned in the course of actual fulfilment of plans. They were also to analyse wage payments in order to assess the efficiency of enterprises.

[1] T. Leszek and S. Pudlik, 'Place', in ZRMPPL, p. 262.

The organisation of settlements has already been described in the previous chapter, where it was noted that the provisions laid down by legislation were not rigorously enforced by the authorities. The 1948 bank reform empowered the NBP to organise and carry out settlements between enterprises in the socialised sector and to exercise supervision over settlements conducted by other banks. On 1 July 1949 a new law was passed,[1] aiming at strengthening bank control through settlements by extending the system of cashless settlements to include unincorporated associations and co-operative and local government firms. Provisions concerning settlements and the holding of cash reserves in the bank were henceforth in general to be more rigorously enforced.

After 1949 the NBP was to pay more attention than before to the mobilisation of 'temporarily free' monetary resources. Partly for motives of control over money and partly as an anti-inflationary device, the bank was to become the only centre of cash reserves in the economy. In 1950 the bank's chairman stressed that a socialist central bank must regard the function of mobilising monetary resources as being on a par with its function of extending and controlling credit.[2] Earlier it was noticed that the monetary reform of 1950 helped to concentrate purchasing power in the banking system at the expense of the public's cash holdings.

In connection with the accumulation of monetary resources in the bank, it must be mentioned that from July 1950 the bank became directly involved in 'cash servicing of the budget' (*kasowa obsługa budżetu*).[3] Before that date budgetary revenue was collected and some budgetary expenditure made through a network of fiscal institutions independent of the bank but each possessing a bank account.[4] The 1948 bank reform imposed upon the bank the duty of servicing the budget directly, but it was not until after 1950 that the bank in fact discharged this duty through special departments for budget servicing. Fiscal functions performed in these departments (for example collection of taxes, control over tax payments) remained separate from the other operations of the bank. In effect, previously

---

[1] 'On the duty of participation in cashless turnover', *DURP* 41 (1949) item 294.

[2] Kostowski, p. 9.

[3] Cash servicing of the budget by the State Bank was first introduced in the USSR in the budget year 1927–8.

[4] W. Miłkowski, 'Bankowa Obsługa Budżetu Państwa i Ministerstw w Latach 1945–1951', *WNBP* 3 (1965) pp. 89–91.

independent units of the budgetary system were now attached to most branches of the bank.[1]

Thus, the importance and scale of operations of the NBP increased significantly. The tables above indicated the bank's growth mainly in terms of credit. Its expansion in terms of branches and employees was equally impressive. In 1948 it had 78 branches, in 1950 373 and in 1952 436.[2] Between 1948 and 1950 the bank's personnel increased more than threefold and from 1949 to 1950 the staff more than doubled.[3] It is worth mentioning here that the employees recruited between 1948 and 1950 were poorly qualified – rarely with higher, more often with only primary education. The ratio of personnel with banking experience to the total staff of the bank fell from 76% in 1945 to 36% at the end of 1949. The staffing policy was designed to give the bank a socialist image by discriminating against old staff and in favour of applicants with peasant and worker family background and Party members. Leading positions were often filled by young people with little banking experience, but with an 'appropriate socio-political attitude'. At the end of 1949 personnel with peasant and worker backgrounds accounted for 43% of total staff and at the end of 1953 for 71%.[4]

The main conclusion to this section is that, following the banking reforms in the early 1950s, the NBP emerged as a large monopolistic credit institution and the centre of cashless settlements. Its chief duty became the control over the activities of enterprises. Other banks served mainly as channels for the distribution of budgetary funds.

It may be noticed that both the Soviet and Polish banking systems were made quite simple by Western standards, consisting of few institutions. This was done as part of the overall centralisation process and was to facilitate monetary control. In the West the usual course of events is for financial development to accompany general economic development and to be characterised by increasing complexity.[5] Indeed sometimes a deliberate creation of a financial struc-

---

[1] For more information see W. Miłkowski, 'Współudział NBP w Kontroli Wykonania Budżetu Państwa', *WNBP* 2 (1953); Z. Karpiński and J. Lindner, *Organizacja Bankowości w Polsce Ludowej* (1954) pp. 65-8; B. Szymot, 'Podstawowe Założenia Wykonania Budżetu Państwa Przez Bank Centralny', *RPEiS* 1 (1962).

[2] Laskowski, p. 27; see also table 22a.

[3] Bank personnel at the end of each year: 1954, 2,366; 1946, 3,823; 1947, 4,407; 1948, 5,677; 1949, 8,206; 1950, 17,751; 1951, 20,294; 1952, 22,927; 1953, 25,546; Laskowski, p. 271.

[4] *Ibid.* pp. 271-3.   [5] See e.g. Goldsmith, pp. 46-8.

ture is encouraged, to increase home savings and harness them to development.[1] This assumes that savings are institution elastic and that a relatively developed financial system is able to allocate resources efficiently. Socialist banking systems appear to have neglected this aspect. Personal savings formed a very small percentage of total bank liabilities (see tables B1a and B1b) and little was done to encourage the banking habit in the population. This may perhaps be explained by difficulties in encouraging saving when per capita income is low and by the fact that complete faith was put in the budget as the instrument for accumulating capital.

From control based on liberal credit to stringent Soviet-type monetary control

(a) The 'signal role' of credit and 'credit automatism'

It has been observed (p. 104) that in the late 1940s attempts were made to free banks from the task of exercising an administrative type of control over enterprises and to link control to credit. In 1949 a system of control emerged which incorporated an original solution to the problem of control, in spite of the fact that Soviet economic methods were at that time generally transplanted automatically into the Polish economy.

In organising the credit system the authorities endeavoured to impregnate credit with the characteristics attributed to it in the Soviet Union (see chapter 2), in particular with that of 'specific purpose', to ensure that credit was granted in a planned way, and not just on the strength of the plan. At first Soviet monetary control was not mechanically adopted.

On 12 April 1949 the CM resolved that turnover credit must be 'tied' to the object of credit and must be given for a specified period. If it was not promptly repaid, it became 'overdue' and its settlement from the current account was to take precedence over all other payments except wages. Also a penal rate of interest was imposed on all outstanding 'overdue credit'. Moreover, the NBP's credit became more differentiated than before 1949, consisting of the following types: (a) 'normative credit' given to supplement own funds ('normal credit' was granted where enterprises had not yet calculated their normative), (b) 'above-normative credit', consisting of transitional

[1] See e.g. Hicks, pp. 51–4.

credit and special credit (see p. 104), (c) credit for exports, (d) credit for imports, (e) credit to be refunded from the investment plan (first mentioned on pp. 121-2), which was a bridging credit extended where an enterprise started an investment project before receiving investible funds (mainly from budgetary sources).

All these credits fulfilled the *qualitative tests* by being given for a specific purpose and, as a rule, for a specific period of time, but enterprises could also get overdue credit, which was not specific and indeed in theory should not have arisen, assuming that they carried out their plans and settled all their debts promptly. Overdue credit, however, did occur when enterprises failed to repay the specific credits enumerated above, and/or overdrew their current account. Banks at the time settled current obligations of clients even if balances on their settlement account were insufficient to meet them. Such a practice led simply to the growth of overdue credit in enterprises with payments difficulties.

Although overdue credit did not possess the socialist attributes as interpreted in the Soviet Union, its existence had a justification based on a view of the 'signal role of credit' popular at that time in Poland. Overdue credit was considered to be a red light, a signal that an enterprise was guilty of mismanagement. Furthermore, as Kucharski explained,[1] its existence suggested shortcomings in particular spheres of management. It could not then arise due to shortages of working capital, as these were settled with the equalisation account of working capital, or because of price changes as losses (and profits) caused by such changes were settled with the equalisation account of price differences. Both accounts, it may be recalled, were operated by the NBP. In this situation overdue credit could only imply that an enterprise was (a) accumulating excessive stocks, (b) financing investment from working capital, or (c) increasing the amount of trade debts outstanding, suggesting a failure of buyers to settle their bills promptly.

In connection with the last point it must be emphasised that banks automatically gave overdrafts to clients with insufficient funds to cover their current commitments (for example the repayment of a specific bank credit, the settlement of accepted invoices or the payment of a tax), so that there were no reasons for enterprises not to settle their accounts promptly. Kucharski commented that 'In these conditions overdue credit became a signal that an enterprise possessed

[1] Kucharski, *Kredyt...*, pp. 144-5.

unjustifiable above-normative stocks or that it employed in an irregular way its working capital to finance investment.' Thus overdue credit indicated specific areas where the institutions to which enterprises were subordinated and the banks could look for instances of mismanagement.

There was one further justification for the above interpretation of the role of credit. As already stated, the NBP operated the two equalisation accounts. From 1949 credit ceased to finance investment in the state sector and the NBP began to acquire a near monopoly of short-term credit. In these circumstances the bank was a sort of central receiving station for 'signals' transmitted by overdue credit, and was in a good position to ascertain the causes of the irregularities which these indicated.

The concept of the signal role of credit, which marked the last attempt before 1957 to offer a Polish solution to credit management in a socialist economy, did not survive beyond 1950, for reasons discussed later. It may be observed that the view which crystallised in 1949 was a logical consequence of the earlier interpretation of the nature of bank control (see pp. 99–100), which stressed that banks should above all supply facts about the management and plan fulfilment of enterprises, pinpointing the areas where improvement in efficiency could take place. There was little faith at the time in the efficacy and desirability of credit restrictions. Indeed banks, for several good reasons, were loath to refuse to lend. Credit was the main source of finance and, as the paramount aim at the time was to revive production, few credit restrictions were imposed in practice, except in the private sector. State enterprises, or even private enterprises carrying out the orders of various state departments, generally found it easy to obtain credit in the quantities requested. Furthermore, as up to 1950 enterprises were combinations integrating a number of factories (p. 78), banks were generally reluctant to restrict credit, lest this might involve cutting off credit from factories needing and deserving it. Also banks were not very concerned about granting enterprises more credit than was necessary, because a surplus of short-term funds was normally paid into the working capital equalisation account operated by the NBP (p. 96). Finally, to implement the signal role of credit, banks pursued a liberal short-term credit policy, not in general restricting credit even to enterprises unable to meet their current payments, so that overdue credit represented the total indebtedness of an enterprise at any time.

To its critics the policy was 'credit automatism', embodying the same deficiencies as the Soviet automatism of 1930, despite significant differences between the 'automatisms' of the two countries.[1] In the Soviet Union, in 1930, the State Bank operated only one account for each enterprise (see pp. 31–2). In Poland in 1949 the NBP held separate accounts for current transactions and for credit. In fact three types of accounts existed: (a) the current (or settlement) account, (b) the specific credit account and (c) the overdraft account, viz. the account of overdue credit.

In the USSR in 1930 credit was not given for a specific purpose, but generally as long as the plan envisaged it (*pod plan*). The NBP, as a rule, granted credit for a specific purpose only. The exception was overdue credit, which had certain characteristics (as a signal) making it useful for the purpose of bank control. As stated earlier, credits were already classified according to their specific purpose and were returnable in a strictly defined period, so that in general they may be said to have possessed the qualities demanded of socialist credit. The exception again was overdue credit. However, whereas in the Soviet Union changes in the current account could not be used for diagnostic purposes concerning the management of enterprises (see p. 32), changes in the overdue credit account performed a useful diagnostic role.

In the USSR invoices were settled regardless of whether the buyer accepted them or not. The NBP, as a rule, did not settle invoices which were not accepted, so that overdue credit could not directly arise as a result of incorrect deliveries. Though the above differences were important, criticisms of Polish automatism were inspired by criticisms referring to the Soviet automatism.[2]

An interesting feature common to both Soviet and Polish credit automatism may be noticed. The abolition of the bill of exchange, which represented both a method of settlement of debts and an instrument of credit, and the divorce of settlements of debts from the mainstream of credit, produced similar difficulties in both countries. Automatic extension of credit to enable enterprises to settle debts,

---

[1] Indeed Kucharski, having discussed these differences (*Kredyt...*, pp. 147–9), concluded that Soviet automatism 'had a completely different character' from Polish automatism.

[2] This is implied in Kucharski's discussion and is specifically stated in other sources, e.g. W. Pruss, 'Rozliczenia Między Przedsiębiorstwami Uspołecznionymi i ich Kredytowanie', *WNBP* 2 (1961) p. 60.

however different it might have been in each country, appeared to be a way of relinking settlements with the flow of credit. The problem of the interrelation between the two is, as will be shown in subsequent chapters, one of the key financial problems of a socialist economy.

(b) From credit automatism to stringent monetary policy

Two main criticisms were levelled against the liberal credit policy of 1949. First, it was pointed out that unrestricted credit, allowing enterprises to settle their debts without encountering any financial difficulties, would have a demoralising effect on their management. The second criticism was more specific. It was thought that if invoices were settled even when the buyer was short of funds then it would be a matter of indifference to the seller whether his customer paid his bills or not. Thus suppliers would lose interest in the ability of the buyers to meet their obligations, thereby weakening the 'mutual control' (see pp. 44–5) between the seller and the buyer. The critics of automatic crediting thought it necessary for suppliers to experience financial difficulties when their clients failed to pay promptly thus forcing the seller to exert pressure on the client to settle.[1]

These criticisms were sound in so far as it was indeed necessary to encourage punctual settlements. There remained, however, the problems of how to inculcate in enterprises a sense of responsibility for payments and how to interest the seller in the buyer's ability to pay. The most obvious solution seemed to be bank sanctions against recalcitrant enterprises, but, as will be shown later, banks were reluctant to impose sanctions and such sanctions as were imposed were generally ineffective. Overdue credit was in fact automatically connected with a bank sanction in the form of a penal rate of interest of 8%, which was double the rate of interest charged on other types of credit, but its effectiveness was weakened by the fact that enterprises in general paid insufficient attention to costs of production. Sanctions based on limitations on the supply of bank credit were feared by the supporters of the signal role of credit, because they might lead to a chain reaction of financial difficulties, which are explained later.

[1] M. L. Kostowski, 'Założenia Nowej Instrukcji Kredytowej', *WNBP* 1 (1951) p. 12.

In 1950 it was decided to eliminate credit automatism by a more fundamental change of the credit system.[1] The concepts of the signal role of credit and of bank control as primarily involving fact-finding were discredited as involving an erroneous interpretation of the role of credit in a socialised economy. The new attitude towards credit was well expressed by Karczmar, who stated that

Credit as an instrument of financial control must not be used exclusively for purposes of registration or diagnosis. Its role lies not merely in the detection of deviations and shortcomings in plan fulfilment by enterprises but also in their rectification. It must encourage enterprises to improve their economic accounting and strictly to observe financial discipline.[2]

It was thought that credit could fulfil this 'active role' if it were given only to finance expenditure arising from correct management, rather than to cover shortages of funds which might be symptomatic of mismanagement.

To this end the credit reforms of 1950-2 were carried out, establishing a credit system closely resembling that of the Soviet Union. One must bear in mind that these changes accompanied a budget reform, the introduction of economic accounting and a currency reform, which was to be a precondition for more effective control by money. They were introduced by the NBP's instructions,[3] and the immediate object was to eliminate credit automatism. First it was decided to change the system of credit on settlements by introducing credit on documents in transit, better known in Poland as the 'inkaso credit' (*kredyt inkasowy*), granted to the seller to bridge the gap between the despatch of goods ordered and the payment of the invoice by the buyer. Initially this credit was not given for a strictly defined period, so that in practice, like overdue credit before 1950, it functioned automatically. At the same time the old overdue credit account became 'overdue credit account B', but did not really differ

---

[1] At the same time it was decided to strengthen 'mutual control' by making 'planned contracts' between enterprises compulsory on 19 April 1950. These were based on production plans of enterprises and their terms were legally enforceable. The practice of planned contracts was copied from the USSR (see ch. 2).

[2] M. Karczmar, 'O Istocie i Funkcjach Kredytu Socjalistycznego', *WNBP* 2 (1955) pp. 71-2. (A similar view was expressed by the author in 'O Umocnienie Roli Kredytu', *Finanse* 4 (1954) p. 38).

[3] Information on these may be found in e.g. Kucharski, *Kredyt...*, pp. 161-4; Jaworski, *Obieg...*, pp. 199-202.

from its predecessor. A new type of overdue credit was granted in 1950 for enterprises failing to fulfil their planned targets. It was entered in 'overdue credit account A' and was in effect the old type of transitional credit, but had nothing in common with the pre-1950 overdue credit and the overdue credit on account B. In addition, a 'seasonal credit' was allowed specifically to finance seasonal stock accumulation. These changes increased the number of types of credit from seven (in 1949) to nine, but did not eliminate credit automatism.

This is said to have been accomplished on 18 April 1951, when the Chairman of the NBP issued an order prohibiting the settlement of current debts from overdue credit (on account B). Overdue credit on account A became known as 'credit for unusual needs' (*kredyt na nadzwyczajne potrzeby*). Credit on settlements (the inkaso credit) ceased to be issued without a stipulation of the time of repayment and was subdivided into two types: credit for settling invoices (*na faktury*), the main type, and credit for purchases by instalments. Credit on invoices was to be repaid within a defined period based on the estimated time needed for settlement of the invoices. If these were not paid punctually the credit was to be terminated, leaving the seller in financial difficulties. After 1951 overdue credit became overdue credit in the strict sense of the word, viz. 'simply credit which had not been settled in a stipulated time'.[1] In consequence, automatic financing of the current obligations of enterprises short of funds stopped in 1951.

Another important change introduced on 18 April 1951 was the order of payments to be observed by enterprises whose current account balances were insufficient to meet all their debts, viz. when, in theory, some 'incorrectness' occurred in their management. It was modified on 12 December 1951 by resolution 877 of the Presidium of the Government,[2] which laid down the following sequence of settlements: wages, budgetary obligations, depreciation payments, payments of overdue bank credit, payments of overdue settlements (for example of overdue invoices) together with penalties for not settling promptly, other financial obligations including payments for current invoices, viz. payments for deliveries. Both the order of 18 April and the resolution of 12 December, following the practice

[1] Karpiński and Lindner, p. 99.
[2] 'On the principles of settlements for supplies and services made between units of socialised economy.' *MP* 103 (1951) item 1500.

of the Soviet Union,[1] relegated payments for deliveries to last place, so that a buyer who was short of funds could not pay his invoices because other payments had priority. In theory, this arrangement was to act as a stimulus for the seller to take action against a defaulting buyer. At the same time the buyer who failed to settle promptly had to pay the seller a penalty of 18% per annum on the amount of the overdue debt.

The main object of resolution 877 was to improve the functioning of settlements in general.[2] Buyers were presumed to have accepted invoices if within three days (previously a five day rule applied) they failed to refuse acceptance, but they could refuse acceptance for more reasons than previously (compare p. 95). It was thought that such an arrangement would strengthen 'mutual control'. Thus the system of settlements established in 1951, and especially the new order of payments, reinforced the credit restrictions discussed above. In theory, 1951 marked the end of the liberal credit policy and the beginning of stringent credit considered at the time essential to effective monetary control.

Between 1951 and 1952 the number of types of credit rose to seventeen (see table 24). The basis of division continued to be the purpose of credit, but this time defined more specifically. For example, the number of 'above-normative credits' rose from three to six: special and seasonal credits were replaced by separate credits financing specified types of stocks, such as stocks of final products, stocks of semi-finished products or stocks of raw materials. Similarly credits on settlements were divided into three types, according to the mode of settlement used. Thus separate credit was given to finance settlements by the acceptance of invoices method, which was the main credit on settlements known as 'credit on invoice debts' (*na należności fakturowe*), being given to the seller on the strength of prompt payment by the buyer. The other two were: credit for purchases by instalments and credits for other settlements (e.g. by letters of credit – the *akredytywa*). The group of credits called 'others' in table 24 consisted of a variety of credits, such as credit to finance

---

[1] The idea of a fixed order of payments originated in the Soviet Union in February 1929. Up to 1954 the order which applied there was: payments of wages and similar claims, payments to financial organs (mainly taxes), depreciation, bank debts, payments for deliveries of goods. Atlas (1947 ed.) pp. 255–6.

[2] In 1951 alternative methods of settlements to *inkaso* were introduced, but in practice they did not play an important part in payments of state industrial enterprises.

Table 24

Summary of the types of credits granted by NBP in 1952

Main groups of credits	Number of types of credit in each group	Percentage of total short-term credit
Normative	1	21.1
Above-normative	6	47.9
On settlements	3	15.7
For imports/exports	2	3.7
Overdue	1	8.6
Others	4	3.0
Total	17	100.0

Source: W. Jaworski, *Obieg Pieniężny i Kredyt*, p. 201.

investment expenditure until finance was available from appropriate sources, or credit for advances made for future agricultural deliveries (*na kontraktacje*). The group also included a type of credit called 'miscellaneous credits' (*kredyty różne*), which in turn were specified in accordance with the purpose for which they were advanced, e.g. credit for wage payments, or for overdue debts from buyers (*kredyt na przeterminowane należności fakturowe*). Different types of credit were entered on separate credit accounts.

The fragmentation of bank credit which emerged in 1952 was to achieve the following basic objectives: (*a*) to give bank credit socialist characteristics, especially of being specific purpose, specific term and planned credit; (*b*) to facilitate the management of working capital in enterprises and ensure bank control over it; (*c*) to improve the signal role of credit in the sense that, with a wide subdivision of credit, non-repayment of a specific type of credit in a stipulated period was thought to signify an irregularity in the sphere of activity which the credit specifically financed.

The 1951–2 credit reforms copied the principles which operated in the Soviet credit system, a fact which was usually acknowledged by Polish economists.[1] After 1951 there was no important difference between the principles of credit in Poland and in the Soviet Union. Thus both Polish and Soviet banks applied the same *qualitative tests* before extending or refusing credit.

Important changes relevant to monetary control also occurred in

[1] See e.g. M. L. Kostowski, 'Nowe Zasady Kredytowe', *Finanse* 1 (1952) p. 33.

the early 1950s in the sphere of credit planning.[1] Very briefly, attempts at credit planning were first made in 1947; in 1948 and 1949 the NBP did in fact produce credit plans, which were summaries of the credit plans of banking institutions, consisting of balances of planned loan requirements and the resources available to cover them. The plans were not 'directive', but served mainly for purposes of information or 'orientation'.[2] Directive credit planning was introduced between 1950 and 1951, when the NBP worked out plans on the basis of which credit limits (*limity kredytowe*), viz. maximum limits beyond which specific types of credit could not be granted to an enterprise, were imposed on banks. These limits were directive in the sense that they represented the chief method of fulfilment of the credit plan and had to be strictly observed by banks. Not all credits, however, were subjected to limits; they were imposed only on credit whose amounts could reasonably be foreseen. As a rule, normative and above-normative credits, except 'credit for unusual needs', were subject to limits; for other credits so called 'control figures' were given, estimating merely the total indebtedness of an enterprise at the end of a period (they were, for example, used in connection with import or export credit or in cases of credit for agricultural contracts).

[1] Information on this may be found in U. Wojciechowska and W. Szczegielniak, 'Finanse' in *ZRMPPL*, pp. 349–60; Kucharski, *Kredyt...*, chapter 5; Jaworski, *Zarys...*, pp. 185–8.
[2] Wojciechowska and Szczegielniak, p. 353.

Appendix to chapter 5

Summary of institutional changes in the credit system since 1939
(*Principal credit institutions*)

Banks	1939	1945–8	1948–52	1952–5
State	Bank of Poland[1] Nat. Econ. Bank	NBP Nat. Econ. Bank	NBP Investment Bank	NBP Investment Bank[5]
	State Ag. Bank	State Ag. Bank	Ag. Bank BCT[4]	Ag. Bank[5]
Co-operative	Co-operative banks LSCs[2]	The Co-op Bank	Rural Co-op. bks.	Rural Co-op. bks.
Municipal	Municipal bks. Mun. savings bks.	Municipal bks. Mun. savings bks.	The Mun. Bank	
Joint stock	Joint stock bks. Banking houses	Trade Bank UWCB[3]		

Notes:

[1] The central bank (private joint stock company but co-operating with the government).

[2] Loans and savings co-operatives.

[3] Union of Workers' Co-operatives Bank.

[4] Bank of Craft and Trade.

[5] Investment finance institutions.

6

Monetary control in practice

Introduction

This chapter deals mainly with the practical application of the principles of credit control discussed in earlier chapters, covering roughly the period of forced industrialisation of the Polish SYP and incorporating some Soviet comparisons for the post 1931 period.

The fulfilment of the gigantic tasks of the plan (p. 108) required a supreme effort from the economy, an effort which is usually demanded only in periods of emergency. Dziewanowski observed that 'While launching the SYP the Party attempted to create an almost mystical atmosphere resembling, to some extent, that which prevailed in the Soviet Union during the first two five year plans.'[1] In chapter 5 an outline was given of the administrative reforms leading to the centralisation of national economic management considered necessary in the campaign to industrialise. Planned targets were worked out by the SCEP and economic ministries and passed on to enterprises in the form of commands for fulfilment. Planned output became the key economic goal; its fulfilment became the measure of economic achievement and the main basis for remuneration. Planning acquired war-time characteristics in the sense that in managing the economy the authorities used 'methods based on moral and political exhortation, on legal and administrative directives, on various means of para-economic compulsion and not on economic incentives'.[2]

The study attempted below is severely limited by the availability of material. From 1949 to 1956 publications on banking and credit generally consisted of either a repetition or an interpretation of laws

[1] Dziewanowski, p. 226.
[2] O. Lange, 'W Sprawie Doraźnego Programu', *ŻG* 14 (1956) p. 1. See also 'Rola Planowania w Gospodarce Socjalistycznej (1957)' in *Pisma Ekonomiczne i Społeczne 1930-60* (*PES*) (1961), esp. pp. 138-9.

or regulations concerning banks, or an abstract elaboration of the principles of socialist credit outlined in the preceding chapters. Economists in general were obliged (at least in their publications) to follow the Party line and to be in agreement with the Soviet version of Marxism–Leninism. One of their most important roles was to show how well the socialist system worked – 'the need for an apologia for the socialist economy superseded the need for analysis'.[1] In consequence the period was sterile with regard to the development of economics. 'The place of lively scientific thought was often taken by dogmatic and schematic repetition of well-worn, officially accepted formulae'.[2] In the realm of applied economics the key difficulty was the shortage of statistical data. Between 1951 and 1955, for example, the Chief Statistical Office ceased to publish its Year Books and so the main source of quantitative data ceased to exist. 'The economist found himself in the situation of a chemist who was refused permission to use his laboratory, of a doctor who had lost access to his clinic, or an astronomer who was forbidden to look at the sky.'[3] Much more information on the period was forthcoming after 1955, when economists were allowed to write freely, but this information was largely in terms of critical comments and suggestions for future reforms, rather than quantitative data.

The emergence of trade credit

The stringent credit control mentioned in the preceding chapter eliminated automatic granting of bank credit to enterprises, which were now, in effect, faced with the need to fulfil their plans with less funds than in the pre-1951 period. This was to be achieved through better overall management of enterprises. Indeed, it must be remembered, the stringent monetary control was introduced in order to encourage enterprises to improve their financial management.

The actual results of the policy were in general disappointing. From 1951 onwards a new financial phenomenon appeared, namely a rise in overdue trade debts of enterprises, viz. debts which occurred owing to the failure of buyers to settle their obligations with

[1] E. Lipiński, 'O Przedmiocie Ekonomii i Prawach Ekonomicznych', *Ekonomista* 5 (1956) p. 17.
[2] O. Lange, 'Aktualne Problemy Nauk Ekonomicznych w Polsce', in *PES*, p. 394.
[3] *Ibid.* p. 393.

Table 25a

Overdue indebtedness of enterprises settling through NBP 1951–5

Date	Overdue debts[1]	Overdue credits[2]	Changes in settlements and remedial action
31.3.51	–	1	
30.6.51	–	49	End of overdue credit on account B (18.4.51)
31.12.51	62	70	New order of settlements (12.12.51)
30.4.52	70	73	
31.12.52	54	64	BMS began to operate in 1953
30.6.53	42	56	General clearing action by NBP Easier bank credit for trade creditors
31.7.53	49	66	
31.12.53	40	48	General clearing action by NBP
28.2.54	46	67	
31.3.54	42	59	Easier bank credit for trade creditors
30.6.54	38	56	General clearing action by NBP
31.7.54	44	63	
31.12.54	34	52	General clearing action by NBP
28.2.55	42	59	
30.4.55	34	51	General clearing action by NBP

Notes:

[1] Overdue debts, viz. sums owed to enterprises (mainly for deliveries which were not settled promptly), as a percentage of the total value of debts owed to enterprises.

[2] Overdue credits, viz. sums owed by enterprises (mainly for deliveries which the enterprises failed to settle promptly), as a percentage of the total value of debts owed by the enterprises.

Sources: M. L. Kostowski, 'Znaczenie Nowej Kolejności Regulawania Zobowiązań Płatniczych', *WNBP* 6 (1956) pp. 280–1; M. L. Kostowski, 'Rozwój Systemu Rozliczeń Płatniczych w Polsce Ludowej in *RPGS*, pp. 63–4.

sellers. The latter became in effect involuntary creditors of their customers. It may be recalled that trade credit was, strictly speaking, illegal in Soviet-type economies. However, it never really disappeared in practice, being officially tolerated over short periods (determined by the transit of documents in settlements). 'Illicit' trade debts were the immediate outcome of the policy of stringent bank credit and the order of settlements, which put the payments of invoices last on the list of priorities (see pp. 131–2). Thus enterprises in financial difficulties simply failed to settle their bills within a stipulated period and in

Table 25b

Overdue indebtedness of socialised enterprises
1951–4

Year	Overdue trade debts[1]	Overdue trade credits[2]
1951	58.2	63.0
1952	59.3	62.2
1953	43.8	47.5
1954	34.8	51.1

Notes:
[1] As a percentage of total trade debts.
[2] As a percentage of total trade credits.
Source: P. Sulmicki, 'Finansowanie Srodków Obrotowych'
in *FPL 1944–1960*, pp. 317 and 321.

turn left the supplier short of funds.[1] Such action ultimately penalised enterprises which, though innocent of mismanagement, could not meet their financial obligations because of the default of their customers. It must be remembered that enterprises were not permitted to carry cash reserves, their place being taken by bank credit. Thus even well managed enterprises 'suffered for the sins of others'.[2] This led to a continuous chain reaction of inability to pay, resulting in a very serious rise in the total illicit indebtedness shown in tables 25a and b.

The more detailed table 25a refers to the ratios of overdue indebtedness, which consisted mostly of trade debt, but also included other obligations (for example to the budget) of enterprises conducting their settlements through the NBP. Thus the table only reflects the growth of overdue trade indebtedness of socialised enterprises, whereas table 25b shows the actual overdue trade indebtedness of socialised enterprises. It is assumed that the figures in table 25b refer to the balances at the end of particular years.[3]

---

[1] Enterprises accumulated overdue trade debts in spite of an 18% penalty (payable to the bank) imposed on them, for reasons discussed later.
[2] M. Karczmar, 'O Usprawnienie Rozliczeń Miedzy Przedsiębiorstwami', *Finanse* 1 (1954) p. 4.
[3] The proportion of working capital financed by overdue credit is difficult to specify, because of the lack of reliable data for the early 1950s. Sulmicki (p. 325) estimated that in the years from 1951 and 1955 trade credit amounted respectively to 17.0, 17.8, 12.7,

The failure to settle debts promptly became general rather than exceptional among state enterprises.[1] Thus, compared with the 1949–50 period, enterprises could still automatically finance their expenditure over and above the balance on their settlement account, but finance now came mainly from trade credit instead of bank credit.[2] It was trade credit and not bank credit which provided the 'financial slack' in the economy. At the same time the policy of stringent bank credit failed to make the supplier exert pressure on his customer to settle promptly and thus failed to fulfil one of the basic aims of the 1951–2 reforms. According to Kostowski, 'The appearance of overdue trade indebtedness disorganised the financial management of enterprises. It had a demoralising effect on enterprises and a destructive effect on financial control, which in turn led to the undermining of the principles of economic accounting and to unplanned distribution of monetary resources between enterprises.'[3]

The rise of overdue trade indebtedness may be regarded as an indicator of shortcomings in the management of the economy. It is, however, impossible to say what specific shortcomings it indicated. It could indicate mismanagements on the part of enterprises. It could equally indicate faults in planning, especially the planning of working capital, resulting in shortages of working capital in individual enterprises, or the fact that enterprises met unforeseen difficulties in plan fulfilment.[4] Overdue trade debts were a much less specific 'signal' of

11.6 and 10.5% of total current liabilities of socialised enterprises. It is therefore possible that overdue trade credit covered on the average about 6 to 10% of working capital. Compare with table D2.

[1] The reasons why it was possible for enterprises to expand overdue indebtedness are explained in the course of the chapter.

[2] It must be pointed out that credit restrictions were also to some extent outweighed by granting bank credit for wage payments. In spite of bank control of wage payments, wages were in practice paid, even when enterprises had spent their wage funds. Credit for wages could be obtained easily and was sometimes used to finance expenditure other than wages. (See M. Karczmar, 'Problemy Reformy Systemu Kredytowego', *WNBP* 3, (1957) p. 110, also in *Finanse* 3 (1957). The credit in question was, however, very small – in 1952 it amounted to only 0.4% of total credit granted by NBP. Credit for wage payments was the only type of credit which was used in Poland but not in the USSR.

[3] L. Kostowski, 'Rozwój Systemu Rozliczeń Płatniczych w Polsce Ludowej', in *RPGS*, p. 64.

[4] For reasons described in the introduction to this chapter, criticisms of payments difficulties on the whole neither were searching nor offered effective solutions to the problem. Whereas some authors indicated that the difficulties might be due to a variety of causes in the functioning of the financial system as a whole (e.g. M. L. Kostowski,

mismanagement in enterprises than the overdue credit balance in the 1949–50 period. It was noticed that overdue trade debts could arise in enterprises innocent of mismanagement. They arose, however, in a system of centralised planning aimed at a more automatic functioning of the economy, so that they could also be regarded as indicative of faults in the planning mechanism in general. This point is elaborated at the end of the chapter.

By 1952 it became quite common for state enterprises not to settle their debts promptly. Blockages in payments became so serious that emergency action to ease the payments situation had to be undertaken. It was appreciated that the blockages could be eliminated by a return to the 1949–50 system of credit automatism, but the system, together with the concept of the signal role of credit, had been discredited so that the immediate problem was to make the existing arrangements work more efficiently without changing their fundamental premises. Paradoxically the banks were now simultaneously to continue to apply the *qualitative tests* for credit, which resulted in credit shortages, and to take steps to reduce the accumulation of overdue trade debts.

The measures taken to unblock payments can be described here only in general terms. Up to 1955 they were based on the introduction of settlements by setting off debts and on an easier credit for settlements, especially credit for involuntary trade creditors (viz. those who expected payments for deliveries from enterprises failing to settle in a stipulated time).[1] There were three ways in which clearing of debts began to operate from 1953 onwards. Enterprises having mutual trade dealings could arrange with the bank for bilateral setting off of debts, settling the balances periodically (*rozliczenia saldami*). Such arrangements were not common. More important systems of setting off debts were organised by the NBP on a multilateral basis, viz. involving several enterprises in the process of debt clearing (for example a group where A owed money to B, B owed money to C and C owed money to A). The basic form of multilateral clearings was to be a continous clearing (*kompensaty*

'Zagadnienie Przeterminowanych...' *WNBP* 12 (1952), others tended to put the blame mainly on mismanagement in enterprises and the failure of enterprises to fulfil their plans (e.g. M. Karczmar, 'O Usprawnienie..., esp. p. 5).

[1] These changes in settlements were made by an order of the Minister of Finance 'On different forms of settlements arranged by NBP for some deliveries and services.' Issued on 17 April 1953, *MP* 64 (1953) item 780.

stale), organised by establishing Bureaux of Mutual Settlements (BMS) in some branches of the bank.[1] This form of settlement presented problems: much labour was needed to operate the bureaux and it was difficult to select enterprises to participate in such continuous clearings. Twenty bureaux were nonetheless established in 1953, but their activity 'never went beyond the stage of trials and experiments'.[2] The most important clearings became non-continuous multilateral clearing actions (*kompensaty jednorazowe*) organised twice a year, after which, as may be seen from table 25a, overdue indebtedness temporarily fell.

Blockages in payments were further alleviated after 1953 by a relaxation in the 'qualitative tests', resulting in a more lenient granting of bank credit for settlements, particularly to involuntary trade creditors. After April 1953 'credit on overdue debts' (see p. 133) was granted more generously than before. Thus enterprises which involuntarily financed their defaulting buyers now received bank credit, enabling them to meet their obligations. In effect bank credit began to be granted specifically to counteract the growth of trade credit. The ratio of bank credit for settlements to total trade credit rose significantly after 1952, being 27.5% in 1951, 28.3% in 1952, 55.0% in 1953, 56.2% in 1954 and 59.3% in 1955.[3] The more liberal attitude of banks was reflected in a rise in the relative importance of credit on settlements after 1952, as shown by table 26.[4] The proportion of credit on stocks (mainly normative plus above-normative) declined steadily. It is also interesting to note that the share of overdue credit actually rose in 1952, in spite of an attempt to check it (see pp. 130–3), remaining at a relatively high level after that year. Moreover, payments blockages encouraged a more liberal attitude by banks towards granting credit generally, which is discussed below.

---

[1] BMS (in Polish Biura Wzajemnych Rozliczeń, in Russian Biura Vzaimykh Raschotov) were first set up in the USSR in 1931. See Ikonnikov, p. 388. *Gosudarstvennyi Bank SSSR*, pp. 115–16. On their introduction in Poland see J. Szyrocki, 'O Biurach Wzajemnych Rozliczeń', *Finanse* 1 (1954).

[2] Jaworski, 'Zarys...', p. 194.   [3] *Ibid.* p. 200.

[4] The share of credit on settlements in the total short-term credit given to industrial enterprises rose from 22.5% in 1952 to 27.7% in 1953, 39.2% in 1954 and 40.2% in 1955. W. Jaworski, 'Funkcja Rozdzielcza Kredytu', *Zeszyty Naukowe SGPiS* 45 (1963) p. 16. The ratio of credit on settlements to the total short-term credit issued by NBP rose from 15.7% at the end of 1952 to 22.9% at the end of 1955. Z. Fedorowicz, 'System Kredytowy a Budżet Państwa', *WNBP* 3 (1957) p. 120.

Table 26

The structure of total short-term credit 1951–5
(*In percentages of the total*)

Type of credit	1951	1952	1953	1954	1955
Normative	22	20	21	25	27
Above-normative	51	48	46	41	37
On settlements	15	15	22	23	23
Overdue	8	14	9	9	12
Others	4	4	2	2	1

Sources: W. Jaworski, *Zarys Rozwoju Systemu Kredytowego w Polsce Ludowej*, p. 201. Also *Finanse* 4 (1958) p. 15.

The 18% penalty imposed on those who failed to settle their debts promptly proved to be of little effect. As the failure to settle promptly became commonplace for many enterprises, the penalties paid tended to be offset by penalties received, making little or no impact on costs of production. Further, up to 1954, trade enterprises preferred to pay the 18% penalty for trade credit rather than 4% interest for bank credit, because bank interest was a charge on cost and affected the size of the bonus (*premia*) for staff, whereas penalties were charged against profits.[1]

As can be seen from tables 25a and 25b, the various actions against blockages decreased the level of overdue indebtedness but did not solve the problem of trade indebtedness. Successive clearing actions had the immediate effect of lessening the problem, but this was only temporary, for there was a regular re-expansion of overdue trade credit, which had to be dealt with by fresh clearing operations. Thus, though some overall improvement did take place between 1951 and 1954, the problem of illicit finance of enterprises by trade credit remained unsolved until the end of 1955.[2] Moreover, the NBP's clearing actions involved the bank in considerable extra costs.

It may be interesting to observe at this stage that the phenomenon of the growth of overdue trade indebtedness was not peculiar to Poland. It occurred at the time in other East European economies and was well known in the Soviet Union for some time. Though a detailed Russian–Polish comparison of the phenomenon is beyond the scope of this work, it may be useful to give a brief account of the

[1] Karczmar, 'O Usprawnienie...', pp. 10–11. [2] This is discussed in chapter 7.

problem in the Soviet Union. The main difficulty here is the lack of readily available data, particularly such as are used in tables 25a and 25b. It seems that though the Polish data are not as adequate as one could wish, they enable the problem to be seen more clearly than do the Soviet data and descriptive accounts.

There are indicators that after the 1931–2 credit reforms Soviet enterprises experienced considerable difficulties in securing finance, ultimately relying on trade credit involuntarily given by suppliers.[1] Continuous exhortation of enterprises by the authorities to improve their 'payments discipline', commonly encountered in the relevant literature, was largely inspired by the growing chain of payments stoppages. One way of solving the problem was to relax monetary control, extending credit for 'business needs' as they arose in enterprises, and hence relinquishing the idea of credit as a coercive device. This course was not followed; instead the authorities endeavoured to improve the efficiency of settlements mainly by setting up various ways of settling by setting off debts, which have already been discussed.

In 1932, viz. shortly after the credit reform, there was, according to Atlas, a significant rise in overdue debts to suppliers, which undermined control by the rouble and especially bank control through settlements.[2] The Soviet answer to the problem was, in the main, to establish a system of clearing of debts through the BMS. Indeed the growth of the bureaux may be a rough indicator of the intensity of the problem of overdue payments in the USSR. The first bureau was set up in 1931 in the leather industry. Later the State Bank developed them in some other industries. Their number rose steadily in the 1930s – there were 23 of them in 1935 and 36 in 1936. There was a sharp rise in overdue debts during the war and more bureaux were set up to alleviate the problem of payments, especially in heavy and munitions industries. In 1941 there were 41 bureaux and 153 in 1946. The most significant expansion came in the early 1950s, as a result of which in 1953 and 1954 there were about 700 bureaux.[3]

8.3% in 1937 and 11.1% in 1940 of settlements carried out by the

[1] Z. V. Atlas (1947), pp. 226–7 and 285–6.

[2] *Ibid.* p. 226. For this state of affairs the author blamed overpayment of wages by enterprises, non-fulfilment of qualitative and quantitative planned indices, poor stock control and financing fixed investment from working capital, pp. 285–6.

[3] *Ibid.* p. 239. *Gosudarstvennyi Bank SSSR*, p. 115.

State Bank were by setting off debts. This form of settlement became more popular during the war, accounting for 16.4% of all settlements in 1946. In the 1950s the percentage began to expand, reaching 45% in 1955.[1] Kazantsev[2] mentioned that before 1954 overdue indebtedness by buyers applied also to well-run enterprises which failed to exert pressure on their customers to settle promptly. Thus a chain of payments difficulties (*tsepochka neplatezhei*) arose (compare with p. 141). The growth of overdue trade debts in the USSR was the chief reason for the reform of settlements which was enacted on 21 August 1954 and which is explained later.

The effectiveness of the Soviet system of setting off debts in dealing with overdue trade debts is difficult to ascertain, again because of a lack of data over a reasonably long period. However, some authors claimed that there was some positive effect, suggesting that overdue debts were lower where a system of setting off debts operated.[3] Certainly Soviet writers ascribed greater effectiveness to the BMS than did Polish writers.

'Credit liberalism'

'Credit liberalism' is a term sometimes applied in Polish literature to the attitude of banks towards granting credit in the period between 1951 and 1956. It does not refer to a deliberate credit policy, but to a banking practice which contravened the officially adopted credit principles and policy. Credit liberalism, therefore, described the execution of what was supposed to be a stringent credit control adopted in the early 1950s. It was an interesting phenomenon, because the policy, which started as a reaction against credit automatism, paradoxically led to liberal credit practices.

'Credit liberalism' was different from the liberal credit policy pursued before 1951 (see pp. 126–7). Its key cause was the

[1] See Ikonnikov, p. 371; *Ekonomicheskaya Entsiklopedia* (1962) pp. 170 and 211.
[2] A. Kazantsev, Voprosy Effektivnosti Vzaimnykh Paschotov', *DiK* 19 (1955) pp. 15–16.
[3] The ratios of overdue payments to total payments settled through BMS in 1952, 1953 and 1954 were 8.4%, 6.4% and 5.1% respectively, *Ibid*. p. 13. See also A. Kazantsev, 'O Chem Govorit Praktika Postoianno Deistvuyushchikh Zachotov', *DiK* 4 (1956) pp. 11–14; G. Shvarts, 'Ekonomicheskaya Osnova Vzaimnykh Raschotov', *DiK* 4 (1956) p. 21. The above figures and other data given in Soviet sources are not adequate for any definite pronouncement to be made concerning the effectiveness of setting off debts.

blockages in payments mentioned earlier. The execution of monetary control based on stringent credit rested with banks, and in particular with the NBP and its numerous branches. After the problem of overdue trade credit emerged and blockages in payments threatened financial chaos, the responsibility for solving these problems and improving the efficiency of settlements was once again given to the NBP. The bank was thus faced with a difficult situation, having to achieve two objectives which in practice proved to be conflicting.

Earlier it was shown that attempts to unblock payments by means of clearing operations and easier credit on settlements were only partially successful. Though the extent of the problem was lessened it still remained. Branches of the NBP (simply called banks in this context) were given special targets regarding the settlements of their clients, designed to ensure prompt payment of debts. They soon realised that restrictions of credit further accentuated the problem of settlements and thus were disinclined to impose them. Other important reasons for credit liberalism, most of them connected in some way with settlements and trade credit, are to be found in the behaviour of superior organs of enterprises, of enterprises and of banks themselves.

Occasionally, when the banks were prepared to impose restrictions on lending, they were pressed by the ministries concerned to give way and advance credit, sometimes in order to finance unjustified accumulations of stocks.[1] Thus in effect bodies such as ministries, anxious to avoid payments blockages within their organisation, made it difficult for banks to exercise stringent credit control.

Often enterprises failed to apply for bank credit to which they were entitled. This failure fully to utilise bank credit was caused by three factors. First, enterprises in general showed little interest in financial management. 'As a result enterprises are not only disinterested in the conditions of credit or the rates of interest, but worse still, are completely disinterested in obtaining credit at all.' Enterprises learned that they could function without bank credit.[2] Indeed bank credit gradually began to lose its importance as a source of finance for working capital. Its ratio to the total working capital of enterprises tended to fall, being 56.1% in 1950, 53.4% in 1951, 54.6% in 1952, 50.7%

[1] Karczmar, 'Problemy...', p. 112.
[2] *Ibid.* p. 109. Similar ideas were expressed by the author earlier in 'O Umocnienie Roli Kredytu Jako Instrumentu Kontroli Finansowej', *Finanse* 4 (1954) p. 45.

in 1953, 47.9% in 1954 and 44.5% in 1955.[1] Fiszel suggested that trade credit was a chief source of working capital finance in industry. At the end of 1952 40% of working capital in the iron and steel industry was covered by trade credit. He mentioned a steel works, whose funds for working capital came from: own funds 4.5%, trade credit by suppliers (viz. debts owed by the enterprise to its suppliers) 62%, bank credit 18.5% and overdue bank credit 15%.[2] Secondly, some enterprises did not resort to credit finance in order to avoid bank control. Karczmar spoke of 'a purposeful escape from bank credit'[3] and Fiszel contended that enterprises preferred the 'illegal' trade credit which was not associated with bank control. The third reason for not fully utilising credit was ignorance on the part of enterprises as to the purposes for which bank credit could be claimed. Enterprises could not properly digest the volume of financial regulations imposed on them.

Faced with this attitude to credit on the part of enterprises, banks found it difficult to counteract the growth of trade indebtedness and at the same time faithfully to apply the *qualitative tests* of credit. They often strongly encouraged their clients to apply for credit, giving rise to what was often called '*polityka dokredytowania*', which may perhaps be translated as 'the policy of upcrediting', described as 'squeezing credit into enterprises, often against their will, solely in order to avoid the non-fulfilment of targets of settlements by enterprises credited by a bank'.[4] Pruss commented that 'There thus developed a situation where it was not the enterprise which took pains to obtain credit but the bank which took pains to grant it.'[5]

Some blame for credit liberalism was put on the banks, or rather on the attitude of their staff to credit control. Bank staff were blamed for not knowing how to credit enterprises (for example, credit was sometimes given to finance stocks which should not have been

---

[1] Jaworski, 'Zarys...', p. 199. The author suggested that the largest fall was in industrial enterprises. Sulmicki's data (op. cit., p. 325) of the proportion of credit to total liabilities of socialised enterprises do not show such a definite trend as Jaworski's data: (in %) 48.4 in 1951, 52.8 in 1952, 53.8 in 1953, 52.2 in 1954 and 49.0 in 1955. However, Sulmicki showed (p. 323) a steadily falling credit finance of 'tangible assets' for respective years: (credit as percentage of tangible assets) 48.4 (31.6), 47.5 (30.6), 45.7 (29.8) 43.4 (22.4), 38.5 (21.5). Data in brackets refers to industrial enterprises only.
[2] H. Fiszel, 'W Sprawie Oddziaływania Prawa Wartości na Produkcję', *Ekonomista* 1–2 (1954) p. 170.   [3] Karczmar, 'O Umocnienie...', p. 10.
[4] Malesa, 'Krztałtowanie się Należności i Zobowiązań Inkasowych w Okresie Lat 1954–1956', *WNBP* 7 (1957) p. 352.   [5] Pruss, 'Rozliczenia...', p. 61.

6

financed from borrowed funds)[1] and tended to undervalue the importance of credit control. It was suggested that credit liberalism was caused by 'the lack of faith in the possibility of influencing business matters by credit'.[2] The application of sanctions by banks was ineffective. In theory banks could refuse to renew the cash float of an enterprise, refuse to make a payment from its settlement account, curtail or stop credit. In practice these sanctions were used very rarely. Often an attempt to use them resulted in intervention on behalf of enterprises by their superior bodies (e.g. economic ministries). Jaworski claimed that banks were too easily swayed by such interventions; he also put some blame for liberal credit attitudes on excessively detailed credit regulations and overcentralisation in the structure of the NBP.[3]

Banks, moreover, made little use of interest rates in crediting state enterprises. It has already been observed (pp. 52–3) that interest rates were neglected for purposes of control. They were regarded as a price of banking services, low interest being taken as an indicator of increasing efficiency of banking and considered helpful to enterprises in keeping their costs down. The long-term trend was towards low interest rates. Compared with other periods, rates of interest were lowest during the SYP. They were rigidly maintained at 2% on normative credit, 4% on above-normative credit and 8% on overdue credit. Thus the rates actually charged had little effect on enterprises, because they were low and inflexible – but it must also be remembered that in a system of planning based on physical allocation of resources, emphasising the fulfilment of physical rather than financial targets, any system of interest rates must have a limited impact.

For the reasons outlined, credit policy could not ensure that aggregate monetary expenditure was kept within the limits prescribed by plans. In this context it is relevant to note that the control of wages, which was not linked with monetary control, was equally ineffective in making certain that incomes rose as planned and in step with changes in productivity. Overpayment of wages (caused mainly by the fact that the tasks of the SYP were being fulfilled by a large amount of overtime working) was not in practice stopped by bank

[1] Karczmar, 'O Usprawnienie...', p. 10.
[2] L. Szyszko, 'Kilka Uwag na Temat Dyskusji w Sprawie Reformy Polskiego Systemu Kredytowego', Zaszyty Naukowe *SGPiS* 35 (1961) p. 103.
[3] Jaworski, 'Zarys...', pp. 211–13.

control, in spite of the fact that between 1953 and 1954 attempts were made to strengthen it. Indeed banks tried to stop enterprises from overspending their wage funds, and often bank–enterprise relations in this connection were strained, but superior organs of enterprises made a practice of 'legalising' excessive wage payments.[1] Inflationary pressure, which existed throughout the period of the plan,[2] had to be controlled by central planning measures to change wages and prices[3] and to scale down investment plans (especially in 1954 and 1955). Neither credit restrictions nor attempts to stop wage payments succeeded in curbing the expenditure of enterprises made in accordance with their planned output targets.

To conclude, credit liberalism on the part of banks had a number of immediate causes. Some proximate causes are suggested in the last section of this chapter. Above all, the increase in trade indebtedness convinced bankers that credit restrictions would be harmful in the circumstances of the early 1950s. As one banker put it: 'excessive crediting was less dangerous than insufficient crediting'. Thus the principles of credit were not strictly obeyed. Yet it would be incorrect to say that monetary policy became liberal, in the sense of creating some 'financial slack' enabling enterprises to receive all the bank credit they needed. Clearly if that were the case the problem of settlements and trade credit would not have arisen or been so severe. Such credit liberalisation as did occur was calculated to retard the growth of overdue trade indebtedness, which allowed enterprises to bypass bank control, and which was the key pointer to basically stringent credit conditions. It would later be argued that the *qualitative tests*, based mainly on planned targets, were not realistic and that even more liberal credit policy would have been justified.

It would be interesting to ascertain whether there was an analogous occurrence of 'credit liberalism' in the Soviet Union. Information on the subject does not really allow a firm conclusion. There are, however, indications that the credit principles were not strictly

[1] For more details see e.g. 'Perspektywy Bankowej Kontroli Płac', *WNBP* 6 (1957) esp. p. 274.
[2] It was caused mainly by the ambitious investment programme of the plan, the policy of industrialisation and the neglect of agriculture. Kucharski, 'Pieniądz...', pp. 275–7.
[3] On 3 January 1953 money wages were increased by approximately 30% and prices by approximately 40%. Thus there was a fall in real wages and in the purchasing power of cash balances held by the population. For more details see Kucharski, 'Pieniądz...', pp. 278–80.

applied in the Soviet Union either, in the sense that credit restrictions were rarely used as sanctions against insolvent enterprises.

Between 1932, viz. just after the 1931 reforms, and 1940 short-term credit rose by 420.9%. This was a high rate of expansion, which, however, should not be interpreted as indicative of a liberal credit policy. It may be partly explained by increases in production and price levels. Much of the expansion was due to adjustments in the credit system occurring after 1932. Credit was allowed to be given on some stocks whose finance was overlooked by the authorities between 1930 and 1932 and above all there was a move to expand credit finance (in preference to 'own funds') of the working capital of firms not affected by seasonal fluctuations (see p. 42). Some of these adjustments were also calculated to prevent stoppages of settlements, but not enough credit was given to achieve this object; the authorities were seeking the solution of the problem not in easy credit but in clearings of trade debts.[1] Payments difficulties made banks unwilling to impose credit sanctions on defaulting enterprises, but there is little evidence of generally liberal lending particularly after moves made to improve credit planning and control over firms following the abolition of rationing in the mid 1930s.[2]

The high rate of credit expansion between 1940 and 1950 (see table D1 Appendix D) can be partly explained by the more liberal finance policy which prevailed during the war and up to the 1947 currency reform. Credit was not, however, granted liberally enough to prevent severe payments difficulties. These were alleviated, especially in the heavy and armaments industries, by settlements through the newly created BMS.

In the early 1950s the rate of credit expansion slowed down. The choice of period intervals in table D1 was dictated by the data available and not by logic. In fact credit expansion after 1950 and up to 1956 slowed considerably, only to accelerate after 1955, perhaps partly as a result of the August 1954 act, which allowed banks to extend credit more leniently than before to firms categorised as

---

[1] Shenger, pp. 132–3; G. Shvarts, *Beznalichnyi Oborot i Kredit v SSSR* (1963) pp. 156–9; M. B. Bogachevskii, *Finansy i Kredit SSSR* (1969) pp. 46–8.

[2] However, after 1935 some food processing enterprises were allowed to receive more liberal credit than before (planned credit limits were lifted and not reimposed until 1953). This was mainly due to difficulties experienced in the planning of credit limits and severe payments difficulties (thus bank credit was merely substituted for trade credit).

'well-managed'.[1] Moreover, a change in the method of settlements by setting-off debts, introduced in the mid-fifties, incorporated a small extension of credit to pay the balance of debts cleared periodically by the State Bank.[2]

Thus in the Soviet Union the high rate of expansion of total credit did not necessarily imply liberal credit, certainly not as liberal as during the 1930–1 period, and not liberal enough to prevent blockages in payments. Indeed, table D1 suggests that credit expansion basically followed the growth of stocks (rising ratio of stocks in total working capital). Also some legal substitution of credit for other sources of finance took place. On the other hand, the *qualitative tests* were not applied as rigorously. Had they been more rigorously utilised payments difficulties would simply have become worse.

Mechanical crediting

'Credit automatism' in East European literature usually describes a specific organisation of bank credit in a particular period of time. It has been noted that credit automatism in the Soviet Union followed the 1930 credit reform and lasted until 1931; in Poland it existed between 1949 and 1950.

Polish automatism was allegedly eliminated by the 1951 reforms, which introduced stringent credit and the cessation of automatic bank overdrafts. Indeed credit automatism, in the sense in which it was then described, was eliminated, but it may be argued that a new type of automatism took its place.

It has already been explained how restrictions on the automatic accumulation of overdue bank credit were compensated for by an unwarranted rise in overdue trade credit. This was but one manifestation of the new brand of automatism. From the early post-war years the authorities searched for rules of behaviour for both enterprises and banks, to govern the granting of credit. The implementation of such rules continuously eroded the discretionary powers of banks and their customers. It may be argued, for example, that the introduction of the normative of working capital brought a significant

---

[1] This act is later discussed in greater detail.
[2] Clearings through BMS were replaced by 'decentralised clearings': clearing accounts were opened by the bank for each enterprise, net balances of indebtedness usually being settled every 3–5 days. For details see e.g. Shenger, pp. 155–68.

mechanical element into crediting by banks as early as 1947. Banks, as a rule, could grant only above-normative credit, which began to be continuously subdivided into more narrowly defined credit groups. Whereas before 1950 credit regulations were tolerable, leaving some discretion to the banks, after 1950 they were expanded, leaving little or no scope for initiative on the part of the banker.

The main causes of mechanical crediting were the system of credit planning and the detailed regulations concerning credit and settlements. Banks in general could only grant credit within planned credit limits and on terms outlined in regulations handed down by the headquarters of the NBP. Credit plans entitled enterprises to some types of credit, provided there were no faults in their plan fulfilment. 'The limits of utilisation of credit were determined by financial and credit plans, and the cost of credit by the planned cost of production.'[1] Thus, in effect, credit plans distributed credit, while banks acted merely as credit dispensers whose chief duty was to ascertain that the applicants possessed the right prescriptions. Indeed, in 1956, economists criticised banks for being merely 'offices' (*urzędy*).[2]

The interpretation of the principle of specific purpose of credit (see p. 51) accentuated the automatic dispensation of credit. Credit could be granted only for purposes explicitly specified in the NBP's instructions and to the exclusion of other purposes which might have been economically justified. This led to what was sometimes called 'the filing of credits' (*szufladkowanie*), suggesting that operations concerning various types of credit were kept in different files or, if we translate the term literally, in different drawers.[3] This clearly was inconsistent with the tenets of the 'real bills' theory, which presupposes the banks' discretion in deciding what are legitimate business needs and gives banks the right to refuse credit. The narrow interpretation of the test of specific purpose also made banks lose sight of the overall state of business in enterprises, because each time a credit was requested they had to examine only a small part of their client's activity. This made it difficult to exercise effective monetary control and at the same time imposed a strain on the resources of banks. Also there was little or no cohesion between monetary control

---

[1] A. Zwass, 'Ewolucja Kierunków Kontroli Bankowej', *WNBP* 10 (1963) p. 379.

[2] H. Fiszel, 'O Prawdziwy Rachunek Gospodarczy', *ND* 5 (1956). Reprinted in his book *Zagadnienia Cen i Rachunku Ekonomicznego* (1958) p. 101. See also M. L. Kostowski, 'Aktualne Zagadnienia Systemu Kredytowego', *WNBP* 1 (1957) p. 1.

[3] J. Szyrocki, 'System Kredytowy Może Być Prosty', *ŻG* 21 (1957) p. 4.

and the control of wage payments, in spite of the fact that whatever the 'drawer' from which credit was extended, it ultimately satisfied a general financial requirement of enterprises.

To conclude, the credit system which emerged in 1952 and which survived until 1955 with only minor alterations, imposed upon both enterprises and banks the necessity to behave mechanically when dealing with credit finance. Strict observance of plans and regulations was thought automatically to ensure correct credit management. This significantly impaired monetary control by banks, which had to grant enterprises various types of credit, regardless of whether they were generally well or badly managed. Each credit application in practice demanded of a banker, not an analysis of the whole business performance of the applicant, but a probe into a narrow aspect of the enterprise's activity in isolation from all other aspects. At the same time credit planning and various banking regulations and instructions severely limited the 'operative autonomy' of both banks and enterprises, infringing one of the key principles of economic accounting.

The nature of bank control and its effectiveness

It has previously been noted how the emergence of trade credit, 'credit liberalism' and mechanical distribution of credit by banks dissipated monetary control and frustrated the stringent credit policy. The breakdown of monetary control also had an important effect on the nature of bank control in general. The NBP developed techniques of control which were not directly connected with credit. Bankers were encouraged to familiarise themselves with the details of the business of enterprises under their control. Unable to rely on credit to signal specific areas of mismanagement[1] in enterprises, they began to devote much time to reviewing and checking documents, accounts or reports of their clients. They developed a form of co-operation with enterprises known as 'reviews' (*lustracje*), in which bank officials discussed with enterprises ways of improving the management of the latter. Reviews had no direct connection with

[1] J. Wierzbicki claimed that credit lost its 'signal' role, explaining in a footnote that 'credit showed continuously such considerable shortcomings that it was impossible to draw from this any specific conclusions.' 'Zagadnienia Samodzielności Finansowej Przedsiębiorstw Państwowych w Polsce', *RPiE* 1 (1960) p. 151.

crediting, and after 1952 were replaced by conferences, where general management problems were discussed by bank directors and individual enterprises or groups of enterprises.

Bank inspections became another important technique of control. They started in 1952 and were more directly connected with granting credit by banks than reviews or conferences. Their basic aim was to check whether the information contained in documents and reports presented to the bank by enterprises corresponded with the facts (for example by checking the value or quality of stocks) and whether enterprises were creditworthy. They were also carried out independently of credit applications, probing into the more general aspects of management of enterprises; for instance, to discover the reasons for financial difficulties such as excessive trade indebtedness.

The chief remedial measure used by banks was 'intervention'. The bank, having discovered shortcomings or faults in the activity of an enterprise, intervened directly (rather than by using sanctions, such as restricted and/or more expensive credit) with the staff concerned, exhorting it to amend its ways or, in more serious cases, reporting the matter to a superior body of the enterprise in question. Sanctions were generally considered by banks after interventions had not produced desired results, but, as already mentioned, in practice were rarely used at all.

In the process of controlling enterprises the attention of banks was focused on stocks. Banks endeavoured to make enterprises improve their stock management, so as to avoid excessive accumulation of unsaleable stocks. Stock control was also ultimately to lead to a reduction of the share of stocks in national income. The special attention paid to stocks in conferences, inspections and interventions was, to some extent, due to the fact that credit on stocks formed the main part of all credit (see p. 142 and table 26).

It may be concluded that during the SYP control was exercised by banks not by using credit as the main weapon, although in theory this should have been the case, but by direct intervention in the management of enterprises. This type of control was often called administrative, as distinguished from economic, control. Banks were, in effect, institutions supervising enterprises and often participating directly in their management (e.g. in the realm of stock control).

An assessment of the effectiveness of bank control is very difficult, as there are no quantitative studies specifically dealing with the problem. The ineffectiveness of monetary control has already been described. In evaluating the effectiveness of bank control in general let us look at two issues, namely the efficiency of enterprises and the problem of stock accumulation.

It has already been stated that banks were to exercise 'management control', designed to improve the efficiency of enterprises. During the SYP enterprises failed as a rule to achieve the increases in efficiency which were planned for them (viz. fulfil their plans for lowering production costs), though in general they fulfilled their quantitative plans of production. For example, for 1952 the plan set a target for cost reduction in industry of 5.5%. The actual reduction was only 2.8%. The figures for 1953 were 4.5% and 3.5% respectively.[1]

The impact of bank control on stock management is difficult to ascertain, because of the lack of adequate data. The ratio of the increase in stocks and reserves to national income fluctuated, not showing any definite tendency to fall.[2] Planned accumulation of stocks by enterprises was regularly exceeded by actual accumulation, the rise in stocks in the SYP being four times higher than planned.[3] According to Gluck, a Vice-Chairman of the NBP, the actual rise in stocks surpassed the planned rise by 50% in 1953; 22% in 1954 and 127% in 1955.[4] This, however, does not conclusively indicate the ineffectiveness of bank control, particularly as plans for stock increases were not realistic,[5] and changes in the rate of stock accumulation might be caused by a variety of factors, of which perhaps the most important in a planned economy are changes in technology, plans and demand. To get a clearer picture, the impact of bank control on the usefulness of accumulated stocks may be examined. Some stocks were superfluous, viz. they were unusable or unsaleable, chiefly because of their poor quality. It was the bank's duty to stop the growth of such stocks mainly by refusing to finance them. However, the quantity of such stocks in the socialised sector was

[1] B. Blass, 'Znaczenie i Drogi Walki o Obniżenie Kosztów Własnych Produkcji w Przemyśle', *Finanse* 4 (1954) p. 55. The actual reduction in costs may appear impressive, even if the fall was short of the planned target. It must, however, be remembered that these costs did not fully reflect the capital input and ground rent (p. 109).
[2] It was (at 1956 prices) 4.3% in 1950, 6.7% in 1951, 7.4% in 1952, 11.1% in 1953, 7.0% in 1954 and 1955. GUS – *RS 1961*, p. 56.
[3] Kucharski, '*Pieniądz...*', p. 266.
[4] L. Gluck, 'Zagadnienie Zapasów w Gospodarce Narodowej', *WNBP* 2 (1959) p. 61.
[5] Kucharski, *Pieniądz...*', p. 266.

rising in the SYP; it amounted to 2.5 bil. zł. in 1953 and to 3.1 bil. zł. in 1955. This represented a small (2.7% and 3.1% respectively) but rising proportion of total stocks.[1] Furthermore, stocks for which credit could be granted included those which should more appropriately have been classified as superfluous. Ficowski estimated that at least 2 to 3% of stocks credited should have been classified in that category. Thus, in 1955 superfluous or useless stocks amounted to at least between 4.6 and 5.3 bil. zł., which was between 4.5% and 5.2% of total stocks.[2] Ficowski further suggested that banks were well aware of the problem of their clients' stocks. 'The banking apparatus studied, analysed and intervened. It would be unjust to the conscientious bank officials to assert that their interventions never had any effect. Nevertheless the effect on the scale of the economy as a whole was rather slender.' He added that if banks had not acted to improve the management of stocks 'the results would have been even worse'.[3]

The fundamental reasons for the breakdown of monetary control

Some indications were given above that bank control did not in practice have much effect on the management of enterprises. However, these were not specifically indicative of the effectiveness of bank control, but could be regarded as pointing to a general weakness in the management of the economy. It must be remembered that, according to socialist theory, bank control played an important part in national economic management. Indeed, the failure of monetary control and the ineffectiveness of bank control in general may perhaps be better understood after a brief examination of other aspects of economic activity relevant to the behaviour of banks *vis-à-vis* enterprises.

The policy aiming at a rapid industrialisation of the economy and the system of planning adopted help to explain why enterprises gave

[1] S. Ficowski, 'Struktura Zapasów w Gospodarce Narodowej w Latach 1950–1955', *WNBP* 1 (1957) pp. 24–5.

[2] *Ibid.* pp. 25–6. The author claimed that the waste entailed in the accumulation of such stocks in the SYP was equivalent to housing for 170,000 people.

[3] *Ibid.* p. 26. Ficowski blamed the lack of effectiveness of bank action on stocks on banks using administrative methods of control rather than economic incentives.

priority to output, often regardless of costs. Enterprises had little incentive to increase their efficiency. Their economic and financial plans, consisting of a number of detailed tasks, frequently not properly co-ordinated or consistent, were imposed upon them from above, forcing them to concentrate on the fulfilment of some targets while neglecting others. In practice, the emphasis was on the attainment of quantitative targets, such as output, often disregarding its quality or saleability and with little consideration for such factors as cost, profit, the state of indebtedness to other enterprises and stock accumulation, which were of special interest to banks. With the planners strongly favouring output targets at the expense of financial targets, it was likely that basing the *qualitative tests* for granting credit on planned targets would lead to a shortage of finance during plan fulfilment. As enterprises had no financial reserves, but were to use bank credit for the purpose, and as the *qualitative tests* in effect amounted to a stringent credit control geared to planned and not actual needs, it was inevitable that shortages of finance would have to be covered by the creation of unplanned claims in the form of mainly illicit trade credit, the accumulation of which did not lead, as it might in the West, to bankruptcy.

As already mentioned (p. 136), the economy of the SYP resembled a war economy, its main feature being physical and arbitrary distribution of resources. The possession of money by enterprises did not enable them to purchase means of production or to exercise choice between markets. Money at the time served only as a unit of account. All the other functions attributed to it in socialist literature it fulfilled imperfectly. This impeded the exercise of both 'mutual control' and monetary control. The contracts into which enterprises had to enter failed, in practice, to produce the effects expected of them in theory. The rationing of materials prevalent during the SYP reduced them to a formality devoid of economic meaning.[1] Enterprises had little or no autonomy in making decisions and relations between buyers and sellers had to conform to detailed regulations. The quality of the products was controlled by planned 'norms'. One consequence of this was mechanical acceptance of deliveries. Sellers in general could not stop deliveries even to bad debtors. In many cases this was because the customers were in a monopoly position and hence there were no alternative markets. Equally enterprises could not look for alternative sources of supply,

[1] L. Horowitz, 'Zarządzenia czy Umowy', *GP* 4 (1956) pp. 49–55.

158   MONETARY CONTROL IN PRACTICE

because their suppliers were often in a position of monopoly.[1] This explains further the inability of suppliers to influence the punctuality of settlement by buyers. The 'automatism of deliveries' was often seen as a root cause of mechanical crediting. Gluck, a Vice-Chairman of the NBP, considered the automatism of deliveries, together with payments of wages regardless of the financial state of the employer, and the rigid order of settlements, to be responsible for the malfunctioning of the credit system.[2]

Enterprises had to contend not only with detailed planned targets, but also with voluminous regulations embracing every aspect of their activity. Ficowski compared the complex of financial instructions and regulations to a jungle, in which directors of enterprises and their financial teams wandered with no hope of rescue.[3]

The autonomy of enterprises was further fettered by various types of 'controls' described on pages 43–50 and shown in chart C1. What impact they had on the activity of enterprises in practice is difficult to say. Unfortunately, no cost-benefit studies of these 'controls' were made. There are, however, indications that in general inspections by various control bodies were expensive and troublesome to enterprises, but ineffective. The most useful information comes from Jankowiak, who produced data on the subject based on a survey of enterprises in the Poznań area, conducted between 1955 and 1956 by the Higher School of Economics in Poznań.[4] Financial 'controls'[5] (by the Ministry of Control, Ministry of Finance Inspectorates, Financial Departments of National Councils, Inspectorates of economic ministries, organs of social control and banks – see chart C1) were frequent and costly. Excluding banks, the control organs carried out on average twelve controls annually per enterprise, at a total cost of 80 working days. In some cases the number of 'controls' exceeded 20, so that on average every month two institu-

[1] Pruss, 'Kredyt...', p. 99.
[2] L. Gluck, 'Nowe Kierunki Systemu Kredytowego', *WNBP* 7 (1957) p. 329.
[3] A. S. Ficowski, 'O Nowy System Finansowania Przedsiębiorstw', *ŻG* 19 (1956) p. 5.
[4] L. Jankowiak, 'Przerosty Kontroli Finansowej', *ŻG* 25 (1956); 'W Sprawie Przerostów w Kontroli Finansowej', *WNBP* 2 (1957); 'Istota i Zadania Kontroli', *Finanse* 10 (1957); 'Kontrola Finansowa Przedsiębiorstw Gospodarki Uspołecznionej' *RPiE* 1 (1958).
[5] The term 'financial control' in this context embraces bank control, but it is mostly concerned with various forms of inspections or enquiries designed to ascertain whether the controlled enterprises obeyed financial laws and regulations (e.g. concerning accounting techniques, taxation or settlements).

tions carried out control (lasting an average of 4 days) in the same enterprise, causing serious disruption in its work. Often different control bodies probed into the same or similar matters. Jankowiak concluded in his studies that controls were too costly, carried out too often by too many bodies, unco-ordinated and not systematic. As far as their effectiveness is concerned, a number of controls carried out by financial organs were 'positive', in the sense of actually revealing some shortcoming in management. In one article[1] he suggested that only 25% of 'controls' were positive, but on the basis of data (from the survey mentioned) given in his later article it appears that 41% of controls by financial organs were positive (32% of bank inspections were positive).[2] He stressed that he found no evidence to suggest that financial control raised efficiency or 'socialist morality' in enterprises. Inspections of various organs were not, as a rule, concerned with raising efficiency, but with ensuring that enterprises obeyed rules and regulations. The chief *de facto* objective of the work of control organs was not the elimination of irrational decisions, therefore, but the enforcement of regulations.[3]

On the subject of bank control Jankowiak was especially critical, concluding that:

Experiences so far, however, revealed that banks have expanded their control to limits which, in respect of the enterprises controlled by them, amount to a kind of tutelage leading to a distortion of the sense and aim of the control. This tutelage inhibits the self-management and operative autonomy of enterprises and its effects are considerably smaller than expected.[4]

In some ways bank control had the undesirable result of contributing to the lack of interest of enterprises in financial management, already mentioned in connection with 'credit liberalism'. The wide scope of management control by banks, including direct participation in settlements of debts and stock formation, caused many enterprises to neglect problems of finance, leaving the bank to cope with them.[5]

---

[1] Jankowiak, 'Istota...', p. 30.   [2] Jankowiak, 'Kontrola...', p. 253.
[3] Florczak, 'Aby Kontrola Była Kontrolą, *ŻG* 20 (1956).
[4] Jankowiak, 'Kontrola...', p. 276. The number of bank 'controls' was difficult to determine. They were, however, very numerous.
[5] This was especially true as regards settlements. Jaworski and Przywecki ('Bank a Samodzielność Przedsiębiorstwa', *ŻG* 25, 1956, p. 4) wrote: 'we have developed a conviction that an enterprise may be functioning properly without the necessity of bearing any responsibility for its payments situation.'

Anomalies in the budgetary mechanism, which functioned slowly and rigidly, were partly responsible for the financial difficulties of enterprises. For example, budget subsidies financing planned losses or supplementing 'own' working capital of enterprises were not promptly paid, causing shortages of funds in enterprises.[1] The way in which normatives of working capital were planned in practice resulted in a further financial difficulty. The determination of the normative by superior bodies of enterprises (e.g. ministries) was 'mechanical and unrelated to the actual needs of enterprises'.[2] Ficowski added that the size of the normative ultimately depended on the availability of budgetary finance, suggesting that 'the normatives which are fixed for enterprises do less and less represent economically justified needs of enterprises because the normative proposed by the ministries undergoes mechanical cuts by superior bodies in accordance with the actual financial possibilities of the state budget'. He further remarked that 'The phenomenon of mechanical "cuts" of normatives on all tiers has become a common occurrence.'[3] Enterprises in turn did not always try to estimate their normative requirements properly. In order to protect themselves against possible cuts and to secure greater independence from bank finance, they sometimes endeavoured to raise their estimates of the normative above the level which was economically justifiable.[4] Thus on the whole, the normative and its finance functioned imperfectly.

Two further points on the autonomy of banks may be added to those already mentioned earlier, so as to throw more light on the performance of the banks as regards the control of enterprises. First, bank control, stressing in particular management control, was beyond the capacity of banks. As early as 1946–7, when this type of control was exercised only in key industries, banks found it difficult to cope with.[5] After 1950 bank control was extended to all enterprises on economic accounting, its main burden falling on the NBP, which

[1] Karczmar, 'O Usprawnienie...', pp. 13–14. During the SYP enterprises had to rely increasingly on budget funds to supplement increases in their working capital (viz. in normatives). As stated on p. 111, the amount of accumulation left to enterprises declined, making it impossible to satisfy working capital needs from net profits.

[2] Karczmar, 'O Umocnienie...', p. 45.

[3] Ficowski, p. 5. See also 'O Rewizję Zasad Finansowania Przedsiębiorstw', *WNBP* 11 (1956).

[4] T. Choliński, 'O Nowe Formy Finansowania Przedsiębiorstw', *Finanse* 1 (1957) p. 33.

[5] The exercise by banks of such control in these industries meant 'the acceptance of responsibilities beyond their strength'. Kucharski, *Kredyt...*', p. 123.

was given a monopoly of short-term credit.[1] From interviews conducted on the subject, it appears that bankers in general readily accepted the idea of control over the activity of enterprises, as it enhanced their importance in the economy. Many, in order to acquaint themselves with the problems of enterprises, began to spend more time in factories than in banks. Many were overwhelmed with the magnitude of their task. One banker suggested that, faced with the problems of control of enterprises, he and his colleagues had a feeling of 'complete helplessness'.[2] In particular, the staff of the NBP had difficulty in adjusting to their new tasks, for their experience lay mainly with central banking operations, such as financing the government or rediscounting bills presented by other financial institutions. Compared with the staff of specialised state banks (e.g. the NEB), they had little or no experience before the war of assessing the prospects and management problems of enterprises.

The recruitment of new staff presented considerable difficulties, as there was a general shortage of skilled and educated manpower, particularly with managerial know-how. In fact it was this shortage, as stated earlier (p. 102), which was primarily responsible for imposing upon banks the management control of some state enterprises in the immediate post-war period. As a result, banks had to recruit staff with poor qualifications, especially after 1949 when the personnel of the NBP rose sharply and when the social and political background of applicants became of key importance. In 1951, out of a total intake of staff of 2,543, only 22 had higher education. In 1952 only 11.3% of staff had higher education and 18.8% had only primary education, the respective figures for 1953 being 10.6% and 27.6%.[3] There was no improvement in the quality of recruitment during the SYP. In June 1957 only 10% of the NBP's staff had higher education, while 35.2% had only primary or incomplete secondary education. In 'operational branches', viz. in banking establishments

---

[1] In the course of 1950 the number of enterprises subjected to control by NBP rose by 6,500. Kostowski, 'NBP w Latach...', p. 9.

[2] Interview material. Kucharski ('Ku Czemu Zmierza Reforma Systemu Kredytowego?' *WNBP* 9 (1957) p. 375) suggested that 'Those who worked in the NBP in the first years of its direct crediting remember the tremendous enthusiasm and devotion of staff which emanated from the importance of tasks connected with bank control.' Gradually, however, the enthusiasm waned 'with the growing conviction that "you cannot hit your head against a brick wall".'

[3] Laskowski, pp. 271–2.

other than the headquarters, the corresponding figures were 6.7% and 37.8%. In those branches, 64.4% of the directors did not have higher education and 11.7% had not completed their secondary education.[1] Though these figures do not directly indicate the banking or managerial ability of bank employees, they do perhaps point out a contrast between the type of personnel employed by banks and the expected requirements emanating from the socialist principles of bank control. Bank employees, especially those engaged in crediting, were in theory expected to possess not only the necessary banking skill, but also the ability to improve the management of enterprises along a path consistent with plans and the national interest.

Secondly, the difficulties experienced by banks were exaggerated by the change from the Polish road to socialism to the mechanical acceptance of the Soviet principles of finance. Few Poles knew the Soviet banking and financial principles and even fewer knew the banking practice involved in their implementation. For example, a quick switch from monetary control based on the Polish interpretation of the signal role of credit and the acceptance of the Soviet type of bank control produced some confusion in the relationship between banks and enterprises.[2] This contributed to the magnitude of overdue debts accumulated in 1951 and persisting at a high level till 1955, but the significance of the element of lack of expertise in Soviet financial methods is difficult to estimate. The phenomenon of illicit trade credit, as was shown earlier, occurred in the Soviet system as well, and we may advance the hypothesis that it was primarily a product of the system of economic planning and finance, coupled perhaps with the policy of forced industrialisation. On the other hand, one gets the impression that the State Bank in the USSR coped more effectively (through the BMS) than did the NBP in the period 1951–2, possibly because by then it had had a lengthy experience of the problem, gained in an evolutionary way.

The speed with which the NBP had to change its banking practice must have contributed to the confusion in payments and credit. Furthermore, it is problematical whether Soviet banking methods and practice were in all cases suitable for the Polish banking system, which, up to 1949 or even 1950, had successfully evolved its own *modus operandi*. Rejman observed that 'The deterioration of the

[1] Laskowski, 'Program Polityki Kadrowej w NBP i Jego Realizacja w Roku 1958', *WNBP* 1 (1959) p. 13.
[2] Kostowski, 'Założenia...', p. 12.

work of the apparatus of NBP emerged in an obvious and indisputable manner only in the period of mechanical copying of foreign formulae in the period of excessive centralisation.'[1] A Vice-Chairman of the NBP stated that 'in this period the bank widely utilised the experience of the State Bank of the USSR which undoubtedly was of great help in shaping socialist methods and forms of action on the economy, although there was also the phenomenon of not taking sufficiently into account the specific conditions in which our economy and our banking system functioned'.[2] In a later article he was even more critical of 'too direct copying' of some Soviet solutions to problems of banking and credit, which were 'not applicable to the specific conditions of our economy'.[3]

The circumstances outlined in this chapter lead us to the following broad conclusions. First, the practice of credit finance, and in some respects finance in general (for example, the finance of normative working capital), contradicted the accepted theory of socialist finance. Secondly, banks found it impossible, largely because of blockages in payments and the increase in trade credit, to carry out the stringent monetary control adopted in the early 1950s. Crediting of enterprises was mechanical and bank credit never in fact served as the instrument of bank control, which was based on methods divorced from credit and often involving a duplication of the managerial functions of enterprises. Thirdly, bank control, and in particular monetary control, was not in general effective. In the circumstances of centralised planning the theory of monetary control proved unrealistic. The authorities, as it were, expected the lubricating oil to improve significantly the mechanical performance of an engine suffering from faulty design. Finally, the administration of bank finance and control, especially if contrasted with its insignificant results, must have involved considerable cost. Kucharski aptly observed that 'the credit system fulfilled a role of a "pop gun" which, although it was never actually used to fire live ammunition, was nevertheless equipped with precision-made, expensive sights.'[4]

[1] F. Rejman, 'W Sprawie Branżowego Banku Rolnego', ŻG 4 (1957) p. 6.
[2] L. Gluck, 'Działalność NBP w Dwudziestoleciu Polski Ludowej', Finanse 7 (1964) p. 20.
[3] '25 Lat NBP', Finanse 3 (1970), p. 8.
[4] Kucharski, 'Ku Czemu...', p. 375.

PART III

Reforms of banking and monetary control during
attempts at decentralised planning

7

A prelude to decentralisation – credit reforms at the end of the Six Year Plan

Introduction

Political and economic events in Poland after the mid-fifties are on the whole well known in the West and no comprehensive account of them is given here. In general, it was thought that both political and economic changes were necessary for the country's further progress. Attempts to bring about such changes started after the Twentieth Congress of the Soviet Communist Party, held in February 1956, heralded a new political situation in the East European communist bloc. In this new political situation Poland, like other non-Soviet socialist economies, was presumably able, within the framework of the commitments to the Warsaw Pact, to experiment with economic solutions to problems which had no precedent in Soviet experience. It is by no means clear, especially in view of the Czech (1968) and Hungarian (post-1965) economic experience, what were the limits of economic autonomy in Poland. Nevertheless, it is clear that these limits widened considerably compared with the period of the SYP, especially between 1956 and 1958.

In discussion on the economic model in Poland, the principle that a socialist economy must be centrally planned was not questioned, even by the extreme group of economists, called 'the value men' (*wartościowcy*), who advocated the utilisation of the market mechanism in planning. It was generally agreed that the number of directives handed down to enterprises by superior bodies must be reduced, but at the same time that the state should not relinquish its central control over enterprises. The way out of this dilemma was seen in the use of new techniques of economic control.

A distinction is often drawn in socialist economic literature between 'administrative planning' and planning by 'economic means'. The main feature of the former, which in Lange's view normally characterised a war economy, was the use of 'para-economic compulsion', based on orders of the political authorities disregarding economic laws. Planning by economic means, on the other hand, was based on the application of economic laws and stimuli. 'By using economic methods planning utilises the automatic character of human reaction to certain incentives.'[1] The use of the terms 'administrative methods' and 'economic methods' was widespread, in spite of the realisation that a precise distinction between them might not be possible.[2] It appears that measures which, when imposed on a subordinate body (e.g. an enterprise) by a superior body (e.g. a ministry or the central planning body), leave the former with no alternatives, were called administrative, whereas the essence of economic means was to allow a subordinate body the freedom to choose a solution from a number of alternatives. In short, administrative planning relied on the use of commands or directives, planning by economic means on the motivation of autonomous enterprises.

It was generally agreed that more emphasis must be put on planning by economic means, with a reduction in directives being balanced by the deployment of financial instruments of control, such as prices, credit, taxes and interest rates. In other words, in the future more use was to be made of the market mechanism in national economic management. Indeed, the 'value men', represented by Kurowski and Popkiewicz,[3] advocated a primary role for the market mechanism in distributing national resources. The central planning authority was necessary as a guardian of the public interest and could control enterprises indirectly by controlling the market, viz. through monetary and fiscal policies.

Many prominent economists (Lange, Lipiński) envisaged a more limited use of the market mechanism, suggesting reforms which were to result in a model described later in a comprehensive essay

---

[1] Lange's views on economic laws are fully expounded in his book *Ekonomia Polityczna* (1959), ch. 3. On p. 59 he defined economic incentive: 'A situation which stimulates people to realise an aim of economic activity is called an economic incentive.'

[2] The difficulty of distinguishing between the two terms was discussed particularly by W. Brus (*Ogólne Problemy Funkcjonowania Gospodarki Socjalistycznaj* 1961, p. 123), who suggested (p. 236) that 'The application of economic methods depends on the utilisation of a regulated market mechanism in order to influence the independent decisions of enterprises.'

[3] S. J. Kurowski, 'Demokracja i Prawo Wartości', *Kierunki* 14 (1956) p. 9. 'Rynek i Plan', *TL* 6 February (1957); 'Model a Cele Gospodarki Narodowej', *ŻG* 7 and 12 (1957); J. Popkiewicz, 'Prawdziwa Rentowość', *TL* 5 January (1957); 'Biurokracja czy Rynek', *ŻG* 26 (1957) p. 7.

on decentralisation by Brus. Its main characteristics were: (*a*) only the most important decisions, such as the rate of growth of the national income, the division of the national income between consumption and investment or the distribution of investment among various branches of the economy, were to be decided at the central level and incorporated in the national economic plan; (*b*) the central planning authority was to plan not by issuing directives, but by using economic methods; (*c*) enterprises were to aim at maximum profit; (*d*) money was to assume 'an active role', prices becoming the most important means of influencing the decisions of enterprises.[1] In essence Brus' model was a 'model of a planned economy using the market mechanism', controlled by the state, in the sense that the state would, in general, be responsible for shaping the structure of prices, which would have a parametric character.

It is interesting to note that in debates on financial issues (budget, credit, banking) it was often assumed that the economy would in the future move towards greater utilisation of market methods of control; that enterprises would acquire some measure of profit motivation, that they would become more autonomous and capable of planning and financing at least a substantial part of their fixed investment from internally accumulated funds, of deciding on the working capital required to fulfil their plans (many advocating the abolition of the normative) and of choosing their own methods and order of settling debts.[2] Furthermore it was believed that in the new 'model' enterprises would become sensitive to financial stimuli, which would serve as alternatives to commands.

The period after 1955 was one of continuous economic changes and the chapters which follow describe and analyse adjustments made in the banking system and methods of monetary control in chronologically succeeding economic reforms. It must be borne in mind that the key common element of the reforms was the aim of

---

[1] Brus, p. 258. Advocating the use of the market mechanism in planning, Brus thus summarised (p. 238) his basic view on prices: 'The utilisation of the market mechanism necessitates the transformation of the prices of capital goods into *sui generis* prices which equilibrate the supply and demand and represent to a producer and above all to a user the true indicators of alternatives of choice in given circumstances shaped by the general decisions of the plan.' Lange also emphasised a need to set prices at a realistic level as a prerequisite to planning by economic methods, See e.g. 'Rola...', pp. 145–7.

[2] For a detailed review of the debate on general and especially financial problems of the mid-fifties see Podolski, ch. 7, esp. pp. 177–214.

achieving a more efficient economic system by methods which invariably included some reorganisation of financial management.

The principle of differentiation

The years 1956–8 are usually regarded as those in which the important economic reforms began, but as far as banking is concerned reforms bringing some degree of decentralisation occurred in 1955. These followed similar Soviet reforms,[1] which received wide publicity in Poland. Though in some way still belonging to the period when Soviet methods were slavishly copied, they nevertheless produced a significant breach in the rigidity of contemporary principles of banking and finance and in this sense may be regarded as a harbinger of a new era. In Poland all the reforms were introduced on 2 July 1955.

The first reform brought in an important new credit principle – that of differentiation by the bank between 'well-run enterprises' and 'badly-run enterprises'.[2] The criteria to be used in this differentiation were the fulfilment of plans for lowering the costs of production and for accumulation, and in some cases the quantity and quality of stocks.[3] Enterprises considered by the bank to be well-managed were to receive certain privileges, i.e. they could obtain unrestricted credit for wage payments and overdue trade debts. With respect to badly managed enterprises, the bank was to apply the existing sanctions more rigorously and was also equipped with new sanctions. For example, credit for wage payments could only be given to such an enterprise at the request of its superior body (e.g. the ministry).[4] The bank could also insist that the enterprise settle

[1] Resolution of the CM of the USSR and the CC of the Party 'On the role and tasks of the State Bank of the USSR' passed on 21 August 1954. *Direktivy KPSS*, vol. 4 (1958), pp. 279–95.

[2] Resolution 526 of the Presidium of the Government 'On the strengthening of the activity of the NBP to improve the economic accounting and financial discipline of enterprises.' The resolution was not officially published, but it is often quoted in the relevant literature. The principle of differentiation was adopted by Czechoslovakia in 1955, Hungary in 1956 and Rumania and Bulgaria in 1957.

[3] In the USSR the criteria were the same, with the exception of stocks.

[4] It may be noted that a link, albeit weak, was introduced between crediting and wage payments. Strangely, wage payments were not a criteria for deciding whether an enterprise was well-managed, but only well-run enterprises could easily obtain credit for wage payments. However, resolution 526 did in general terms urge integration of credit control with wage control.

its debts by letters of credit (known as the *akredytywa* method), which guaranteed payment for goods delivered.[1] The reform did not make a significant immediate impact on bank control. For instance, badly-run enterprises could still, in practice, easily obtain credit for wage payments, through ministerial intervention.[2] Neither the immediate impact nor the details of the reform were as important as its interesting new emphasis on the overall performance of the credit recipient. So far bank control had been fragmented and unrelated to the overall performance of the enterprise. The connection between the ease with which bank credit could be obtained and the fulfilment of the plan for lowering costs of production is also significant, because the latter was a better indicator of the efficiency of an enterprise than the fulfilment of the output target. Finally, at least for well-run enterprises, the reform implied less management control by the bank. The most important corollary of the new principle in the field of crediting was that well-managed enterprises could now quite automatically obtain credit for overdue trade debts (viz. they could easily replace trade credit, which they gave involuntarily, by bank credit).

The principle of differentiation remained operative in banking practice in later years. Perhaps the most vital problems of implementing it were the criteria used in differentiation and the way in which they were applied. In this respect an important question, namely how deeply banks were to probe into the management of enterprises to ascertain whether they were efficient, was not specifically answered. To take an example, one of the criteria for differentiation was the plan for lowering the cost of production, but it was not clear whether the fact of non-fulfilment or persistent non-fulfilment of plans was sufficient evidence for classifying an enterprise as badly-run, or whether the banks were to ascertain whether there might have been some external diseconomies (or even the malfunctioning of parts of the whole economic system) which accounted for it. In other words, enterprises could be inefficient for objective as well as subjective reasons. In proposing the principle of differentiation little attention was given to this and in general the principle stimulated little discussion. Nevertheless, it may be regarded as a small step towards banks participating in determining the legitimate business needs of their clients – a step consistent with the 'real bills' doctrine.

[1] Previously *akredytywa* was only a method of settlement (rarely used in Poland) without being a sanction (see p. 132).   [2] Jaworski, '*Zarys...*', pp. 205 and 209.

The new order of settlements

The second reform of July 1955[1] was designed to eliminate overdue trade credit and encourage prompt settlements of invoices. The period allowed for the acceptance (or rejection) of invoices was lengthened from three to five days, to enable the buyer to refuse deliveries which did not correspond with the order. The most important measure was a change in the order of payments from the current account of an enterprise unable to settle all its obligations, the new order being: wage payments and insurance contributions, budgetary obligations, payments for goods and services, depreciation, bank credit, other obligations. Thus payments for deliveries now received priority over such payments as bank credit and depreciation.[2] The reform made a significant impact on overdue trade debts in the economy, largely because it eliminated the chain reaction of trade indebtedness.[3] The fall in overdue trade is reflected in tables 27a and b, which may respectively be compared with tables 25a and b in chapter 6 (pp. 138 and 139).

The reform of settlements had an interesting effect on the structure of bank credit (see table 27c). The fall in overdue trade credit was to some extent balanced by a rise in overdue bank credit. Largely because of the lengthening of the period of acceptance, credit for settlements rose. Credit for overdue trade debts was volatile, showing a very dynamic rise in 1956 as compared with 1955; its

[1] Resolution 527 of the Presidium of the Government 'On the principles of settlements for deliveries and services' *MP* 66 (1955) item 861.

[2] Compare with the old order given on p. 131. The order provided by the Soviet reform of 1954 was: wages and similar payments, payments for deliveries of goods and services, depreciation, bank obligations, other payments. *Direktivy KPSS* vol. 4, p. 290. Though the law specifically did not say so, payments into the budget were made before payments for deliveries.

[3] There was also a fall of overdue trade debts following the similar reform in the Soviet Union. Taking overdue indebtedness of Soviet enterprises settling through the State Bank as 100 on 1 July 1954, the figures for 1 February 1955, 1956 and 1957 were 43.6, 39.1 and 34.0 respectively. The source (*Gosudarstvennyi Bank SSSR*, pp. 121–2) does not quote figures for corresponding changes before 1954. It may be noted that settlements by setting off debts also changed in the USSR – BMS were superseded by so called decentralised clearings. In September 1957 there were only two bureaux left in existence (compare p. 144). On changes in Soviet settlements see e.g. *Gosudarstvennyi Bank SSSR*, pp. 123–30; M. Atlas, *Razvitie Gosudarstvennogo Banka SSSR* (1958), pp. 297–312.

Table 27a

Overdue indebtedness of enterprises settling through NBP 1955–7

Date	Overdue debts[1]	Overdue credits[2]	Change in settlements
31.7.55	44	59	
31.8.55	31	46	New order of settlements and easier
31.12.55	16	18	bank credit on overdue trade
31.12.56	17	12	credit introduced 2.7.55
31.12.57	15	11	

Notes:
[1] As a percentage of total debts.
[2] As a percentage of total credits. For explanatory notes see table 25a.
Sources: as in table 25a, R. Malesa, 'Kształtowanie się Należności i Zobowiazań Inkasowych w Okresie Lat 1954–1956', *WNBP* 7 (1957) p. 353; W. Jaworski, *Obieg Pieniężny i Kredyt*, p. 131.

Table 27b

Overdue trade indebtedness of socialised enterprises 1954–7

Year	Overdue trade debts[1]	Overdue trade credits[2]
1954	34.8	51.1
1955	18.4	19.3
1956	20.3	14.6
1957	19.5	13.2

Notes:
[1] As a percentage of total trade debts.
[2] As a percentage of total trade credits.
Source as in table 25b.

continued liberal extension (compare ch. 6, p. 142) also helped to reduce overdue trade indebtedness in 1955–6.

These two reforms thus liberalised credit policy, at least for well-managed enterprises, reflecting a recognition that monetary control was too stringent (though ineffective, because of the compensating variation of overdue indebtedness) and that the credit principles (viz. the *qualitative tests* of credit) were too rigidly interpreted.

Table 27c

Some changes in credit granted by NBP after 1955 reform of settlements

	Credit in 1956	
Type of credit	1954 = 100	1955 = 100
Credit on settlements	149	122
Credit for overdue debts[1]	102	277
Overdue credit	153	106

Note:
[1] In 1956 the ratio of this credit to total credit was only 1.2% and its ratio to credit on settlements was 5.3%.
Source: R. Malesa, 'Rozwój Działalności Kredytowej NBP w Ostatnich Dwóch Latach', *WNBP* 8 (1957) p. 396.

Credit for small investments

The third reform concerned investment finance. After 1949 investment in the state sector was financed from non-returnable budgetary allocations (see pp. 111–12). Investment projects were not decided by enterprises but by their superior planning organs and had to be included in the investment plan before they could be undertaken.

A breach, albeit very insignificant, in this system occurred shortly after 1949. As early as 1950 some local government and co-operative enterprises were allowed to undertake capital projects outside the limits of the investment plan – called non-limited investments – which were financed from profit or credit repayable from profit. In 1951 the right to undertake non-limited investment was extended to all enterprises, but the values of such investment were set at a very low level and funds for it could come only from such sources as gifts (special contributions from society) or insurance indemnities. In 1953 the sources were widened to include, among other things, a part of the profit of local, trading and catering enterprises.[1] Although after 1950 there was a continuous expansion of non-limited investments, their total was very small. In 1953 they accounted for only 1.2% of total investment in the economy and in 1954 for 1.8%.[2]

[1] For more information see R. Szarota, 'Rozwój Systemu Finansowania Inwestycji w Dwudziestoleciu', *Finanse* 7 (1964) pp. 36–7; Szyrocki, *Samofinansowanie...*, pp. 140–1.   [2] GUS – *RS 1955*, p. 139.

Table 28

Credit for quick-yield investment 1955–7

(*million zloty*)

	1955	1956		1957			
		half I	half II	Qtr I	Qtr II	Qtr III	Qtr IV
Credit allowed during the year	4.8	39.4	269.0	187.4	305.5	271.9	88.8
Credit balance (end of year)	I		165			611	

Sources: M. Kunicki, 'Rozwój Inwestycji Szybkorentujących Się', *WNBP* 2 (1962) pp. 73 and 75; W. Pruss, 'Kredyt Bankowy i Polityka Kredytowa', in *FPL 1944–1960*, p. 93.

Nevertheless some regarded them as the origin of the later decentralisation in decision taking concerning investment.

On 2 July 1955 a further step was taken in permitting state enterprises to invest outside the investment plan. The CM passed a resolution allowing enterprises to undertake small investment projects which would quickly raise the rate of growth of production (especially of consumer goods), eliminate bottlenecks in enterprises and retard the rate of capital consumption – evident at the time in many enterprises.[1] An important condition for such investment was that it was to yield a quick profit. Indeed these projects were later (after 1956) often called 'quick-yield investments' (*inwestycje szybkorentujące się*). Their key novelty was their finance by short-term credit (repayable within a year),[2] carrying a low (2% per annum) interest rate and issued by the NBP.

Thus, once again, it became accepted that credit had a role to play in investment finance. This does not tally with the 'real bills' theory of credit, which insisted on the desirability of extending credit only against a self-liquidating security and (in conditions of a capitalist economy) regarded investment financing by banks as speculative.

[1] Resolution 508 'On the principles of undertaking and financing some small investment projects in the sphere of mechanisation and improvement of production, rationalisation of production and production of by-products in popular demand.' *MP* 65 (1955) item 851.

[2] Short-term credit was justified by the contention that its repayment might be made soon after completion of investment, from profits to which it had given rise.

Nonetheless, it may be argued that in a socialist economy credit finance of investment is, in view of the absence of a capital market, more desirable than budget finance. This point is further elaborated later.

Initially the impact of the reform was very insignificant.[1] The upper limit of credit for quick-yield investment was 100,000 złoty (500,000 złoty in key industries). At the end of 1955 the total debt outstanding for this type of investment was small (see table 28). The slightness of the impact was caused mainly by the fact that it was a timid reform, allowing too small investments repayable over too short a period. Also enterprises did not often know what types of investment in practice came within the category of quick-yield investments.

To further encourage this type of investment, on 14 April 1956 the authorities introduced an amendment to the 1955 reform,[2] raising the limit of investment (to 500,000 złoty in general) and allowing the NBP discretion to vary it. The period of credit repayment was also extended to two or three years, depending on the industry. The law also enumerated nine specific areas (for example, mechanisation of production processes, commencement of production of by-products) in which quick-yield investment could be undertaken. More emphasis was put on the necessity of these investments being capable of yielding a quick profit. Banks could refuse credit if they were not satisfied with the technical and economic documentation of projects or the general efficiency of management in an enterprise.

Data on quick-yield investment are not given in official statistical information and rarely appear in works on banking and investment. The statistics assembled in table 28 must be approached with caution. For instance, it is difficult, in view of all the circumstances outlined above, to reconcile the figure for credit allowed in 1955 with the figure for credit outstanding. It is possible that the total credit allowed differed from the total credit actually taken up by enter-

[1] W. Jaworski, 'Rola Kredytu Krótko-terminowego w Finansowaniu Drobnych Inwestycji', *Finanse* 6 (1955) pp. 64–5; Z. Szymczak, 'W Sprawie Finansowania Inwestycji z Zakresu Modernizacji i Mechanizacji', *MG* 8 (1957) p. 55.

[2] Resolution 182 of the CM 'On the principles of realisation and finance of some small investments in the sphere of mechanisation and rationalisation.' *MP* 35 (1956) item 417. More detailed regulations based on the above law were issued by the Chairman of the SCEP and the Minister of Finance on 11 May 1956, *MP* 41 (1956) item 519.

prises, i.e. that enterprises did not use all the credit which they were permitted to take up.[1]

The table suggests that a significant expansion of quick-yield investment credit took place in the second half of 1956. This was mainly due to the more liberal provisions of the law of 14 April 1956. Expansion of credit in 1957 also caused by other factors, notably the extension of quick-yield investment credit to some co-operative undertakings. The striking expansion in the second quarter can be explained by the fact that many enterprises decided to use credit to finance investments which were excluded from the investment plan (normally financed by budget grants). On the other hand, the marked decline in credit allowed in the last quarter of 1957 was due to restrictions imposed by the CM in August 1957 on investment financed by credit, because of a rapid rise in credit in the previous two quarters and because demand for credit was considerably greater than supply.[2]

Thus the situation in the field of this new credit was not stabilised. In spite of rapid growth between 1956 and the last quarter of 1957, the total investment financed by short-term credit was relatively small.[3] Nevertheless, as far as the principles of credit finance were concerned, the July reform permitted (or more strictly permitted the acceptance as a principle, rather than an exception) the finance of some investment of state enterprises by credit. It also began the erosion of the principle that the central bank should be primarily an institution for financing exclusively temporary shortages in working capital, for the NBP became now a bank granting both short-term and investment credit, thus bringing the strict division of function between the NBP and the IB to an end.

The three reforms mentioned above made a significant breach in the rigidity of contemporary principles of finance. Though there was a need for such reforms in Poland, they were not so much a genuine answer to this need as a continuation of a mechanical acceptance of Soviet methods of finance as a blueprint to be followed by socialist

[1] W. Lissowski and S. Baran ('O Szybką i Gruntowną Zmianę Systemu Planowania i Finansowania Inwestycji i Remontów', GP 12, 1956, p. 2) report that in the first nine months of 1956 the sum total of credit allowed by NBP for this type of investment was 120 mil. zł., of which only half was actually utilised.

[2] For more details see Kunicki, pp. 74–5.

[3] Considering for example that total investment expenditure at current market prices in 1955, 1956 and 1957 (in mil. zł.) was 37,476, 50,402 and 62,619 respectively (GUS – RS 1959, p. 65).

economies in general. In short, it is debatable whether such reforms would have occurred in Poland had similar changes not happened in the Soviet Union. Nevertheless, they brought a measure of decentralisation and some of their provisions continued to be applied in later years, when Poland could more freely undertake economic changes on her own initiative.

8

In search of a monetary policy in decentralised planning

1. An experiment with stringent monetary control

Introduction

(a) The Party's attitude to reforms

In 1956 the Party committed itself to political and economic reforms,[1] but it did not put forward a coherent plan for them, nor did it appear to have a long-term economic policy. At no time was the Party favourably disposed towards the radical reforms of the economic system advocated, for instance, by the 'value men'. On the other hand, it is difficult to perceive any alternative positive attitude or policy concerning the problem of decentralisation.

Promises of reforms, and indeed the enactments of reforms discussed below, were the main factor defusing an explosive situation in 1956. It seems that after 1956 the Party 'played by ear', changing its tune as soon as it was faced with the loss of central control over some aspect of economic development or management. This nervous approach to reorganisation is illustrated later. As the Party began to regain its strength with the progress of time after 1956, its attitude increasingly revealed itself as orthodox and more decidedly critical of demands for radical reform. This was not a sudden change, but a gradual process which occurred between 1959 and 1960. As early as 1957 the Party supported police intervention in the tram conductors' strike in Łódź and closed down '*Po Prostu*', a leading radical student journal. In 1958 there were considerably more signs of counter-reforms and pronouncements by the Party, which suggested that it was not prepared to tolerate significant deviations from pre-1956 centralised planning, but simply wanted to eliminate the overgrowth of bureaucracy characteristic of national economic management. At the end of 1958, for instance, Szyr, the Chairman of the ECCM,

[1] See for example 'Uchwała o Sytuacji Politycznej i Gospodarczej Kraju i Zadaniach Partii', *ND* 7–8 (1956) pp. 196–219.

179

strongly condemned demands for autonomy of enterprises as 'revisionist in character'.[1] The inflationary pressure of 1959 (discussed later) finally removed any lingering doubts within the Party that centralised control over the economy must be firmly maintained.

(b) No comprehensive economic changes

The reforms of 1956 and later years were concerned mainly with granting enterprises new rights to manage their production and finance, without radically changing other spheres of national economic management. There was no fundamental change in the price system. The Party firmly resisted the idea of enterprises being permitted to fix the prices of some of their products.[2] Prices remained centrally controlled and based on orthodox principles. Many prices were raised to enable some deficit enterprises to cover their costs, but this did not ensure that in general prices reflected values in exchange. In such a situation it was hard to see profits as good indicators of the efficiency of enterprises and effectively to base incentives on profit. Furthermore, prices were of dubious value as a guide in making rational investment decisions. Thus the price system did not offer a foundation conducive to the delegation of decision taking from central planning authorities to enterprises.

Though changes were made in the upper tiers of the planning apparatus, the relationship of enterprises with these higher levels was not clearly defined. A law of 15 November 1956[3] abolished the SCEP, which had often been blamed for developing excessively detailed plans, and in its place established the Planning Commission (PC) attached to the CM. The PC was to start functioning in January 1957, but its competence vis-à-vis central administrations and enterprises was not made clear. Moreover, the policy of the authorities concerning the role of economic ministries and central administrations did not seem to be consistent with the delegation of decision-taking powers to enterprises. Central administrations began their transformation into associations (zjednoczenia) of enterprises in

---

[1] E. Szyr, Nowe Elementy w Planowaniu i Zarządzaniu (1958) pp. 7–9.

[2] See e.g. S. Jędrychowski (the Chairman of the SCEP), The Fundamental Principles of Economic Policy in Industry (Warsaw, 1957) p. 11; E. Szyr, pp. 7–9.

[3] 'On the establishment of the Planning Commission attached to the Council of Ministers and on the abolition of the State Planning Commission.' DURP 54 (1956) item 244.

1958.[1] In theory, they were to be horizontal integrations of enterprises and serve as administrative organs, representing both state interests and the interests of their members. In practice, they inherited the functions of central administrations and received additional powers to distribute the profits of enterprises between various special funds (to be discussed). The functioning of the associations was not intended to diminish the autonomy of enterprises, but their precise *modus operandi* in relation to member enterprises was not clearly specified. In practice, the associations continued to function like the central administrations which they superseded – merely providing a channel through which ministries intervened in the management of enterprises.

Finally, the concept and the status of the enterprise remained unchanged. The enterprise, still generally a single plant unit and comparatively small,[2] was the basic production unit of the economy and no definite programme for the concentration of enterprises was put forward. There was, however, some tendency to concentrate small enterprises into larger units. Furthermore, many small state enterprises ceased to be tied to the central budget (viz. to pay taxes and receive subsidies from the central budget); instead, they were placed under the authority of local governments and tied to local budgets.[3] Thus only the most important and the larger enterprises in 'key industries' continued to settle with the central budget.

(c) *Enterprises: new rights and their erosion*

Towards the end of 1956 the authorities decided to free enterprises from the multitude of directive indices and binding regulations to which they had hitherto been subjected. The most important

[1] They were created following resolution 128 of the CM 'On the changes in the organisational structure of state key industry', passed on 18 April 1958 (not published in official law publications).

[2] In 1960 the average size (in terms of employees) of an enterprise in the socialised sector was 423 and in the state sector (embracing the largest enterprises) 733. Enterprises employing less than 500 comprised 81.2% of all enterprises in the socialised sector and 63.9% of state enterprises. State industrial enterprises employing less than 500 comprised 63.5% of all state industrial enterprises; 9.5% employed more than 1000 workers. GUS – *RS 1968*, pp. 149–50; *CSYP 1968*, p. 98.

[3] See Pirożyński and Winter, ch. 3. Whereas in 1955 the budgetary expenditure of local authorities accounted for 14.8% of state budgetary expenditure, in 1958 the ratio rose to 24.0% (*Ibid.* pp. 53 and 70).

legislative measure to this effect was resolution 704 'On the extension of rights of state industrial enterprises', passed by the CM on 10 November 1956.[1] The national economic plan was to have only eight directive indices, so that enterprises were empowered to produce their own technical–production–financial plans, subject only to eight decisions handed down by superior organs: (a) the value of total output, (b) the output of the most important products, (c) the limit of the wage fund, (d) profit (or loss), (e) payments into the budget, (f) budget grants for investment subjected to limits, (g) financial limit for capital repairs, (h) the normative of working capital. These were, moreover, to serve as indicators of the success of the management of enterprises.[2] In separate enactments enterprises received new rights increasing their financial autonomy. These are discussed in later sections.

Workers' councils[3] were a further innovation in the management of enterprises. They were defined by Gomułka, the new secretary of the CC of the Party, as 'autonomous, democratic institutions of workers, set up to co-manage individual establishments of work'.[4] It was not evident from his pronouncements whether they were to function basically in an advisory capacity or were to form a co-partnership with directors. Their sphere of interest was to extend to such matters as cost of production, productivity, elimination of a labour surplus, appointment of managing staff and labour discipline.

In trying to ascertain how much autonomy enterprises did, in fact, enjoy after the enactments of 1956 in non-financial spheres of management (viz. in such matters as planning of output, employment or quality), it must be observed that the law of 10 November 1956 still left the most important managerial decisions subject to dictates of superior organs. Given the interrelationship between various aspects of an enterprise's activity, even in theory, the autonomy of the enterprise remained quite limited. Even so they were freed from a multitude of directives, gaining some rights which they did not possess before; they could, for instance, decide on the size and structure of their employment, as long as they did not exceed their

[1] *MP* 94 (1956) item 1047.

[2] Enterprises continued to pay most attention to the criterion with which they associated greatest benefit – the target of production. M. Misiak, 'Sprzeczności Bodźców', *ŻG* 12 (1961) p. 4. Z. Madej, 'Hierarchia Kryteriów', *ŻG* 26 (1963) p. 1.

[3] The law on workers' councils was passed on 19 November 1956, *DURP* 53 (1956) item 238.

[4] W. Gomułka, 'Węzłowe Problemy Polityki Partii', *ND* 6 (1957) p. 15.

wage fund; they could fail to fulfil plans for output of products for which there was no demand.

There is no evidence to suggest that the newly acquired autonomy had a significant impact on the work of enterprises. In many cases the autonomy was ephemeral, having little or no impact, and in some cases (e.g. in the choice of markets) economic realities (e.g. monopoly conditions; rationing) rendered it quite insignificant. A sample survey by the Economic Council, conducted mainly in 1957 and 1958, to determine the degree of self-management of enterprises, revealed that, although they did gain more autonomy in some matters (for instance, decisions on output and range of products), the degree of autonomy acquired was less than was implied by the law of November 1956.[1] In some spheres of management (such as employment, changes in design of products) which, according to the law, were not to be subject to directive indices, the superior organs of many enterprises still exercised a considerable degree of control.

After 1956 the number of directive targets which could be handed down to enterprises grew steadily. On 30 May 1957 the CM introduced an extra directive target, the 'wage fund for office workers'. Further limitations on the autonomy of enterprises in the field of employment followed in 1958 when, largely as a result of the confusing situation referred to above, the CM imposed limits on the size of employment in enterprises.[2] This illustrates a point mentioned earlier, that the authorities tended to impose central control as soon as an undesirable, though perhaps predictable, situation occurred. Reverting to old practices, rather than searching for new solutions, was the key method of coping with economic difficulties. This was the path followed with workers' councils, whose desire for independence (of Party cells and trade unions) largely contributed to their amalgamation in 1958 into 'conferences of workers' self-management', embracing the councils, the Party and trade union organisations. Thus autonomous workers' councils, hailed as the symbol of 'democratisation' of management, ceased to exist. As will be seen later, a similar erosion of autonomy took place in the realm of investment by enterprises.

The number of directive indices rose in 1958. For instance, in

[1] Some data on the survey are given in B. Gliński, *Teorie i Praktyka Zarządzania Przedsiębiorstwami Przemysłowymi* (1966), pp. 296–305.

[2] Resolution 42 'On the policy of employment in socialised production enterprises', passed on 28 February 1958.

addition to limits on employment, both the size of the development fund (which is explained later) and production for exports were expressed in terms of directives. Various limits imposed on enterprises were, in effect, directives,[1] stretching the number of indices binding on enterprises in 1958 to 19.[2] Ministries showed a tendency to control the production of enterprises by issuing directives in addition to those prescribed by law, so that there was a wide gap between the number of directive indices *de jure* and the number *de facto*.[3]

Early in 1959 it became generally recognised that the decrease in the use of directives was an illusion. With the increased use of commands came 'a miraculous multiplication' of new regulations and paperwork, which further decreased the scope for self-management in enterprises.[4] Though enterprises were still, in theory, encouraged to show initiative, in reality they possessed very little scope for doing so.

The inflation of 1959, the causes of which are discussed later, finally dispelled any illusions about the Party's attitude to decentralisation and ended the government's flirtation with the delegation of decision-taking from central authorities to enterprises. Reliance on centralised planning as a socialist method of management was declared and the Party expressed the need for 'increasing the role and widening the competence of the PC'.[5] Thus the strengthening of centralised control became the Party's chief anti-inflationary weapon.

(d) Profitability and self-finance

Profit and financial incentives based on profit were to play a vital part in decentralised planning. Before 1957 profit was regarded merely as an indicator of the efficiency of enterprises. Most of the

---

[1] Some authors reported a growing confusion as to which targets were directives and which were 'orientational', viz. calculated to serve as a guide to enterprises. See M. Misiak 'Dyrektywne Fikcje', *ŻG* 38 (1959) p. 5.

[2] T. Gradowski and A. Kiernożycki, 'Wskaźniki Dyrektywne Planu a Samodzielność Przedsiębiorstwa', *GP* 10 (1959) pp. 12–15. See also J. L. Toeplitz, 'Narada Plus Skargi', *ŻG* 47 (1960) p. 2.

[3] Gradowski and Kiernożycki, p. 14.

[4] 'O Samodzielności Przedsiębiorstwa w Praktyce', *Finanse* 10 (1959) pp. 68–9.

[5] Resolution of the Third Plenary Session of the Central Committee of the Polish United Workers' Party on the tasks arising from the economic situation, *ND* 12 (1959) p. 38. In June 1960 the CM issued an order (*DURP* 31 (1960) item 171) formally giving the PC wide powers in the sphere of planning.

INTRODUCTION 185

profit was absorbed by the budget, so that there was no direct
connection between the size of profit and the ability of enterprises
to finance their development by devoting part of it to investment.
Enterprises had little discretion in the distribution of profit, and there
was no effective link between its size and the remuneration of staff
and employees, in spite of the existence of the factory fund (see
p. 114). After 1957 it was the intention of the authorities to make
profit the basis of a system of incentives to management (by allowing
self-finance) and to employees (through participation in its distribution).

It is difficult to ascertain precisely what happened in the realm of
profitability of enterprises, largely because of inadequate data. In
general, between 1956 and 1960 profitability of enterprises rose.
Financial accumulation of enterprises also rose[1] (though rather
erratically), due to a combination of factors, such as changes in the
structure of production (the share of products bringing higher
accumulation, mainly consumer products, in the total industrial
production increased), a rise in prices,[2] some overfulfilment in
production plans and increases in labour productivity.[3] The share
of profits in total accumulation rose, whereas the share of the turnover tax, which before 1956 absorbed well over 90% of accumulation,
steadily declined to 56% of accumulation in 1960.[4] A large proportion of profits, however, was absorbed by the budget.[5] Table 29
shows the amount of financial accumulation ultimately left to the
enterprises (as opposed to the amount taken by the budget). Thus, in
the period 1956–60 profitability of enterprises in general rose,

[1] For details see E. Winter, 'Akumulacja Finansowa w Latach 1955–1960', *Finanse* 7
(1964) pp. 43–4.
[2] Between 1956 and 1961 industrial prices rose by 26.1% (taking 1956 = 100, the prices
index was 107.9 in 1957, 108.5 in 1958, 112.1 in 1959, 113.2 in the first half of 1960,
126.4 in the second half of 1960 and 126.1 in 1961). In the same period, prices of capital
goods rose by 54.8% and consumer goods prices by 9.3%. A. Płocica, 'Jeden czy Dwa
Poziomy Cen', *Finanse* 1 (1965) p. 29.
[3] For more details see Rada Ekonomiczna, *Sytuacja Gospodarcza Kraju w Roku 1958*
(1959) pp. 9–10; Winter, 'Akumulacja...', pp. 43–9.
[4] For data see GUS – *RSF 1945–1967*, pp. 178–9. Profits refer to net profits (viz. profits
less losses). Financial accumulation was distibuted between turnover tax, profits and
'budget differences', which were payments into the budget (positive differences) or
payments from the budget (negative differences) caused by the pricing of sales.
[5] State enterprises paid 71.2% of profit into the budget in 1959 and 70.1% in 1960.
Thus less than 30% of profit was retained by enterprises for internal distribution.
GUS – *RS 1961*, p. 415.

Table 29

Distribution of financial accumulation between the budget and enterprises in the state sector 1955–60

(*Percentage of total accumulation in the state sector*)

	Financial accumulation	
Year	Absorbed by the budget	Retained by enterprises
1955	96.6	3.4
1956	92.6	7.4
1957	88.1	11.9
1958	84.5	15.5
1959	83.8	16.2
1960	81.1	18.9

Source: E. Winter, 'Akumulacje Finansowa w Latach 1955–1960', *Finanse* 7 (1964) p. 52 (the author used data supplied by the Ministry of Finance).

marking an important step towards the attainment of one of the essential prerequisites of self-finance postulated in the debate on the economic 'model'. It now remains to be seen to what extent enterprises were able to utilise their retained profits independently.

Resolution 460, passed by the CM on 19 November 1957[1] laid down that profits were to be divided between (*a*) the factory fund, (*b*) the development fund (which was newly created), (*c*) reserve funds and (*d*) payments to budget or superior organs. Thus the profits retained by enterprises were to be distributed mainly through the special funds.[2]

Employees were to share in the profits through the factory fund. Reserve funds were to be formed not in enterprises, but in ministries and central administrations (later in the associations of enterprises). The development fund (DF) represented the authorities' solution to the problem of giving enterprises some scope for deciding upon and financing their expansion. As shown in chart 1, the fund was

[1] 'On the principles of distribution of profit and the finance of working capital' (in units subordinated to ministries of various key industries which are enumerated in the title), *MP* 94 (1957) item 550.

[2] Also known as 'decentralised funds' (as opposed to 'centralised funds' such as the budget or the banking system) or 'specific purpose funds' (*fundusz celowe*).

Chart 1

Sources of funds and expenditure of the development fund in state enterprises

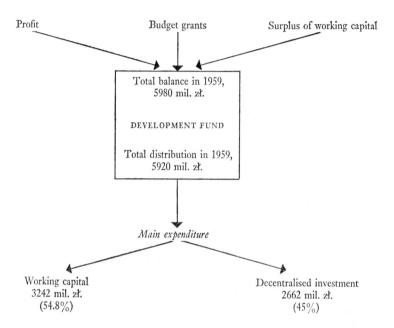

Main sources

Profit   Budget grants   Surplus of working capital

Total balance in 1959,
5980 mil. zł.

DEVELOPMENT FUND

Total distribution in 1959,
5920 mil. zł.

Main expenditure

Working capital   Decentralised investment
3242 mil. zł.   2662 mil. zł.
(54.8%)   (45%)

formed from payments from profits or from specific-purpose grants (to deficit enterprises) and from surplus working capital.

At first the planning of the fund was complex, but in essence the actual amount transferred to it was decided by a superior body following a request by an enterprise.[1] Its planning was changed on 13 October 1958, the change to apply from the beginning of 1959.[2] Deciding to relate the DF more directly to profit, the CM laid down that 'The appropriate association determines the size of the development fund of the enterprise expressed as a percentage of planned profit of the enterprise after subtracting the planned sum of the

[1] For details see Szczepański, pp. 208–10.
[2] Resolution 392 of the CM 'On the principles of division of profits, equilibrating differences in covering deficits, financing working capital, investment and repairs in industrial enterprises, and on the principles of financial management of associations in industry for the year 1959.' *MP* 88 (1958) item 491.

Table 30

Analysis of expenditure from the development fund in state enterprises 1958–61

(*a, mil. zł.; b, percentages of total distribution*)

		Distribution						
	Total transfers	Total	On investment		On working capital		Other	
Year	a	a	a	b	a	b	a	b
1958	3,930	3,760	1,882	50	1,828	49	50	1
1959	5,980	5,920	2,662	45	3,242	55	16	0
1960	8,510	7,674	2,908	38	4,549	59	217	3
1961	9,562	9,027	4,594	51	4,182	46	251	3

Source: GUS – *RS 1967*, p. 579.

factory fund.' Thus the most vital decision concerning the formation of the fund was to be made not by the enterprise but by the association and no specific criteria for doing this were given.[1] Moreover, to prevent enterprises from trying to achieve profits 'at all costs', verification of profit (*weryfikacja zysku*) was introduced. Before the apportionment of profit between various funds, the authorities were to verify the profit by deciding what was the 'correct profit', attributable to a true rise in productivity, and what was the 'incorrect profit', attained in a manner which was against the public interest and contrary to regulations (for example, derived through misuse of assets). No specific criteria of verification were established and so a new element of uncertainty was introduced into the activity of enterprises, taking an edge off the incentives based on profit and creating new administrative problems.[2] Furthermore, it was still problematical whether, in allocating money to the DF, associations were to reward good management and effort by enterprises by

[1] The size of the fund (and other funds) was determined, as a rule, for one year. Enterprises were thus never certain how much money they were likely to have to invest over a period longer than a year.

[2] Criticising the system of incentives in 1960 C. Bobrowski (Rozwój Planowania w Polsce Ludowej, *Ekonomista* 5 (1964) p. 999) commented that 'The care (perhaps too petty and detailed) to eliminate from profit those components which could not be attributed to the enterprise created burdensome controls and a complicated system of calculations which diminished the "readability" of incentives.'

higher allocations, or whether they were to be guided mainly by the needs (for example, for investment) of enterprises. However, whatever problems existed about the formation of the fund, it did represent a pool of money for capital expansion. Some factual information on the distribution of the fund is given in chart 1 and table 30. More information on the subject is given in the sections dealing with the finance of working capital and investment.

Some general changes in banking and banking practice

(a) The structure of the banking system

Between 1956 and 1961 some important changes occurred in the structure and functions of banks. They were brought about mainly by a change in agricultural policy and in the finance of investment.

Tables 31 and 32 show that, both in terms of credit and the size of employment, the NBP was still the dominant bank in the economy, but its importance in relation to other banks decreased after 1955, so that there was some decentralisation in the credit system in this respect. However, in 1960 over 76% of credit was granted by the bank. The bank's status as central bank was confirmed by its new statutes,[1] which asserted its competence in the fields of credit and settlements and, as before, gave it wide powers of control over the banking system and over its customers.

The most important change in the function of the bank was the finance of decentralised investment by long-term credit. It was observed in the previous chapter that in 1955 the bank began to grant credit for quick-yield investments. After the introduction of decentralised investment in 1958, the finance and control of this investment became the bank's new function.[2] The share of investment credit in the total credit granted by the bank rose from less than 0.2% in 1955 to 6.8% in 1960.[3] More details on this aspect of its activity are given later, especially in the section of this chapter dealing

---

[1] The law of 2 December 1958, 'On the National Bank of Poland.' *DURP* 72 (1958) item 356 (also published in *WNBP* 1, 1959).

[2] Earlier, by an order of the Minister of Finance issued on 4 November 1957, 'On the determination of the competence of banks in the sphere of investment finance' (*MP* 89, 1957, item 532), the NBP was allowed to finance decentralised investment in enterprises of local authorities, co-operatives, private industry, handicrafts and trade.

[3] GUS – *RSF 1945–1967*, p. 234.

Table 31

Credit institutions 1955–60
(*Credit balances at the end of the year*)

	1955		1960	
	bil. zł.	%	bil. zł.	%
Total:	67,109	100.0	154,257[1]	100.0
NBP	59,686	88.9	117,353	76.1
IB	3,580	5.3	14,371	9.3
AB	3,124	4.7	15,207	9.9
SLCs	719	1.1	3,743	2.4

Note:
[1] The total includes credit by the Common Savings Bank (14 mil. zł.) and the Hire Purchase Bank (3,569 mil. zł.) which started to grant credit in 1960.
Source: GUS – *RSF 1945–1967*, p. 234.

Table 32

Employment in banks 1956–60

	1955	1956	1958	1959	1960
Total	50,491	50,075	49,394	48,714	50,020
NBP	24,843	24,410	21,557	21,045	21,014
IB	4,234	4,045	3,236	2,902	2,959
AB	2,518	2,674	3,432	3,440	3,656
SLCs	8,232	8,413	8,569	9,022	9,545

Sources: GUS – *RS 1957*, p. 303; *RS 1958*, p. 360; *RS 1960*, p. 427; *RS 1961*, p. 408.

with decentralised investment. Thus, though long-term credit was a small part of its business, the bank became a universal bank, capable of providing enterprises with short-term as well as long-term finance.

The IB continued to be the main channel of budgetary finance. Its credit activity changed in that it lost some business to the NBP,[1] but became the main supplier of long-term credit for housebuilding, which was the main reason for the expansion of its credit shown in table 31.[2]

[1] In 1959 the NBP took over the financing (by long-term credit) of those investments, previously financed by the IB, which were decided by enterprises (viz. decentralised investments). [2] For details see Niemski, p. 473.

After 1956, as part of a general drive to increase agricultural production, it was decided to create specialised banking institutions for agriculture. Gradually, between 1956 and 1960, the AB began to take over from the NBP the custom which it had lost between 1951 and 1953, extending short-term as well as long-term credit to state agricultural enterprises, co-operatives and private undertakings,[1] and in 1959 it began to refinance SLCs. Thus the AB ceased to be a narrowly specialised investment bank and became a universal bank servicing agriculture.[2] Its operations expanded very rapidly,[3] its credit activity more than doubling between 1955 and 1960 (see table 31).

Another significant change in the realm of agricultural finance was the replacement of RCBs by SLCs,[4] thus reversing the change which followed the 1948 banking reform (p. 115). SLCs were associated in the Union of SLCs set up in 1957 with one headquarters and seventeen branches, one in each voivodship. The co-operatives were mainly to finance the rural economy, by issuing short and long-term loans. Their credit was refinanced mainly by the NBP until January 1959 and afterwards by the AB. After 1956 credit granted by the SLCs expanded quickly (see table 31), though its share in the total credit of the economy was small.[5] More information on crediting agriculture is given in Appendix A.

Thus after 1956 some decentralisation, in the sense of delegation

---

[1] By the order of the Minister of Finance already quoted (*MP* 89 (1957) item 532), the AB was empowered to finance investment throughout agriculture, viz. from state farms to peasant holdings.

[2] Of East European countries only Poland and East Germany established a universal bank for agriculture. In Czechoslovakia greater centralisation of banking took place at this time – the Czech State Bank (Statni Banka Ceskoslovenska) as a result became the monobank, having taken over the activity of the Investment Bank, which was abolished in 1959.

[3] Its balance sheet totals rose from 9,686 mil. zł. in 1955 to 35,753 mil. zł. in 1960 and 42,074 mil. zł. in 1961, K. Niemski, 'Bank Rolny w Swietle Bilansów Rocznych', *WNBP* 7 (1960) p. 322; 'Bilans Banku Rolnego za Rok 1961', *WNBP* 7 (1962) p. 312. The number of its branches rose from 267 in 1955 to 291 in 1956 and remained at this level until 1960, GUS – *RS 1957*, p. 302. For expansion in staff see table 32.

[4] Their establishment was confirmed by the law of 29 May 1957, 'On the change of the decree of 25 October 1948 on bank reform'. *DURP* 31 (1957) item 136. Further legislation on them was issued later, *DURP* 20 (1960) item 121, articles 32–36 and *MP* 79 (1963) item 386.

[5] The co-operatives also expanded in terms of employees (see table 32) and the number of their branches rose from 1285 in 1957 to 1359 in 1960 (1471 in 1961), GUS – *RS 1960*, p. 427; *RS 1962*, p. 429.

of banking activity to specialised banks, did take place, reducing somewhat the dominance of the central bank. Also, diversification of banking services took place in some instances (in particular in the operations of the NBP and the AB). In agriculture there was a return to the system of banking which broadly had operated before 1949. In consequence, the division of function between banks, where the NBP acted as the bank of short-term credit and the specialised banks as investment finance institutions, became less strict. All banks now acquired the characteristics of universal banks, financing both the short and long-term needs of their customers.

The structure of the liabilities of the banking system also began to change, with deposits of enterprises becoming more important and budgetary deposits declining. Currency in circulation rose appreciably, largely due to increased activity in consumer sales (for details see table B11).

There was also a move to provide some decentralisation within the structure of the NBP. Specialist branches of the NBP were set up in some localities, attempting to adapt their services to the requirements of their customers. Furthermore, though headquarters control was still basically very strong, the NBP's branches could make decisions concerning their customers more autonomously than in the past. Some aspects of this will be discussed later, especially when dealing with the form and methods of bank control.

(b) Towards simpler credit practice

Some changes in banking were designed to simplify the work of the banker, freeing him from some administrative tasks in dealing with enterprises. At the same time there was a move to give enterprises greater financial autonomy.

Enterprises and their banks were to enter into 'general credit contracts' which, in theory, were to define business relations between the two parties. However, there is no evidence to suggest that in practice the credit contract was more than a mere formality with perhaps some legal, but little economic meaning. Credit continued to be given according to general laws and regulations concerning banking.[1]

[1] Credit instructions were periodically issued by the NBP to its branches and to enterprises. One such instruction issued in 1965 (Instrukcja Służbowa Nr. A8 *Kredytowanie Przedsiębiorstw Uspołecznionych*) was examined by the author. It suggested that a

Table 33

Classification of short-term credit in 1952–7 and in 1958

1952–7		1958
Main groups of credit	No. of credits in a group	Types of credit[1]
Normative credit[2]	1	Normative credit[2]
Above-normative credit	6	Above-normative credit
Settlements	3	On trade debts by buyers For other settlements
Other credits	4	Special credit Payments credit
Credit for imports/exports	2	
Overdue credit	1	Overdue credit

Notes:
[1] With no sub-divisions.
[2] Explained on pp. 200–4.
Sources: W. Pruss, 'Zmiany w Systemie Kredytowania Działalności Eksploatacyjnej Przedsiębiorstw Uspołecznionych', *WNBP* 2 (1958) pp. 35–43; W. Jaworski, *Obieg Pieniężny i Kredyt*, pp. 201 and 226.

Some simplication in crediting did, however, take place. An instruction from the NBP laid down that after 1 January 1958 six types of credit would be distinguished,[1] and the old, detailed classification of credits would be abandoned. The first three types of credit, listed in column 3 of table 33, were granted generally. Normative credit financed shortages of normative working capital[2] and the above-normative credit financed all above-normative stocks. Credit for loans to buyers (*na należności od odbiorcow*) replaced the old credit on invoice debts, becoming the main credit for settlements (compare p. 132). It was granted to the seller only on 'correct' debts,

---

credit contract 'determines the basic rights and obligations of the creditee and the Bank' (p. 6), but these rights and obligations were in general defined in various banking laws and regulations leaving little scope for independent contracting between the parties. Moreover, the contract was to follow a 'pattern' which could, however, be supplemented by clauses taking account of specific conditions of an enterprise.
[1] W. Pruss, 'Zmiany w Systemie Kredytowania Działalności Eksploatacyjnej Przedsiębiorstw Uspołecznionych', *Finanse* 2 (1958).
[2] Changes concerning normative credit are discussed in detail later.

viz. not on overdue trade indebtedness, but only to cover a permissible gap between the receipt of goods by the buyer and his settlement of the invoice. This provision was an important part of the stringent credit policy discussed in detail later. These three kinds of credit were issued on the basis of quarterly credit requests made by enterprises and approved by banks. The remaining three credits were given in exceptional circumstances. Credit for other settlements financed mostly advance payments on agricultural contracts; special credit financed special actions such as sales (viz. stock clearance); and payments credit (*kredyt płatniczy*) covered some 'urgent payments' when there were no funds on the current account. This last credit functioned very much like an overdraft allowed on the current account for a specific purpose.[1] It was repaid automatically as soon as funds flowed into the account.

In trade and co-operative enterprises, by way of experiment, from January 1958 credit was paid into the current account, separate accounts for each type of credit being abandoned. The experiment proved successful and later (1962) crediting on current account became operative in all enterprises.[2]

The principles of credit most affected by the 1958 changes were those of specific purpose and security of repayment. Up to 1958 the principle of specific purpose of credit was narrowly interpreted leading to excessive classification of credit (see pp. 51, 132–3, 152–3). In 1958 banks were instructed to take into account the whole of the activity of the enterprise before granting credit, and to differentiate between well-run and badly-run enterprises according to the principle adopted in 1955 (pp. 170–1), Banks were now to interpret the principle of specific purpose broadly, by giving credit to cover expected shortages of funds, thus enabling production to continue uninterrupted. Well-run enterprises were to get credit on more favourable conditions than badly-run enterprises. In view of this it is difficult to understand why the authorities retained a classification of credit by purpose, defining the conditions under which these credits were to be extended. The classification by purpose continued to lead to 'dispersion of credit decisions' – credit decisions being undertaken separately and at various times for each type of

---

[1] For more details on these credits see Pruss, 'Zmiany...', pp. 35–43; Jaworski, 'Obieg...', pp. 225–31.

[2] J. Lenczewski, 'Kredytowanie Przedsiębiorstw w Rachunku Bieżącym', *WNBP* 5 (1962) esp. p. 228.

credit.[1] Thus, a reasonable explanation of changes in the principle of specific purpose is perhaps to say that there has been a significant erosion of the interpretation based on detailed credit classification and a move, consistent with the tenets of the 'real bills' theory, to allow the banks more discretion than before in ascertaining whether a credit applicant's overall performance justifies the extension of a specific credit.

After January 1958 short-term credit could be granted not only, for instance, to finance an accumulation of stocks, but also to accommodate enterprises anticipating certain financial needs. Thus, to use Polish terminology, credits, and in particular the above-normative credit, ceased to be simply self-liquidating (called 'refund') and became 'anticipatory', granted on the basis of quarterly credit requests prepared by enterprises. This affected the interpretation of the security of credit. Instead of looking for a particular existing asset as a security of repayment banks began to estimate the general ability of their customers to repay loans.

Thus, on the whole, crediting became more rational and credit operations became administratively simpler and less labour consuming.[2]

(c) Settlements

An important step towards giving greater financial autonomy to enterprises was made in the realm of settlements, when on 1 July 1958 a law concerning 'Monetary settlements by units in the socialised sector of the economy' was passed.[3] It was followed by two orders issued by the Minister of Finance on 13 August 1958.[4] Many fundamental principles of socialist settlements remained unaltered

---

[1] R. Michejda, 'Warunki Skutecznego Działania Kredytu Bankowego w Praktyce', Poznań Economic Society, *Rocznik Ekonomiczny 1961/1962*, p. 226.

[2] This helps to explain the tendency shown in table 32 for banks as a whole, and NBP in particular, to employ less staff in the late 1950s.

[3] *DURP* 44 (1958) item 215. The law repealed existing legislation on settlements.

[4] 'On the principles of cash management by units of socialised economy.' *DURP* 54 (1958) item 263. 'On forms of settlements for deliveries and services between units of socialised economy.' *DURP* 54 (1958) item 264. For more information on settlements see Jaworski, 'Obieg...', pp. 120–5; Kostowski, 'Rozwój...', pp. 67–77; W. Pruss, 'Funkcjonowanie Systemu Rozliczeń Pieniężnych' in *RPGS*, pp. 121–3; Karczmarek, pp. 43–5.

(enterprises were, for instance, still obliged to keep their money in the bank in a single settlement account), but there were some new provisions permitting practices hitherto prohibited. Enterprises were allowed to make advances on orders in cases determined by the CM and to make larger cash payments than before (up to 1500 złoty), provided that cash was withdrawn from the current account for the purpose of the payment.

The provisions of greatest interest to us, however, were those which were designed to make enterprises rather than banks more responsible than before for financial management and, in particular, for prompt payments. Enterprises were allowed to choose the method of settlements which best suited their particular circumstances. They could choose between the *inkaso* (viz. the acceptance of invoices) method, credit transfer requests, cheques and letters of credit. Furthermore, the compulsory order of payments from the current account was abolished (compare pp. 131–2 and pp. 172–4).

Greater freedom of settlements for enterprises did not mean that banks now became completely passive suppliers of payments services. They were empowered in cases of 'undisputed indebtedness' to carry out settlements on behalf of enterprises on their own initiative. Nevertheless, there was a definite move now for banks to give payments services rather than to control the whole mechanism of payments. Banks thus ceased to be the key organisers of settlements, playing a more passive role in the economy's payments system. Greater freedom in the realm of settlements was, in theory, a significant gain by enterprises.

As regards changes in settlements which were designed to encourage enterprises to settle promptly, the authorities decided that 'mutual control' between enterprises should be strengthened. In general, payments for deliveries were to be made within five working days from the day of the receipt of relevant documents (e.g. the invoice). Failure to settle within the stipulated time entailed a 12% per annum penalty receivable by the seller. In the previous system of settlements overdue trade indebtedness carried an 18% penalty receivable by the debtor's bank.

Surprisingly enough, the newly gained freedom in the sphere of settlements made little impact in practice. Logically, one would have expected enterprises to take advantage of the new laws after 1958 and to manage their settlements more autonomously, leaving less discretion in this respect to banks. More specifically, significant switching was expected from the mechanical bank manipulation of settlements, entailed in the *inkaso* system, to simpler and quicker methods, such as cheques or credit transfer requests. However, enterprises generally continued to use mainly the *inkaso* method of settlements, often showing inability to manage their payments.[1] In 1966 79.9% of all settlements were still carried out by the *inkaso* method.[2]

The reasons for this conservative attitude on the part of enterprises are not completely clear. Wierzbicki suggested that the main reason was that the *inkaso* allowed enterprises to leave to their banks the maintenance of the accounts involved in settlements, simplifying the calculation of penalties for a failure to settle debts promptly.[3] Znaniecki, on the other hand, stressed inertia on the part of both enterprises and banks, stating that the *inkaso* had become a habit formed as a result of lengthy compulsory use.[4] Kaczmarek[5] thought that banks failed to give the alternative methods of settlement sufficient publicity to make them more popular.

Similarly, measures to strengthen mutual control did not, on the whole, prove successful. The effect of the seller's action on the buyer was not strong enough to eliminate overdue trade indebtedness.[6] The financial stimulus to settle promptly contained in the 12% penalty did not exert a significant impact, as many enterprises at first failed to calculate and collect penalties from their defaulting debtors. Though there was a marked improvement in this respect later, in 1962 the Ministry of Finance found it necessary to make calculation and claiming of penalties compulsory.[7] Nevertheless, doubts persisted about the power of the penalty to encourage punctual settlements. An interesting view on the subject was expressed by Slipko, who claimed that there were important disincentives to demanding prompt repayment by buyers: (*a*) enterprises

[1] J. Mazur, 'Jak Usprawnić System Bankowej Obsługi Rozliczeń Pieniężnych', *WNBP* 8 (1960) pp. 374–5.

[2] M. Znaniecki, 'Krytyczne Uwagi o Inkasowej Formie Rozliczeń', *WNBP* 4 (1967) p. 133. Writing in 1966, E. Kaczmarek ('Rozliczenia Między Jednostkami Gospodarki Uspołecznionej', *WNBP* 5 (1966) p. 167) claimed that in the socialised sector about 90% of all settlements were carried out by the *inkaso* method.

[3] K. Wierzbicki, 'Bank a Przedsiębiorstwo', *ŻG* 11 (1963) p. 7.

[4] Znaniecki, pp. 133–4.   [5] Kaczmarek, 'Rozliczenia...', p. 168.

[6] Further discussion of this phenomenon and statistics of overdue indebtedness are given in the context of stringent monetary policy, p. 204 et seq.

[7] Pruss, 'Funkcjonowanie Systemu...', p. 133; Wierzbicki, p. 7.

received 12% penalty rates, but could obtain credit on overdue debts at the rate of 3%,[1] (b) by insisting on prompt payments enterprises worsened their relations with customers. Thus selling enterprises did not insist on punctual payment.[2] Jaworski noticed that suppliers were loath to claim penalty rates when their customers (presumably trading enterprises) found it difficult to sell the products supplied to them.[3]

There were two more fundamental reasons for the continued weakness of mutual control. First, enterprises did not possess the ultimate deterrent against their persistent bad debtors, namely the stoppage of deliveries. In this respect little had changed as compared with the pre-1958 period when, as observed earlier (pp. 157–8), deliveries were made automatically, viz. regardless of whether the customer could settle or not.[4] Many enterprises enjoyed monopolistic power either as buyers or as sellers. There was also rationing of many raw materials and other products. The main reasons for the authorities' reluctance to permit stoppage of deliveries were that this could have had politically and socially undesirable consequences, such as non-fulfilment of plans, stoppages of production and redundancies.[5]

Prompt payments may also be said to be a function of the availability of funds. As is shown later, the stringent monetary policy adopted in the late 1950s was a significant factor in the payments difficulties encountered by enterprises.

Extension of credit finance of working capital

(a) The planning of working capital

Before moving to purely financial aspects of working capital, let us outline the important reforms in its planning introduced on 19 November 1957.[6] In spite of the fact that the institution of the normative had not proved successful (see p. 160), it was

---

[1] It is not clear to what period of time the author referred. This point was likely to be stronger in the post 1961 period, during the lenient credit policy, than earlier, during the stringent credit policy, as explained later.

[2] Slipko, 'Zbędna i Kosztowna Praca', ŻG 15 (1963) p. 6.

[3] Jaworski, 'Obieg...', p. 132.

[4] Pruss, 'Funkcjonowanie...', pp. 129–30; 'Rozliczenia...', esp. p. 63.

[5] Michejda, 'Warunki...', p. 225.

[6] MP 94 (1957) item 550. The law is first quoted on p. 186.

retained,[1] but enterprises were as a rule to determine their own normative requirements, instead of having them imposed 'from above'.[2] It is difficult to ascertain how far this principle applied strictly in practice. It was feared that enterprises might be tempted to set their normatives at an arbitrary 'convenient' level. For instance, because finance for normative needs could be obtained more easily than above-normative finance and was less costly, some enterprises might raise their normatives above the justified minimum level. On the other hand, enterprises with ambitious investment plans might present lower than necessary normatives, hoping to channel working capital into investment. To discourage this the reform provided that enterprises were to be guided in planning their normatives, by methods of 'normatising' suggested by their superior bodies. The main safeguard, however, was bank control over normatives. Banks could question the size of the normative and in cases of discrepancy between the enterprise's assessment and the bank's the latter prevailed, in the sense that the bank extended credit according to its own assessment. Thus, although enterprises did gain more autonomy in deciding their normatives, their autonomy was hardly complete. According to a survey of the Economic Council, in 1959 31% of enterprises in the sample had their normatives imposed by their superior bodies, 2.8% had them determined by the bank, 56% drew them up with the co-operation of the bank and 10.2% planned them autonomously.[3]

Soon after the introduction of the new way of planning working capital, difficulties began to arise. The general tendency was for enterprises to overstate their normative requirements. In industry the actual rise in normatives was significantly higher than the rise estimated by various ministries. Szczepański quoted some figures suggesting that the discrepancy varied on the average from 25% in the light industry to 189% in the building industry, but warned that the figures must be interpreted with extreme caution mainly because many industries experienced a shortage of stocks before 1958

[1] For discussions on the usefulness of the normative see Podolski, pp. 190–7. Of the socialist countries only Hungary abolished the normative in 1957, but reestablished it in 1962. Czechoslovakia adopted a similar solution to Poland's – namely the normatives subject to bank 'opinion'. In the USSR the normative continued to be determined by superior organs of enterprises and to be a directive task.

[2] This provision conflicted with the earlier resolution (p. 182), which laid down that normatives were to be directive targets handed down from above.

[3] Gliński, p. 303. The survey was first mentioned on p. 183.

in relation to their planned tasks.[1] Nevertheless, part of this unplanned expansion was evidently because enterprises tended to
include in their normatives stocks which were 'not correct' and
stocks which were previously excluded from crediting by banks.[2]
Thus normatives were used as a way of obtaining funds for stocks
for which finance was not available.[3] Such a situation implied that,
despite safeguards, the planning of normatives did not work effectively. By way of remedy it was decided to strengthen the safeguards,
largely at the expense of enterprise autonomy. On 24 December 1958
the Minister of Finance issued more specific regulations concerning
the methods of normatising,[4] although in March 1961 he stipulated
that these were to be treated as a framework within which enterprises were to plan their normatives.[5] External control over normatives was further increased by the introduction in 1959 of blocking
of enterprises' working capital funds by their associations, which
transferred the blocked funds to a special bank account,[6] and by
partial coverage of normatives by bank credit, which is further
elucidated later.

(b) Credit finance of normatives

The normative, apart from being a way of estimating the volume of
working capital needed over a period, remained an important
institution for purposes of finance. Normative and above-normative
requirements continued to be financed in different ways. The law of
19 November 1957 laid down that deficits or increases in normatives,
previously financed mainly from the budget, were to be financed
from the DF and bank credit. Surpluses of working capital and sums
released due to lowering of normatives were no longer to be absorbed

[1] Szczepański, p. 215.

[2] T. Choliński, 'Srodki Obrotowe Przedsiębiorstw', *Finanse* 7 (1958) p. 29. The author
advocated the adoption of some 'guiding indicators' on methods of normatising. This
advice was later followed by the authorities.

[3] More is said about the practice of excluding stocks from crediting in our discussion of
the stringent monetary policy below.

[4] 'On the principles of normatising and determination of constant liabilities in state
enterprises', *MP* 10 (1959) item 35. The Minister again specified that the normative
determines 'constant needs of enterprises in the field of working capital.'

[5] 'On the guiding principles of normatising...', *MP* 27 (1961) item 131.

[6] Blocking took place when the associations observed that normatives were excessively
high, or at the request of appropriate banks.

by the budget, but to remain in enterprises, in the DF. However, if they were not in need of funds, any surplus was to be taken over by ministries or central administrations.

The main source of increases in normatives was to be the DF, viz. basically there was to be self-finance of normatives. Money from the fund was to go in the first place to finance working capital, and only the residual was to be used to finance fixed investment. This arrangement was thought to provide what became known as the 'interplay between stocks and investment'. The authorities realised that enterprises had a strong propensity to invest in fixed assets. By giving working capital the first claim on the DF (so that only what was left of the fund could be spent on fixed investment), they hoped to make enterprises economise on stocks by planning normatives at the lowest possible level. In practice, however, the interplay was not very effective. Earlier it was observed that the DF did not really reflect the performance of enterprises and failed to have a strong incentive effect and that, in fact, normatives tended to be planned at a high level. Indeed it is hard to see why the interplay was not allowed to take place without normatising, particularly in view of the lack of success in using the normative in the past.

Credit (normative credit) was a supplementary source of finance, used when the DF was insufficient to cover the normative requirements.[1] It was to be repaid from the DF and was granted in anticipation of future accumulations of money in the fund. Following the above-mentioned reform the role of normative credit was increased. Before 1958 this credit was given in the main to trading and co-operative enterprises. In 1958 it became an important credit given to industrial enterprises – its size, compared with other types of short-term credit, is shown in table 34. In the early 1950s less than 0.5% of credit granted to industrial enterprises was normative.[2]

After 1958 the role of credit in financing the working capital of industrial enterprises further increased when the authorities began to experiment with a compulsory partial coverage of normatives by credit. This innovation had already started in 1958, chiefly in coal-mining enterprises. In 1959 more enterprises in key industries (and especially in the light and timber industries) had to resort to credit

---

[1] In trading enterprises, however, 70% of the normative could be financed by bank credit.

[2] Jaworski, 'Funkcja...', p. 16. In 1955 the figure was 0.1%; 49.6% was above-normative and 40.2% credit on settlements.

Table 34

The structure of short-term credit granted to socialised enterprises in industry 1958–60

(*a, mil. zl.; b, percentage of total*)

Year	Total a	Normative a	Normative b	Above-normative a	Above-normative b	On settlements a	On settlements b	On current account[1] a	On current account[1] b	Others[2] a	Others[2] b
1958	32,912	3,824	11.6	13,209	40.1	10,410	31.6	3,039	9.2	2,430	7.4
1959	36,547	5,340	14.6	14,579	39.9	11,857	32.4	2,116	5.8	2,655	7.2
1960	45,710	5,589	12.2	16,541	36.2	18,454	40.4	2,692	5.9	2,434	5.3

Notes:
[1] Mainly for co-operative enterprises.
[2] Consisting mostly of overdue credit.
Source: Material supplied by NBP.

finance of normatives, their own funds being absorbed by the budget.[1] This change largely explains the rise of approximately 40% in normative credit between 1958 and 1959 (shown in table 34).[2] In 1961, following the order of the Minister of Finance issued on 25 February 1961 'On the partial coverage of the normative of working capital by own funds and constant liabilities',[3] compulsory partial coverage of the normative was extended to more industrial enterprises (in coal mining, heavy industry, building, transport). Most enterprises affected by the order could use their own funds to cover only 70% of the normative, but in some industries enterprises could cover more or less of the normative by their own funds (e.g. in the building industry 75%, in heavy industry 50%). Though not all industrial enterprises were obliged to resort to compulsory credit finance, it may be claimed that 1961 marked the acceptance of the partial coverage of normatives by credit as a principle of working capital finance. Thus credit was accepted as an important source of normative finance, viz. a source of finance for the constant (e.g. non-seasonal) needs of enterprises, which previously could be covered only from their own funds.

[1] Szczepański, p. 268. For the effect on budget revenue see GUS – *RS 1961*, p. 396.
[2] Some rise in credit could have been due to the over-estimation of normative requirements; it is not known to what extent banks detected wrong estimates and refused credit in consequence.   [3] *MP* 24 (1961) item 115.

Chart 2

Principal sources of finance for increases in working capital in socialised industrial enterprises before and after 1957

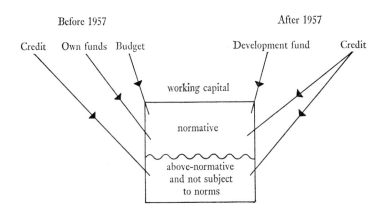

The acceptance of this principle was motivated by three considerations: (*a*) the desire to extend bank control to enterprises which might otherwise not resort to credit finance, (*b*) because it was widely accepted that monetary control could be effective only if credit was an important (viz. large) source of finance, (*c*) as a way of helping to eliminate excesses of funds, which was also an aim of the stringent monetary control discussed later.

Changes in the finance of the normative meant that, as far as existing enterprises were concerned, the direct link between enterprises and the budget was abandoned (see chart 2). Budgetary funds still flowed to finance working capital (in deficit or new enterprises), but, as a rule, they were paid into the DF. Thus after 1957 working capital was financed mainly from own funds and bank credit in the proportions shown, for key industries, in table 35. The somewhat erratic changes in own funds and the role of overdue trade credit are explained in the next section.

To conclude, changes in the planning of the normative were not fundamental and indeed, for many enterprises, the normative was still externally determined. On the other hand, in the field of working capital finance direct links with the budget were severed, bank credit increasingly being used as a substitute for budget finance. Bank control over the planning and finance of working capital gradually

Table 35

Sources of finance for working capital in key industries 1958–60

Year	Total bil. zł	%	Own funds[1] bil. zł	%[3]	Bank credit bil. zł	%[4]	Others[2] bil. zł	%[5]
1958	92.6	100	47.7	51.5	23.3	25.2	21.6	23.3
1959	103.0	100	51.3	49.8	30.0	29.1	21.7	21.1
1960	131.8	100	66.5	50.5	38.9	29.5	26.4	20.0

Notes:
[1] Including constant liabilities.
[2] E.g. trade credit, including overdue trade credit.
[3] In industry as a whole in 1957–9 the ratios were 49.6, 43.3 and 42.4% respectively.
[4] In industry as a whole in 1957–9 the ratios were 29.1, 30.1 and 31.0% respectively.
[5] In industry as a whole in 1957–9 the ratios were 21.3, 26.6 and 26.6% respectively.
Source: J. Szczepański, *Finansowanie Środków Obrotowych*, p. 280. Data in the notes, taken from A. Zwass, 'Poziom i Struktura Zapasów w Gospodarce Krajów Socjalistycznych', *GP* 11 (1961) p. 54, may not be strictly comparable with the data in the table.

increased, thereby limiting the autonomy of enterprises in this sphere of management.

Stringent monetary policy

(a) Its underlying philosophy

In the debates on the economic 'model' which started in 1956, there was widespread agreement that banks should use economic methods of control rather than directly interfere in the operation of enterprises. Credit, it was postulated, should assume an active role, becoming the chief weapon of bank control. Although, as has been shown earlier, there was a relaxation of control by banks in the field of settlements, on the whole the scope of bank control over enterprises increased after 1956. Banks now controlled the planning of normatives, and were to assess the overall performance of enterprises before giving credit for above-normative needs and settlements. This widening of the scope of bank control was done for a purpose. It was assumed that after 1956 enterprises would be more autonomous and less contrained by directives and that it was therefore necessary to use banks to ensure that they did not act against the public interest and contrary to plans and government policy. This function, not in any sense a new one, banks were to fulfil more effectively than before 1956.

In practice, it appeared that whereas enterprises did not achieve the degree of self-management postulated, banks did gain a wider scope for control over them and some measure of autonomy in exercising control. It was claimed that 'The bank today is not, as it was in the past, a guardian and a supervisor of careful fulfilment of the plan by enterprises, but can and does influence the determination of tasks and the appropriate proportions of means necessary for their fulfilment.'[1]

The post 1957 banking policy, conceived mainly by the NBP, was in essence to exercise bank control, chiefly by economic means of control. More specifically, between 1957 and 1961 a stringent monetary policy was implemented. Its philosophy was not fundamentally different from that of the policy of the early 1950s. Enterprises were to obtain finance only for activities which were economically justifiable. Financial difficulties were, in theory, to cause enterprises to improve their management. Thus strict limitations of external finance, such as bank credit, were regarded as effective in eliminating shortcomings in the management of working capital, or more specifically in bringing about better stock management. Credit restriction was to last until the shortcomings had been eliminated. Thus there was a significant element of what was previously called 'coercive credit control'.

A further similarity between the two stringent monetary policies was the emphasis on action through the supply of credit rather than the cost of credit.[2] However, whereas in the early 1950s credit was cheap and becoming cheaper, after 1956 interest rates in general rose and there was an attempt to combine stringent credit with dear credit and a more flexible use of interest rates. In 1958 rates of interest on normative credit and credit for settlements rose from 2% to 4%, and on overdue credit from 8% to 12%. Banks could also use interest rates more flexibly; for instance, enterprises mismanaging their stocks could be charged rates between 6% and 10%.[3] In practice

---

[1] Michejda, 'Warunki...', p. 244.

[2] Though higher interest rates were sometimes considered to be a part of the stringent credit policy – see, for example, Szczepański, p. 234.

[3] Here the principle of differentiation between well-run and badly-run enterprises (ch. 7) had some impact.

higher interest rates were not, as a rule, charged in 1958, but greater use was made of this weapon in later years. In 1959 higher charges were imposed on 600, and in 1960 on 720, enterprises.[1] It must, however, be stressed that though dear credit was an element in the monetary control of the late 1950s it was not a vital one. The authorities doubted the efficacy of interest rates as a control instrument. A survey by the Economic Council confirmed their doubts by revealing that in 81% of cases where higher interest rates were charged they did not have the desired effect on the management of enterprises.[2] This ineffectiveness was attributed to the fact that raising interest rates had very little effect on the total costs of enterprises, because rates were still relatively low in spite of the increase, and because in many enterprises bank credit was not deployed in a large enough quantity.[3] It may be noted that the small impact of changes in interest rates on total costs is often given as one of the main reasons for the weakness of the interest incentive effect in Western economies.

The novelty of the post-1957 stringent monetary policy was to be found in the new environment in which it was to function – an environment where enterprises were to have a greater profit motivation than before and were freer to make autonomous decisions. Furthermore, banks were to interpret the *qualitative tests* more broadly, by executing the policy on the basis of the examination of the overall performance of their customers and not simply on the basis of only one aspect of their activity in isolation from all others. In this respect the retention of the classification of credit, mentioned earlier, could be interpreted as an inconsistency between the principles and the administration of credit.[4]

[1] Szczepański, p. 238. No further details are given in the source. In 1961, when the stringent monetary policy was being modified (this will be discussed), of 3639 cases of bank action in industry 2611 (72%) involved credit limitation, 7 the stoppage of credit, 42 crediting under guarantee of repayment by a superior body, 339 compulsory repayment of debts and 640 (18%) increases in interest rates. M. Krzak, *Polityka Finansowa*, in *Polityka Gospodarcza Polski Ludowej*, part II (1962) p. 215.

[2] Michejda, 'Warunki...', p. 226.

[3] Estimates suggest that in the late 1950s bank interest charges in industrial enterprises were about 1% of total costs. However, in trading enterprises their effect was much greater: 6.8% of total costs for retail enterprises and 15 to 40% in wholesale trade (in 1958) Jaworski, *Obieg...*, p. 152.

[4] However, the granting by banks of a single general credit was opposed by some on the grounds that it might lead to overcrediting and weakening of credit control. See e.g. W. Jaworski, 'Przyczynek do Zagadnienia Zasad Kontroli Bankowej', *Finanse* 9 (1958) p. 21.

In exercising stringent monetary control banks were armed with various sanctions which were not basically different from those which banks in theory had at their disposal in the early 1950s. The sanctions included compulsory transfers from current account to repay overdue credit, limitations of further credit, crediting under a guarantee of repayment by a superior body, or stoppage of credit, but this only in unusual cases of chronic mismanagement by enterprises.[1]

Finally it must be emphasised that the monetary policy adopted in 1958 should not be confused with the stringent credit policies sometimes used in capitalist economies. The policy was not designed to affect the level of aggregate demand nor, more specifically, to serve primarily as an anti-inflationary device. Tight short-term credit was to be a weapon used continuously to control the efficiency of enterprises. Aggregate spending was determined mainly by national economic plans. Thus the overall strategy of socialist monetary control did not alter, although its tactics were somewhat different.

(b) *Its implementation*

The stringent monetary policy, introduced by the credit instruction mentioned on p. 193, was to start from January 1958. Banks were asked to estimate the extra-bank finance available to enterprises and to help eliminate 'excessive liquidity' (*luzy finansowe*).[2] 'Excessive liquidity' was never clearly defined and it was difficult to establish which items it specifically included and how it was to be eliminated. In general, the items which could account for excess liquidity were provisions for unpaid obligations, or unpaid obligations such as payments into the budget which should have been settled, depreciation payments, payments to superior organs, payments on insurance premiums or wages. It was felt that outstanding obligations constituted too large a source of funds, but little specific information on this was given. However, the broad philosophy of excess liquidity was quite straightforward. In order to make a credit squeeze effective it was necessary to check possible alternative sources of finance. Without excessive liquidity enterprises would seek credit regularly, thereby subjecting themselves to bank control. Thus the elimination

---

[1] Pruss, 'Zmiany...', p. 45.

[2] The direct translation of '*luzy finansowe*' would perhaps be 'financial looseness' or 'financial loose ends'. For details see e.g. T. Choliński, 'O Ekonomicznym Oddziaływaniu Banku na Gospodarkę Przedsiębiorstwa', *Finanse* 5 (1958); Pruss, 'Niektóre Problemy...', pp. 548–9; 'Zmiany...', p. 44.

of excess liquidity became the first key ingredient of the stringent credit policy.

In 1958 and 1959 attempts were made to channel some excessive liquidity into the budget, largely by reducing 'constant liabilities', normally regarded by enterprises as part of own funds. On 24 December 1958, by order of the Minister of Finance,[1] the number of items regarded as constant liabilities was actually extended, but the liabilities were now to be planned at a minimum level. The net result was a decrease in the liquidity of enterprises, reflected mainly in a falling proportion of own funds to total liabilities, although, as stated earlier, own funds were also affected by the substitution of credit for own funds in financing normatives. From 1957 to 1959 the percentage of own funds to the total finance of working capital in socialised enterprises fell from 47.0 to 42.4.[2] In view of all the circumstances this did not represent a substantial squeeze on own funds. Indeed, in his study of the finance of working capital Szczepański concluded that excess liquidity had not been completely eliminated in the late 1950s, largely because of the tendency to raise normatives above their correct level.[3]

An estimate of excessive liquidity was made by Kostowski, whose calculations are shown in table 36. Shortages of working capital equalling 17.1 bil. zł. led to a rise in overdue (viz. unauthorised) credit equal to 13.4 bil. zł., the difference (3.7 bil. zł.) indicating excess liquidity.[4] Various items in the table, and the reasons for the shortages of funds leading to the rise in overdue debts, will be better understood after the discussion of the effects of the stringent monetary policy, which follows.

The second key ingredient of the stringent monetary control was the strengthening of the mutual control between buyers and sellers discussed earlier (pp. 196–8). In particular it was assumed that the supplier would, in his own self-interest, exert sufficient pressure on the buyer to settle debts for deliveries promptly. This was to prevent

---

[1] *MP* 10 (1959) item 35. For the title see p. 200.

[2] The percentages in the years between 1957 and 1960 were: 1957, 47.0; 1958, 45.2; 1959, 42.4; 1960, 45.2 (Sulmicki, 'Finansowanie...', p. 319, table 13). For figures referring to enterprises in key industries see table 35.

[3] See p. 249 and Szczepański, pp. 268–9.

[4] Szczepański estimated that excessive liquidity (*nadwyżka finansowa*) in industry was (in bil. zł.) 4.7 in 1958, 6.2 in 1959 and 7.9 in 1960, but his method of calculation was not given. 'Próba Oceny Efektywności Polityki Finansowania', *Zeszyty Naukowe SGPiS* 45 (1963) p. 59.

Table 36

Shortages of working capital funds and their finance by overdue credit
(*Balances at the end of September 1960*)

Cause of shortages of funds	bil. zł.	Overdue credit	bil. zł.
Deficit of own funds not subject to credit	1.8	trade credit	10.2
		bank credit	2.6
Exclusion of stocks from credit	3.0		
Overdue trade debts not compensated by bank credit	10.5	unpaid budgetary obligations	0.6
Limitations of credit	1.0		
Use of working capital to finance investment	0.8		
Total	17.1		13.4

Source: M. L. Kostowski, 'Problematyka Funkcjonowania Systemu Rozliczeń Pieniężnych', *WNBP* 3 (1960) pp. 111–12.

the expansion of illicit trade credit for buyers and therefore it may perhaps be regarded as part of a general move to check excess liquidity, paving the way to an effective monetary control.

The third key ingredient of the policy was the actual credit squeeze. The general principle here was that only the correct or 'justified' activity of enterprises was to be financed. The credit squeeze was to be implemented by the 'exclusion of incorrectness' (such as superfluous stocks) from finance. It was suggested that extending credit only for purposes economically justified was designed to create quasi-market conditions in which financial difficulties would encourage enterprises to improve their efficiency so as to avoid stoppages of production caused by lack of funds.[1]

Two aspects of the credit squeeze may be distinguished: the principal aspect was the refusal of banks to credit stocks recognised as incorrect; secondly, to make the squeeze on credit on stocks meaningful, credit for settlement purposes was to be curtailed. Enterprises found it more difficult to obtain payments credit. Also credit to enterprises which became involuntary trade creditors, viz. 'credit on overdue debts' was, as a rule, to cease.[2] The inability to obtain credit on overdue trade debts was to encourage the seller to

[1] A. Zwass, 'Propozycje Usprawnienia Systemu Rozliczeń', *WNBP* 8 (1962) p. 358.
[2] Up to that time such credit could be obtained easily, especially by enterprises regarded as well-managed.

exercise more vigorous mutual control on the defaulting buyer. Thus during the stringent monetary policy bank credit was to be isolated from the process of settlement of (overdue) trade debts. Banks were also warned to beware of the remnants of the old credit liberalism (ch. 6). They were not, for example, to fix their credit limits at some 'loose' or 'convenient' level, but at a minimum level.[1] Thus the effectiveness of the stringent credit control was in theory to depend on the reliance of autonomous enterprises, increasingly profit motivated, on bank credit as the only external form of finance balancing expenditure with revenue. It is interesting to observe that in the West too there is a growing conviction that the vital preconditions of effective monetary policy are low company liquidity (as measured by either the ratio of current assets to fixed assets or current assets to current liabilities) and the degree of dependence of companies on bank finance.[2]

In practice, after January 1958 banks focused their attention on what has become their main area of interest, the management of stocks. They began to distinguish strictly between stocks which were correct and qualified for credit and stocks which were incorrect and excluded from crediting. In this respect banks behaved consistently with the 'real bills' doctrine as outlined in chapter 1. However, they refused to credit incorrect stocks, irrespective of the causes of the incorrectness. Such stocks were not taken into account in dividing stocks into normative and above-normative. Thus correctness of stocks had to be established before a more specific division of stocks, from the point of view of their role in production, was made. This was really the kernel of the stringent monetary control – the inability to obtain credit for incorrect stocks was intended to goad enterprises into better stock management and, on the macroeconomic scale, to reduce the share of national product absorbed by increases in stocks. Thus the bank control embodied in the policy was essentially 'coercive control' by credit.

The preoccupation of banks with stocks was not fully consistent with the principle of differentiation; enterprises possessing incorrect stocks were to get the same treatment irrespective of whether they

---

[1] L. Gluck, 'O Srodkach i Sposobach Realizacji Zadań Banku w Dziedzinie Pieniężno-Kredytowej', *WNBP* 3 (1959) p. 118.

[2] See e.g. A. D. Bain *The Control of the Money Supply* (London, 1970) pp. 108–14; E. Eshag, 'The Relative Efficacy of Monetary Policy', *Economic Journal*, June 1971 esp. pp. 299–302.

were on the whole well or badly-managed. This may have been a contributory factor in the lack of progress towards better integration of monetary control with wage control. After the acceptance of this principle there was a move to organise operations in branches so as to obtain a comprehensive picture of the economic situation of the enterprises controlled. On 8 March 1957 the NBP issued an instruction (A/17) giving branch directors autonomy in organising wage control, but underlining that the control should be a function of credit departments aiming at a comprehensive analysis of the performance of enterprises. Few branches in practice made wage control a function of credit departments; the function was performed in separate departments or departments dealing with payments.[1] Wage control was still a separate type of control relying on its specific sanctions.[2] The authorities continued to encourage a closer integration between credit and wage controls, by allowing banks (in the NBP's instructions: A/11 of July 1958 and A/9 of June 1959) to use credit sanctions against enterprises showing serious faults in managing their wage funds. However during the stringent monetary policy credit restrictions on such enterprises were neither automatic nor widely used.

[1] For more details see L. Nowakowski, 'O Wlasciwe Ustawienie Bankowej Kontroli Fundusz Plac', *WNBP* 9 (1957) pp. 420–2.

[2] Briefly, a law of 18 January 1957 (*MP* 1957 item 57) laid down that if the wage fund was overpaid and the overpayment was not 'justified' by superior organs and banks then the enterprise was given an opportunity to rectify it from 'savings' generated within a quarter. Until then it paid interest rates (18% p.a.) on the amount overpaid and bonus payments to office workers were suspended. Control was not effective. 'Justifications' were too easy, 'savings' resulted from technical factors (e.g. too low plans) rather than rises in labour productivity, and interest payments were not a deterrent. (For details see R. Malesa, 'Bankowa Kontrola Funduszu Plac w Roku 1957', *WNBP* 12 (1957) pp. 552–3; M. Szudek, 'Uwagi o Dotychczasowym Systemie Kontroli Fundusz Plac', *WNBP* 5 (1958) pp. 225–6; R. Malesa and S. Sikora, 'Zmiany w Bankowej Kontroli Funduszu Plac Przedsiębiorstw Przemyslowych', *WNBP* 9 (1958) pp. 423–6) Wage control was modified in June 1958 (*MP* 48 (1958) item 278), when the concept of 'savings' and penalty interest were abolished, and the need was emphasised for *associations* to make certain that the wage funds of enterprises were planned at a level which would prevent easy 'justification' of overpayments on the grounds of unrealistic plans. Overpayments of wage funds continued, however, to be a regular occurrence in the late 1950s. Justifications of overpayments were still made and an upward 'correction' of the wage fund was automatically obtained if production plans were overfulfilled. See Malesa and Sikora, pp. 425–6; S. Frankel, 'Niedoskonala Kontrola', *ŻG* 34 (1959) p. 6; B. Blass, 'Problemy Krztaltowania i Kontroli Funduszu Plac', *Finanse* 3 (1964) pp. 1–8.

8

Table 37

Above-normative stocks outstanding at the end of the year in socialised industry

(*a, bil. zł. ; b, percentages of total in each year*)

	1958			1959			1960		
	Total	Excluded from credit		Total	Excluded from credit		Total	Excluded from credit	
Stocks	*a*	*a*	*b*	*a*	*a*	*b*	*a*	*a*	*b*
All industries	16.2	3.0	18.5	13.1	1.9	14.5	18.4	2.8	15.2
Key industries	14.9	2.2	14.8	12.2	1.3	10.7	17.3	2.2	12.7

Source: J. Szczepański, 'Próba Oceny Efektywności Polityki Finansowania, *Zeszyty Naukowe' SGPiS* 45 (1963) p. 52; *Finansowanie Środków Obrotowych Przedsiębiorstw Przemysłu Kluczowego*, p. 257.

The degree of credit squeeze during the stringent monetary policy was not uniform. This is to some extent reflected in table 37, showing that the year in which the banks refused to credit the highest proportion of above-normative stocks was 1958, but the table does not fully reflect the development of the policy. The credit squeeze was most intensive up to mid-1959, when banks attempted rigorously to exclude incorrect stocks from crediting[1] and otherwise endeavoured to restrict credit, so as not to let enterprises have excessive liquidity. In 1959 a crack appeared in the policy in the shape of permission by the CM for banks to credit some excessive stocks. Partly to clear the backlog of superfluous stocks accumulated in previous years (and especially in 1957) and partly to release stocks to satisfy the demand for commodities created by the inflationary pressure of 1959, the authorities decided[2] to tackle the problem of accumulation directly. This they did by carrying out a special once-and-for-all action to liquidate excessive stocks by reporting them to trading enterprises, which were to organise their sale, and, in some cases, by writing them off for scrap. It was within the framework of this decision that banks were allowed to credit excessive

[1] But they did not prevent enterprises from including some incorrect stocks in their normative working capital (see p. 200).

[2] Resolution 151 of the CM. For more information see M. Osiecki, 'Zapasy Gospodarczo Nie Uzasadnione w Latach 1962–1964 i Przyczyny Ich Powstania', *WNBP* 9 (1965) p. 310; Szczepański, *Finansowanie...*, p. 262.

stocks in a manner quite contrary to the principles of stringent monetary control. Thus in 1959 generally less stocks were excluded from crediting than in 1958 and 1960 (see table 37). The crack was, however, temporary. In 1960, though they continued to finance stocks declared superfluous in 1959, banks refused as a rule to credit incorrect stocks detected in 1960. Thus essentially the stringent monetary policy continued, but with a difference. In 1960 it became less rigorous than before mid-1959. Gluck, the Vice-Chairman of the NBP, called this variant the policy of 'maximum effectiveness of every złoty'.[1] In deciding on whether to credit stocks or not, banks were to pay more attention than before to the principle of differentiation. They were to be more lenient towards the crediting of stocks whose incorrectness resulted not from mismanagement but from external factors, such as changes in demand. In short, the effective monetary policy starting in 1960 was fundamentally the stringent policy, but with a more flexible interpretation by banks of the incorrectness of stocks. In considering credit applications banks relied less on the mechanical exclusion of stocks from crediting and more on a premeditated judgement. This was thus yet another move in giving the banks more scope for interpretation of the *qualitative tests* of credit. Also from 1960 credit for settlements was granted more liberally than in previous years, with well-managed enterprises now able to obtain credit to finance overdue trade debts by defaulting buyers.[2] The ratio of credit on settlements to total trade debts (viz. debts owed to sellers by buyers) in industry was 50.9% in 1958, 42.4% in 1959 and 53.7% in 1960.[3] In 1961 credit control was further liberalised and, as shown in the next chapter, ceased to be stringent.

(c) Its effects

In assessing the effectiveness of the stringent monetary control we meet the difficulty which has already been encountered in assessing it in the early 1950s – namely the lack of criteria for evaluating its effect in isolation from numerous other factors affecting the management of enterprises.

[1] L. Gluck, Węzłowe Zagadnienia w Pracy NBP w Roku 1960, *WNBP* 3 (1960).

[2] By the same token a change occurred in the attitude towards mutual control between sellers and buyers, but, as already noted, this control has not in fact been effective in any case.

[3] Data supplied by NBP. In key industries the corresponding ratios were 54.3%, 48.9% and 62.7%. Szczepański, *Finansowanie* ..., table 31, p. 283.

Table 38

Changes in stocks and reserves in the national economy 1955–61

(*bil. zł. at current market prices*)

Year	(i) Planned rise	(ii) Fulfilment	(iii) (ii) − (i)	(iv) (ii) × 100 / (i)
1955	4.9	16.0	11.1	326.5
1956	3.7	15.0	11.3	405.4
1957	9.3	25.7	16.4	276.3
1958	11.2	23.7	12.5	211.6
1959	15.6	21.6	6.0	138.4
1960	18.4	25.5	7.1	138.5
1961	17.0	32.9	15.9	193.5

Sources: J. Wierzbicki, 'Zapasy w Gospodarce Polskiej w Latach Ostatnich', *WNBP* 1 (1963) p. 17; M. Osiecki, 'Przyrost Zapasów a Dochód Narodowy w Polsce w Latach 1961–1965 na Tle Porównań z Zagranicą', *GP* 6 (1967) p. 17.

The management of stocks was, as stated before, the main target of the policy. Table 37 shows the stocks which banks refused to credit; the data in Table 38 reflect the behaviour of stocks in general. The ratio of the rise in stocks to the national income did not show a consistent tendency to decrease, being (at 1956 prices) 7.9% in 1957, 7.1% in 1958, 6.0% in 1959 and 6.8% in 1960.[1] The good performance in 1959 can be explained mainly in terms of inflationary pressure and bad climatic conditions, leading to low stocks in agriculture, food and fuel industries.

Table 38 compares the actual with planned changes in stocks, showing that targets for stock accumulation were consistently surpassed.[2] Discrepancies between targets and fulfilment were substantial, though they decreased in 1958–9, largely because after 1957

[1] GUS – *RS 1961*, p. 56. At current market prices the percentage ratios of stock increases to national income were (figures in brackets showing planned ratios) 8.2 (3.4) in 1957, 7.1 (3.4) in 1958, 5.9 (4.8) in 1959, 6.9 (4.8) in 1960 and 7.6 (4.2) in 1961. M. Osiecki, 'Proporcje Między Przyrostem Zapasów a Składnikami Dochodu Narodowego', *WNBP* 12 (1964) p. 422.

[2] In the Five Year Plan 1956–60 the planned rise of stocks was 36.8% and the actual increase (end of 1960) 56.1% at 1956 prices and 96.2% at current prices. Corresponding figures for stocks in industry were 39.2%, 50.5%, 116.3%. Szczepański, *Finansowanie* ..., p. 250.

there was a tendency to plan stocks at a higher (more realistic) level than before. In industry in the period under discussion production in general rose faster than planned, but the rate of stock building was faster than the rate of increase in output.[1]

On the whole the information on stocks given above is not very helpful in assessing the efficacy of stringent credit control. The behaviour of stocks shown in table 37, for instance, tells us little about the effectiveness of the policy on stock management. Variations in stocks excluded from crediting were caused by changes in credit policy (pp. 212–13) rather than in the quality of management. The rest of the data quoted does not conclusively indicate the impact of the policy, for reasons similar to those discussed in chapter 6. First, behaviour of stocks in any economy is one of the least predictable items in economic development. The fact that stock accumulation can be affected by a variety of factors makes the planning of stocks very difficult. Accurate planning, both on the macroeconomic scale and in enterprises, can take place only in conditions of reasonable certainty on the demand as well as the supply side of production. Enterprises, however, functioned in conditions of considerable uncertainty, caused above all by frequent changes in plans and uncertainties on the supply side. The chief causes of excessive accumulation of stocks between 1957 and 1961 were changes in production plans (especially in heavy industry) and in the technology of production. Equally serious causes were shortages of supplies, occurring for diverse reasons such as: a general shortage of certain materials relative to the demand for them, unreliable deliveries from subcontractors, deliveries of products of poor quality or wrong specifications. General shortages in supplies, moreover, tended to foster the hoarding of stocks by enterprises able to secure deliveries. On the demand side factors affecting stocks were: poor quality, the lack of consumer demand (for example when consumers preferred an imported product to home produced goods) and inaccurate predictions of changes in demand.[2]

---

[1] According to J. Wierzbicki ('Zapasy w Gospodarce Polskiej w Ostatnich Latach', *WNBP* 1 (1963) p. 19) between 1956 and 1961 industrial production rose by 85.3% and stocks by 124%.

[2] On uncertainty in the operations of enterprises see W. Samecki, *Ryzko i Niepewność w Działalności Przedsiębiorstwa Przemysłowego* (1967) esp. chapters 3–6. Economists writing at the time on the problem of stock formation invariably emphasised such factors as plan changes, inadequate organisation of supplies and poor predictions of

Data comparing the actual stock accumulation with planned accumulation must be interpreted with caution. Plans for stock building were worked out by the PC at a minimal level, to allow for a greater expansion of consumption and fixed investment. On the other hand, decentralisation in the management of stocks (more freedom for enterprises to plan their stocks) gave enterprises, whose stocks were low before 1956, encouragement to replenish them in order to ensure continuity of production.[1] As stated earlier, in spite of bank control, enterprises managed on the whole to set their normatives at a higher level than necessary, sometimes including stocks which would not otherwise have been financed.

Thus there is no conclusive evidence to suggest that the stringent monetary control resulted in a marked improvement in stock management in enterprises. Equally it is difficult to say how much more badly enterprises would have managed their stocks had there been no strict bank control preceding the issue of credit. These observations on stocks also lead us to propose that it was not reasonable to expect the policy to have a significant effect on the management of stocks.[2] The policy could at best be a palliative, not a cure for stock building in enterprises and against the excessive share of stocks in the national income.

Stringent monetary policy had some undesirable effects, which both disorganised payments and weakened bank control. It did leave many enterprises short of funds to which they could legitimately turn when in need of finance to fulfil their plans. Shortages of funds (see table 36) did not result in stoppages of production or bankruptcies of enterprises, but led, as in the early 1950s, to the accumulation of illicit indebtedness.

The basic sources of working capital finance (see table 35) were own funds, bank credit and 'other sources', which included an increasing proportion of unplanned finance, of which the most important (see tables 36 and 39) was overdue trade credit, viz. money

demand, rather than mismanagement by enterprises. See e.g. Gluck, 'Zagadnienie...'; Kucharski, 'Czy Zapasy Hamują Rozwój', ŻG 16 (1960) p. 1; Wierzbicki, 'Zapasy...', p. 19 et seq.; Szczepański, 'Próba...', pp. 47–8; *Finansowanie...*, pp. 249–51.

[1] Szczepański, *Finansowanie...*, pp. 249–51.

[2] Referring to stock management before 1959, Gluck quite rightly observed ('*Zagadnienie...*', p. 66) that 'The characteristic feature of the attempts made so far to improve the management of stocks was to endeavour to cure the symptoms of mismanagement but not to eliminate its causes'. The stringent monetary control was indeed yet another manifestation of this feature.

Table 39

Composition of overdue credit in industrial enterprises 1959 and 1960

	31.12.1959		30.9.1960	
	bil. zł.	%	bil. zł.	%
Total	10.0	100.0	13.4	100.0
Trade credit	6.4	64.0	10.2	76.1
Bank credit	2.4	24.0	2.6	19.4
Obligations to budget	1.2	12.0	0.6	4.5

Source: M. L. Kostowski, 'Problematyka Funkcjonowania Systemu Rozliczeń Pieniężnych', *WNBP* 3 (1961) p. 111.

owed to suppliers which should already have been paid.[1] As in the early 1950s, during the stringent monetary policy of 1958–60 there was a large accumulation of overdue trade debts, illustrated by tables 40a, 40b and 41. Tables 40a and b, which are the continuation of tables 25a and b and 26a and b, are given to enable comparisons with overdue trade indebtedness before 1958. However, they do not cover the full period of the policy because of the lack of comparable material for 1959 and 1960.[2] They both show a significant rise in overdue indebtedness after 1957, viz. after the introduction of the policy. In our study of the impact of the policy, much use will be made of material referring to industrial enterprises, where the growth of overdue trade debts was particularly striking,[3] because of the availability of better data (including data kindly supplied by the NBP) dealing only with industrial enterprises after 1957.

Table 41 shows that in industry trade credit expanded steadily, about half of it being overdue. Between 1958 and 1959 the proportion

---

[1] For comparison with the finance of working capital in the USSR (including finance from unwarranted funds) see table D2.

[2] A Vice-Chairman of the NBP quoted a long series of percentages of overdue credit in total credit liabilities of (presumably socialised) enterprises, but gave little specific information concerning the data. The percentages are: 22 in 1958, 40 in 1959; 43 in 1960, 45 in 1961, 34 in 1962 (the start of lenient credit policy), 19 in 1963. Gluck, 'Działalność...', p. 26.

[3] Overdue credits as a percentage of total credits (viz. figures corresponding to column 3 in table 40a) at the end of 1957 and 1958 were 15 and 32 in industry and 7 and 16 in trade (source as in table 40a).

Table 40a

Overdue indebtedness of enterprises settling through NBP 1957–9

	Overdue debts[1]	Overdue credits[2]	
31.12.57	15	11	Stringent credit control applied from January 1958
31.3.58	23	25	
31.12.58	40	22	
31.3.59	36	33	

Notes:
[1] As a percentage of total debts.
[2] As a percentage of total credits. For explanatory notes see table 25a.
Source: W. Jaworski, 'Rola Banku w Likwidacji Przyczyn Wzajemnego Zadłużania się Przedsiębiorstw', *WNBP* 11 (1959) p. 544.

Table 40b

Overdue trade indebtedness of socialised enterprises 1957–9

	Overdue trade debts[1]	Overdue trade credits[2]
1957	19.5	13.2
1958	34.1	21.7
1959	37.8	28.0

Notes:
[1] As a percentage of total trade debts.
[2] As a percentage of total trade credits.
Source as in table 25b.

of overdue credit to total trade credit rose, falling slightly after 1959. The ratio of overdue trade credit to short-term bank credit in industry was quite high: 13.4% in 1958, 17.5% in 1959 and 16.9% in 1960.[1]

Though the problem of the accumulation of trade credit did not appear to be as acute as in the early 1950s (especially 1951–3), it was nonetheless serious. Failure by some enterprises to settle promptly led to a chain reaction producing financial difficulties generally. As

[1] Data supplied by the NBP.

Table 41

Trade credit in industry
(*Balances at the end of the year*)

	1958		1959		1960	
	bil. zł.	%	bil. zł.	%	bil. zł.	%
Industry:						
Total	8.8	100.0	11.9	100.0	15.0	100.0
Overdue	4.4	50.0	6.4	53.5	7.7	51.5
Key Industries:						
Total	7.2	100.0	10.1	100.0	12.7	100.0
Overdue	3.5	48.8	5.3	52.2	6.3	49.6

Source: Data supplied by the NBP; J. Szczepański, *Finansowanie Środków Obrotowych*, p. 283.

explained earlier, even enterprises innocent of mismanagement (at least up to mid-1959) were denied credit from banks against overdue trade credit, so as to encourage them to exert pressure on their defaulting debtors. Here again a situation arose where an attempt to separate settlements from bank credit led to difficulties in the shape of blockages in payments. The payments problem would have become even more serious than indicated in tables 40a and b and 41 had there been no liberalisation of credit policy in 1960, allowing some involuntary trade creditors to receive bank credit, viz. credit on overdue debts. It may also be noted that, whereas in the early 1950s some of the overdue trade indebtedness could be explained in terms of a compulsory order of payments (see pp. 131–2 and 172–4), after 1957 enterprises were free to decide their own priorities. It seems that they preferred to settle other obligations before settling with their suppliers. For instance, as illustrated in table 42, enterprises showed greater preference for overdue trade credit to overdue bank credit.[1] Explaining this choice of settling with suppliers last, Pruss commented that 'Consequences of conflicts with employees, superior bodies or financial organs are as a rule more acute than conflicts with

---

[1] Overdue trade debts and overdue bank credit were the largest overdue obligations of enterprises (see table 36). The former rose faster (by 44.8% in 1959 and 20.7% in 1960) than the latter (by 6.7% in 1959 and −11.8% in 1960).

Table 42

Overdue indebtedness during the stringent monetary policy 1958–60

	1958	1959	1960
(a) Overdue trade credit (mil. zł.)	4,415	6,392	7,713
(b) Overdue bank credit (mil. zł.)	2,290	2,443	2,155
(c) $a + b$	6,705	8,835	9,868
(d) $\frac{a}{a+b} \times 100$	65.8	72.3	78.2

Source: Data supplied by the NBP.

suppliers'.[1] Thus overdue trade debts accumulated, in spite of attempts to strengthen mutual control (p. 196). Trade creditors moreover displayed little enthusiasm in pressing their debtors for payment, partly because they received penalty interest at 12% on overdue debts while obtaining bank credit at 4% interest.[2]

The lack of adequate statistics prevents a systematic evaluation of the impact of the expansion of overdue trade credit on the finance of total working capital of enterprises. Winter estimated that in 1958 funds, including largely overdue trade credit, financed 43%, and overdue bank credit 6%, of *increases* in working capital.[3] Sulmicki's data suggest that overdue trade credit expressed as a percentage of the working capital of socialised enterprises was 1.5 in 1956, 1.3 in 1957, 2.4 in 1958 and 3.6 in 1959.[4] Thus after 1957 the percentage ratio rose substantially, but was still rather small.

From Szczepański's calculations it appears that 3.8% of the working capital of enterprises in key industries in 1958 was financed by overdue trade credit; in 1959 and 1960 the ratio rose to 5.1% and 4.8% respectively.[5] Thus overdue trade credit was by no means a

[1] Pruss, 'Zmienność Potrzeb Kredytowych Przedsiębiorstwa', *WNBP* 5 (1965) p. 141.
[2] K. Czyżniewski, 'Przyczynek do Dyskusji Na Temat Systemu Rozliczeń', *WNBP* 3 (1963) p. 120.
[3] The development fund provided 12% and 39% came from bank credit. E. Winter, 'W Jakim Kierunku Zreformować System Finansowy Przedsiębiorstw', *Finanse* 1 (1960) p. 19.
[4] Sulmicki, 'Finansowanie . . .', p. 319. On the basis of data supplied by the NBP and GUS – *RS 1968*, p. 576 the percentage for industrial enterprises in 1960 was 5.1.
[5] Ratios of overdue trade plus bank credit to total working capital were 6.2% in 1958, 8.7% in 1959 and 6.9% in 1960. Szczepański, *Finansowanie . . .*, pp. 282–3.

large source of working capital finance, though it was large considering that it was an illicit form of finance.

Was the rise in overdue trade debts in any way indicative of deteriorating management of enterprises? This is an interesting question, answers to which are very difficult, if not impossible, to test. Certainly in a capitalist system this type of insolvency would generally indicate the failure of management to adapt effectively to market conditions and might, in some cases, threaten the existence of firms. It is not impossible for an enterprise in a socialist economy to accumulate trade debts because of its poor management. However, the rise in overdue trade debts in the late 1950s was a general occurrence and there were no indicators that a significant general deterioration in management of enterprises did occur at the time. Apart from the tight credit policy, the possible causes of overdue debts might be (*a*) mistakes or inaccuracies in planning of working capital and (*b*) inaccurate estimates of credit requirements by enterprises and banks.[1] Both (*a*) and (*b*) occurred continuously and there is no evidence that their extent increased between 1958 and 1960. However, the lack of flexibility in monetary control which was evident, at least in some stages of the stringent credit period, was likely to heighten their impact on the financial results of enterprises. Thus it appears that, though there may have been some other contributory factors to the growth of overdue trade indebtedness, the primary factor was the tightness of bank credit.

Expansion of overdue trade credit, although it did not have the consequences which it might have had in a capitalist system, namely insolvency leading ultimately to bankruptcy, did reduce the potency of bank control. The squeeze on both the excess liquidity of enterprises and bank credit, without producing any appreciable improvement in stock management, led to the expansion of overdue trade credit and an escalation of payments difficulties. Thus the monetary policy simply resulted in a substitution of unplanned forms of finance for planned. It was this particular effect, rather than the absence of evidence that stock management had improved, which caused the abandonment of the policy in 1961.

[1] Another reason, mentioned by Czyżniewski ('Przyczynek...', p. 119), for the existence of overdue debt was that payments from the budget or superior organs to enterprises entitled to them were not prompt. This occurred continuously and not just during the stringent credit period.

(d) Monetary policy as an anti-inflation device

With the failure of the policy an interesting experiment in socialist monetary control came to an end – an experiment in which banks endeavoured, by basing control mainly on credit, to use 'economic' as opposed to 'administrative' means of control. This, together with the failure of the stringent monetary control of the early fifties, invites comment on the use of monetary policy as a stabilisation device. As already stated, some Western economists (see pp. 54–5), though realising that the primary cause of inflation in the Soviet economy was 'overfull employment planning', often considered monetary policy as an anti-inflation weapon.

The nature of inflation is one of the most debatable economic topics and cannot be fully discussed here. It is assumed here that inflation in Soviet-type economies is in the main excess demand inflation and that the unplanned overpayment of wages, which is a chronic phenomenon, does not necessarily indicate cost inflation, but appears mainly as a symptom of planning output targets without sufficient and/or realistic assessment of the means to fulfil them and without consistent coordination of these means. Inflation is thus assumed to be of the demand-pull variety, caused partly by the system of planning and incentives and partly by the policy of rapid industrialisation, which includes priority for the development of capital goods industries. Polish experience (and indeed Soviet experience, though it has not emerged as clearly there) suggests that monetary control is powerless to affect aggregate spending, which has been determined by national plans and not influenced by financial stringency.

In a given situation (viz. given plans of production, the price level, the rate of change in labour productivity) the finance of a socialist enterprise is chiefly demand determined. The coercive element in monetary control, whereby credit restrictions were to lead to improvements in management (viz. were expected to affect real variables), was inconsistent with this, assuming a causal relation going from financial to real variables. Though some Western theories stipulate the existence of such causation (see theories summarised under A on pp. 6–7), in Soviet-type planning there clearly was no causal relationship between monetary and real processes.

The tendency to plan output targets at a high level and the means to fulfil them at a relatively low level, allowing for an optimistically low rate of stock building, resulted in unrealistic financial plans. Thus in the overall financial set-up the application of the *qualitative tests* of credit, based mainly on planned targets, inevitably resulted in a shortage of funds. Though the tests were not strictly applied, monetary control was not slack in relation to the demand for finance. Its continued stringency was indicated by the spontaneous growth of unplanned financial claims. Indeed in a system where banks were the only financial institutions and their credit was to serve as the financial reserve of production units, which could possess only a small cash float, one would expect the demand for funds to press mainly on bank credit. One would, therefore, expect banks to become the 'lender of last resort' to enterprises. The fact that trade credit and not bank credit in effect fulfilled the function of the lender of last resort was a measure of the stringency of monetary control. Had banks applied their *qualitative tests* more strictly and fully utilised credit sanctions, the problem of payments and the accumulation of illicit claims would simply have become worse. In view of the fact that credit had little effect on real processes it would have been more efficient to relax credit policy sufficiently to prevent the chain reaction of stoppages in payments by defaulting buyers. This could only have been done by giving banks considerable autonomy in interpreting the *qualitative tests* and by relinquishing credit as a corrective device, retaining it mainly as a diagnostic device (compare pp. 126–30).

At this stage it may be useful to state more precisely the difference of view between the author and Western studies of Soviet-type monetary control. The overall financial management was slack and ultimately the total supply of finance adjusted itself to the actual rather than planned transactions requirements. However, if the supply of credit is considered in isolation from other financial flows then it was not flexible and did not adjust liberally to transactions requirements. If it contributed at all to the overall slack it did so only indirectly, in so far as it encouraged the development of unwarranted compensatory financial flows. Thus the difference of view turns on the nature of the financial mechanism, rather than on the question of the overall result of financial management. The understanding of the financial mechanism is vital because it reveals the 'balloon effect'[1]

---

[1] The term inspired by A. B. Cramp, 'Two Views on Money', *Lloyds Bank Review*, July 1962, p. 5.

in Soviet-type finance, where pressure on one part of the financial mechanism is relieved by bulging out elsewhere. Consequently grave doubts must be cast on the efficacy of anti-inflationary financial policies and the wisdom of viewing monetary policy as an instrument of macroeconomic control.

(e) Comparison with the West

It is interesting to note that in Western economies effects similar to those mentioned above are stressed in theories already outlined in chapter 1 under point C (pp. 7–8). It is claimed that, given a demand for credit, action on a narrowly defined money supply leads to the development of new borrowing and lending channels and the creation of new financial instruments, making monetary control ineffective. Non-bank financial intermediaries (e.g. finance houses, insurance companies – see pp. 10–11) in particular are said to be able to activate 'idle money balances', thereby frustrating monetary policy.

The relation between the expansion of trade credit and the effectiveness of monetary policy in the West is complex and debatable.[1] It may be noted that in the West trade credit is a relatively larger source of finance for firms than bank credit, though exact estimates of its size do not exist. The Radcliffe Committee reported (para. 304) that in the UK in 1956 trade credit given by companies quoted on the Stock Exchange alone was more than the total credit granted by the clearing banks. In Canada in 1960 bank loans were 4.5% and accounts payable 6.1% of total balance sheet liabilities of non-financial corporations.[2] In contrast in socialist economies bank credit is usually a more important source of funds than trade credit (see tables 35, 48a and b, and for Soviet data table D2 in Appendix D).

The possibility of destabilisation through trade credit in the West was recognised long ago. J. S. Mill (in *Principles of Political Economy*, vol. III), for instance, was impressed by it. More recently the Radcliffe Committee was convinced that, especially when monetary policy was intended primarily to affect bank credit, 'In conditions of boom it [trade credit] can be used to finance a continuing expansion,

---

[1] Compare two studies: R. G. Lipsey and F. P. R. Brechling, 'Trade Credit and Monetary Policy', *Economic Journal*, December 1960 and J. B. Coates, 'Trade Credit and Monetary Policy', *Oxford Economic Papers* 1 (1967).
[2] *Report of the Royal Commission on Banking and Finance*, p. 34.

even when bank credit is being contracted, so long as business expectations remain sanguine.' (para. 300). The Canadian Royal Commission on Banking and Finance also reported (pp. 38, 87, 429) expansion of trade credit in times of monetary restraint, observing that there was then a tendency towards 'taking' rather than granting the credit. In general, however, it is non-bank financial inter-mediaries, operating quite often outside the scope of monetary control, which are blamed for frustrating restrictive monetary measures.

In Soviet-type economies, due to the rigid structure of financial institutions, unplanned generation of finance cannot occur through spontaneous adjustments in the structure and methods of operation of financial institutions.[1] In the circumstances, the accumulation of overdue trade credit appears to be an understandable development, suggesting that even in a planned economy the financial 'market' adjusts itself in an unplanned way to requirements primarily deter-mined by real variables.[2]

It may be of interest to add here that the frustrating effect of unplanned accumulation of trade credit has also been noted in Yugoslavia, where the banking system is much more diverse and flexible than a Soviet-type system, though not in any way approaching the complexity and adjustability of Western-developed systems. Attempts to use monetary policy as a stabilisation device, which have gradually evolved since the mid-fifties, have been offset in recent years by a growing indebtedness caused, as in other East European economies, by the failure of 'illiquid' firms to settle promptly with suppliers. The Yugoslav economy has been consider-ably opened up in recent years, and cannot therefore easily adopt easier credit to unblock payments,[3] especially during inflationary pressure. In 1970 the decision was taken to adopt credit sanctions against 'illiquid' firms, in the hope that this would force them to improve their management.[4] This, in essence, is the formula of Soviet-type stringent credit control and it will be interesting to see how effectively it will perform in a 'socialist market economy'.

[1] Though it must be remembered that the BMS and other new settlement practices developed as a direct consequence of the accumulation of unplanned finance.
[2] Such behaviour is consistent with the Western 'Banking School' monetary theory (see pp. 13–14).
[3] It will be seen in chapter 9 that such a solution was adopted in Poland and other East European countries.
[4] See Hauvonen, esp. pp. 592–3.

In a sense East European monetary experience tends to support the view of the Radcliffe Committee (see pp. 7–8) concerning the concept of money in the context of monetary control. Even if we allow the existence of self-managing enterprises responsive to financial stimuli – a situation which may at some future date occur in socialist planning – control over the supply of money, narrowly defined as consisting of currency in circulation and bank deposits, may not be sufficient to ensure the effectiveness of monetary policy.

Clearly, overdue debts and especially overdue trade credit proved to be good substitutes for money. Thus, for purposes of effective monetary control of spending by enterprises, a wider range of assets than currency and bank deposits may be considered to constitute money, and monetary control should therefore aim at control over money in that broad sense.[1] Indeed, this was in essence the approach to monetary control in the 1958–61 period in Poland, when the authorities attempted to combine the credit squeeze (viz. 'exclusion' from crediting) with the squeeze on excess liquidity in enterprises and to discourage the accumulation of trade debts. What frustrated this approach was the absence of an effective link between monetary and real processes.

The use of economic means of control in Poland rested on the assumption that *de facto* decentralisation of decision-taking would take place and that a significant degree of profit motivation would be introduced into the management of autonomous enterprises, making them more sensitive to financial stimuli. Much blame for the lack of success of the policy must necessarily be attached to the failure to grant enterprises autonomy and to their paying more attention to the fulfilment of their output indices than to the attainment of high profits or to their financial state. Reforms in banking and credit were too far ahead of reforms in the general management of production to be effective. With the end of the stringent monetary policy there arose once again the problem of the nature and methods of bank control, and the role in it of bank credit, which are discussed in the next chapter.

---

[1] Even so, the control of illicit trade credit may prove singularly difficult to achieve. In the West overdue trade credit may lead to bankruptcy; in Soviet-type economies, where bankruptcy virtually does not exist, there does not appear to be an obvious 'economic' check to the expansion of trade credit when other sources of credit are restricted.

Credit finance and the control of investment

(a) Credit finance of investment 1955–7

It has already been mentioned that in the decentralised economic 'model' which was under discussion after 1956 enterprises were to be given scope for self-management. One way in which self-management was to be extended was to allow enterprises to decide upon and finance independently of the central planning authorities a part of their investment which became known as 'decentralised investment'. Such a reform naturally involved substantial readjustment of the existing Soviet-type investment planning and finance mechanism.

Yet the authorities did not appear to have any premeditated comprehensive policy concerning the devolution of decision-taking in investment and frequent changes in this sphere suggested a 'nervous approach'.[1] Non-limited investment, which before 1955 was very small (see p. 174), rose appreciably, especially in 1957.[2] Enterprises could, in addition, undertake quick-yield investment financed from bank credit. Thus between 1955 and 1957 enterprises had a little more scope than before in deciding their investment. Though the bulk of investment was still centrally planned and budget financed, investors (viz. enterprises for whom investment was allocated) began to be more involved in the process of investment.[3] The availability of funds for investment began to be more dependent on actual progress in the execution of investment projects, rather than on limits determined in investment plans. An interesting innovation in this respect was short-term credit granted to facilitate speeding up of the completion of projects. It was given by banks financing investment (viz. banks other than the NBP) after they were satisfied that credit would indeed speed up completion, benefiting the economy as a whole (for example, increasing productivity or exports). No data are available on the amount of such credit, but

[1] R. Michejda, 'Uwagi na Temat Obecnego Systemu Finansowania Inwestycji', *WNBP* 6 (1969) p. 287.
[2] In the years 1955–7 its ratio to total investment in the socialised sector was 8.0%, 5.2% and 10.0% and in the state sector 4.5%, 2.3% and 5.8% respectively. GUS – *RS 1957*, p. 180; *RS 1958*, p. 193.
[3] Changes in this area were introduced on 4 February 1957 'On the principles of finance of limited investment.' *MP* 12 (1957) item 82. For more details see K. Czyżniewski, *Efektywność Form Finansowania Reprodukcji Środków Trwałych* (1966) pp. 136–42.

Table 43

Expansion of investment credit for socialised enterprises 1955–7

	1955	1956		1957	
	mil. zł.	mil. zł.	Rise[2]	mil. zł.	Rise[2]
Credit by all banks[1]	2,335	4,874	209	5,935	254
Credit by NBP[1]	103	1,325	1,286	1,526	1,482

Notes:
[1] Credit balances outstanding at the end of the year.
[2] Taking 1955 = 100.
Source: GUS – *RSF 1945–1967*, pp. 230 and 234.

there is no evidence to suggest that it was significantly large. Indeed, little precise information is available on the finance of investment in general between 1955 and 1957. A variety of sources began to be used, suggesting that financing had become haphazard and complicated.[1]

Table 43 indicates that in this period there was an expansion in credit finance of investment, especially pronounced in 1956, and shows the growth of investment credit granted by the NBP. However, in spite of its expansion, investment credit was still a relatively unimportant source of finance for the economy's capital expansion. In the absence of adequate data on the finance of investment up to 1961, this may be indicated by the ratio of the increase in investment credit to the total expenditure on investment and capital repairs in the socialised sector by the whole financial system, which rose from, on the average, less than 0.5% in 1952–5 to 4.5% in 1956, falling in 1957 to 1.7%,[2] when restrictions were imposed on credit finance following its fast growth in 1956 (see p. 177).

[1] K. Czyżniewski, *Efektywność Form Finansowania Reprodukcji Srodków Trwałych* (1966) p. 142.
[2] GUS – *RSF 1945–1967*, p. 14. The comparable ratio for budget grants for respective years was 64.9%, 68.3%, 71.3%, the remaining finance being mainly depreciation. Reasonably detailed statistics on investment finance were obtained only for years after 1960. The data on which the above ratios are based are available for the 1950s and 1960s. In answer to the author's enquiry GUS kindly confirmed that, though the data lacked some cohesion and involved some overlapping, they did quite accurately reflect changes in the finance of investment and capital repairs. The ratios are used in later chapters for comparative purposes.

(b) Decentralised investment and bank credit 1958–60

After 1957 attempts were made to change the planning and finance of investment. On 19 November 1957 the CM passed a resolution[1] introducing a new division between centralised and decentralised investment. The distinction between limited and non-limited investment ceased to operate and quick-yield investment became part of decentralised investment. Centralised investment, consisting of projects (such as new factories or large expansion of existing ones) undertaken on government initiative, continued to be financed by budget grants. Decentralised investment was to be initiated by enterprises themselves,[2] involving mainly modernisation, replacement of worn-out equipment and mechanisation of production processes. Though it is possible to regard it as a continuation of non-limited investment, its size, sudden growth and increased scope made it a new phenomenon. The most important information on it is given in tables 44a and b, which suggest that in the socialised sector it accounted for quite a sizeable proportion of the total (36.8% in 1959).[3] It was proportionally greater in the co-operative sector than in the state sector, and was less pronounced in industry than in the economy as a whole.

The law of 19 November 1957 laid down that decentralised investment was to be financed from the newly created investment fund and bank credit. The fund could be composed of (*a*) part of the depreciation payments which an enterprise was allowed to keep, (*b*) payments from the DF and (*c*) other payments (e.g. from the sale of superfluous fixed assets, insurance indemnities). Money in the investment fund (kept in the bank) earned a rate of interest.[4] From our point of view

[1] Resolution 467 'On the sources of finance of investment and capital repairs.' *MP* 96 (1957) item 557.

[2] Enterprises did not always, however, exercise unfettered choice. In some cases decentralised investment was a continuation of projects already begun under central planning and budget financed. One problem which soon emerged, and which continued for some time, was the absence of clear or objective criteria for distinguishing centralised from decentralised investments. Z. Sałdak, 'Zalety i Wady Inwestycji Zdecentralizowanych', *ŻG* 21 (1959) p. 5; K Czyżniewski, 'Z Zagadnien Reprodukcji Prostej...' part III, *Finanse* 9 (1964) p. 34; *Efektywność...*, p. 207.

[3] Though larger decentralised investment was implied in many 'model' discussions. Lissowski and Baran (p. 6) proposed a 50%–50% division between state and enterprise investment.

[4] The law of 27 March 1958 'On the determination of rates of interest and charges of state banks,' *MP* 42 (1958) item 239 envisaged interest rates for all special funds of 1%

Table 44a

Investment in the socialised sector 1957–60

(*Current market prices; a, mil. zł.; b, percentages of total*)

	Total a	Decentralised a	Decentralised b	Total a	Decentralised a	Decentralised b
				Investment in industry		
1957	53,925	5,403[1]	10.0	–	–	–
1958	59,309	14,595	24.6	26,598	7,441	27.6
1959	72,926	26,863	36.8	33,246	9,554	28.7
1960	82,552	29,851	35.2	36,364	9,293	25.6

Note:
[1] Non-limited investment.
Sources: GUS – *RS 1958*, p. 193; *RS 1960*, p. 78; *RS 1961*, p. 73.

Table 44b

Investment in the state sector 1957–60

(*Current market prices; a, mil. zł.; b, percentages of total*)

	Total a	Decentralised a	Decentralised b	Total a	Decentralised a	Decentralised b
				Investment in industry		
1957	51,485	2,982	5.8	–	–	–
1958	55,010	10,296	18.7	24,838	5,681	22.9
1959	66,994	20,931	31.2	31,192	7,500	23.8
1960	75,665	22,964	30.3	34,500	7,429	21.5

Sources: GUS – *RS 1958*, p. 193; *RS 1960*, p. 78; *RS 1961*, p. 73.

the interesting provision was the possibility of financing decentralised investment by credit, which was to be medium-term with a maximum period of repayment of five years (ten years in exceptional circumstances). Repayments were to be made from the investment fund or, if that was insufficient, from the current account. Banks could demand that a certain proportion of decentralised investment should be

to 3%. An order of the Minister of Finance of 12 April 1955 (*MP* 48 (1958) item 253) fixed the rate for the investment fund at 2%.

Chart 3

Sources of finance of decentralised investment and capital repairs in 1959

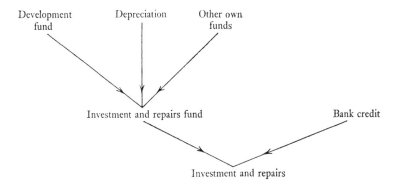

Development fund | Depreciation | Other own funds

Investment and repairs fund   Bank credit

Investment and repairs

covered from own funds of enterprises and, before agreeing to extend credit, were to analyse the purpose and the efficiency of projects.

On 13 October 1958 the CM introduced important changes and modifications in the financing of fixed capital investment, to apply from 1959.[1] Decentralised investment and capital repairs were to be financed from a newly created 'investment and repairs fund' (IRF) and from bank credit (see chart 3). The innovation here was the finance of repairs from the same source as net investment, giving enterprises a new freedom of choice between repairs and new installations. The IRF was formed from a part of the depreciation fund, a part of the DF and other own funds. It was to be kept in a bank account earning interest.

Data on the actual structure of finance of decentralised investment are difficult to find, but it is certain that credit became an important source of funds.[2] Investment credit grew at a very fast rate (see table 45) and the NBP became an increasingly important supplier until

[1] Resolution 392 (see p. 187), whose other provisions should be borne in mind in this context.

[2] Kucharski (*Pieniądz. . .*, p. 235) gives the following structure of finance of investment by enterprises (not specifying what enterprises) (in percentages):

	1958	1959	1960
Own funds	78.8	80.5	78.5
Credit	21.2	19.5	21.5

Table 45

Expansion of investment credit to socialised enterprises 1957–60

	1957	1958	1959	1960
Total credit[1] in mil. zł	5,935	8,326	11,193	14,493
index 1955 = 100	254	357	479	621
index 1957 = 100	100	140	189	244
Credit by NBP[1] in mil. zł.	1,526	3,486	6,740	8,012
as % of total	25.7	41.9	60.2	55.3

Note:
[1] Balances outstanding at the end of the year.
Source: As in table 43.

1959 (compare also with table 43). However, as a source of finance of gross investment in the economy as a whole, investment credit continued to be relatively unimportant, the budget and depreciation being the chief sources of investible funds. The ratio of the rise in investment credit to the investment expenditure of the financial system (compare with p. 228) in the years 1958–60 remained steady at 3.3%.[1]

(c) Bank control of decentralised investment

Potentially investment credit could serve as an important instrument of control of aggregate investment expenditure. In practice it was not used specifically for that purpose, first because the amount of credit for investment was, as stated previously, relatively small and secondly because finance (e.g. the availability and the cost of credit) was not adequately linked with real investment processes. The authorities preferred to control the level of investment directly. Credit did not even become an important instrument of control over decentralised investment.

[1] The comparable ratio for budgetary expenditure in the three years was 61.5%, 63.1% and 56.1% respectively and for the DF 2.6%, 3.1% and 3.0% respectively. GUS – *RSF 1945–1967*, p. 14.

The actual experience of decentralised investment cannot be described here in detail. Broadly speaking, in 1958 enterprises enjoyed some autonomy in this respect. There was a tendency to make the finance available to enterprises for investment purposes the effective limit of decentralised investment. Two major constraints on the autonomy of enterprises in this respect were: (a) the size of special funds, which was fixed by the superiors of enterprises and (b) the fact that before granting credit banks endeavoured to make certain that the investment decisions of enterprises did not conflict with general directives of government economic policy. Total credit for decentralised investment was, however, determined by the funds held in the accounts of enterprises in banks. Thus in 1958 there was, at least in theory, no rigid limit to the amount of decentralised investment, the crucial factor being the size of investible funds accumulated by enterprises.

In actual fact, enterprises showed an insatiable appetite for investment and tended to accumulate funds quickly.[1] They did not always plan their investment in a satisfactory way, sometimes undertaking projects known as 'wild investments' (*inwestycje dzikie*) recklessly. The blame for this was mainly attached to uncertainty and instability surrounding enterprises, which were never sure how much of their current income (profit) they would be allowed by their associations to retain for development purposes, because the size of the DF (and other special funds) was planned for one year only. This militated against enterprises having a long-term development programme. There were also frequent changes in the plans of enterprises, and in government policy concerning their autonomy. The price system, moreover, offered the enterprises no rational guide to investment decisions. Thus in estimating their investment for a current year, they took a chance, planning it at a high level, often without proper preparation, hoping somehow to obtain finance if their funds proved inadequate.[2] The main thing was 'to get a foot in the door' by having a project started. Czyżniewski stressed that there was

lack of synchronisation between physical and financial investment activity. Enterprises, wishing to secure prompt deliveries, order machines and equipment months before the beginning of a planning year – not knowing

[1] As a rough indicator of this we may take the percentage ratio of deposits, other than current account deposits, to total deposits in the banking system which, in the years 1957–61, was 6.2, 12.5, 16.5, 21.5, 23.6 respectively. GUS – *RSF 1945–1967*, p. 232.
[2] Szczepański, *Finansowanie...*, p. 261.

at the time what financial resources could be at their disposal.... It is assumed that if an order has been accepted then its finance will be found.[1]

The crucial test for the new investment policy came in 1959. A drive towards a higher rate of investment started as early as the second half of 1958. The national economic plan for 1959 envisaged a rise in net investment of 13.5%, which meant that the share of investment in the national income would rise from 15.7% in 1958 to 16.8% in 1959.[2] In fact, in 1959 investment tended to grow at a rate faster than planned. From table 44a it may be seen that investment in the socialised sector rose between 1958 and 1959 by 23%, the rise in decentralised investment being 84.1%. The level of investment planned by enterprises was impossibly high. The investment boom led to a dangerous inflationary situation. In the building industry wage funds were 'seriously overspent' and stocks of building materials fell to 'below the necessary minimum level'.[3]

Of the measures undertaken to curb inflation those designed to stop the investment boom were particularly stressed. In 1959, at the III Plenary Session of the CC of the Party, it was decided to plan investment with greater care, improving control (including bank control) over investment processes.[4] The government put into operation 'the action of investment revision', calculated to select for execution only the most profitable projects,[5] and imposed restrictions on decentralised investment. Tables 44a and b show that the rate of growth of investment in 1960 fell significantly compared with 1959 (in the socialised sector the rate was 23% in 1959 and 13.2% in 1960, and in the state sector it was 21.6% in 1959 and 12.9% in 1960). Restrictive policies on investment applied most severely to decentralised investment; the ratio of decentralised to total investment in the socialised sector rose by 84.1% in 1959, but by only 11.1% in

[1] Czyżniewski, 'Z Zagadnień...', p. 35; *Efektywność* ..., pp. 274–5.

[2] 'Zadania Narodowego Planu Gospodarczego na Rok 1959', *GP* 12 (1958) p. 1. Private consumption was also to increase, from 70.3% of national income in 1958 to 71.1% in 1959. The government hoped to achieve both rises by special efforts to reduce stocks in the economy (vide stringent credit policy).

[3] Szarota, 'Rozwój...', p. 41.

[4] *ND* 12 (1959) pp. 36–7. Disinflationary measures included tax increases on peasants and tightening up on wage payments.

[5] For information on the action see e.g. M. Bartnicki, 'Powszechna Akcja Rewizji Inwestycji', *ND* 9 (1960) pp. 3–12; J. Ciahunowicz, 'Wstępne Wyniki Powszechnej Akcji Rewizji Inwestycji', *GP* 12 (1960) pp. 7–11; S. Jędrychowski, 'Bieżąca Sytuacja Gospodarcza', *GP* 7 (1961) p. 4.

1960 (the corresponding figures for the state sector were 103.3% in 1959 and 9.7% in 1960). In industry decentralised investment actually fell in 1960 compared with 1959.

Restrictions on decentralised investment were not of a general financial nature, like a credit squeeze or high interest rates, but took the form of a direct curb on the freedom of enterprises to undertake and finance such investment. There was a retreat from the idea of self-finance of enterprises towards greater central control over investment, accompanied by protests claiming that devolution of investment decisions was in itself a useful practice and that disturbances in the economy were a consequence of a variety of factors, including a lack of a clear cut government policy. What was needed was not restrictions on investment, but the creation of a more stable environment conducive to a rational attitude towards investing.[1]

Three ways in which restrictions on decentralised investment were imposed may be distinguished. First, beginning in 1960, the total decentralised investment in the economy was limited in terms of a directive target in the national economic plan, which meant that total investment by enterprises could not exceed a limit imposed by the plan. This limit in turn automatically fixed the amount of bank credit which could be extended for investment purposes, because the total of own funds planned for investment plus bank credit could not exceed the limit. Thus the total credit allowed was the difference between the limit and the funds accumulated by enterprises for investment finance. In fact, in an order issued by the Minister of Finance on 17 December 1959[2] the NBP was given the specific task of adhering to a stated limit of investment credit. In practice, the use of planned limits was not confined to total investment – limits on decentralised investment were also set for individual enterprises.[3]

The second way of curbing decentralised investment was by direct intervention of superior organs, which began to occur on an increas-

---

[1] A plea for more stability and certainty in the circumstances surrounding enterprises was continually made. See. e.g. J. Niewiadomski, 'Reforma Zasad...', *Finanse* 2 (1958) p. 26; W. Lissowski, 'Problem Inwestycyjnej Samodzielności Przedsiębiorstwa Przemysłowego', *GP* 4 (1959) p. 28; W. Dudziński, 'Inwestycje Zdecentralizowane – Rozdział Zamknięty', *ŻG* 18 (1960) p. 6; J. L. Toeplitz, 'Na Co Czekają Przedsiębiorstwa', *ŻG* 20 (1959) p. 4; Saldak, p. 5.

[2] 'On the methods and control of finance for decentralised investment in 1960'. *MP* 1 (1960) item 2.

[3] Czyżniewski, 'Realizacja Inwestycji Zdecentralizowanych w Pierwczym Półroczu 1960 Roku', *WNBP* 10 (1960) pp. 467–8.

ing scale in 1959. Associations in particular began to regulate investment activities of enterprises. As already mentioned, many of them
continued to act in the same way as their predecessors, viz. central
administrations. Having themselves little autonomy, they were
often a medium through which economic ministries and the PC
transmitted their decisions.[1] From 1959 onwards associations were
intervening not only in the distribution of money between special
funds but also in the utilisation of these funds and especially the DF.
Here again they were used merely as a tool of economic ministries.
Thus, paradoxically, decentralised investment was subjected to
centralised planning and control after 1959.[2]

The only form of investment which was not affected by planned
limits was quick-yield investment. The law of 19 November 1957
incorporated quick-yield investments into decentralised investment,
but after 1959 they again became a separate category of investment
financed by bank credit. On 16 May 1960 a resolution of the CM
specifically laid down that quick-yield investment could surpass
the limit for decentralised investment set in the national economic
plan. It encouraged investment in machinery and scientific equipment, stating that 'The condition for the realisation and finance of
investments mentioned in this resolution is the agreement of the
bank to finance investment and the acceptance by enterprises of
bank control over the investment.'[3]

Investment restrictions were imposed by either prohibition or the
blocking of funds – the latter method being more generally used.
Associations ordered banks to block investible funds of some enterprises and, on the strength of these frozen funds, to extend finance to
others. The blocking of finance, regarded by the authorities as an
effective method of adjusting the flow of funds to the needs of enterprises, was a crude weapon of financial control which met widespread criticism. Przywecki, a deputy director of the department of

---

[1] A. Płocica, 'Na Co Czekają Zjednoczenia', ŻG 21 (1959) pp. 1 and 3; U. Wojciechowska,
'Czynniki Określające Fundusz Rozwoju', Finanse 8 (1961) esp. p. 29. See also J.
Toeplitz, 'Co z Tą Samodzielnością,' ŻG 18 (1959) p. 6; J. Boguszewski, 'Inwestycje
Zdecentralizowane a Bank Finansujący', ŻG 24 (1959) p. 4.

[2] Dudziński (p. 6) claimed that in 1960 investment by enterprises was decentralised only
'in nomine'.

[3] Resolution 167 'To facilitate the realisation of quick-yield investments, investments
connected with technical progress and other decentralised investments'. MP 52 (1960)
item 245. In 1959 the credit allowed for these investments was 702.8 mil. zł. and in 1960
532.5 mil. zł. Kunicki, pp. 73–7. Also compare pp. 175–7.

investment of the NBP, thought blocking a dangerous practice which should have been used only in exceptional circumstances, instead of being a 'safety valve for clumsy management of associations'.[1]

Blocking ran counter to decentralisation, to which the government committed itself after 1956. Admittedly enterprises still possessed the right to accumulate investment funds and to ask for investment credit. This, however, did not constitute freedom to invest, in the same way that the possession of investible funds did not necessarily mean the ability to invest. In this way blocking diminished the autonomy of enterprises, reducing their incentive to save.

The third way in which the authorities exercised restrictions on decentralised investment was through bank control. Banks were involved in the operation of the two forms of restraint discussed above, but there were also changes specifically relating to bank control over investing enterprises.

It may be useful at this point to assemble and expand information on the bank control of investment, by first glancing at the control of centralised budget-financed investment, before proceeding to the control of decentralised investment. In the late 1950s specialised banks, and in particular the IB, continued to serve mainly as budgetary institutions distributing finance for centralised investment. There was, however, some change of emphasis in the control administered by them; notably control was based less on checking documents in order to ascertain that investments were carried out in accordance with 'the investment code', and more on research into actual economic problems of investment.[2] Nevertheless, the control continued to have a supervisory and administrative character, embracing every stage of investment activity. It was never primarily based on the use of financial instruments, such as the supply of funds and/or interest rates. A common criticism of such control was that its scope was too wide, surpassing the possibilities of its effective fulfilment. This was especially true after 1959, when cuts in investment had to be made as part of the disinflationary policy. As a result the IB in particular became a sort of licensing bureau – rejecting some projects, modifying others, questioning costing procedures and reviewing estimates.[3]

---

[1] S. Przywecki, 'Niektóre Problemy Dotyczące Finansowania Inwestycji', *WNBP* 4 (1959) p. 178.

[2] Czyżniewski, *Efektywność...*, p. 163.

[3] A. Wołowczyk, 'Bankowa Kontrola Inwestycji', *Finanse* 9 (1961) esp. p. 89.

Returning now to the problem of bank control of decentralised investment, it may be observed that at first bank finance of this kind of investment was rather disorganised, as all banks were engaged in supplying investment credit. From 1959 onwards the principle that investment credit should be given to an enterprise by the bank financing its working capital was firmly established. Thus one bank supplied the total credit requirements of the enterprise and exercised bank control. Such a solution had been postulated in the debates on the economic 'model', implying that the principal bank engaged in the control of decentralised investment should be the NBP, which (according to table 45) extended 60% and 55% of investment credit in 1959 and 1960 respectively.[1] In extending credit banks were to ensure that investment was in the public interest and that enterprises had chosen the most advantageous projects. To use the Polish terminology, they were to ascertain that proposed investments possessed the characteristics of 'purposefulness' (*celowość*) and 'effectiveness' (*efektywność*). Again, a distinction was made between preliminary control (ensuring that the project would be profitable and that it was well documented), current control (to make certain that the project was being carried out according to plan and that planned costs of construction were not surpassed) and subsequent control (ascertaining whether the estimated efficiency of investment was actually being achieved).

The finance of investment widened the scope of the NBP's control, imposing on the bank the burden of familiarising itself with the vast and complicated subject of the economics and technology of investment. It is difficult to assess how initially the NBP coped with its new task. It had more autonomy of lending in 1958 than in later years; it is not clear how its branches actually interpreted the requirements of purposefulness and effectiveness.

Some attempt was made to use credit as a means of control. As a rule, banks financed projects only to the value agreed beforehand. Thus if, for instance due to some delay or problems of construction, there was a rise in costs, enterprises had to find the extra funds from other sources (for example the current account), with the result,

---

[1] The concentration of both long and short-term credit and of bank control in one bank constituted a step towards the Leninist ideal of a single all embracing bank and bank control. The concentration of banking was less noticeable in Poland than in some other communist countries, especially Czechoslovakia and Albania, where in 1959 a single bank emerged supplying long and short-term credit.

usually, of a decline in profits and in the factory fund. However, these 'economic methods' of control were not in general successful, especially in cases of enterprises making large profits.[1] During the implementation of decentralised investment much bank control was of audit or supervisory nature, based on checking documents and calculations.

After restrictions on decentralised investment were introduced in 1959 bank control became more automatic. The necessity to adhere to planned limits, mentioned earlier, decreased the autonomy of banks in extending credit. However, the main factor which reduced their autonomy was the blocking of investment funds by associations. Blocking and unblocking served as pointers to the distribution of credit so that, in effect, the main direction of credit was determined not by banks but by the associations.[2] In general, in granting credit the key factor was not the purposefulness and effectiveness of investments, but the need of banks to keep within the limits of credit imposed from above and not to counteract the policy of superior organs of enterprises. Credit in such a situation could not serve as an effective means of control.

At the same time from 1960 the authorities imposed on banks additional duties regarding the control of decentralised investment. From January 1960 enterprises had to notify banks about all their contracts concerning investment. Banks were to ratify such contracts, after checking whether they complied with regulations. Such a procedure existed before 1957 but was then suspended, only to reappear in 1960.[3] In addition banks were to supervise practically every stage of the investment process, largely in order to ascertain that investment was taking place according to regulations and policy. In particular, they were carefully to analyse all investment proposals. To that end very onerous tasks were imposed on them in 1960 by the V Plenary Session of the Party's CC. In their 'preliminary control' banks were to examine such things as: existing productive reserves in enterprises, to see whether investment was really necessary and whether it would be economical (modernisation rather than new installations were preferred); the possibility of shortening the period

[1] Czyżniewski, *Efektywność...*, esp. pp. 179 and 192.
[2] This was accentuated by J. Boguszewski, 'Kilka Uwag o Kredycie Inwestycyjnym', *WNBP* 5 (1961).
[3] M. Jaslar, 'Bankowa Notyfikacja Umów a Legalność Działalności Inwestycyjnej', *Finanse* 6 (1961) p. 19.

of completion; the likelihood of investment leading to the production of important substitutes for other goods.[1] To carry out such evaluations banks needed to have considerable technical knowledge. In the case of the NBP especially, which possessed little investment experience compared with specialised banks, this necessitated an intake of extra technical and engineering staff, though in theory the lack of expertise was to be solved by inter-bank co-operation of a more intensive nature than before.

Thus from 1959 banks began increasingly to be used as departments vetting the investment projects of enterprises, focusing their attention on individual projects rather than the performance of the enterprises undertaking them (which is always helpful to banks in ascertaining the credit-worthiness of their clients). Przywecki aptly commented that banks attempted to exercise control by putting themselves in the place of actual investors.[2] Such a solution to control over decentralised investment limited the autonomy of enterprises, imposing on banks a function which they could not effectively fulfil, because of the lack of sufficient capacity in terms of staff and expertise. The imposition of excessive control responsibilities upon banks had an interesting harmful effect, namely that other bodies engaged in planning and costing investment projects tended to become lax in discharging their duty, trusting that the banks would in any case rectify any shortcomings.[3]

[1] Z. Saldak, 'Rola Banków w Realizacji Inwestycji', ŻG 41 (1960) p. 1.
[2] S. Przywecki, 'Niektóre Problemy Inwestycji Przedsiębiorstw na Przełomie Roku 1960/1961', WNBP 1 (1961) p. 6.
[3] Czyżniewaki, Efektywność..., p. 186.

9

In search of a monetary policy in decentralised planning
II. The adoption of lenient credit control

Background information

(a) Status quo ante 1961

During the period 1961–5 covered by this chapter, few fundamental economic changes occurred. The chapter is mainly devoted to an account of the adoption of lenient monetary control and its consequences and to changes in investment planning and finance.

During this period the United Workers' Party consolidated its political hegemony, showing little enthusiasm for major reforms. It was thus, broadly speaking, a period of stabilisation of the conditions which had emerged by 1961, described in the previous chapter. Planning continued to be centralised, based on the use of directive (or *de facto* directive) indices. Common complaints about it included excessive arbitrariness in the formulation of plans and their frequent alterations. The autonomy of enterprises continued to be limited by the use of directives and through interventions by associations and banks in particular. Indeed, some authors were convinced that autonomy declined during the period under discussion.[1] After their incorporation into the conferences of workers' self-management (see p. 183) workers' councils remained ineffective, a situation which was lamented in a cycle of articles in *ŻG* entitled 'Why the cucumber does not sing?'.[2]

(b) What role for the association?

One development in industrial administration which may be singled out was the growing preoccupation with the status and functions of

---

[1] A. Bober, 'Samodzielność a Inicjatywa', *ŻG* 27 (1964) p. 3.
[2] See *ŻG* e.g. 6, 7, 9, 10 (1962); the summary of the debate in 27 (1962).

the association of enterprises. It may be postulated that after the failure of the attempt to delegate decision-taking powers from the top tiers of the planning apparatus (viz. PC and economic ministries) to the enterprise, viz. to the lowest level of the planning apparatus, a different form of decentralisation began to be considered, notably the delegation of decision-taking to the intermediate level, the association. At the same time it was urged that greater autonomy of the association should not occur at the expense of the autonomy of the enterprise. Towards the mid-1960s it became clear that the government was seriously contemplating an experiment in decentralisation involving more autonomy for the association, but no clear-cut policy on the problem emerged. For instance, Szyr, the Vice-Chairman of the CM, forecast a transition to a system of management involving more autonomous associations and enterprises, expressing a conviction that it was possible to grant more autonomy to both associations and enterprises.[1] He emphasised the need for associations to employ economic means of control over member enterprises. At the same time Trendota, a Vice-Minister of Finance, warned against the danger of giving associations more financial power over enterprises, on the grounds that this might militate against financial autonomy in enterprises.[2]

Legislation concerning the association was capable of wide interpretation. In most legal contexts it was stressed that, like the enterprise, the association was a legal person functioning on economic accounting, but it was not clear how this provision was to be interpreted. The law of 16 February 1960[3] declared that the object of the association was to create conditions under which enterprises could fulfil their plans, stating that: 'The activity of the association must not limit the legally determined autonomy of its member enterprises.' The very next sentence, however, claimed that 'The association can conduct its own economic activity.' Resolution 404 of the CM, passed on 11 October 1961,[4] gave the association what may

[1] E. Szyr, 'O Roli Zjednoczenia i Przedsiębiorstwa',*ND* 6 (1964), pp. 69–71. This view was not shared by all economists. Some believed that an increase in the autonomy of the association must detract from enterprise autonomy. E.g. T. Kierczyński and U. Wojciechowska, *Finanse Przedsiębiorstw Socjalistycznych* (1965) pp. 361–2.

[2] J. Trendota 'Warunki Sprawności Systemu Finansowego',*ND* 6 (1964) pp. 118–19.

[3] 'On the change of the decree of 26 October 1950 on state enterprises'. *DURP* 9 (1960) item 57.

[4] 'On the financial economy of associations of enterprises embraced by the central plan.' *MP* 79 (1961) item 329.

appear to be complete control over the financial affairs of enterprises. It laid down that 'associations carry out financial policy in relation to their member enterprises'. The resolution gave the associations wide control over various aspects of financial management, including payments discipline, debts and bank credit. These, it may be noted, were the traditional areas of interest of banks. Finally, the formal position of the association *vis-à-vis* economic ministries and the PC was not clearly defined.

Considerable disappointment was expressed in economic literature about the actual performance of associations. In fact, they did not display much initiative, failing to act like autonomous economic units. As already observed in the previous chapter, they constituted mainly an executive organ of economic ministries. They themselves were the victims of the whole system of centralised control, in which most of the important decisions were taken by the PC and ministries, and associations served only as a channel of communication with enterprises. They were said to fulfil a 'transmitting function', acting like a post box through which enterprises received decisions on matters of fundamental importance.[1] Some critics of associations stressed imperfections in the way they dealt with the plans of enterprises and the haggling that went on between associations and enterprises about the planned targets arbitrarily distributed by associations to their members, which tended to weaken financial stimuli, among other things.[2]

Thus in the period under discussion associations functioned imperfectly, though plans were made to transform them into more effective economic units capable of autonomously taking and executing economic decisions.

(c) *Special funds and profitability*

After 1960 few alterations occurred in the financial management of enterprises. The blueprint for the 1960s (up to 1966) became resolution 387 of the CM, passed on 17 November 1960, entitled

---

[1] For details see W. Głowacki, 'Gorzkie Żale Dyrektorów', *ŻG* 46 (1961) p. 9; 'Zjednoczenie i Integracja', *ŻG* 10 (1962) p. 5; Z. Madej, 'Funkcjonowanie Gospodarki Narodowej' in *Polityka Gospodarcza Polski Ludowej* (1965) vol. 3, p. 62.

[2] W. Dudziński, 'Zjednoczenie czyli Rozdzielnia Niedoskonała', *ŻG* 45 (1961) p. 1. Szyrocki, *Samofinansowanie...*, p. 156.

9

'On the principles of financial management of state industrial enterprises and their associations embraced by the central plan.'[1] This was a lengthy document dealing comprehensively with various aspects of financial management, some of which are separately discussed in this chapter. At this stage it may be noted that the number of special funds which enterprises could form was increased to six: DF, depreciation fund, IRF, factory fund, fund for premiums for office workers and factory house fund. Associations could set up three basic funds: reserve fund, investment fund and administration fund. Enterprises and associations could also have a fund for technical progress and other specialised funds. Details of all these funds cannot be given here, but some of them are further discussed because of their significance in financing investment and working capital. The creation of a large number of specialised funds reflected the authorities' desire to set up a system of 'specialised stimuli' for enterprises. Economists frequently criticised the ineffectiveness of incentives based on a variety of funds whose size was unrelated to profit, and instead advocated the creation of a single 'synthetic index', such as a rate of profit.[2]

As far as the profitability of enterprises was concerned, there was some reversal of trends visible between 1957 and 1960. Briefly, financial accumulation on socialised enterprises stagnated between 1961 and 1963, but rose in 1964 and 1965 (see table 46). The post-1955 tendency to allow enterprises to retain a growing proportion of financial accumulation[3] did not continue. Between 1961 and 1964 enterprises and their superior organs retained approximately the same proportion of financial accumulation, which was likely to be a little lower than the proportion retained between 1959 and 1960. In 1965 the proportion rose (table 46) when the authorities changed their attitude to self-finance, anticipating the reforms discussed in the next chapter. Thus, with the exception of 1965, there was a retreat, though not a drastic one, from self-finance. This was reflected in the formation and distribution of the DF, shown by table 47.

[1] *MP* 91 (1960) item 411.

[2] Profit (or some index of profitability) and its possible use in planning were widely discussed at the time. The discussion gathered momentum in 1964 and continued up to the reforms of 1965 and 1966. From about 1962 Soviet debate on profit (including Liberman's views) received much publicity in the Polish economic press.

[3] The trend is shown by table 29, which is not strictly comparable with table 46, because the latter refers to state enterprises only. However, the two indicate broadly how the accumulation was distributed.

Table 46

Financial accumulation of socialised enterprises and its distribution between the budget and the enterprises and their superior bodies 1961–5

		Financial accumulation			
		Absorbed by budget		Retained by enterprises	
Year	Total bil. zł.	bil. zł.	%	bil. zł	%
1961	132.5	110.5	83.4	21.9	16.5
1962	133.6	112.5	84.2	21.0	15.7
1963	132.5	112.8	85.1	21.1	15.9
1964	155.4	132.1	85.0	24.3	15.6
1965	169.8	141.6	83.4	29.0	20.5

Note:
The sum of accumulation absorbed by the budget and retained by enterprises may not add up to the total. This is caused by a variety of reasons (see source p. 161), but mainly by the arrangement of transfers by enterprises of their accumulation to the budget or other bodies.
Source: GUS – *RSF 1945–1967*, p. 193.

Table 47

Analysis of expenditure from the development fund in state enterprises 1961–5

(*a, mil. zł. ; b, percentages of total distribution*)

		Distribution of the fund						
	Total transfers	Total	On investment		On working capital		Other	
Year	a	a	a	b	a	b	a	b
1961	9,562	9,027	4,594	50.9	4,182	46.3	251	2.8
1962	9,629	10,121	3,435	33.9	5,689	56.2	997	9.9
1963	10,311	10,056	3,381	33.6	6,258	62.2	417	4.1
1964	9,463	9,374	2,876	30.7	6,155	65.7	343	3.7
1965	12,960	12,377	3,200	25.9	8,883	71.8	294	2.4

Source: as in table 30.

Before 1961 the fund grew continuously (see table 30), but after that year its growth was less dynamic and regular.

It may be observed that the size and sources of the fund continued to be arbitrarily controlled by superior authorities and were not systematically linked with profit, though profit was the major source of the fund.[1] As shown by table 47, it financed mainly working capital; a decreasing proportion of the fund was allocated to investment. In distributing the fund between working capital and investment the authorities endeavoured to implement the idea of interplay between stocks and fixed investment (see p. 201).

Credit and the finance of working capital

The main source of finance of working capital in the period under discussion were bank credit and own funds (see tables 48a and b). The tendency to decrease budget financing of working capital continued and, in fact, between 1962 and 1965[2] budget expenditure on working capital was less than 1% of total budgetary expenditure. The proportion of working capital financed from bank credit was quite steady between 1961 and 1962, 1963 and 1965, but it was significantly higher in the latter period than in the former.[3] This may be explained mainly by the imposition of a new requirement of a partial coverage of the normative of working capital by bank credit, for the same reasons which were mentioned in the previous chapter (pp. 201–3), and also by a relaxation in credit policy, which is discussed below.

It may be recalled that partial coverage of normatives by credit became an accepted principle of finance in 1961, but was not extended to embrace all industrial enterprises. In 1963 (after an order of the

[1] Szyrocki *Samofinansowanie*..., pp. 213–14 and 239–41; Szczepański, *Finansowanie*..., p. 296.

[2] 1961 was exceptional as relatively large sums were advanced to enterprises (8766 mil. zł. viz. 3.8% of budgetary expenditure) to finance their working capital. This was connected with the partial coverage of normatives introduced in some industries. The authorities supplemented own funds of some enterprises to the required amount. In 1962 budget grants for working capital amounted to only 0.8% of budget expenditure, GUS – *RS 1966*, pp. 523–5.

[3] The proportions in key industries were 33.8% in 1961, 34.5% in 1962 and 41.6% in 1963 (Szczepański, *Finansowanie*..., p. 302). They are comparable with those given in Table 35.

Table 48a

Finance of working capital in socialised enterprises 1961–5
(*Balances at the end of the year*)

Year	Total	Bank credit	Own funds	Trade credit[1]	Others[2]
			In mil. zł.		
1961	367,669	134,717	111,677	43,008	78,267
1962	399,816	144,664	121,100	43,465	90,587
1963	458,132	183,442	125,825	44,199	104,666
1964	479,644	195,325	125,548	49,788	108,983
1965	524,681	211,534	142,205	56,496	114,441
			In percentages		
1961	100	36.6	30.4	11.7	21.3
1962	100	36.2	30.3	10.9	22.7
1963	100	40.0	27.5	9.6	22.8
1964	100	40.7	26.2	10.4	22.7
1965	100	40.3	27.1	10.8	21.8

Notes:
[1] This includes all obligations, including overdue payments of enterprises to their suppliers.
[2] For example provisions for payments or unpaid obligations with respect to e.g. wages or the budget.
Source: GUS – *RSF 1945–1967*, p. 167.

Minister of Finance of 12 March 1963) nearly all industrial enterprises were obliged to finance a proportion (usually at least 25–30%) of the normative by bank credit. According to Albrecht, the Minister of Finance, during the year 1963 15 bil. złoty of credit was granted as a result of the extension of this requirement.[1]

It may be mentioned here that in 1962 credit practice was further simplified – the principle that all credit for working capital should be granted on the current account became generally accepted. This was the outcome of experimenting with crediting on the current account mentioned in the last chapter (p. 194). The use of one account for crediting did not end or change the classification of credits, which continued to serve as a guide for banks in ascertaining the credit needs of their customers.

[1] J. Albrecht, 'Niektóre Problemy Pracy Aparatu Bankowego w Roku 1964', *WNBP* 1 (1964) p. 2.

Table 48b

Finance of working capital in socialised enterprises in industry 1961–5

(*Balances at the end of the year*)

Year	Total	Bank credit	Own funds	Trade credit	Others
			In mil. zł.		
1961[1]	171,461	57,049	65,651	16,607	32,154
1962	179,267	59,804	72,177	15,326	31,960
1963	211,844	84,946	74,562	15.220	37,116
1964	210,938	86,488	67,561	16,402	40,487
1965	229,967	92,381	74,377	18,165	45,044
			In percentages		
1961[1]	100	33.3	38.3	9.7	18.8
1962	100	33.4	40.3	8.5	17.8
1963	100	40.1	35.2	7.2	17.5
1964	100	41.0	32.0	7.8	19.2
1965	100	40.2	32.3	7.9	19.6

Note:

[1] In 1960 the comparable figure for working capital was 150,523; bank credit was 45,710, which was 30.4% of working capital (*GUS – RS 1968*, p. 576; data supplied by the NBP). Source: GUS – *RSF 1945–1967*, p. 168.

Lenient monetary control

(a) A departure from control by the supply of credit

In the early sixties it was generally realised in East Europe that monetary control based on the use of credit restriction as a corrective device was a failure in conditions of socialist planning and that the *qualitative tests* of credit requirements linked mainly to planned targets, did not always realistically assess the 'business needs' of enterprises. Consequently there was pressure throughout the Soviet bloc, including the USSR,[1] for liberalisation of the criteria for granting credit. Some easing of credit took place in all socialist countries, with Rumania and East Germany adopting

[1] In the USSR perhaps the best case for this was put by Shenger, esp. Essays 5, 6, 11.
V. Batyrev, 'Niektorye Voprosy Dal'neishego Razvitiya Kreditnykh Otnoshenii, *DiK* 12 (1964), in urging more liberal credit, claimed that bank control was possible even if banks granted credit on 'incorrect' stocks (pp. 12–14).

the most lenient credit policies and the Soviet Union relaxing credit to a lesser extent. The Polish experience, discussed in detail below, represents the middle of the road.

It was observed above that credit became a more important source of finance of working capital than before. One of the reasons for this was to ensure adequate bank control, and especially control by credit. However, the expansion of credit finance of working capital was accompanied after 1962 by a departure from the practice, followed during the stringent credit period, of using the supply of credit as a key control instrument. As early as 1960 there was some liberalisation of the stringent monetary control (see p. 213); a further relaxation followed an instruction (A47) from the Chairman of the NBP issued 3 January 1961, which suggested that banks should not automatically impose credit restrictions on 'incorrect' stocks or trade debts. The bank realised that restrictions on credit supply did not prove effective, mainly because enterprises could, without severe consequences to themselves, finance their expenditure mainly through overdue trade credit.

Three points need to be accentuated in connection with the new strategy of the bank. First, bank control in general was not to be abandoned or relaxed, and its objectives remained unaltered – stock management, for instance, continued to be regarded as of primary importance in bank control, as was stressed by Żebrowski, the Chairman of the NBP.[1] Only the methods of bank control changed. The emphasis shifted from restrictions on the supply of credit to other methods, which are specified below. Banks could still restrict the quantity of credit to badly-managed enterprises, but were not now compelled to do so.

Secondly, it now became possible to obtain credit to finance 'incorrect' activity. A change of attitude in this respect on the part of the authorities was heralded by Blass, a Vice-Chairman of the NBP, who stressed the importance of direct control by banks of the stock management of enterprises.[2] Banks were, for example, to assist enterprises in the annual disclosure and sale of super-fluous stocks,[3] to stop them from producing goods not in demand

[1] 'Zadania Banków w Roku 1963', *WNBP* 1 (1963) pp. 2 and 6.
[2] B. Blass, 'Zadania Banku w Roku 1961', *WNBP* 3 (1961).
[3] This move was a development of the 1959 action on stocks (see p. 212). In 1961 it became a permanent annual requirement, T. Choliński, 'Próba Oceny Przebiegu Realizacji Postanowień Uchwały, Nr. 151 KERN', *WNBP* 3 (1961).

and to help in planning their normatives. Stringent monetary control was said to have been enforced too rigorously especially as, in some circumstances, more rather than less credit was needed to help enterprises over their difficulties. Thus Blass encouraged a more liberal expansion of credit on overdue trade debts, as well as credit on stocks, including 'incorrect' stocks. Crediting 'incorrect' requirements meant the demolition of an old established principle that financial restrictions must apply until the 'incorrectness' is eliminated.

In connection with credit on stocks, in January 1962 the NBP issued a new credit instruction, changing the classification of stocks for purposes of finance.[1] Banks had to distinguish between correct stocks, qualifying for finance, and incorrect stocks, excluded from finance. The division between normative and above-normative stocks concerned only those stocks which qualified for finance. The new instruction brought in a new principle, that incorrect stocks were to be part of above-normative stocks.[2] But, as already stated, banks were still to endeavour to eliminate the holding of such stocks by enterprises. To this end they were to co-operate with enterprises and choose the most effective way of doing so.

The third aspect of the policy is closely connected with the second. Banks were encouraged to look for measures of control likely to yield the maximum effect upon enterprises. As already stated, restrictions on the supply of credit were among the measures which could be used, but in general there was a realisation that this was an unsuccessful control method likely to create payments difficulties. Credit was to be granted in quantities which would ensure its optimum effectiveness on enterprises, and the interpretation of this was left to the banks. In cases of badly-run enterprises banks were to use a package-deal of measures likely to be effective.[3] Thus credit pressure was to be replaced by what became known as 'concentrated interventional

---

[1] W. Pruss, 'Nowa Instrukcja Kredytowania Działalności Przedsiębiorstw Uspołecznionych', *WNBP* 1 (1962); L. Bogobowicz and J. Koziciński, 'Uwagi na Tle Funkcjonowania Nowej Instrukcji Kredytowej', *NWBP* 12 (1962).

[2] Thus if working capital subject to norms was W and the normative was N, then normally above-normative working capital would be $W-N$. But if some stocks, X, were not justified, then the normative would be decreased by X (viz. $N-X$) and so the above-normative working capital would be $W-(N-X)$.

[3] A. Żebrowski ('Nasze Zadania w Roku 1962', *WNBP* 1, 1962, p. 3) referred to this as 'the postulate of unity of credit policy', suggesting a more 'elastic' credit policy based on a mixture of 'exclusion from credit', interest rates and bank interventions.

pressure' and by higher interest rates. It was generally thought that banks could recognise shortcomings in enterprises and choose an appropriate mixture of remedial measures, without necessarily cutting the supply of credit.

Though it is difficult to see precisely what was meant by 'incorrect' activity in the context of credit practice in the sixties, the possibility of crediting such an activity marked an important turning point in the socialist theory of monetary control. In terms of Western economic concepts, it may be said that there was a move towards a more consistent application of the 'real bills' doctrine. Banks now had greater autonomy in assessing the legitimate business needs of enterprises and in so doing could use criteria other than strict fulfilment of planned targets, which constituted the essence of the orthodox *qualitative tests*, but which, due to the lack of co-ordination between them, did not always help to determine the demand for credit realistically. Furthermore, the move may be interpreted as the beginning[1] of official recognition of the fact that financial restrictions were impotent in an economic system where the availability of finance had little or no influence on real processes in enterprises, or, in other words, where the amount of finance was demand determined rather than demand determining.

It may be noted that the new monetary policy permitted a closer integration of the control of wage payments and other forms of bank control, though wage control still remained a separate control system relying on its specific sanctions. Important changes in this control were introduced in the early 1960s in three enactments,[2] the most significant being the law of 21 December 1963, which attempted to transfer some of the burden of wage control to associations and to stop automatic expansion of wage funds following overfulfilment of output targets (see note 2 p. 211). The law referred to the enterprises (numbering about 1600 and producing approximately 50% of the total output in socialised industry) in key industries, laying down that 'justifications' for wage over-payments and 'corrections' of wage funds were primarily the responsibility of associations, which had to cover the overpayments from special reserve funds. Banks in this respect were to signal

[1] As will be seen later, credit liberalisation was by no means complete.

[2] 2 June 1960 (*MP* 54 (1960) item 257); 27 March 1962 (*MP* 29 (1962) item 123); 21 December 1963 (*MP* 4 (1964) item 15).

the overpayments, making certain that associations obeyed the relevant regulations. Thus after 1963 there existed two systems of wage control: the above mentioned one and bank control, where, as before, banks were engaged in justifications of overpayments and corrections (quite automatic in the case of plan overfulfilment). In both cases unjustified overpayments carried a penalty, in terms of suspension or reduction of bonus payments for office workers.[1] In general, in deciding their attitude to a particular enterprise banks took into account its overall performance, including the management of wages. Furthermore the laws of 27 March 1962 and 21 December 1963 allowed the banks to use credit sanctions (e.g. higher interest rates) against clients showing serious mismanagement of wage funds, in addition to the normal sanctions prescribed by regulations concerning wage control, which the banks had to follow passively, having no right of discretionary action.[2]

Though the supply of credit was not now regarded as an important instrument of control, enterprises were still required to work out their quarterly credit needs, which helped banks to set credit limits. As will be shown later, banks were not always ready to extend credit above these limits, so that the lenient credit control was not a policy of unrestricted credit.

It is important to realise that the lenient monetary policy was not the same thing as the easy credit conditions sometimes practised in the West. It was not intended to raise aggregate spending in the economy, but amounted merely to a change in the technique of microeconomic control by banks over enterprises. As is shown later, the policy was combined with the use of higher interest charges, an unusual combination in the context of a market economy, but not totally devoid of rationale in socialist planning.

[1] Wage overpayments still presented a problem (see e.g. budget speeches, *Finanse* 1 (1962) pp. 2–3; 1 (1964) p. 4). Control of wage payments by associations resulted in a smaller amount of overpayment than direct bank control. For information on wage control see H. Holdys, 'Zasady Bankowej Kontroli Funduszu Płac', *Finanse* 1 (1961); Jaworski, *Obieg...*, pp. 88–92, *Bankowość w Gospodarce Socjalistycznej* (1967) pp. 105–8; Blass, 'Problemy...', pp. 1–12; B. Fick, 'Nowy System Kontroli Funduszu Płac', *ŻG* 2 (1965) pp. 1 and 9, 'System Kontroli Funduszu Płac', *ŻG* 18 (1969) p. 7.

[2] The use of higher interest rates against enterprises mismanaging their wage funds was never automatic and in practice applied in only a few cases where very serious faults occurred.

(b) The structure of credit

The remainder of this section probes deeper into the nature and consequences of the lenient monetary policy. Data given in tables below broadly indicate the effect on the structure of credit. Tables 49a and b suggest that it was in general easier to obtain credit on stocks; the proportion of credit on stocks to total credit to industrial enterprises increased from 54.3% in 1960 to 59.8% in 1961, rising further in subsequent years (see table 49b). Some of this rise (especially between 1962 and 1963) was due to the compulsory partial coverage of normative working capital by credit, mentioned earlier. After 1962 the supply of normative credit in industry was relatively stable (see table 49c) and the rise in credit on stocks was largely due to expansion in above-normative credit. As already observed, this credit could now be used to finance incorrect stocks. This factor contributed to the expansion of credit on stocks, though its precise contribution is difficult to evaluate, because of the lack of data.[1]

Credit on settlements behaved erratically (see tables 49a, b and c), which is to be expected for this type of credit. Its ratio to total short-term credit fell over time. Table 50 shows that in fact enterprises received steadily less credit in relation to their trade debts. Thus, as regards settlements, the lenient credit policy did not appear to be very liberal; there was no indication of automatic finance of trade debts. The main reason for utilising less credit on settlements was the relaxation of credit on stocks (viz. normative and especially above-normative credit). Easier credit on stocks raised the excess liquidity (see pp. 207–8) of enterprises, thus lowering their demand for credit on settlements.[2] Largely for the same reason there was a sharp fall in overdue credit (table 49c).

An important role in the lenient monetary control was to be played by payments credit, which was granted in exceptional cases from 1958 onwards (see p. 194). In the new approach to credit finance this credit was designed to help enterprises overcome

---

[1] In key industries between 1961 and 1963 incorrect stocks amounted to 21.7%, 22.9% and 22.2% respectively of above-normative working capital. In these three years credit financed 78.9%, 88.2% and 91.8% of above-normative working capital. Szczepański, *Finansowanie...*, p. 289.

[2] *Ibid.* pp. 301 and 305.

Table 49a

Short-term credit to socialised enterprises 1961–5

(*Balances at the end of the year : a, mil. zł. ; b, percentages of total*)

Year	Total a	Credit on stocks a	b	On settlements a	b	Other credit a	b
1961	134,717	97,366	72.3	31,616	23.5	5,735	4.3
1962	144,664	112,282	77.6	30,319	21.0	2,063	1.4
1963	183,442	145,391	79.3	34,515	18.8	3,536	1.9
1964	195,325	154,913	79.3	35,422	18.1	4,990	2.5
1965	211,534	171,812	81.2	35,102	16.7	4,620	2.2

Source: GUS – *RSF 1945–1967*, p. 167.

Table 49b

Short-term credit to socialised enterprises in industry 1961–5

(*a, mil. zł. ; b, percentages of total*)

Year	Total a	Credit on stocks a	b	On settlements a	b	Other credit a	b
1961	57,049	34,135	59.8	21,382	37.5	1,532	2.7
1962	59,804	40,024	66.9	18,536	31.0	1,244	2.1
1963	84,946	62,856	74.0	20,373	24.0	1,717	2.0
1964	86,488	64,058	74.1	20,711	24.0	1,719	2.0
1965	92,381	71,731	77.6	18,903	20.5	1,747	1.9

Source: GUS – *RSF 1945–1967*, p. 168.

short-term difficulties in payments. In a letter written to banks on 23 December 1962 the Chairman of the NBP requested that the banks be lenient in giving credit, in particular payments credit, in order to lessen temporary difficulties of settlements. Up to the end of the first quarter of 1963 it was not made clear how payments credit was to function and banks were uncertain how to operate it,[1]

[1] For more information see R. Michejda, 'O Ewolucji Organizacji i Kontrolnej Funkcji Kredytu', *WNBP* 8 (1963) p. 312; M. Znaniecki, 'Funkcjonowanie Kredytu Płatniczego', *WNBP* 1 (1964); Pruss, 'Zmienność . . .; M. Rajczyk, 'Kredyt Płatniczy na Pokrycie Przejściowych Trudności Płatniczych – w Teorii i w Praktyce', *WNBP* 8 (1966), p. 315.

Table 49c

The structure of short-term credit granted to socialised enterprises in industry 1961–5

(*Balances at the end of the year ; a, mil. zł. ; b, percentages of total*)[1]

Year	Normative a	Normative b	Above normative a	Above normative b	On settlements a	On settlements b	Payments credit a	Payments credit b	Overdue a	Overdue b	Others a	Others b
1961	9,214	16.1	24,921	43.7	21,382	37.5	26	0.0	1,374	2.4	132	0.2
1962	11,240	18.8	28,784	48.1	18,536	31.0	190	0.3	610	1.0	444	0.7
1963	29,017	34.2	33,839	39.8	20,373	24.0	612	0.7	323	0.4	782	0.9
1964	28,300	32.7	35,758	41.3	20,711	23.9	946	1.1	226	0.3	547	0.6
1965	30,075	32.6	41,656	45.1	18,903	20.5	866	0.9	159	0.2	722	0.8

Note :

[1] Total given in tables 48b and 49b.
Source: Data supplied by the NBP.

Table 50

Percentage ratio of credit on settlements to total trade debts[1] in the socialised sector 1961–5

(*Balances at the end of the year*)

Year	All enterprises	Industrial enterprises
1961	36.8	50.8
1962	34.0	43.1
1963	33.8	41.0
1964	32.3	40.8
1965	29.8	35.3

Note :

[1] Debts outstanding to suppliers.
Source: GUS – *RSF 1945–1967*, pp. 167 and 168.

but more information was given in a circular of the Planning Department of the NBP issued on 30 March 1963, laying down that the credit might be claimed at any time for any type of temporary payment difficulties. It was granted for short periods of 10 to 15 days, after which time it was compulsorily repaid. If after that period an enterprise continued to have unpaid obligations, then its payments difficulties were regarded not as temporary but as permanent and the enterprise was encouraged to review its estimates for other types of credit, or possibly to improve its management. Indeed, one of the key problems in giving payments credit was to decide whether an enterprise had a temporary or a more permanent financial difficulty. If payments difficulties were not considered temporary, banks did not as a rule grant the credit, but took some other action. There was, however, no possibility of extending the credit to finance persistent deficits. As is shown later, a controversy developed about whether banks extended the credit liberally enough. At this stage it may be observed that although the rate of growth of this kind of credit was very dynamic,[1] its balance was small (table 49c) compared with total credit and credit on settlements.

In conclusion, the data in this section suggest that the lenient monetary policy manifested itself mainly through more liberal credit on stocks and payments, the former being quantitatively the more significant.

Before further discussing the new Polish monetary policy, a digression on contemporary developments in the Soviet Union may be of interest. Unfortunately the lack of readily available data and the rather sketchy nature of other Soviet information on the subject permit only a vague account.

There are indications that some relaxation of credit occurred, beginning in the late fifties. Between 1958 and 1964 it worked mainly by granting credit in the course of 'decentralised settlements' and in the course of the application of the principle of differentiation. Data in tables D1 and D2 suggest, however, that the crediting was somewhat erratic, not revealing a stable pattern. After 1964 there was a more decided movement towards more liberal crediting. In December 1963 banks were allowed to grant credit (up to 30 days) to ease the payments problems of firms and the September 1965 plenary session of the CC urged not only the extension of credit finance but also a more liberal credit policy.[2]

Total credit after 1964 expanded at a high rate relative to the rate in the early 1960s, credit on stocks, in particular, showing a high rate of growth, in spite of the fact that on the average the growth of total working capital was faster than the growth of the

---

[1] Taking 1962 as 100, the index of expansion of this credit was 322 in 1963, 498 in 1964, 456 in 1965, 554 in 1966, 1040 in 1967 and 800 in 1968.

[2] See e.g. Vorob'ev, pp. 113–15; H. D. Barkovskii, *Organizatsiya i Planirovanie Kredita* (1968) pp. 80–90; Bogachevskii, pp. 55–9; 210–12.

share of stocks in working capital (table D1). This may be explained by the extension of credit finance (replacing 'own funds') of non-seasonal working capital and by a more liberal granting of credit on stocks in general, especially to well-managed enterprises.[1] There was an increase in credit 'on turnover', which was not subject to limits but was estimated in plans in terms of 'control figures'. Banks were not strict with firms whose credit balances surpassed the figures – a not uncommon occurrence.[2] Credit could also be obtained specifically to ease payments carried out by setting off debts. These reached their peak between 1956 and 1958, when they accounted for over 46% of all settlements. The ratio then declined to 42.9% in 1964, falling to a little over 30% after 1965.[3]

(c) The impact of lenient monetary control on the accumulation of trade debts

Lenient credit policy was a negative policy in the sense that it was brought in primarily to stop the accumulation of overdue trade credit which occurred during the stringent monetary policy and which was made possible by the weakness of 'mutual control', viz. by the failure of the supplier to exert pressure on his customer to pay his debts promptly. This departure from the stringent monetary control may indeed be interpreted as a recognition by the authorities that the consequences of the failure of enterprises to settle trade debts were not severe enough to deter them from

[1] Also the credit totals on the basis of which table D1 was compiled include short and medium-term credit on 'quick-yield' investment projects. The amount of such credit was very small but growing (esp. after 1955), reaching over 3% of total credit in 1967 (TsSU –NKh v 1967, p. 892).

[2] This credit was usually granted 'on special loan accounts' and its expansion in the 1960s was calculated partly to ensure uninterrupted payments. See e.g. M. Pessel' and I. Shraiber, 'Nazrevshie Voprosy Kreditovaniya i Raschotov', DiK 5 (1963), p. 25.

[3] Vorob'ev, p. 129, Barkovskii, p. 65; Zakharov, 'O. Beznalichnykh Raschotakh', DiK 5 (1970) p. 38 gives an interesting table, classifying settlements by sources of payment, which shows the role of credit increasing and a falling off of settling by clearing debts and from own funds (in percentages, balances at the end of September).

	1965	1966	1967	1968
Credit	41.6	42.8	43.3	49.0
Own funds	47.7	46.9	46.5	41.6
Clearing account	10.7	10.3	10.2	9.2

Table 51

Trade credit in industry (balances at the end of the year)

(*a. mil. zł.* ; *b, percentages of respective totals*)

	1961		1962		1963		1964		1965	
	a	*b*	*a*	*b*	*a*	*b*	*a*	*b*	*a*	*b*
Industry										
Total	16.6	100.0	15.3	100.0	15.2	100.0	16.4	100.0	18.2	100.0
Overdue	9.3[1]	55.8	7.0[1]	46.0	4.0	26.4	2.9	17.9	1.8	9.7
Key industries:										
Total	14.4	100.0	12.8	100.0	12.9	100.0	–	–	–	–
Overdue	3.8	26.4	5.1	39.8	3.2	24.8	–	–	–	–

Note:

[1] In 1961 and 1962 all *non-inkaso liabilities* (*zobowiazania pozainkasowe*) were counted as overdue trade credit. This somewhat overstated overdue indebtedness and made the figures not strictly comparable with the other years.

Source: Data supplied by the NBP; J. Szczepański, *Finansowanie Srodków Obrotowych,* p. 303.

the practice and could not be made sufficiently serious to discourage the accumulation of illicit finance during a credit squeeze. Our main concern here is to assess the extent to which easier bank credit did assist the payments situation. Other changes and their effects are considered later.

Data in tables 51 and 52 suggest that the lenient monetary control did have a significant impact on the overdue indebtedness of industrial enterprises. Table 51 shows that the ratio of overdue trade credit to total trade credit fell continuously and by a substantial amount. A comparison with table 41a makes the point even more *vivid* Thus between 1960 and 1965 the ratio fell from 51.5% to 9.7%.[1] Tables 48b and 52 show that overdue trade credit financed a

[1] 1960 rather than 1961 is chosen for comparison, for reasons obvious from table 51. In key industries the ratio fell from 49.6% in 1960 to 24.8% in 1963. No data were obtained for 1964 and 1965. A rise in the ratio in 1962 (table 51) is explained by failure to fulfil plans for accumulation in key industries. Liberalisation of stringent monetary policy in 1961 had a significant impact on key industries. Szczepański, *Finansowanie...*, p. 303. The ratio of overdue trade debts (viz. sums owed to enterprises) to total trade debts in industrial enterprises did not perform as impressively. Between 1960 and 1965 it fell from 30.7% to 17.2%. Data supplied by the NBP.

Table 52

Overdue indebtedness of industrial enterprises in the socialised sector 1961–5

(*Balances at the end of the year*)

	1961	1962	1963	1964	1965
(*a*) Overdue trade credit (mil. zł.)	9,263[1]	7,044[1]	4,025	2,943	1,766
(*b*) Overdue bank credit (mil. zł.)	1,374	610	323	226	159
(*c*) $a + b$	10,637	7,654	4,348	3,169	1,925
(*d*) $\dfrac{a}{a+b} \times 100$[2]	87.1	92.0	92.6	92.9	91.7

Notes:

[1] Inclusive of *non-inkaso liabilities* (see table 51).

[2] The ratio in the key industries was 74.5% in 1961, 91.1% in 1962 and 94.1% in 1963. Szczepański, *Finansowanie...*, p. 304.

Source: Data supplied by the NBP.

declining proportion of working capital,[1] and its ratio to total short-term credit in industrial enterprises fell continuously from 16.9% in 1960 to 16.2% in 1961, 11.8% in 1962, 4.7% in 1963, 3.4% in 1964 and 2.0% in 1965. Tables 49c and 52 also show a remarkable improvement in overdue bank credit, whose ratio to total short-term credit fell from 4.7% in 1960 to 0.2% in 1965. Indeed an examination of table 52 suggests that enterprises were much keener to repay bank credit promptly than to settle overdue trade obligations. This propensity was stronger now than it was in the five years of stringent monetary control (compare table 52 with table 42 on p. 220).[2]

Thus, though lenient monetary policy resulted in a significant reduction in overdue trade and bank indebtedness, it did not eliminate overdue trade indebtedness completely. Overdue trade credit was still a problem, albeit reduced to bearable dimensions, implying that the policy did not achieve a full liberalisation of credit, which would have led to a complete substitution of bank credit for trade

[1] In industrial enterprises 5.1% in 1960, 5.4% in 1961, 3.9% in 1962, 1.9% in 1963, 1.4% in 1964 and 0.8% in 1965. Note 4 on p. 220; table 48b; data supplied by the NBP.

[2] It must be remembered that a compulsory order of payments no longer applied (see p. 196).

credit. Often enterprises which were not refused credit by their banks had overdue non-bank obligations, in spite of the fact that trade credit, when overdue, was subject to penalty interest.[1] One explanation of this was that enterprises which had used up their credit limits had to apply for extra credit, thus submitting themselves to bank control.[2] Jaworski claimed that enterprises sometimes preferred overdue trade credit to bank credit, because their suppliers might not claim penalty rates (or not charge full penalty rates) and because it was a way of avoiding bank control.[3] Sometimes banks had to encourage enterprises to make extra requests for credit. A controversy on how liberal or lenient the credit policy should be in a socialist economy is discussed in a separate section.

It may be more interesting to observe that in the Soviet Union too the more liberal approach to credit, mentioned earlier, is often approvingly given as a reason for the decline of trade credit finance.[4] Table D2 shows that, in general, the expansion of bank credit as a source of finance of working capital coincided with the fall in trade credit, though the reductions were not large; this suggests that payments difficulties still continued but were less serious than before.

(d) The nature of bank control and its effectiveness

Action through the cost of credit. It was noted that the stringent monetary control of the 1950s was mainly based on restrictions on the quantity of credit, to the neglect of the cost of credit. In the late 1950s interest charges were raised and their more active use was widely advocated in the discussion on the 'economic model'; nevertheless interest rates as a weapon of control played a role subsidiary to that of the quantity of credit. In the new approach to monetary control interest rates began to gain prominence as an instrument with which banks could usefully affect the management

---

[1] A study conducted in a branch of the NBP revealed that 25 out of 28 enterprises controlled by the branch had overdue debts in 1964, in spite of the fact that the bank had never refused their requests for more credit.

[2] Viz. credit was granted more liberally than before but there was no automatic expansion of credit to cover the needs of enterprises.

[3] W. Jaworski, 'Kryterium Płynności a Oddziaływanie Banku na Przedsiębiorstwa', *WNBP* 7 (1967) p. 282.

[4] Vorob'ev, p. 109; E. Mitel'man, 'Razvitie Printsipov Pryamogo Bankovskogo Kreditovaniya', *DiK* 5 (1970) pp. 22–3.

of enterprises. Thus, the lenient monetary control was gradually becoming a dearer credit control.

The relevant legal provisions are not very helpful in assessing the role of interest rates. Legislation on interest charged by banks, certainly from 1958 onwards, quite specifically allowed banks the discretion to charge differentiated rates within certain limits or up to a maximum limit.[1] This power was confirmed in resolution 347 of the CM, passed on 8 November 1962[2] permitting banks to grant credit at preferential rates or penal rates up to a limit of 10%. In this context we must distinguish clearly between two types of rates which may both be described as penalty rates. First, there were penal rates associated with the appearance of a particular incorrect debt, for example overdue debt (either to the bank or to the supplier). Such penalty rates applied before 1961 and continued to operate during the lenient monetary policy. Secondly, there were what, in order to distinguish them from the above-mentioned penalty rates, we shall call higher rates. Banks could use interest rates more flexibly than before, depending on their evaluation of the management of enterprises. Thus they could apply the principle of differentiation by charging well-managed enterprises lower rates than normal (in general 4% on short-term credit and 3% on investment credit) or by charging badly-run enterprises higher rates than normal. Thus higher interest rates could be imposed on all credit granted to an enterprise and their imposition was at the discretion of the bank. During the lenient monetary policy these discretionary higher interest rates became more important.

With regard to the actual development and organisation of the more flexible interest rate policy, though its legal foundations were laid in the late 1950s it was not until the early 1960s that the banks received encouragement to make more active use of this weapon. Quantitative information concerning its actual implementation is scarce. The Chairman of the NBP revealed that in the last quarter of 1962 higher rates were imposed on 623 enterprises and in the corresponding quarter of 1963 on 751. In these periods the sum

[1] MP 42 (1958) item 239; MP 48 (1958) item 283; MP 5 (1960) item 21; MP 12 (1960) item 55.

[2] 'On interest rates on credit granted by state banks...,' MP 84 (1962) item 391, with more detailed provisions in an order of the Minister of Finance of 12 December 1962, MP 89 (1962) item 418. Moreover an order of the President of the NBP of 31 January 1963 empowered banks to threaten higher interest rates so as to mobilise enterprises to put right their shortcomings. Michejda, 'O Ewolucji ...,' p. 312.

of credit subject to higher rates was 9.8 and 14 billion złoty. In 1963 higher interest charges were used in respect of 9.3% of all enterprises and 11.7% of all credit granted.[1]

In theory, higher rates were to encourage more efficient financial management in enterprises by acting on profits – either directly or through costs. We may reflect that action through the quantity of credit (for example a credit squeeze) also basically acts on profits. Shortages of funds in a socialist economy were likely to lead not to insolvency in the Western sense, but to an accumulation of overdue debts and to penalty interest on them. Action through higher interest rates could, however, be preferable to action through a credit squeeze, because it might not lead to blockages of payments on the scale usually produced by a reduction in the supply of credit. Finally, it must be remembered that the effectiveness of any action on profits rests on the assumption that enterprises are *de facto* sensitive to such actions.

In 1963, in order to strengthen the effectiveness of higher interest rates (and penalties for overdue credit), they came to be regarded as 'extraordinary losses' (*straty nadzwyczajne*) chargeable directly on profits.[2] Banks could, however, also give rebates (*bonifikaty*) on higher interest rates when enterprises responded positively to bank actions rectifying their shortcomings. Thus the rebates became a reward, although banks sometimes paid them in order to correct an unjustifiably high increase in interest charges.[3]

Other methods of control. In addition to interest rates, banks used 'administrative methods' of control, such as direct interventions in the management of enterprises, inspections and reporting to superior organs. With less weight attached to control by the supply of credit greater emphasis was put on these measures. A survey by the WNBP on bank control over the financial management of enterprises[4] revealed that banks tended in the first place to use

---

[1] A. Żebrowski, 'Dwadzieścia...', p. 216. In a different context Żebrowski suggested that in 1963 higher interest rates were imposed on 20% more enterprises and that the amount of credit subject to increased charges rose by 44% (as no base year is specifically given it is assumed that the rises refer to periods between 1962 and 1963) *WNBP* 6 (1964) p. 178.   [2] Hitherto interest charges were a part of costs.

[3] T. Sawicz, 'O Oddziaływaniu Kredytowym', *WNBP* 5 (1967) p. 188.

[4] Forty-one branches (viz. approximately 10% of all branches) returned questionnaires addressed to directors of branches of the NBP. See W. Kiezuń, 'Oddziaływanie Banku na Sytuacje Gospodarczą i Finansową Przedsiębiorstw', *WNBP* 5 (1965) pp. 145–9.

administrative means of control, such as 'letters of intervention' addressed to an enterprise, or to its director, or to the director with a copy to a superior organ, or to superior organs (association, party committees, national councils or control bodies such as the Supreme Chamber of Control) and conferences with the management of an enterprise.[1] The survey showed that 38 banks (out of 41) used interventions as a method of control, 33 regarding this form of action as one of the first steps to be taken. Thirty-three banks intervened by reporting enterprises to their superior organ.[2] It is interesting to observe that 29 banks intervened by reporting to a local Party committee, 7 regarding this action of primary importance. It appears that in practice there was a definite order in which various forms of direct control or intervention were used. Bank action usually started with talks with enterprises and only after that were the administrative means mentioned above resorted to. A disadvantage in using these was that they were largely *ex post* measures. Considerable time often elapsed from the time of the discovery by banks of shortcomings in the management of enterprises to the time of actual implementation of an intervention. Thus sometimes interventions were proceeded with even when enterprises had eliminated the causes of shortcomings.[3]

According to the survey, economic methods (interest rates and credit restrictions) were used only after it became clear that administrative measures would not be effective. The most popular economic measures were higher interest rates. These were used by 39 banks and 35 regarded them as a primary economic method of control. Credit restrictions were imposed by 21 branches, but only 2 thought them of primary importance, which confirms the general strategy of the lenient monetary control discussed earlier.

The impact on stocks. In attempting to assess the effectiveness of bank control during the lenient monetary policy it must be reiterated

---

[1] There were many variations on the methods of intervention mentioned.

[2] It may be noted that bank directors were in close contact with political organisations. This is one of the interesting points emerging from a comprehensive study of the work of bank directors conducted by W. Kiezuń (*Dyrektor*, 1968). Bank directors often held important posts in local Party organisations (see esp. pp. 270–7). They spent between 9% and 12% of their working time in contacts with national councils and local Party committees and about 1% with a central Party organ (p. 108).

[3] E. Bautro, 'Niedociągnięcia w Organizacji Działalności Kredytowej Oddziałów Operacyjnych', *WNBP* 12 (1967) pp. 517–18. R. Napiórkowski, 'Pozaekonomiczne Srodki Oddziaływania NBP', *WNBP* 1 (1968) p. 15.

Table 53

The rise in stocks and reserves in the national economy 1961–5

(bil. zł. at current market prices)

Year	(i) Planned rise	(ii) Actual rise	(iii) (ii) − (i)	(iv) $\frac{\text{(ii)} \times 100}{\text{(i)}}$
1961	17.0	32.9	15.9	193.5
1962	23.4	21.5	−1.9	91.9
1963	18.1	34.9	15.9	187.8
1964	24.4	36.0	11.6	147.6
1965	29.1	44.5	15.4	152.9

Source: Osiecki, 'Przyrost...', *GP* 6 (1967) p. 17. Compare with table 38.

that the relaxation of credit restrictions was effective in significantly reducing the level of overdue trade credit. The main question which one would wish to examine now is the extent to which the new strategy of bank control, based on higher interest charges and administrative measures, helped to foster greater efficiency in enterprises. Banks continued to exercise 'planning control' and 'management control' (terms explained on pp. 47–8) and to be particularly interested in the stock management of enterprises.

Stock control is a very complex problem already touched on in previous chapters, where it was noticed that examination of the behaviour of stocks told us little about the effectiveness of bank control in this sphere. Stocks remained a problem for economic planners. As before, the share of the rise of stocks in national income fluctuated, being 8.1% in 1961, 5.1% in 1962, 7.3% in 1963, 7.5% in 1964 and 8.3% in 1965.[1] In general it was considered that the ratio was too high. In industry the rate of increase in stock accumulation was higher than the rate of increase in production. Although in some circumstances such behaviour could be justified, it was thought that the gap between the two rates of growth was too high and that the rate of increase in stocks should have been lower.[2]

---

[1] GUS – *RS 1968*, p. 78. Values at 1961 prices. The low ratio in 1962 was caused by bad climatic conditions reducing stocks in agriculture and disorganising transport, leading to a dangerous fall in stocks of fuel and raw materials in industry.

[2] Osiecki, pp. 18–19. The author concluded that stock formation in Poland compared favourably with that in other socialist countries, but unfavourably with that in advanced capitalist economies.

A comparison of table 53 and table 38 shows that there continued to be a wide gap between the planned rise in stocks and the actual rise (except in 1962 – see note 1 on p. 264) mainly for the same reasons as in previous periods. Excessive rises in stocks and the existence of superfluous or incorrect stocks continued to present a problem, but there was a slight improvement in this area in the 1960s. For instance, the percentage ratio of incorrect[1] stocks to total stocks in socialised industry was 6.7 in 1961, 6.1 in 1962, 6.5 in 1963 and 5.2 in 1964.[2] The fall in the ratio which occurred in 1964 was in the main caused by the special action to reduce incorrect stocks (see p. 249) and the creation of special institutions ('stocks exchanges') designed to eliminate them.[3]

Economists writing on the problem of stock formation continued to emphasise that stocks were a variable dependent on many factors, but mainly on those beyond the scope of direct bank control.[4] In the early 1960s studies of the causes of incorrect stocks in heavy, chemical and light industries revealed that among the most common causes were changes in plans, resulting in limitation, delay or cessation of production, other changes in plans and non-fulfilment of plans, technological difficulties in starting new production and inadequate organisation of the supply of raw materials.[5] Trendota

[1] Incorrect stocks in the contemporary nomenclature included 'unnecessary stocks' (viz. stocks not needed to fulfil planned tasks) and 'superfluous stocks' (viz. stocks in excess of the 'economically justified' level). According to L. Siemiątkowski, the future Chairman of the NBP, these stocks did not necessarily include all stocks which were actually incorrect; see 'Ekonomiczne Problemy Bankowej Klasyfikacji Zapasów', *WNBP* 9 (1965) pp. 290–2.

[2] T. Choliński, 'Aktualne Problemy Upłynnienia Zapasów Zbędnych i Nadmiernych', *WNBP* 8 (1965) p. 268; M. Osiecki, 'Zapasy Gospodarczo Nieuzasadnione w Latach 1962–1964', *WNBP* 9 (1965) p. 310.

[3] Specialised institutions for clearing incorrect stocks were set up and in 1964 were centralised in the Common Council, which was to initiate and co-ordinate actions to eliminate incorrect stocks. For further information see Choliński, 'Aktualne...', pp. 268–70, 'Zagospodarowywanie Zapasów Nieprawidłowych – Problem Nadal Istotny', *WNBP* 4 (1968), pp. 152–4.

[4] See e.g. Z. Fedorowicz, 'Normatywy, Zapasy, Inwestycje Przedsiębiorstw,' *Finanse* 3 (1965) p. 2; L. Szyszko, 'Cele i Metody Polityki Kredytowania', *Finanse* 12 (1965) pp. 3–5. Szyszko concluded that 'The formation of stocks depends chiefly on matters which lie beyond the sphere of functioning of credit.'

[5] For more details see Osiecki, 'Zapasy...', pp. 311–12; Choliński, 'Zagospodarowywanie...', pp. 151–2. Gluck ('Działalność...', p. 25) stated that in 1963 in heavy industry 42.6% of superfluous stocks were caused by changes in plans, 22% by difficulties connected with new methods of production, 11.6% by mistakes in deliveries and 4.6% by cancellations of orders.

of the Ministry of Finance did, however, blame the ease with which above-normative credit could be obtained for excessive stock accumulation, although he did not elaborate the point.[1]

Our conclusion on the effect of bank control over stocks in enterprises is the same as that reached in the previous chapter. There were no definite signs that the control was effective, but on the other hand it is difficult to say to what extent the stock position would have been worse had there been no bank control over that aspect of management.

The general impact of bank control. An assessment of the effectiveness of bank control over the general financial management of enterprises again presents many problems. It must be remembered that enterprises continued to be subjected to 'controls' other than that of their banks and laid greater emphasis on the fulfilment of targets such as output, rather than on financial targets (e.g. profit) or on financial matters such as the maintenance of payments discipline. Directors of enterprises, for instance, were rarely personally engaged in financial management, preferring to delegate this function to their subordinates (heads of accounting and finance sections).[2] Misiak suggested that enterprises were interested only in the fulfilment of plans in physical terms, regarding financial management as mere 'bookkeeping matters'.[3] A search for a systematic study of the effectiveness of bank control proved fruitless. During the lenient monetary policy evaluation of bank control became more difficult than before, because banks no longer had a uniform approach to control. Different banks (viz. different branches of the NBP) used different criteria in assessing the work of enterprises and different methods of action, which could yield different effects on enterprises. Bearing this in mind let us synthesise some, albeit rather scattered, information on the subject.

There were no indications that bank control significantly improved the management of enterprises. There were some comments to the effect that banks could not successfully carry out the kind of control whose scope was very wide, embracing practically every aspect of

[1] J. Trendota, 'IV Plenum KC PZPR i Zadania Aparatu Finansowego', *Finanse* 10 (1965) p. 7.

[2] Z. Grzybowski, 'Współpraca Oddziału NBP z Przedsiębiorstwem Przemysłowym' *WNBP* 3 (1962) p. 129.

[3] M. Misiak, 'Naczynia Niepołączone', *ŻG* 38 (1964) p. 1.

management.[1] Grzybowski believed that the time at the disposal of bankers permitted only a superficial analysis of the business of enterprises; too superficial for effective control.[2] Bankers (mainly credit inspectors) themselves believed that they were not able (given that they had to control more than one enterprise, spending on the average seventy-five days a year on each) to get to grips with the crucial problem of costs and their analysis in enterprises under their control.[3] As mentioned earlier, during the lenient monetary policy banks received more autonomy in choosing the methods of control. It thus became very important to base control on a sound knowledge of enterprises' business, but, as will be shown later, decisions of banks were often arbitrary.

The survey, mentioned on page 262, did not reveal anything specific on the effectiveness of bank control. Reporting results of the survey Kiezuń commented that 'the determination of a direct causal connection between bank action and economic efficiency of an enterprise is extremely difficult and often completely impossible'. Agreeing with this, Napiórkowski suggested that an enterprise was simultaneously subjected to various stimuli by various institutions (banks, superior organs, Party cells, national councils). 'Some stimuli act in a parallel way, but others cross. To deduce what is the result of what, is not easy.'[4] Nevertheless, some banks did offer quantitative indications (in terms of, for example, sales of unwanted stocks, or a fall in overdue trade indebtedness) of the efficiency of their action. Thus, clearly, in some cases, bank control was effective, but these cases are hardly sufficient to make a generalisation on the effectiveness of bank control.

As regards the effectiveness of methods of control over enterprises, some banks regarded administrative means as most effective – others economic means. However, on balance the economic methods were

[1] Napiórkowski claimed that there was a 'dispersion of attention on the part of both the controller and the controlled' which prevented the control from attaining positive results. 'Pozaekonomiczne...', p. 15.

[2] Grzybowski, p. 30 et seq. The author included investment control in his discussion. He thought that bank control was ineffective also because enterprises were not sufficiently interested in financial matters and often did not even know the regulations concerning credit and investment finance.

[3] M. Misiak, 'Bankowcy o Analizie Kosztów', ŻG 50 (1964) p. 6. The article is a summary of views expressed by bankers at a conference on the analysis of costs.

[4] R. Napiórkowski, 'Niektore Aspekty Kredytowego Oddziaływania Banku', WNBP 9 (1966) p. 365.

considered to be most effective.[1] Perhaps the most interesting finding of the survey was that banks showed considerable autonomy and initiative in devising forms of action against enterprises, many of them using quite original combinations of control measures.

Official statements on bank control usually explicitly or implicitly expressed confidence in the efficacy of the control. During the lenient credit policy this was especially evident in connection with the use of interest rates as a weapon of control. Żebrowski, for instance, considered that the use of higher interest charges in 1962 and a wider use of 'interventional action', independent of credit, were a marked success.[2] Albrecht, the Minister of Finance, encouraged further use of interest rates, claiming that their effectiveness was enhanced by regarding them as 'extraordinary losses' (see p. 262).[3]

There were, however, a number of pronouncements in economic publications suggesting that the impact of bank control on the efficiency of management of enterprises was very limited. One author argued that the central authorities' view, attributing effectiveness to bank control, was in fact incorrect.[4] Misiak was also sceptical about the potency of bank control and indeed the whole financial 'control' of enterprises. He maintained that higher interest charges on credit had very little impact on the profits of enterprises – they were not widely imposed, but were confined to a small group of enterprises.[5] Though banks could still use credit restrictions, they rarely did so for fear of a conflict with the enterprise and very often with an association, ministry or local authority. They imposed restrictions more readily against enterprises which were small, of local importance or co-operative.[6] Misiak thought that the basic reason for the

[1] Economic methods (especially interest rates) were thought to be most effective by fifteen branches, twelve chose administrative measures and eleven mixed administrative and economic. Three did not specify.

[2] 'Zadania...', pp. 2–3.   [3] Albrecht, p. 3.

[4] E. Bożyczko, 'Nadrzędna Jednostka czy Równorzędny Partner', ŻG 15 (1963) p. 6. This was one of the articles in a debate on 'the bank and the enterprise' discussed below.

[5] An empirical test on the effectiveness of interest rates was not carried out until 1966, revealing a very limited effect of interest charges on the profitability of enterprises covered by a survey. See H. Błaszak, 'Oprocentowanie Kredytu Jako Srodek Oddziaływania na Gospodarkę Przedsiębiorstw, WNBP 4 (1968) pp. 142–50.

[6] No data for the period 1961–5 were found to confirm this point. However, a later study (1966) based on a small sample survey showed that enterprises in key industries were subjected to sanctions less frequently than other enterprises. M. Boruń, 'Oddziaływanie Banku na Jednostki Gospodarki Narodowej', WNBP 1 (1967) pp. 30–1.

ineffectiveness of bank control was the general weakness of financial instruments in economic management. 'There is but a minimal connection between credit, interest rates and other conditions of credit finance and the fundamental, material stimuli: wages, bonuses and prizes.'[1] His main thesis was summed up in the title of his article – 'Unconnected vessels'; one vessel being the production of output, on which remuneration depended and to which enterprises attached primary importance, the other being financial arrangements, which were neglected by enterprises. Insufficient links between the two rendered financial action on efficiency impotent.

Some argued that instead of leading to improvements in management, bank sanctions frequently led to changes in staff. 'Often, however, the application of increased pressure on an enterprise ends, not with the elimination of causes which had led to credit restrictions, but with a change in the personnel of financial management.'[2]

Strained bank-enterprise relations. The implementation of the lenient monetary control resulted in what may probably be described as an undesirable effect – certainly undesirable if the need for greater autonomy in enterprises is accepted as a reasonable postulate. It has already been observed that banks received more autonomy in choosing their control measures and tended to substitute direct methods of control for control through the quantity of credit. A consequence of this was, to use expressions of contemporary economic debate, a rise in the 'control function' of banks and a contraction in their 'service function' (viz. giving advice or a service at the request of an enterprise). This inspired a debate on the bank-enterprise relationship, which was unique in the sense that, whereas hitherto monetary debates were the province of bankers and academics, in this particular debate representatives of enterprises were key contributors.

The debate, mainly in *ŻG*, revealed a strained relationship between banks and their clients. The representatives of enterprises, drawing mainly on their actual experience of bank control, made two main points: (*a*) banks had an excessively authoritarian attitude towards enterprises and (*b*) they applied their coercive measures often without sufficient appreciation of the fundamental problems facing enterprises.

[1] Misiak, 'Naczynia...', p. 2.   [2] Grzybowski, p. 127.

It was suggested that in imposing sanctions banks acted as an 'organ of state power', against which there was in practice no redress; attempts at appeals merely brought home to the appellants the attitude of banks that 'the client is never right'.[1] Banks' 'infallibility' was considered to be responsible for the indifference on the part of enterprises towards bank control, which was thought to be inflexible and carried out without sufficient regard to such problems facing enterprises as irregular deliveries, frequent alteration of plans by superior bodies,[2] dissatisfaction with the determination of normatives of working capital and too many regulations. They called for the 'economic role of banks', especially in view of the fact that control was also exercised by other bodies. Zamoyski, on the example of wage control, bitterly criticised banks for imposing sanctions on enterprises even when shortcomings in their management were not entirely their fault. In a paragraph entitled 'the blacksmith was guilty so the cobbler was hanged' he was especially critical of sanctions leading to changes in personnel.[3]

Replies by bankers were too frequently confined to wishful thinking about what the control should be, rather than what it actually was. However, the banks made three main points. First, the essence of the conflict between enterprises and banks was the 'deadly sins' of enterprises: the tendency to fix normatives of working capital at too high a level, the treatment of the plan for stock accumulation as a superfluous formality, the lack of care to eliminate unnecessary stocks, 'too laconic' justification of investment programmes and poor estimates of costs.[4] Secondly, directors of enterprises were said to show unwillingness to discuss problems with banks, preferring to give priority to the organisation of production rather than financial management.[5] Thirdly, banks sometimes appeared to be 'organs of power', because in exercising control they had to take into account macroeconomic considerations, such as the total money flow, and the fulfilment of national plans. Bankers rarely admitted that they might have been unreasonable or wrong in their actions. Referring to bank –

[1] Wierzbicki, p. 7. The author's contentions were supported by letters in *ŻG* 26 (1963) p. 7 by Bożyczko, (p. 6) and by M. Boruń, 'Odformalizować Przepisy...', *ŻG* 38 (1963) p. 4.

[2] It was reported that in a Łódź enterprise the plan was changed 30 times. 'Dyskusja w Łodzi', *ŻG* 8 (1964) p. 7.

[3] F. Zamoyski, 'Niekonsekwentne Sankcje', *ŻG* 20 (1963) p. 2.

[4] 'Dyskusja w Łodzi', p. 7.

[5] W. Pruss, 'Organ Władzy czy Pomocy', *ŻG* 21 (1963) p. 5.

enterprise relations, the Chairman of the NBP stressed a need for closer future co-operation to eliminate conditions in which banks appeared as organs of power carelessly using sanctions and requests.[1]

An impression left by the debate is that enterprises found bank control unnecessarily onerous. This merely confirms the impression that, in general, viz. not solely during the lenient monetary policy, relations between enterprises and banks were often strained. Banks attempted to exert pressure to improve efficiency in enterprises by acting on areas of management which the enterprises regarded as of secondary importance. Some bank decisions were arbitrary and yet enterprises could not question them, due to the 'infallibility' image projected by banks. On the last point it may be interesting to note that in 1966 Napiórkowski, a banker, expressed the opinion that bank action could be misguided and unfair to enterprises, observing that 'It is well known that members of credit commissions draw different conclusions on the same subject and the bank director has yet another opinion.'[2] In a later article he criticised what he called 'the culture of bank action', suggesting that the attitude of banks towards enterprises was sometimes tactless.[3]

Lenient credit *v* credit automatism

In the preceding section it was noted that lenient monetary control did not amount to a completely liberal extension of credit and that the problem of overdue trade credit, though significantly alleviated, still existed. Indeed banks did not consider credit ease to mean liberal credit, but there was some doubt as to the correct interpretation of the relinquishing of the supply of credit as a key control instrument.

It became generally accepted that credit restrictions were not an effective method of control in the existing 'model' of a socialist

[1] A. Żebrowski, 'Zadania NBP w Roku 1964', *WNBP* 2 (1964), p. 39.

[2] Napiórkowski, 'Niektóre...', pp. 366–7. In 1966, by way of an experiment, some credit inspectors were asked to evaluate, on the basis of the same set of documents, the credit requirements of an enterprise. Their estimates and proposed course of action 'differed significantly'. In 1967 a banker from Olsztyn suggested that in exercising control banks found it difficult to make the punishment fit the crime, often taking steps the consequences of which they did not bother to foresee. Sawicz, pp. 188–91.

[3] Napiórkowski, 'Pozaekonomiczne...', pp. 17–18.

economy. It became a new orthodoxy, a new conventional wisdom, replacing the orthodox view of the 1950s that a shortage of credit was a potent cure for inefficient management (especially of stocks) by enterprises. Some accepted the new orthodoxy with a sigh of relief, regarding it as the only possible conclusion to be drawn from years of experience of monetary control. Michejda noticed that 'theoretically the bank acts through credit, practically – in most cases through tedious work of auditing, analysis, intervention and so on.[1]

Before going on to discuss some controversial points concerning the new orthodoxy, it is necessary to mention that in the 1960s economists became openly sceptical about credit performing the intrinsic function of control traditionally attributed to it in socialist literature. Basically it became accepted that it was institutions and their operations rather than credit itself which determined the nature of control. In other words, what was vital was not simply credit control but bank control, which might or might not employ credit as its instrument. Michejda commented that 'credit acts on the creditee regardless of its type, regardless of its scope, regardless of its quantity or cost, but through the fact of its existence, through the economic and legal relationship between the debtor and the creditor, and through the authority of the banking institution supplying it and possessing an arsenal of control weapons'.[2] A banker from Szczecin added: 'It seems that the concept of the control function of credit is a traditional concept, shaped by history, but inadequate as regards the economic content of credit operations of banks.'[3]

Though the new orthodoxy was unanimously accepted, there were differences of opinion concerning its policy implications. The purpose of this section is to review these differences and, in doing so, to throw more light on the nature of the lenient monetary policy actually pursued. The debate on the role of credit in bank control still continues and the review goes beyond the time limit accepted for this chapter.

Some postulated that the lenient monetary control was not liberal enough and that the persistence of overdue trade debts was a sign of this. The following premises seemed to be generally agreed upon: (*a*) that in a socialist economy shortages of finance do not inhibit material or real processes; (*b*) a stoppage of credit simply leads to

[1] Michejda, 'Warunki...', p. 230.
[2] Michejda, 'O Ewolucji...', p. 312.
[3] M. Gruba, 'Problem Funkcji Kontrolnej Kredytu', *WNBP* 7 (1967) p. 285.

compensatory finance, like illicit trade credit; (c) the use of overdue trade credit instead of bank credit is undesirable, as it weakens bank control and causes blockages in payments; (d) deliveries are made irrespective of whether prompt payment is assured (viz. a weakness of mutual control or what was often described as the 'automatism of deliveries'); (e) it is not desirable to allow enterprises to maintain cash reserves to cover deficits in payments. Reserves were to continue to be centralised in the banking system and credit was to remain the means of equating receipts with payments.

It was thought that these premises, based on past experience, justified complete liberalisation of monetary policy. The debate was also influenced by experimental credit policies undertaken in the early 1960s in some socialist countries. East Germany and Rumania in particular were reported to have introduced very liberal policies in 1961. In East Germany a simple and quite automatic system of settlements was introduced, whereby banks settled all invoices (debited the buyer and credited the seller) immediately after they were presented for payment and even before buyers had accepted them. Buyers with insufficient funds automatically accumulated bank credit rather than overdue trade credit. Thus there was (between 1961 and 1964) an automatism of settlements, leading to automatic crediting.[1] In Rumania it was also assumed that bank control could be effective only if the bank were the only source of external finance. Banks thus extended payments credit liberally to both buyers and sellers, so that they could meet their obligations. Invoices, however, had to be accepted before being settled by banks. Enterprises short of funds were given credit regarded as overdue credit at high interest rates. The main penalty, therefore, for the inability to pay was high interest charges on overdue credit, which could be lifted only after the causes of the indebtedness had been eliminated. Otherwise credit was extended automatically. Some writers felt that Poland should follow these two countries by liberalising credit more. But how liberal was credit to be?

Perhaps the most radical proposals for liberalisation were made

---

[1] The payments and credit system in East Germany came under severe criticism in 1963–4, as a result of which the system was modified in 1965 to eliminate automatic settlements. After 1964 a lenient credit policy was adopted, based mainly on liberal issue of payments credit. Automatic credit in the early 1960s increased the indifference of enterprises to financial matters. W. Pruss, 'Kredyt i Rozliczenia Pieniężne Przedsiębiorstw Uspołecznionych', part I, *WNBP* 7 (1965) pp. 226–7.

by Jaworski[1] and Czyżniewski.[2] They advised settlements by banks of all obligations except invoices which had not been accepted by buyers, regardless of whether the debtors had adequate funds or not. Thus, in general, the proposals implied a complete abandonment of control by the supply of credit; credit was to be extended without limit and hence there was to be what some critics (e.g. Pruss) called 'credit automatism'. Unrestrained issue of bank credit was to ensure that enterprises did not accumulate overdue trade debts, which would lead to a chain of payments difficulties in the economy.[3] Accumulation of overdue bank credit[4] was to act as a signal of mismanagement in enterprises, calling for immediate intervention by the bank. Basically it may be said that the two authors wanted credit to fulfil mainly its 'signal role' (see ch. 5, pp. 125–7), relying on interest rates and interventions as instruments of remedial action.

Jaworski objected strongly to critics calling his proposed policy credit automatism, claiming that the only experience of true automatism was in the USSR in 1930–1 (see pp. 31, 128–9) and that the term automatism was used merely to discredit the concept of liberal monetary control. Though the credit system advocated by him would not restrict credit, badly-managed enterprises would receive credit on penalty terms, to which they were sensitive. Control over enterprises could still be conducted through interest rates and administrative measures.

Czyżniewski unashamedly agreed that his proposals were for automatism in credit and settlements – 'the only possible solution is the acceptance of the principle of automatic coverage of all obligations from balances on the account of the debtor and from credit granted to him and, in case these are insufficient, from the

---

[1] W. Jaworski, 'Kredytowanie Nieprawidłowych Potrzeb Przedsiębiorstw', *Finanse* 8 (1961); 'Rola Kredytu Bankowego w Procesie Rozliczeń Bezgotówkowych', *Finanse* 5 (1963); *Obieg*..., pp. 167–8; 'Automatyzm Kredytowy i Rozliczeniowy', *WNBP* 2 (1966).

[2] Czyżniewski, 'Przyczynek...'; 'Efektywność Oddziaływania...', pp. 101–20.

[3] Complete abandonment of action through the quantity of credit, coupled with the use of interest rates as the main control weapon, was also suggested by M. Pawlak, 'System Kredytowy a Rozliczenia Między Jednostkami Gospodarczymi', *Finanse* 3 (1964) esp. p. 45; Zwass ('Propozycje...', pp. 360–2) also leaned towards credit automatism with higher interest charges on all credit above credit limits, as did Michejda ('Ewolycja...', pp. 313–15).

[4] In Czyżniewski's proposal overdue credit, called 'special credit' was paid into a separate account and granted on penal terms. See 'Efektywność Oddziaływania...', pp. 110–11.

account of special credit'.[1] His reply to those who objected to mechanical settlements was 'It is necessary to admit openly that such automatism already exists now. However we may wish to describe the phenomenon of unlimited trade credit from suppliers, in reality it amounts to a process of unhampered and uncontrolled inflow of external funds to enterprises.[2]

The scheme presented by the two economists had the basic advantage of being simple and cheap to implement.[3] There were to be no other sources of credit, no chains of payments difficulties and financial analysis would become simpler, allowing banks to choose an appropriate selection of remedial measures. The main dangers were seen in the possibility of over-issue of credit leading to inflation. This last point, however, could only apply on the assumption that there was a link between monetary and real variables (such as is sometimes postulated in some Western theories – see pp. 6–7), whereas in conditions of Soviet-type planning such a link did not exist.

In terms of the 'real bills' doctrine it may be said that these views maintained that, in Socialist planning, legitimate business needs for purposes of obtaining credit were those which arose in enterprises in the course of their fulfilment of planned targets, which neither they nor the banks could alter. Pressure to fulfil (or overfulfil) plans and the planners' preferences, as revealed in the system of material incentives for fulfilment, set the demand for credit, which was thus strictly an endogenous variable, passively adjusting itself to real expenditure at a given price level. It seems that such an interpretation was, in the circumstances, logical and, though monetary policy based upon it would have been very liberal, it cannot be said to imply the existence of 'financial slack' (see p. 54) capable of generating inflation. Monetary policy would simply have been neutral as far as pressure on resources was concerned. Experience seemed to indicate that in the same way as the lack of money did not curtail spending, ready availability of money would not necessarily lead to expenditure; in addition it would be more

---

[1] Czyżniewski, 'Efektywność Oddziaływania . . .', p. 108.

[2] *Ibid.* p. 117. He preferred overdue bank credit to overdue trade credit, as the former was associated with bank control. The expansion of payments credit he also regarded as a symptom of *de facto* tendency towards automatism in settlements. A similar view was expressed by Szyszko, p. 6.

[3] Czyżniewski (pp. 114–17) insisted on simplicity and low cost of settlements.

10

efficient, because it would prevent a disorderly payments system from developing.

These propositions were opposed by Fedorowicz, among others. He did not agree that the burden of disentangling payments difficulties should necessarily fall on banks, urging that more attention should be given to the problem of 'financial liquidity' of enterprises.[1] Ensuring adequate liquidity would involve not simply credit reforms, but 'making the whole system of financing enterprises more elastic'. He saw no reason why, for instance, the payments difficulties of enterprises caused by their associations should be alleviated by bank credit and not by the associations. The main opposition to credit automatism, however, came from two bankers: Pruss[2] and Rajczyk.[3] Basically their solution was not credit automatism, but a liberalisation of payments credit.[4] They maintained that it was very difficult for enterprises (and banks) to set credit limits correctly because, in practice, credit requirements were subject to significant short-term variations. The main causes of payments difficulties were the rigidity of quarterly credit limits and the fluctuations in the demand for credit. The problem could thus be solved by a flexible and liberal extension of payments credit.

The introduction of payments credit to ease payments difficulties in 1963 (pp. 253–6) was considered to have been quite successful in helping to lower overdue trade credit, but banks failed to extend the credit liberally enough to solve the problem of overdue non-bank obligations completely. Pruss, of the Planning Department of the NBP, criticised banks for being too cautious in granting the credit and for fearing that its liberal extension would lead to a 'depreciation of the limit of turnover credit'.[5] Contending that the credit should be

[1] Z. Fedorowicz, 'Teoria Kredytu a Rozliczenia Pieniężne', in *RPGS*, p. 26.

[2] Pruss, 'Zmienność...', pp. 141–5. 'Kredyt i Rozliczenia Pieniężne Przedsiębiorstw', *WNBP* 8 (1965) pp. 261–3, 'Finansowanie...', pp. 121–43.

[3] Rajczyk, pp. 315–21; 'Wysokość Kredytów Przyznanych Przedsiębiorstwu Jako Element Kredytowej Działalności Banku', *WNBP* 3 (1967) pp. 107–13; 'Propozycje Uelastycznienia Techniki Kredytowania Przedsiębiorstw', *WNBP* 7 (1967) pp. 272–6.

[4] It may be noted that both Żebrowski, the Chairman of the NBP ('Bank a Przedsiębiorstwo', *ŻG* 8, 1964, p. 7), and Blass, a Vice-Chairman ('Zadania...', p. 107), opposed automatism in settlements and credit.

[5] Pruss, 'Kredyt...', p. 262. Rajczyk, 'Kredyt...', p. 315, suggested that 'sometimes payments credit was used to finance too much, but more often its scope was too narrow'. In a later article (*WNBP* 7, 1967, p. 272) he claimed that the granting of payments credit was 'treated as a privilege, a sort of prize for an enterprise and because of this is not common'.

given without 'unnecessary formalities', he was convinced that this was the only improvement needed in contemporary credit practice.

Rajczyk regarded failure to repay payments credit promptly (usually within 10–15 days) as the main indicator either that there was something wrong with the management of the enterprise or that the credit limit needed adjustment. He proposed a new banking practice to improve the signal role of credit and at the same time to overcome the accumulation of overdue debts.[1] Enterprises were to have the right to exceed their credit limit and settle all their obligations, on condition that credit above the limit was not to persist for more than fifteen days. If it did, then the bank was to ascertain whether the limit had to be corrected or the credit supply cut, the latter solution applying in cases when mismanagement of the enterprise was the key cause of overdue indebtedness. In such a system overdue trade indebtedness could arise only where it could be attributed to shortcomings in the work of enterprises.

Credit finance and control of investment

(a) New classification of investment

Beginning in 1961 the classification of investment changed.[2] Investment was divided in the first place into investment of the central plan and of the local government plan.[3] The distinction between centralised and decentralised investment was abandoned. Investment of the central plan was subdivided into (a) central investment, (b) investment of associations and (c) investment of enterprises. Broadly speaking central investment included projects of fundamental importance, including building of new factories and reconstruction of large plants of national significance. Investment of associations included projects of importance to the associations, such as plants other than those included in central investment, repair or research establishments benefiting all member enterprises, and social and cultural facilities.

---

[1] Rajczyk, 'Propozycje...', pp. 274–6.
[2] For a full classification of investment see H. Swidziński, 'Zarys Nowego Systemu Inwestycyjnego na Lata 1961–1965', GP 8–9 (1961) pp. 27–31; A. Płocica, 'Polityka Inwestycyjna' in Polityka Gospodarcza Polski Ludowej, part 1 (1965) pp. 263–74; A. Płocica, Inwestycje w Polsce (1967) pp. 35–45.
[3] In the 1961–5 five year plan the proportions were to be 57.2% to 42.8% respectively. Płocica, Inwestycje w Polsce, p. 45, 'Polityka Inwestycyjna', p. 275.

Investment of enterprises was roughly the old decentralised investment, consisting mainly of reconstruction or retooling within existing buildings, mechanisation or modernisation of plants. It also included quick-yield investment.[1]

The novel element in the new classification was investment by associations. Giving the associations the ability to undertake investment was, at the time, the most important manifestation of the authorities' desire to equip the association with a capacity for taking economic decisions. In practice, associations had little autonomy in making investment decisions and there was little difference between central investment and investment by associations from this point of view. The new category of investment further complicated the whole organisation of investment without contributing greater flexibility.[2]

Investment of enterprises was also, in theory, to be autonomously decided by enterprises, but in practice the autonomy of enterprises continued to be limited. In some instances the superior organs of enterprises undertook decisions on projects classified as investment by enterprises.[3] Indeed the authorities often allocated a particular investment project quite arbitrarily to a category, so that the categories of investment did not necessarily reflect different processes of decision taking. In practice, investment of enterprises was dependent not on the availability of finance, but on physical possibilities for the fulfilment of projects.[4]

Tables 54a and b show the relative size of expenditure on these investments. The expenditure of enterprises was about one third of the total gross investment in table 54a. This proportion is rather large compared with that in table 54b because, whereas central investment and investment by associations were largely net values (viz.

[1] In the 1960s there was little change in the legislation concerning this investment. Resolution 28 of the CM (10 January 1961) stressed the importance of projects resulting in higher exports or increased production of import substitutes. *MP* 11 (1961) item 61.
[2] A. Wołowczyk, 'Czy i Jak Kredytować Inwestycje', *Finanse* 6 (1965) esp. p. 45; Czyżniewski, *Efektywność...*, p. 149.
[3] For example, when equipment was acquired (often from imports) by the organs, which then had the task of allocating it to enterprises as part of investment by enterprises. Czyżniewski (*Efektywność...*, pp. 211–12) suggested that 'Instances of purchases of machinery and other equipment in the framework of central investment or investment by associations and then their installation as part of investment of enterprises are not infrequent.'
[4] J. Wierzbicki, 'Finansowanie Inwestycji Zdecentralizowanych', *Finanse* 9 (1965) pp. 6–7.

Table 54a

Expenditure on investment and capital repairs 1961–5

(*a, mil. zl.* ; *b, percentage of total*)

Year	Total a	Central a	b	Associations a	b	Enterprises a	b
1961	76,826	36,875	48.0	11,448	15.0	28,503	37.1
1962	83,730	42,440	50.7	13,068	15.6	28,222	33.7
1963	87,023	45,305	52.1	13,286	15.3	28,432	32.7
1964	91,107	45,599	50.0	14,785	16.2	30,723	33.7
1965	102,388	48,461	47.3	17,223	16.8	36,704	35.8

Source: GUS – *RSF 1945–1967*, pp. 19, 22–4.

Table 54b

Investment expenditure 1961–5

(*a, mil. zl.* ; *b, percentages of total*)

Year	Total a	Central a	b	Associations a	b	Enterprises a	b
1961	58,747	36,875	62.8	10,253	17.5	11,619	19.8
1962	64,608	42,434	65.7	11,952	18.5	10,222	15.8
1963	67,807	45,263	66.8	12,635	18.6	9,905	14.6
1964	69,390	45,564	65.7	14,063	20.3	9,763	14.1
1965	75,885	48,455	63.9	16,371	21.6	11,059	14.6

Sources: as in table 54a, also GUS – *RSIiST 1946–1966*, pp. 281, 283, 285, 286.

exclusive of capital repairs), more than half the total capital expenditure of enterprises was on repairs. Spending by enterprises on net fixed investment was the smallest of the three categories of capital expenditure shown in table 54b, the largest being central investment. The proportion of investment by enterprises to total investment failed to grow, which was against the postulates of those advocating greater autonomy (and self-finance) for enterprises.

(*b*) *Credit and the finance of investment*

The finance of investment was based on principles which emerged in the 1959–60 period, though there were some minor modifications in their application. Regulations concerning the main aspects of

Table 55

Finance of expenditure on investment and capital repairs in state enterprises,[1] *1961–5*

(*a, mil. zl. ; b, percentages of totals*)

Source of finance	1961		1962		1963		1964		1965	
	a	*b*	*a*	*b*	*a*	*b*	*a*	*b*	*a*	*b*
Depreciation	12,108	42.5	12,225	43.3	13,735	48.3	15,061	49.0	24,125	65.7
DF or profit	5,475	19.2	4,134	14.6	3,980	14.0	3,438	11.2	3,829	10.4
Bank credit	1,770	6.2	2,269	8.0	2,370	8.3	3,617	11.8	3,705	10.1
Other[2]	9,150	32.1	9,594	34.0	8,347	29.4	8,607	28.0	5,045	13.7
Total	28,503		28,222		28,432		30,723		36,704	

Notes:
[1] Viz. investment by enterprises.
[2] Including working capital spent on repairs, budget grants, sales of fixed assets.
Source: GUS – *RSF 1945–1965*, p. 24.

investment finance were issued in two laws: resolution 387 of the CM, already referred to, and resolution 21 'On the principles of financing investment and capital repairs in state enterprises in 1961.'[1] Central investment was financed mainly by budget grants and also from depreciation,[2] whereas investment of associations was financed from their investment fund (viz. mainly budget grants and depreciation of enterprises, of which the fund was made up) and budget grants extended through the IB. Investment of enterprises was financed from the IRF[3] and bank credit advanced by the NBP. Credit continued to finance quick-yield investments. Thus bank credit was used only as a supplementary source of investment finance in state enterprises (viz. decentralised investments in the pre-1961 terminology). Table 55 shows that only a small, but up to 1964 rising, proportion of capital expenditure was covered by credit.

[1] Issued on 10 January 1961, *MP* 11 (1961) item 60.
[2] So called 'centralised depreciation' (*amortyzacja scentralizowana*), viz. depreciation of enterprises taken over and distributed by central authorities.
[3] Resolution 387 (*MP* 91, 1960, item 411) laid down that the IRF was to be formed from that part of depreciation fund (depreciation charges) which remained in the enterprise, from the DF, from the surplus of working capital created by lowering of normatives during a year, from sale of fixed assets, from the reserve fund and the investment fund of the association and from other sources specified in separate regulations.

Table 56

Finance of expenditure on investment and capital repairs in the state sector[1] 1961–5

Sources of finance	1961	1962	1963	1964	1965
In mil. zł.					
Budget grants	63,551	65,449	68,224	68,811	74,661
Depreciation	25,305	34,557	36,172	39,798	50,355
DF or profit	5,486	4,198	4,103	3,525	3,958
Bank credit	1,801	2,316	2,394	3,630	3,722
Other[2]	14,000	15,049	13,650	16,696	12,878
Total	110,143	121,569	124,543	132,460	145,574
In percentages of total					
Budget grants	57.7	53.8	54.8	51.9	51.3
Depreciation	23.0	28.4	29.0	30.0	34.6
DF or profit	5.0	3.5	3.3	2.7	2.7
Bank credit	1.6	1.9	1.9	2.7	2.6
Other[2]	12.7	12.4	11.0	12.6	8.8

Notes:
[1] Excluding social, political and professional organisations.
[2] Including sales of fixed assets and funds from working capital.
Source: GUS – *RSF 1945–1967*, pp. 18–19.

The importance of bank credit as a source of investment finance in the economy as a whole was very small. This may clearly be seen from tables F1a and F1b in Appendix F, which show that between 1961 and 1965 credit financed only about 4% of gross investment in the socialised sector. In the state sector (see table 56) only about 2% of gross investment was financed from credit. Indeed credit in this period was (especially in 1961–63) a relatively less important source of investment finance than in the period immediately preceding 1961. The ratio of the rise in investment funds advanced by the financial system, comparable to that used in chapter 8 (pp. 228 and 232), was 1.2% in 1961, 2.4% in 1962, 2.2% in 1963, 2.7% in 1964 and 3.1% in 1965.[1] Only in the case of investment by enterprises, where bank

[1] The corresponding percentage ratio for budgetary finance was 56.3, 51.9, 52.8, 50.4, 49.6 and for the DF 4.0, 2.7, 2.6, 2.1 and 2.1. The low figure for credit in 1961 may be explained by the fact that in that year enterprises received relatively high budget grants and were allowed to spend considerably more from the DF (funds blocked in 1959 and 1960 were, in some cases, released).

Table 57

Investment credit granted to the socialised sector

(*Balances at the end of the year: a mil. zł.; b percentages of total*)

	1961		1962		1963		1964		1965	
	a	b	a	b	a	b	a	b	a	b
Total	15,843		18,832		21,652		25,334		30,063	
Granted to industry[1]	6,138	38.7	6,700	35.6	6,929	32.0	8,195	32.3	8,739	29.1
Granted by NBP	7,929	50.0	8,609	45.7	8,996	41.5	10,233	40.4	10,890	36.2

Note:
[1] State industrial enterprises and industrial and commercial co-operatives.
Source: GUS – *RSF 1945–1967*, pp. 230, 234, 236.

credit was a recognised form of finance, did credit cover on the average about 9% of the expenditure on investment and capital repairs in the early 1960s (table 55). Table 57 shows that credit for state industrial and commercial enterprises, most of which were credited by the NBP, expanded at a slower rate than credit for other enterprises (especially for building co-operatives). This helps to explain why the share of investment credit granted by the NBP declined (compare with table 45).

Thus investment was financed mainly from centralised sources and especially from the budget. Extensive use of credit finance did not take place, though this was frequently proposed, particularly in debates on the economic 'model' in the late 1950s.

The financing of the bulk of investment by interest-free budget grants continued to be criticised in the 1960s, on the grounds that it led to wasteful investment. It encouraged what was popularly described by an untranslatable phrase, '*zaczepjanie się*' viz. 'hooking on' to, or 'putting one's foot in the door' of, the investment programme by wilful underestimation[1] of costs and/or overestimation of investment efficiency. Once a project was incorporated into the

[1] Many economists believed that enterprises wilfully underestimated their investment costs. A. Paszyński, for example, claimed that investors deliberately 'obscured' calculations in order 'to enter the plan' ('Odwrócony Porządek', *Polityka* 43, 1963, p. 3). Some were more benevolent. Bobrowski, for instance, suggested ('Rozwój...', p. 998) that 'Conscious lowering of investment costs in quite rare, but insufficient care to include in estimates full costs is more than a common phenomenon'.

investment plan it had a good chance of ultimate completion. Budget finance, it was thought, encouraged many enterprises 'to hook on' without prior evaluation of real capital needs, mainly because the cost of investment was not directly borne by enterprises and associations. It was pointed out that enterprises had a different attitude to the 'investment złoty' (viz. złoty financing investment) and to the 'turnover złoty' (viz. złoty financing working capital); the former was regarded as being somewhat cheaper.[1] As a result there was 'deconcentration' of investment in the economy; at any time there were too many projects in relation to the potential for their fulfilment, engaging resources excessively in work-in-progress.[2] Also, existing capital assets were not properly exploited.[3]

(c) Bank control of investment

Bank control of investment continued very much in the same way as described in the preceding chapter, relying on such control methods as the blocking of funds of enterprises and examination of the costing and documentation of projects. The use of non-credit finance limited the scope for using financial stimuli based on credit for purposes of control.[4] Control of investment by using financial instruments was also difficult because of a dichotomy in the planning of investment; investment plans were drawn by the PC, but the finance necessary to fulfil them was organised by the Ministry of Finance, the two processes being poorly co-ordinated.[5] The possession of investible funds did not necessarily permit enterprises to undertake investment and a shortage of funds did not necessarily constitute an effective restriction of investment.

---

[1] Czyżniewski, *Efektywność Form...*, p. 193.
[2] W. Szyndler-Głowacki, 'Inwestycje', *ND* 3 (1966) pp. 30–7.
[3] For details see Z. Sałdak, 'Zamrożone Miliardy', *ŻG* 1 (1962) p. 6; M. Kabaj, 'Zmianowość Inwestcje Rezerwy', *ŻG* 33 (1962) p. 5. *ŻG* published a series of articles in 1963 called 'Imprisoned might' on the problem of unutilised assets (see e.g. *ŻG* 22, 23, 28, 30, 31, 32). In the 1960s a clearer picture than before began to emerge of the economy's fixed capital, as a result of the valuation of assets undertaken between 1960 and 1961.
[4] In some cases the scope of this direct (viz. non-financial) control was extended. In 1963 the NBP was given the additional task of carrying out a 'deeper analysis' of 100 large scale enterprises, so as to ascertain if, for example, they could produce new assortments of goods, or whether their investment programmes were realistic. 'Bank a Przedsiębiorstwo', p. 7.
[5] M. Jaslar, 'Bodźce w Inwestycjach, *Finanse* 9 (1964) p. 3.

The effectiveness of bank control of investment is difficult to assess. Banks did make a contribution, though quantitatively small, to the lessening of the pressure on resources, by stopping some investment projects. It was reported that in 1963 the IB stopped 2.4 bil. złoty of investment because of inadequate documentation. The corresponding figure for 1964 was 1.4 bil. złoty.[1] When banks decided that documentation was inadequate they usually blocked the investment funds (which, in the case of central investments, were included in planned investment limits) until the necessary documentation was supplied. In practice banks were very reluctant to release the blocked funds. 'In this respect we observe, from year to year, rising bureaucracy, excessive centralisation and unnecessary detail.'[2] In general, banks appeared to be more successful in preventing overexpansion of some types of investment than others. In 1962 expenditure on central investment was 98% of planned investment expenditure, but other types of investment showed overfulfilment of plans: 114% for investment by enterprises, 140% for investment of enterprises and associations under local authorities, 130% for investment in the co-operative sector.[3] On balance, bank control of investment did serve as a way of checking expenditure – in the sense that spending on investment would have been greater had there been no bank control. It must be remembered, however, that bank control was designed to ensure the purposefulness and efficiency of investment (see p. 238). In this respect the control was generally considered to be ineffective.

There were numerous complaints of instances of 'wild investments', viz. projects which were badly prepared, carried out by enterprises without bank permission and financed from illicit sources (e.g. working capital). Quantitative estimates of the extent of such investments are not available, but, judging from various remarks on the subject, one gets an impression that they posed a serious problem. Jankowska wrote that 188 inspections of enterprises (state,

[1] W. Szyndler-Głowacki, p. 35. Considering that total investment expenditure in the socialised sector was app. 107 bil. zł. in 1963 and 111 bil. zł. in 1964, this was a small proportion. On the other hand other banks (NBP, AB) may also have stopped some projects. A. Wołowczyk and T. Zaczek wrote ('Kierunki Usprawnień Działalności Inwestycyjnej', *Finanse* 8, 1964, p. 34) that a lack of adequate documentation was revealed by banks in 1962–4 in projects valued at (bil. zł.) 4.4 in 1962, 3.4 in 1963 and 4.6 in 1964, but it is not clear whether the projects were stopped.

[2] Z. Sałdak, 'Inwestycyjny Półmetek', *ŻG* 33 (1963) p. 1.

[3] A. Wołowczyk, 'Realia i Utopie Finansowania Inwestycji', *ŻG* 7 (1964) p. 9.

local government and co-operative) in the Gdańsk region revealed 'serious shortcomings', including wild investments, in the investment management of 70% of the enterprises.[1]

Bank control of investment failed to stop poor costing of projects and to ensure rational choice. The general tendency was for actual investment costs seriously to exceed planned costs.[2] It is, however, questionable to what extent bank control could be expected to eliminate or even alleviate these anomalies, whose origin lay in the functioning of the whole system of investment planning and finance. In official pronouncements wide scope for bank control of investment was advocated and its importance was strongly emphasised,[3] but some economists doubted whether it was reasonable to expect banks to control the whole process of investment, and questioned whether bank control could be an effective cure of many anomalies in this sphere.[4]

[1] I. Jankowska, 'Oddziaływanie Banku na Gospodarkę Inwestycyjno – Remontową Kontrolowanych Przedsiębiorstw', *WNBP* 6 (1964) pp. 164–7.

[2] A. Płocica, *Inwestycje w Polsce*, p. 188. Jaslar (p. 12) made the point that bank control in practice was confined simply to seeing that enterprises did not wilfully lower their cost estimates of investment projects.

[3] See e.g. 'W Pryzmacie Finansów', *ŻG* 8 (1963) pp. 4–5 (interview with J. Albrecht, the Minister of Finance).

[4] Misiak, 'Naczynia...', p. 2; Jaslar, pp. 5–12; A. Płocica, *Inwestycje w Polsce*, pp. 188–91; Czyżniewski, *Efektywność Form...*, pp. 274–95.

10

The reforms of 1965: a timid step towards credit finance of investment

Introduction: general objectives of the 1965 reforms

As noted in the previous chapter, there were no major changes in the economy after the 1959–61 developments. Economic planning was *de facto* centralised and the move to change the association into an effective decision-taking unit was not successful. In that chapter our attention was focused mainly on the lenient credit policy and its implications. The general performance of the economy in the period 1961–5 was not assessed. In the present context such an assessment may be useful as a background to the reforms started in 1965.

Economic performance in the early 1960s in Eastern Europe was considered generally unsatisfactory and in the mid-1960s economic reforms became fashionable. The criteria for judging economic achievement were not unanimously agreed upon and the problem cannot be considered in depth. The main indicator of inadequate performance was the slowing down of the rate of growth.

In Poland the essence of the problem was a slower growth of national product, accompanied by a higher investment rate. In most years the rate of increase of investment was higher than that of national income. The share of consumption in national income tended to fall and the share of fixed investment to rise, the gross fixed investment ratio rising from 27.0% in 1961 to 28.8% in 1965.[1] According to Secomski (of the PC), the annual average rate of growth of income actually achieved in the 1956–60 plan was 6.8% and in the 1961–5 plan 5.4%. At the same time the plans for employment were significantly overfulfilled, while the targets for labour productivity were significantly underfulfilled (especially in 1962–3).[2] One

[1] GUS – *RDN 1965–1968*, p. 35. See also e.g. GUS – *RS 1966*, pp. 80–1, *RS 1968*, p. 77.
[2] K. Secomski, 'Na Przełomie Dwóch Planów Pięcioletnich', *WNBP* 7 (1965) pp. 214–16.

important result of these developments was stagnation in the standard of living of the people.[1]

The basic aim of the reforms of 1965 and subsequent years was to lay the foundations for 'intensive growth', by creating the conditions necessary for more efficient utilisation of existing resources and a more effective investment policy. To this end there was to be some decentralisation of decision-taking, largely from the PC and economic ministries to associations and enterprises. Each economic unit was to improve its costing so as to be able to choose the most profitable alternative. Economic stimuli were to be preferred to orders in economic planning; one of the watchwords of the reforms was: 'more economic management, less administrative management'.

The debate on the reforms had started in 1964 when, in June, the IV Congress of the Party expressed a need for change. It was a markedly different debate from that of 1956–8, which was concerned with changing the 'economic model', concentrating mainly on some of the anomalies in the existing 'model' which had become evident during the early 1960s and which the Party or government departments proposed to remedy.

The Party this time, unlike in the 1956–8 period, produced a comprehensive policy on the reform, which was finally expressed at the IV Plenary Session of its CC held on 27–8 July 1965 and which served as the basis for legislation in 1965 and subsequent years.[2] For instance Trendota, a Vice-Minister of Finance (and the Minister in 1969), outlined the proposed financial reforms, most of which later became law,[3] and Majewski, the Chairman of the NBP discussed the possible impact of the proposed financial reforms on the work of the NBP in an interview.[4] Trendota gave an account of general improvements to be introduced in the management of industry, stressing in particular the strengthening of the role of associations. Discussing specific financial matters he envisaged further substi-

---

[1] Real wage per wage earner in each of the years between 1960 and 1965 rose by (in percentages) 1.5, 2.7, 0.3, 2.4, 2.1, 0.0. United Nations, *Economic Survey of Europe* (1968) p. 160.

[2] Information on the decisions of the Congress is based on: *IV Plenum KC PZPR, Podstawowe Dokumenty* (1965); Z. Szeliga, *Kierunki i Założenia Reformy* (1966); J. Boguszewski, *System Finansowy Przedsiębiorstw i Zjednoczeń* (1966).

[3] J. Trendota, 'Jak Usprawnić System Finansowy Przemysłu', *ŻG* 50 (1964) pp. 1 and 6, *ŻG* 51 (1964) p. 4.

[4] 'W Interesie Aktywnej Roli Złotówki', *ŻG* 9 (1965) pp. 1 and 7.

tution of own finance and bank credit for budget finance, the abolition of the normative of working capital; the separation of the investment fund and the capital repairs fund; the formation of the DF from profit and direct finance of investment by enterprises from the fund; the imposition of an interest rate on fixed capital and an increase in the size of special funds of associations. The financial reforms which actually occurred closely followed Trendota's proposals. This economic debate lacked the variety and outspokenness of the 1956–8 debate and in most cases went over ground well explored in the late 1950s. Issues such as, for example, the need to extend credit finance and impose interest rates on capital were widely discussed in the 1950s and the 1964–5 debate did not contribute any new ideas or novel solutions.

The management of enterprises

(a) The association and the enterprise

In the 1965 period considerable emphasis was put on the need to transform associations from passive intermediaries between ministries and enterprises into effective economic units capable of deciding on the economic development of particular sections of an industry. It has already been mentioned that the new concept of decentralisation was based largely on more autonomous associations, whose operations, however, were not to impair the self-management of enterprises, and whose methods in dealing with enterprises were preferably to be economic rather than administrative. The basic production unit, however, continued to be the enterprise, whose size was still relatively small,[1] although amalgamation of small enterprises was encouraged. Associations of enterprises were to create conditions (for example by organising purchases and marketing facilities or by carrying out research) conducive to efficient management of enterprises. The proposed relationship between the association and the enterprise was thus summed up by Trendota:

The association, equipped with more rights and more means of independent action, should ensure a maximum alignment of the interest of enterprises with that of the society as a whole. At the same time we must strive towards the removal of impediments limiting the initiative of enterprises

[1] In 1967 only about 27% of state enterprises employed more than 1000 workers. GUS – *RS 1968*, p. 150.

in order to improve economic results and take advantage of the reserves of production and technical progress.[1]

(b) The index of profitability

Apart from the advantages which were to accrue to them from effective associations, enterprises were to gain greater self-management, largely as a result of reforms in three areas: directive indices, economic incentives and financial norms. The authorities decided to introduce an index of profitability (*wakaźnik rentowności*), which was to play an increasing role in the management of enterprises both as the key indicator of success and as a basis of a system of incentives.[2] To make the index effective, and at the same time to control it and shape it into a more effective criterion for comparisons of efficiency in enterprises, a price reform was to be carried out and an interest rate was to be imposed on the value of fixed assets in the possession of enterprises. Basically, the authorities were to use the price system more flexibly than before in order to utilise it as an incentive, for example, to the production of good quality or modern goods and to adapt it more than previously to changing market conditions. The first changes in prices (factory prices) were not, however, to become effective until after 1 January 1967.

Together with the index of profitability other directive indices were to continue to be used in planning, but their number was gradually to decline. After 1965 national economic plans included, in addition to the index of profitability, other directive indices called 'specialised indices' (in contrast to 'synthetic indices', such as the index of profitability and the rate of profit). These were usually: total output, the output of more important products, the value of production for exports, central and associations' investments, unit costs, wage fund, employment.

(c) The development fund and the self-finance of enterprises

In 1965 it was decided to increase the self-finance of enterprises, relating it more directly to the profitability of enterprises. However,

[1] J. Trendota, 'IV Plenum KC PZPR i Zadania Aparatu Finansowego', *Finanse* 10 (1965) p. 3.
[2] The index was defined as 'percentage of profit to total cost of output sold'. In some cases instead of the index there was to be a rate of profit (*stopa zysku*) viz. 'the percentage ratio of profit to the value of fixed and working capital'. The use of such indices in planning was advocated in Poland in the mid-1950s. For a discussion of them see J. Popkiewicz, *Stopa Zysku w Gospodarce Socjalistycznej* (1968).

in this field wide powers were given to associations. Resolution 276 of the CM, passed on 28 October 1965,[1] gave the association the power to decide on the distribution of profits of enterprises between various special funds including the DF, by fixing the 'norms' determining the size of these funds. In answer to criticisms that in the past such norms were fixed for too short a period, causing uncertainty for enterprises (see p. 233), they were to be set for periods of not less than two years.

The DF continued to be the main basis of self-finance. Its total size was, in theory, to depend on the needs and the size of profit of enterprises. The interpretation of this requirement was left to the association and no specific criteria were laid down. In practice, allocation to DF of enterprises was 'accidental'. The associations were given a norm (for example 70% of profits) to be paid to the budget. This set a maximum limit (viz. 30% of profit) to be divided between the DF of enterprises, which were rarely satisfied with their allocation and haggled for more with their associations.[2]

The above mentioned law introduced some changes in the division of the DF. The fund was to be utilised directly to finance working capital and investment. However, money accumulated in the fund in one year could be utilised only in the subsequent year. To this end the fund was divided into two accounts, A and B. Account A, which could not be spent within a year and did not bear any interest, accumulated funds, for example, from a part of profit (after deductions from profit into the factory fund and payments to the association). Account B earned interest and could be spent on working or fixed capital in a manner to be described later. These changes help to explain the large discrepancy between transfers and distribution in 1966, shown in table 58. The growth of the fund was due largely to the financial reforms and in particular the abolition of the normative (to be discussed) and the transfers to the DF of, for example, balances from the IRF (which was abolished) or funds which had been blocked because of faulty 'normatising' by enterprises.[3]

---

[1] 'On the financial management of industrial associations and their enterprises embraced by central planning.' *MP* 61 (1965) item 316.

[2] U. Wojciechowska, 'Fundusz Rozwoju Przedsiębiorstwa Przemysłowego', *ND* 9 (1966) pp. 33–5.

[3] See Order of the Minister of Finance (26 November 1965) 'On settlements connected with the acceptance of new principles of financial management of state enterprises embraced by central planning.' *MP* 65 (1965) item 367. The large rise in 1966 reflects once and for all transfers into the fund.

Table 58

Analysis of expenditure from the development fund of state enterprises 1965–7

(*a, mil. zł.; b, percentages of total distribution*)

	Transfer from all sources	Distribution of the fund						
		Total	On investment		On working capital		Other expenditure	
	a	*a*	*a*	*b*	*a*	*b*	*a*	*b*
1965	12,960	12,377	3,200	25.9	8,883	71.8	294	2.4
1966	36,968	28,500	8,154	28.6	17,040	59.8	3,306	11.6
1967	21,412	21,222	5,901	27.8	12,546	59.1	2,775	13.1

Note:
Data for 1966 and 1967 are not comparable with 1965 and earlier years (see tables 47 and 30).
Sources: GUS – *RS 1967*, p. 579, 1968, p. 579.

Table 59

Financial accumulation of socialised enterprises and its distribution between the budget and the enterprises and their superior bodies 1965–7

	Financial accumulation				
	Total	Absorbed by the budget		Retained by enterprises	
Year	bil. zł.	bil. zł.	%	bil. zł.	%
1965	169.8	141.6	83.4	29.0	20.5
1966	176.5	139.6	79.1	37.9	21.5
1967	179.4	139.3	77.6	41.3	23.0

Notes and source as in table 46.

Table 59 shows changes in financial accumulation; the overall share in total accumulation retained by socialised enterprises and their superior bodies rose from 20.5% in 1965 to 23% in 1967. Thus, compared with the pre-1965 period, more financial accumulation was left at the disposal of enterprises and associations (compare with table 46). This helps to explain further the increase in the transfers to the DF discussed above.

(d) Self-management in practice

The immediate effect of the reforms was disappointing, particularly because associations failed to become effective, autonomous, economic units capable of controlling enterprises by using economic stimuli rather than administrative orders. In their efforts to become more effective they encountered some resistance from enterprises, which feared further intervention in their day-to-day management. Of more importance, however, was the tendency on the part of the PC, and in particular economic ministries, to perpetuate the old planning practices.[1]

Economic stimuli did not appear to be substituted for directives in managing the national economy. Changes introduced in the price system (in 1967) had little positive effect, largely because of two factors: (a) prices were to be based on 1965 prices, preserving the inadequate relative price structure, and (b) the continued use of directives, discussed below, inhibited any incentive effect which prices could otherwise have had.[2]

Again there was a discrepancy between the number of directive indices prescribed by law and the number used in practice. De facto directive indices sometimes appeared under the guise of euphemisms, such as 'limits' or 'orientational indices'. Strictly speaking the number of de jure directive indices did decline, but this was of no practical significance.[3] Indeed the use of a variety of directives, each having a different degree of 'directiveness', made a precise definition of a directive index difficult. It was attempted by Golinowski, who defined directive indices as 'those indices which are strictly connected with a given sanction (material or administrative) and whose non-fulfilment leads to the imposition of the sanction'. In some enterprises studied by the author in

[1] M. Misiak, 'Aktualne Problemy Reformy Metod Planowania i Zarządzania', ND 9 (1966) p. 82; L. Ząbkowicz, 'Przedsiębiorstwo a Zjednoczenie w Ramach Systemu Zarządzania Przemysłem', GP 10 (1968) p. 30.

[2] For details see W. Sztyber, 'Funkcjonowanie Nowego Systemu Cen', Ekonomista 3 (1969) esp. pp. 700–5.

[3] K. Golinowski, 'Wskaźniki Dyrektywne w Zarządzaniu Przedsiębiorstwami', GP 3 (1969) p. 31.

1968 the number of directives thus defined was about 80, leading him to the conclusion that 'Instead of a postulated fall in directive indices there was a sudden rise.'

The development of the index of profitability in economic management did not significantly raise the profit motivation of enterprises. Because the size of various special funds depended (at least partly) on the fulfilment of the index, enterprises became especially sensitive to it. It proved to be difficult to set the index at a level satisfactory to both enterprises and their superior organs.[1] In particular, enterprises were concerned about changes in profit which were dependent not on their own effort, but on external factors beyond their control (e.g. changes in consumer tastes). They were therefore often dissatisfied with their target of profitability and appealed for it to be altered. Undoubtedly enterprises were not always ready to use such an index, but the fact that they did not have sufficient freedom of action to justify its use was of greater significance. The index of profitability imposed on enterprises new responsibilities, without their having been given new rights. The freedom of enterprises to operate was excessively limited by the use of other indices. Indeed it may be argued that the *raison d'être* of this 'synthetic' index was undermined by persistent use of various specialised targets. These were quite often communicated to enterprises after a delay or 'by installments',[2] frequently leading enterprises to appeal against the 'unreality' of the index in relation to particular specialised indices received and to 'haggling' between enterprises and their associations about the size of the index, ultimately resulting in its alteration.

Frequent changes in the index were a disturbing feature of economic management. It was suggested that in a large majority of enterprises the index was changed two or three times in a year, but there were instances where more frequent alterations were made.[3]

[1] A. Gutowski, 'Wskaźnik Rentowności Czyli Kłopoty Nieprzygotowanego', *ŻG* 21 (1967) p. 1.
[2] K. Przyborowska and F. Zachwieja, 'Problemy Funkcjonowania Nowego Systemu Finansowego Przedsiębiorstw', *WNBP* 10 (1967) p. 411.
[3] Przyborowska and Zachwieja, p. 411; L. Siemiątkowski, 'O Systemie Finansowym Zjednoczeń i Przedsiębiorstw Przemysłu Kluczowego', *WNBP* 6 (1968) p. 224; Napiórkowski ('W Sprawie Syntetycznych Mierników Ekonomicznych Efektow Działalności Przedsiębiorstw', *Finanse* 2, 1969, pp. 35-6) surveyed 166 enterprises belonging to 8 associations in 1967. 159 (viz. 95.4%) had the index changed. The

Studies showed that had indices of profitability been left in their original version many enterprises would have lost between 70% and 100% of bonus payments for employees. However, the changeability of the index had an unfortunate effect, in that many enterprises directed their endeavours more to securing a favourable change in the index, rather than to achieving a real increase in profitability.[1] It also created uncertainty and instability in the management of enterprises and considerably reduced the effectiveness of the financial incentives based on the index.

Moreover, the lengthening of the time horizon of various financial norms set by associations (see p. 290) did not materialise. In general, associations continued the old practice of fixing norms for one year only, but there were also many instances where these norms were altered during the year. There were examples where the norms of transfers from profit to the DF were substantially altered three or four times a year, the final norms often being settled at the end of the year for which they were to apply.[2]

The structure of credit institutions

The 1965 reforms were the only major economic reforms which did not involve a significant change in the structure of banking, although one change worth mentioning was the increasing importance of the Trade Bank (TB). The bank had already taken over some of the activities of the NBP[3] in 1963, mainly those connected with the finance of international trade, and some staff and equipment had been transferred from the NBP to the bank. In 1966 a substantial part of the NBP's assets and liabilities connected with international trade was transferred to the bank.[4] It was now empowered to service,

index was changed once in 20 enterprises (12%), twice in 80 (48%), three times in 48 (28.8%) and four times in 11 (6.6%). In 129 enterprises the index was lowered (in 45 between 25%–50%) and in 30 it was raised.

[1] Siemiątkowski, p. 225.

[2] R. Napiórkowski, 'Kilka Uwag na Temat Funkcjonowania Aktualnego Systemu Finansowego Przedsiębiorstw', *GP* 11 (1968) pp. 20–1.

[3] By order of the Minister of Finance issued on 24 September 1963 'On the transfer by NBP to TB of Warsaw S.A. of assets and liabilities concerning foreign settlements.' *MP* 73 (1963) item 365.

[4] Order of the Minister of Finance made on 18 October 1966 'On the taking over by the TB of Warsaw...,' *MP* 59 (1966) item 283.

Table 60a

Credit granted by the banking system 1965–9

(Balances at the end of the year: a, bil. zl.; b, % of total in each year)

	1960		1965		1966		1967		1968		1969	
	a	b	a	b	a	b	a	b	a	b	a	b
Total	154.8	100.0	277.2	100.0	320.6	100.0	370.0	100.0	422.9	100.0	512.8	100.0
NBP	117.3	76.1	194.3	70.1	194.3	60.6	212.3	57.4	221.0	52.2	455.3	46.7
IB	14.4	9.3	36.3	13.1	55.5	17.3	78.8	21.3	116.7	27.6	165.3	32.2
AB	15.2	9.9	28.4	10.3	35.9	11.2	43.0	11.6	49.4	11.7	60.5	11.8
SLCs	3.7	2.4	11.1	4.0	12.8	4.0	13.9	3.8	12.7	3.0	16.4	3.2
'ORS'[1]	3.6	2.3	6.5	2.3	8.4	2.6	8.3	2.2	9.7	2.3	7.5	1.5
TB	–	–	–	–	13.2	4.1	13.2	3.6	12.7	3.0	14.6	2.8
CSB[2]	0.0	0.0	0.5	0.2	0.5	0.2	0.5	0.1	0.7	0.2	9.1	1.8

Notes:

[1] Hire Purchase Bank 'ORS'.

[2] Common Savings Bank, which started to grant credit on a small scale to individuals.

Sources: As in table 31 and *NBP – Information Bulletin*, 1969, p. 24; 1970, p. 21.

Table 60b

Credit to the socialised sector 1965–7

(*Balances at the end of the year ; a, mil. zl. ; b, percentages of the total in each year*)

	1960		1965		1966		1967	
	a	b	a	b	a	b	a	b
Total[1]	138,757	100.0	242,507	100.0	279,323	100.0	323,676	100.0
NBP	117,127	84.4	193,918	80.0	194,113	69.5	211,556	65.4
IB	11,303	8.1	30,902	12.7	49,415	17.7	72,038	22.3
AB	10,320	7.4	17,673	7.3	22,601	8.1	26,808	8.3
TB	–	–	–	–	13,172	4.7	13,254	4.1

Note:
[1] Includes credit by SLCs (in mil. zl.): 7 in 1960, 14 in 1965, 22 in 1966, 20 in 1967.
Source: GUS – *RSF 1945–1967*, p. 235.

finance and control foreign trade. One mark of its growing importance was the fact that in 1966 it became a branch bank, with four new branches, a fifth being added in 1968. Its relative importance in the banking structure may be gauged by examining tables 60a–b and E1 and E2. Another change of importance was the setting up of a socialised bank, the Hire Purchase Bank 'ORS', in 1960 to grant instalment purchase credit, the amount of which (see table 61a) was steadily maintained at a little over 2% of total bank credit.[1]

Throughout the sixties the banking system expanded in terms of credit, employment and branches. Not all banks expanded at the same rate, so that changes in the relative importance of banks occurred. The main trends in the development of the banking system are reflected in the tables given in this section. These were basically a continuation of the trends already visible in the late fifties (see pp. 189–92). Though the NBP was still the dominant credit institution, its relative importance was declining (see especially tables 60a and b). Most banks were universal banks, though banks other than the NBP and TB specialised in granting long-term finance. The NBP continued to be mainly a short-term credit bank and in 1969 still issued 69% of all short-term credit

[1] Hire purchase in socialist countries is not developed on the scale of Western hire purchase. Rather than to regulate aggregate demand, changes in hire purchase are often brought in to sell durable consumers' goods whose supplies are adequate or excessive on the market.

Table 61a

Credit activity of the NBP 1965–9
(Balances at the end of the year : a, mil. zl. ; b, percentages of total)

	Total	Direct credit						Private sector		Refinance[1]	
		Socialised enterprises									
		Total		Short-term		Investment					
	a	a	b	a	b	a	b	a	b	a	b
1960	124,168	117,127	94.3	109,115	87.9	8,012	6.5	226	0.2	6,815	5.5
1965	220,457	193,918	88.0	183,028	83.0	10,890	4.9	424	0.2	26,115	11.8
1966	236,684	194,113	82.0	182,332	77.0	11,781	5.0	165	0.1	42,406	17.9
1967	271,554	211,556	77.9	197,743	72.8	13,813	5.1	703	0.3	59,295	21.8
1968	309,859	219,721	70.9	202,075	65.2	17,646	5.7	1,287	0.4	88,851	28.7
1969	348,425	237,355	68.1	216,409	62.1	20,946	6.0	1,927	0.5	109,142	31.3

Note:
[1] Refinance of other banks.
Sources: GUS – RSF 1945–1967, p. 234. NBP – Information Bulletin, 1970, p. 43.

Table 61b

Short-term credit to the socialised sector 1965–9
(*Balances at the end of the year*)

	1965	1966	1967	1968	1969
Total (mil. zł.)	212,444	238,069	266,298	284,228	315,268
By NBP (mil. zł.)	183,028	182,332	197,743	202,075	216,409
Percentage of total	86.2	76.6	74.4	71.1	68.6

Sources: GUS – *RSF 1945–1967*, pp. 234, 236, NBP – *Information Bulletin*, 1970, pp. 41, 43.

Table 61c

Investment credit to the socialised sector 1965–9
(*Balances at the end of the year*)

	1965	1966	1967	1968	1969
Total (mil. zł.)	30,063	41,254	57,378	87,994	135,642
By NBP (mil. zł.)	10,890	11,781	13,813	17,646	20,946
Percentage of total	36.2	28.6	24.1	20.0	15.4

Sources: GUS – *RSF 1945–1967*, pp. 234, 236, NBP – *Information Bulletin*, 1970, pp. 41, 43.

originating in the banking system; this, however, was considerably less than in the early 1960s (table 61b). As an investment bank its importance also declined (table 61c), mainly because the expansion of credit finance of investment was faster in the spheres of activity serviced by other banks (especially housebuilding and agriculture) than in the spheres serviced by the NBP (see p. 282).

The structure of the liabilities of the banking system also changed after 1965, though the change was in the nature of an accentuation of trends already visible in the 1965 period (for details see table B1b). The share of deposits of socialised production units in total liabilities rose from 35.0% in 1964 to 46.0% in 1969. This change was due mainly to changes in the financing of capital expansion (covered in subsequent sections of this chapter), which tended towards the replacement of budgetary finance by own funds and credit. Budgetary deposits in banks declined to about

16% of liabilities. It is interesting to note that savings and current deposits of the population reached over 20% of total liabilities in this period, becoming a key source of credit in the economy. The developing banking habit of the population was also reflected in a very low ratio (11% in 1969) of currency in circulation to total deposits.

In view of the evolution in banking in the 1960s shown by tables 60a–b and 61a–c and Appendices B and E it would no longer be accurate to call the banking system a monobank. Banking was still, by Western standards, highly concentrated but in the late 1960s it began to resemble the system operating in the late 1940s more than that of the mid-1950s. The increasing role of banks other than the NBP indeed led to an increase in their refinancing by the NBP. In 1969 as much as 31% of the credit granted by the bank refinanced other banks (see table 61a). Refinancing was mainly direct and not, as in the West, by rediscounting eligible paper presented by the banks. Though the central bank's authority over other banks still rested primarily on a statutory basis, refinancing increasingly allowed the bank to put control over other financial institutions on a more 'economic' basis. Thus the NBP was growing into a 'bankers' bank', which was its main pre-war function and an important function in the immediate post-war period. There was, however, no question of developing a money market on a Western pattern, in order to use refinancing and rediscount rates as key instruments of control.

Credit and the finance of working capital

(a) The abolition of the normative

The debate on the reform of planning and finance of working capital again centred around the institution of the normative of working capital, whose inadequacy, both theoretical and in particular practical, had already been exposed in the debate of the late fifties. Criticisms of it before the 1965 reforms were based largely on the observation that in practice the normative could not be objectively determined and was a device which constantly demanded a high input of labour.[1] It was generally recognised that the enterprise

[1] L. Siemiątkowski, 'Czy Normatyw Jest Przydatny', *ŻG* 40 (1964) p. 8.

did not have any effective incentive to set the normative at a theoretically desirable level and that the control of the normative by external bodies was inadequate, being especially onerous on banks.[1] In spite of bank control over its determination, the normative was set in an arbitrary way and was usually too high. Michalski observed that it impeded the interplay between stocks and investment, saying that

It appears that the competition for finance between stocks and investment is not effective, because funds for stocks may be raised above the level set by the normative without major difficulties from both banking and non-banking sources. The financial normative in the conditions of this interplay became the subject of additional speculation in the distribution of financial indices and hence additional measures to counteract this had to be brought in.[2]

The additional measures were invariably direct controls, such as the prohibition of investment and the blocking of funds.

The proposal to abolish 'normatising' met with general approval, though some economists suspected that formal abolition might not necessarily result in effective changes in the planning and finance of working capital. Szwaja, for example, feared that the elimination of the normative might prove to be a mere 'revolution in nomenclature', because it was not clear what new planning methods of working capital were to replace it.[3] Indeed when the normative was abolished in 1965, after a period of 15 years of incessant criticism, there were no mourners at its passing, but there were sceptics who did not believe that an adequate solution to the planning of working capital would emerge to succeed it.

(b) The finance of working capital

Provisions for the planning and finance of working capital introduced in 1965 no longer included the normative. Banks were still to carry out control of stock management by enterprises and for this purpose a new classification of stocks (discussed below) was adopted. Regu-

[1] Misiak, 'Naczynia...,' p. 2; Czyżniewski, *Efektywność Form...*, p. 262.
[2] Michalski, pp. 254–5.
[3] Szwaja, 'Dwa Negatywy do Propozycji Zmian', *ŻG* 15 (1965) p. 9.

lations brought in in 1965[1] laid down that working capital was to be financed from the DF (account B) and credit. Enterprises were not, however, free to decide what proportion of working capital was to be financed from own funds and what proportion by credit. The proportions were determined mainly by financial requirements concerning the finance of stocks, which were reclassified following the abolition of the normative.

The division of stocks between normative and above-normative could no longer apply and it was decided that the basis of finance was to be the nature of stocks actually held. 'Current stocks' (*zapasy bieżące*), which were correct, had to have 60% coverage from the DF and thus could have 40% coverage by credit, but enterprises were not compelled to finance them by credit – they could finance them all from the DF. In this respect, therefore, enterprises gained some financial autonomy. All incorrect stocks (viz. unnecessary and superfluous stocks) were to be covered by own funds, and all seasonal stocks and reserves by credit. In brief the reforms laid down that the DF was to cover all incorrect stocks and at least 60% of correct current stocks.

Whether this new arrangement was a significant departure from the old is best seen by an evaluation of actual stock management, undertaken later. Theoretically, however, behind the new classification of assets we may discern the old concept of the normative. Current stocks were in effect stocks constantly needed for the smooth running of production and in this sense resembled the normative of working capital.[2] All other stocks were essentially the old above-normative stocks. The main practical problem now was to decide which stocks were current and which were seasonal, unnecessary or superfluous. On 8 December 1965 the NBP issued an instruction (A/8) to its branches concerning the new classification of stocks. The criteria given for the purpose were not objective, leaving wide scope for interpretation. Indeed Majewski, the Chairman of the NBP, specifically anticipated a rise in the number of conflicts between banks and enterprises

---

[1] By resolution 276 (see p. 290) and order of the Minister of Finance (26th November 1965) 'On the determination of partial coverage of working capital of industrial enterprises by own turnover funds.' *MP* 65 (1965) item 368. It is interesting to note than in Hungary and Czechoslovakia the normative was also abolished but, as a rule, the whole of working capital was to be financed from credit. Such a solution was advocated by some economists in Poland in 1956–7.

[2] Wojciechowska, 'Fundusz....' pp. 29–30.

Table 62a

Finance of working capital in socialised enterprises 1965–7
(*Balances at the end of the year*)

Year	Total	Bank credit	Own funds	Trade credit	Others
			mil. zł.		
1965	524,681	211,534	142,205	56,496	114,446
1966	589,777	236,930	162,687	61,605	128,555
1967	649,905	261,934	177,805	67,432	142,734
			In percentages		
1965	100	40.3	27.1	10.8	21.8
1966	100	40.1	27.6	10.4	21.8
1967	100	40.3	27.4	10.4	22.0

Notes and source as in table 48a.

Table 62b

Finance of working capital in socialised enterprises in industry 1965–7
(*Balances at the end of the year*)

Year	Total	Bank credit	Own funds	Trade credit	Others
			mil. zł.		
1965	229,967	92,381	74,377	18,165	45,044
1966	262,664	100,208	87,388	18,766	56,302
1967	288,224	109,680	97,853	21,315	59,376
			In percentages		
1965	100	40.2	32.3	7.9	19.6
1966	100	38.1	33.3	7.1	21.4
1967	100	38.0	33.9	7.4	20.6

Notes and source as in table 48b.

resulting from the new classification.[1] Despite the serious difficulty with classification, greater freedom of finance of current stocks made financing more flexible than before. Having covered its rise in working capital, the enterprise after 1965 could (*a*) aim to spend its funds (from the DF) on investment, (*b*) increase the share of own funds in financing working capital and thereby save interest on bank credit, (*c*) save all funds and earn interest (4%) on the DF.

[1] S. Majewski, 'Zadania NBP w Roku 1966, *WNBP* 1 (1966) p. 4.

The removal of the normative, it was thought, would increase the interplay between stocks and investment, largely by removing the basis for the speculation to which the normative gave rise in practice (see p. 300). Enterprises could no longer include incorrect stocks in their normative nor finance them from credit. Incorrect stocks depleted the DF, leaving less money for investment. It was claimed that this sharpened the stimulus to get rid of unjustified stocks. The interplay was also to be improved by financing investment directly from the DF instead of indirectly through the IRF.

An examination of the sources of finance for working capital after the 1965 reform reveals that little change occurred (see tables 62a and b). In socialised industrial enterprises there was a slight drop in the share of credit in the total finance of working capital, balanced by a slight rise in own finance and 'other' funds (see table 62b).

(c) The lenient monetary policy continues

As regards the short-term credit policy, in general the lenient credit approach continued after 1965, though with some modifications. In an interview entitled 'In the interest of an active role of the złoty' Majewski, the Chairman of the NBP, suggested that stocks considered by banks to be incorrect should not as a rule be credited, but financed from the DF.[1] This was done largely to strengthen the interplay between stocks and investment. However, banks could still grant credit for incorrect requirements (for example overdue obligations) and continue to choose the most effective form of action (which might not include a contraction of credit) against badly-managed enterprises. On the whole, the requirement to finance incorrect current stocks from own funds did not constitute a departure from the lenient monetary policy. Little faith continued to be expressed in variations in the supply of credit as an instrument of monetary control over enterprises, for the same reasons as those given earlier in chapter 8.[2] However, crediting became somewhat more mechanical than before 1965, because once stocks were classified banks had to follow the financial regulations laid down by the new reform. It was still possible to obtain credit even if there were some flaws

[1] ŻG 9 (1965) p. 1.
[2] See e.g. R. Michejda, 'Warunki Zwiększenia Roli Kredytu,' WNBP 3 (1969) esp. p. 98.

Table 63

*The structure of short-term credit granted to socialised enterprises
in industry 1965–7*

(*Balances at the end of the year; a, mil. zł.; b, percentage[1] of total*)

	On stocks[2]		On settlements		On payments		Overdue		Others	
	a	b	a	b	a	b	a	b	a	b
1965	71,731	77.6	18,903	20.5	866	0.9	159	0.2	722	0.8
1966	84,954	84.8	13,611	13.6	1,053	1.0	117	0.1	473	0.5
1967	93,410	85.2	13,922	12.7	1,977	1.8	141	0.1	230	0.2

Notes:
[1] Of the total given in table 62b col. 2.
[2] After 1965 credit on stocks was no longer divided into normative and above-normative
– compare with table 49c. Credit on stocks in this table may be compared with the sum
of normative and above-normative credit in table 49c.
Source: Data supplied by the NBP.

in management (for example the existence of incorrect stocks).
However, this occurred as a last resort, viz. when there was no
money in the DF (account B) and when the association refused
to give help (from the reserve fund, which is explained later).
The credit given in such circumstances was 'special credit', carrying
a penal interest rate of 10%. In some cases banks demanded a guarantee by associations that it would be repaid in a stipulated time.
There was, on the other hand, no move to liberalise credit policy on
the lines suggested by those advocating credit automatism (see
ch. 9, pp. 271–7), though pleas for this continued to be made.[1]
   An examination of the distribution of short-term credit after
the reforms shows that, in general, the trends visible in earlier years
continued after 1965 (compare table 63 with 49c). It was still
recognised that enterprises must be allowed to maintain sufficient
'financial liquidity' so as not to accumulate overdue debts. Table 63
shows that payments credit continued to expand, though its total
amount was small. Nevertheless it played an important part in the
lenient monetary policy, which appeared to proceed along the lines

[1] See e.g. R., Napiórkowski, 'W Sprawie Kredytowania Przedsiębiorstw Uspołecznionych', *Finanse* 12 (1969) pp. 32–7.

Table 64

Overdue indebtedness of industrial enterprises in the socialised sector 1965–8

(*Balances at the end of the year*)

	1965	1966	1967	1968
a. Total trade credit (mil. zł.)	18,165	18,766	21,315	22,846
b. Overdue trade credit (mil. zł.)	1,766	1,186	1,235	728
c. $\frac{b}{a} \times 100$	9.7	6.3	5.8	3.2
d. Total overdue credit[1]	1,924	1,303	1,376	884
$\frac{b}{d} \times 100$	91.7	91.0	89.7	82.3

Note:
[1] Viz. bank credit and trade credit.
Source: Data supplied by the NBP.

advocated by the opponents of full automatism of payments (pp. 276–7).

It may be noted that the abolition of the normative meant that there was now only one kind of credit on stocks (see table 63). This completed the simplification in the classification of credits for stocks, from the six credits operative between 1952 and 1957, through the two credits (normative and above normative) operative between 1958 and 1965, to one credit, starting in 1966.

The lenient monetary policy contributed further to the reduction of overdue trade credit (see table 64). Its ratio to total trade credit in industrial enterprises fell (though there was a small rise in the absolute level of overdue trade debts in 1967). In the years 1966–7 overdue trade credit financed only 0.4% and 0.5% of working capital in industrial enterprises and its ratio to total short-term credit to industrial enterprises fell from 1.2% in 1966 to 1.1% in 1967 and 0.8% in 1968.[1] The sum of overdue trade debt and overdue bank credit fell compared with pre-1965 levels (compare tables 64 and 52) and the ratio of overdue trade credit to the sum of the two credits continued to fall after 1965, suggesting that enterprises did not prefer the illicit trade finance to bank finance as much as in the past (p. 259). Thus the payments situation of

[1] GUS – *RSF 1945–1967*, p. 168 and tables 63 and 64. Compare the figures with those on p. 259.

enterprises continued to improve and the problem of overdue trade indebtedness was now of small dimensions (the ratio of overdue trade credit to total trade credit was 50.2% in 1958, 17.9% in 1964 and only 3.2% in 1968).

It may, therefore, be said that with the development of the lenient credit approach the *qualitative tests* were so modified as to allow adjustment of credit supply to 'business needs', defined not necessarily in terms of planned (viz. 'correct') targets, but in terms of actual needs, even when these arose in the course of deviations from plans (viz. were 'incorrect'). Payments were thus linked with credit so that banks, and not illicit trade credit, increasingly performed the function of the 'lender of last resort'.

(d) Higher interest charges and their effects

The aims of bank control of enterprises did not change. Banks still focused their attention on stock building and tried to make certain that enterprises conducted their general financial management efficiently and behaved in accordance with regulations, especially those introduced in 1965. The main methods of bank action were, as before 1965, administrative intervention and higher interest rates. The emphasis was on the latter and it was hoped that the introduction of the index of profitability would increase the effectiveness of interest charges.

An interesting empirical study was conducted to test the effectiveness of higher interest charges, in 100 enterprises chosen from 41 associations in key industries.[1] The study revealed that basic interest charges had too slight an impact on costs and profits to serve as an economic stimulus. In only 18 of the 100 enterprises were higher interest charges imposed. According to the survey, they did not on the whole have a sufficiently large effect on the index of profitability or the factory fund (which was the source of bonus payments to employees) to represent an effective method of bank control. The survey also revealed that penalties imposed for non-fulfilment of contracts were more effective than penalties imposed by banks, which helps to explain the change in preference by enterprises, from overdue trade credit to overdue bank credit, observed above.

[1] H. Błaszak, 'Oprocentowanie Kredytu Jako Środek Oddziaływania na Gospodarkę Przedsiębiorstw', *WNBP* 4 (1968) pp. 142–50.

The chief reasons why higher interest charges were ineffective were given as: (*a*) indices of profitability were too differentiated; where indices were high the effect of interest charges was usually low, (*b*) interest charges were too low; they could only rise from 4% to 10%, (*c*) banks failed to impose maximum charges on enterprises and were too generous in granting rebates.

The survey was not completely conclusive on the question of the effectiveness of interest rates. First, the population of the sample was small and the survey examined developments in only one year. Secondly, the impact of higher rates on profits or on the factory fund is not an adequate measure of the effectiveness of interest charges, because such charges were invariably linked with other methods of action (for example interventions); also the imposition of higher rates might have had its 'psychological aspects'.[1] Nevertheless, the real impact of interest rates must depend on their effect on profitability and incentives based on it; the study quoted found this impact to be rather small.

As far as the effectiveness of bank control in general is concerned, little can be added to the assessment in the preceding chapter. There were no indications conclusively linking changes in stocks or the accumulation of unwanted stocks with bank control. The interplay between stocks and investment was weak.[2] As in previous periods the increase in stocks was considered excessive, though some improvement has taken place since 1966. Taking 1965 as the base, the index of national income was 106.7 in 1966, 114.0 in 1967, 125.0 in 1968, 131.0 in 1969 and 139.2 (estimate) in 1970. The respective figures for stocks were 112.1, 127.5, 135.6, 147.8 and 158.6 (values at current prices). Stocks as a percentage of national income (current prices) were 8.3 in 1965, 8.4 in 1966, 6.3 in 1967, 6.9 in 1968, 5.1 in 1969 and 6.2 in 1970. The percentage in the 1961–5 plan was 6.8, whereas in the 1966–70 plan it was 6.5. Much of the improvement is due to lower agricultural production (caused partly by adverse weather) in the last two years of the 1966–70 plan.[3] It has been estimated,

---

[1] Blaszak, p. 149. The idea that the imposition of sanctions or the threat of imposition had a psychological effect on enterprises was expressed by a number of authors. However, no examples of this effect were specified and there was no evaluation of the strength of the effect.   [2] This is explained in the last section of this chapter.

[3] J. Radecki, 'Zapasy w Przedsiębiorstwach Uspołecznionych', *Wiadomości Statystyczne* 8 (1971) p. 11. The author concluded that stock building in Poland was greater than in East Germany and Czechoslovakia, but less than in other East European economies. It compared poorly with stock building in capitalist countries.

in a different source, that for each percentage point of growth of total production there was a 1.04% growth of stocks, while the planned target was 0.99.[1] As before 1965 incorrect stocks continued to present a problem, but most of the main causes of their existence were beyond the scope of bank action (for example changes in plans, shortages in supply of raw materials, broken delivery dates). The authorities, however, still insisted on bank control of stock management. The Minister of Finance, for instance, having observed that in spite of some improvements in 1967 and 1968 there were still many shortcomings in stock management, suggested that banks should continue their task of effectively influencing the management of stocks by enterprises.[2] In fact banks devoted much attention to stock management and indeed intensified their interest in the matter after the new classification was introduced in 1965.[3]

Credit and the finance of investment

Much blame for the poor economic performance of the early 1960s was attributed to anomalies in the planning and finance of investment, some of which were mentioned in the previous chapter (pp. 282–3). The suggested financial remedies usually included the imposition of interest rates[4] on capital (first put forward in the debate of the mid-1950s) and a wider use of credit finance in preference to budgetary

[1] T. Choliński, 'Przyrost Zapasów w Bieżącej Pięciolatce', *BiK* 9 (1970) p. 347.

[2] S. Majewski, 'Zadania Banków w Roku 1969', *WNBP* 1 (1969) p. 1.

[3] R. Michejda, 'Pierwsze Doświadczenia...,' *WNBP* 10 (1966) pp. 397–8. So far it has not been possible to quantify the amount of attention paid by banks to different spheres of enterprise management, because of the lack of data. In 1967 Boruń produced figures based on the work of a 'few branches', suggesting that in controlling enterprises the branches spent their time in the following proportions: 5% on formulation of plans, 20% on the utilisation of fixed and working capital, *45% on the structure of stocks*, 10% on the wage fund, 18% on financial discipline, 2% on lowering of costs of production. Boruń, 'Oddziaływanie...', p. 29.

[4] Economists continued to urge the imposition of interest rates on fixed (and in some cases on all) capital. Misiak, '600 Miliardów Czeka na Oprocentowanie', *ŻG* 41 (1964) p. 1, for instance, lamented that Poland, which pioneered theoretical discussions on the problem, was left behind in the field of practical application. Hungary introduced interest charges on fixed and working capital in January 1964, and in the same year East Germany announced its intention of adopting a similar scheme. Indeed, East Germany did introduce interest rates on fixed assets soon after. Bulgaria adopted a somewhat different solution, by imposing a tax (6%) on fixed and working capital.

grants. It was proposed that credit should not only finance investments of enterprises, but also investment by associations and central investment.[1] The preference for credit over budgetary finance was on the grounds that (a) credit had to be returned, whereas budget funds were a gift, (b) credit carried an interest rate, which ensured that the cost of capital was reflected in the total cost of production, (c) the bank control entailed in the issue of credit ensured greater efficiency of investment.[2]

Some economists were not convinced that a change in the method of financing investment would necessarily lead to greater efficiency of investment, rightly pointing out that inadequacies in the realm of investment reflected inadequacies of a more fundamental nature. The costing of projects in particular was poor, resulting in significant differences between actual and estimated costs.[3] The lack of co-ordination between physical investment processes and financial processes was stressed and so was the weakness of financial stimuli, caused largely by the lack of autonomy for enterprises, especially as regards the formation and division of the DF.[4] Sałdak found it difficult to accept, on the basis of past experience of bank control, that the extension of control by credit to investment would improve investment processes, claiming that banks already tried to control too much with too little qualified staff. Credit finance of central investment would simply raise employment in banks, with little economic effect.[5]

The 1965 reforms did not alter the classification of investment into central, by association and by enterprises, but, as shown by table 65, there was a change in the relative size of these investments. Consistently with the declaration of a need for greater self-finance

[1] A. Wołowczyk, 'Czy i Jak Kredytować Inwestycje', *Finanse* 6 (1965) esp. p. 45. Some wanted budgetary finance to remain only for 'priority projects' (estimated at 15% of all investment). M. Krzak and T. Zaczek, 'Jak Usprawnić Finansowanie Inwestycji', *ŻG* 8 (1965) p. 1. The 4th Congress of the Party came out in favour of credit finance of investment, *ND* 7 (1964) p. 183. For the Ministry of Finance view see Trendota, 'Jak...', p. 6.
[2] Some economists felt that bank control (based on economic instruments) over fixed investment was likely to be more effective than monetary control over stocks and that credit policy could regulate production processes only if it were used to finance investment. Szyszko, 'Cele...', pp. 5–7.
[3] Z. Sałdak, 'Kredytować czy Usprawniać', *ŻG* 15 (1965) p. 7.
[4] Jaslar, pp. 3–6; Wierzbicki, 'Finansowanie...', pp. 1–6.
[5] Sałdak, 'Kredytować...', p. 7.

Table 65

Relative size of net investment : central, by associations, by enterprises 1965–7

(a, mil. zł. ; b, percentages of total)

Year	Total a	Central a	Central b	Associations a	Associations b	Enterprises[1] a	Enterprises[1] b
1965	76,743	48,461	63.1	17,223	22.4	11,059	14.4
1966	86,110	46,598	54.1	24,215	28.1	15,297	17.8
1967	92,820	47,709	51.4	29,450	31.7	15,661	16.9

Note:
[1] Expenditure on capital repairs was (in mil. zł.): 20,066 in 1965, 22,036 in 1966 and 24,281 in 1967.
Source: GUS – *RSF 1945–1967*, pp. 22–4.

by economic units, investments by associations and enterprises rose relative to central investment.

Before moving to financial reforms it may be noted that, at last, after a lengthy debate on the subject, an interest rate was imposed on the value of fixed assets in state enterprises.[1] The basic rate was 5%, deductible from profit and paid into the budget, but some enterprises (mainly in heavy industry) were exempted or paid only a 2.5% rate.

Changes in financing investment were brought in on 28 October 1965 by resolution 278 of the CM, 'On the principles of finance of investment and capital repairs of state institutions.'[2] Central investments were to be financed by credit granted mainly by the IB. 'The terms on which credit is issued are determined in the credit contract.' As a rule the credit was not to carry an interest rate, but there were to be instances when interest rates were to be imposed: (*a*) 'The bank charges interest on additional credit granted to cover expenditure in excess of planned costs of investment',

[1] Resolution 279 of the CM passed on 28 October 1965 'On the imposition of interest charges on fixed capital in some state enterprises.' *MP* 61 (1965) item 319. Order of the Minister of Finance (11 November 1965) 'On the imposition of interest charge on fixed assets in state industrial enterprises embraced by central planning.' *MP* 61 (1965) item 324.
[2] *MP* 61 (1965) item 318. Some new provisions on investment finance were also laid down by resolution 276 (see p. 290).

(*b*) 'Interest rates are chargeable on the whole credit during the period after the expiry of the date of repayment set in the credit contract.' However, credit for the financing of investment was not a straightforward credit. 'The investor after the completion of investment repays bank credit from funds granted by a superior body.' Generally the superior body was to be the association, which repaid credit from the so-called account of centralised depreciation, but if the association did not possess sufficient funds, finance was to come from the budget. Some central investments, known as 'priority investments' were to be financed as before from the budget, but bank credit (repayable from future budget grants) could be granted to speed up their completion.

Thus the credit which was proposed for the finance of non-priority central investment was neither truly credit nor the traditional budget grant, but a mixture of the two, usually referred to as 'technical credit'. This form of finance, as opposed to budget handouts, incorporated financial sanctions against, for instance, delays in fulfilment of investment projects or underestimation in costing.

Investment by associations was to be financed from the investment funds of the associations (formed from the part of the depreciation of enterprises absorbed by the associations and supplemented by budget grants) and credit granted by the IB. As a rule, own funds of the association were to be not less than 30% of investment cost. Credit given to associations for purposes of investment (on terms agreed in the credit contract) was to be repaid from the investment fund of the association.[1]

In the case of investment by enterprises, the authorities decided to split the IRF into two separate funds: capital repairs were to be financed from the newly created 'repairs fund' (*fundusz remontowy*), which was to be formed from depreciation charges left at the disposal of the enterprise (viz. decentralised depreciation), whereas new investment projects were to be financed directly from the DF (account B). As before, enterprises could also use credit (granted by the bank financing their working capital – viz. usually the NBP) to finance their investment projects.[2]

---

[1] Other special funds which the association could have were the reserve fund and 'the fund of economic projects of the association'. See *MP* 61 (1965) item 316.

[2] Quick-yield investment remained a separate category and continued to be covered by credit extended by the bank financing working capital requirements and repaid from the DF.

Table 66a

Finance of expenditure on investment and capital repairs in the state sector 1965–7

Source of finance	1965 mil. zł.	%	1966 mil. zł.	%	1967 mil. zł.	%
Budget grants	74,661	51.3	70,662	43.4	69,917	41.1
Depreciation	50,355	34.6	54,190	33.3	59,847	35.1
DF or profit	3,958	2.7	13,327	8.2	14,177	8.3
Bank credit[1]	3,722	2.6	8,590	5.3	12,562	7.4
Other	12,878	8.8	16,064	9.9	13,812	8.1
Total	145,574	100.0	162,833	100.0	170,315	100.0

Note:
[1] Corresponding values in the socialised sector as a whole were: (in mil. zł. and in brackets percentage ratio) 7,431 (4.5), 1,359 (7.4), 20,239 (10.3).
Other explanatory notes and source as in table 56.

Table 66b

Finance of central investment expenditure 1965–7

Source of finance	1965 mil. zł.	%	1966 mil. zł.	%	1967 mil. zł.	%
Budget	35,179	72.6	30,188	64.8	28,214	59.1
Depreciation	13,230	27.3	13,677	29.3	15,432	32.3
Credit	–	–	1,881	4.0	4,063	8.5
Other	52	0.1	852	1.8	–	–
Total	48,461	100.0	46,598	100.0	47,709	100.0

Source: GUS – *RSF 1945–1967*, p. 22.

The actual changes in financing investment after the 1965 reforms are discussed with reference to a number of tables. The effect on the finance of gross investment in the socialised sector as a whole may be seen from tables F1a and F1b, which show the rising importance of bank credit relative to budgetary finance. Up to 1968, however, budgetary allocations were a larger source of

Table 66c

Finance of investment expenditure by associations 1965-7

Source of finance	1965 mil. zł.	%	1966 mil. zł.	%	1967 mil. zł.	%
Budget	3,346	19.4	3,274	13.5	3,745	12.7
Depreciation	12,916	75.0	14,633	60.4	16,452	55.9
DF or profit	–	–	3,812	15.7	4,652	15.8
Credit	–	–	2,480	10.2	4,590	15.6
Other	961[1]	5.6	16	0.1	11	0.0
Total	17,223	100.0	24,215	100.0	29,450	100.0

Note:
[1] Includes a fall in balances on bank accounts of 678 mil. zł.
Source: GUS – *RSF 1945-1967*, p. 23.

Table 66d

Finance of investment and capital repairs in state enterprises 1965-7

Sources of finance	1965 mil. zł.	%	1966 mil. zł.	%	1967 mil. zł.	%
Depreciation	24,125	65.7	23,802	56.9	25,463	57.0
DF or profit	3,829	10.4	9,515	22.7	9,525	21.3
Credit	3,705	10.1	3,454	8.2	3,882	8.7
Other[1]	5,045	13.7	5,075	12.2	5,819	13.0
Total	36,704	100.0	41,846	100.0	44,689	100.0

Explanatory notes and source as in table 55.

investment finance than bank credit. It was only in 1969, when, as will be seen in the next chapter, new moves were made to extend the credit finance of investment, that bank credit (29% of all investment funds) exceeded budget subsidies (22% of investment funds).

Details of the changes in the financing of particular types of investment are given in tables 66a–d and chart 4. According to table 66a, in 1966 and 1967 there was a relative expansion in the finance of gross investment in the state sector from credit and the

Chart 4

*Main sources of finance of investment expenditure: central (C),
by associations (A), by enterprises (E) 1965 and 1967
(approximate proportions of totals)*

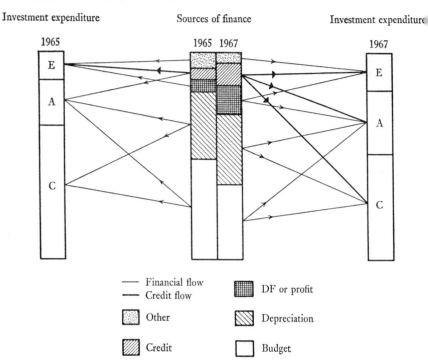

Investment expenditure   Sources of finance   Investment expenditure

DF (compare with table 56).[1] In general, however, the dominant
sources of finance were still the budget (now becoming less significant)
and depreciation. From table 66b it may be seen that bank credit
(for the first time since 1949) became an important source of finance
for central investment. However, the share of credit in the overall
finance of this type of investment was still small, budgetary finance
being the most important source, although declining in importance.
    Table 66c deals with the finance of investment by associations,

----

[1] The ratio of the rise in investment credit to investment funds advanced by the financial
system (see p. 228) was 3.1% in 1965, 6.9% in 1966 and 8.9% in 1967. The respective
ratios for budget finance were 49.6%, 43.4% and 38.9%, and for the DF 2.1%, 5.0%
and 3.3% (compare with p. 281).

showing that after 1965 two new sources of finance appeared, namely the DF (or profit) and credit. Budget finance declined and in 1967 became less important than finance from these two sources. Depreciation, although still the most important source of finance, was declining in importance.

Finally the finance of investment (gross) by enterprises is shown in table 66d (which may be compared with table 55). Here interesting changes emerge: finance from credit in 1966–7 declined a little relative to 1965, but finance from the DF and profit rose significantly. This tallies with our earlier observations on self-finance (pp. 289–91). Depreciation figures as the most important source of funds, largely because the table includes expenditure on capital repairs, which forms a very large proportion of gross investment expenditure of enterprises (see table 65 note 1).

Thus in general as a result of the 1965 reforms credit and funds accumulated internally became more important sources of investment expenditure. Credit began to be substituted for budget finance for central investment and investment by associations. Though budgetary allocations still represented a considerably more important source of finance than credit, this importance was declining. It is interesting to observe that in 1966 budgetary expenditure on investment declined in absolute terms compared with the preceding year for the first time since 1951. Table 67 shows that the ratio of budgetary expenditure on investment to total budgetary expenditure declined after 1965.

The distribution of investment credit after the 1965 reforms is shown by table 68, which once more confirms a significant expansion in investment credit (app. 48% between 1965 and 1967). In absolute terms, the credit expanded in the case of every recipient listed in the table. Housebuilding received the largest proportion of credit, followed by enterprises.

As far as bank control of investment is concerned, there were no important changes compared with the preceding period, except that it was hoped that control would be strengthened through the extension of credit finance of investment and that the imposition of interest on capital would lead to more rational planning and utilisation of investment. Albrecht, in his assessment, thought that interest charges on fixed assets did not lead to better utilisation of fixed capital, but that the new system of finance was proving successful. Investment projects were more realistic and the completion period

Table 67

Budgetary expenditure 1965–9

Year	Total mil. zł.	On gross investment		On net investment	
		mil. zł.	% of total	mil. z..	% of total
1965	288,854	72,852	25.2	67,304	23.3
1966	318,269	68,673	21.6	62,286	19.6
1967	322,006	67,427	20.9	60,238	18.7
1968	326,449	59,700	15.2		
1969	351,546	54,780	15.6		

Sources: GUS – *RS 1967* pp. 558–9; *RS 1968* p. 557; *RS 1970* p. 533.

Table 68

Distribution of credit in the socialised sector 1965–7
(*Balances at the end of the year*)

	1965		1966		1967	
	mil. zł.	%	mil. zł.	%	mil. zł.	%
Total credit	30,063	100.0	41,254	100.0	57,378	100.0
Central investment	–	–	2,203	5.0	4,912	8.6
Associations	–	–	2,910	7.0	6,193	10.8
Enterprises[1]	8,739	29.1	9,318	22.6	10,734	18.7
Housebuilding	14,559	48.4	17,729	43.0	23,031	40.1
Agricultural institutions[2]	2,299	7.6	3,519	8.5	4,199	7.3
Others	4,466	14.8	5,575	13.5	8,309	14.5

Notes:
[1] Including industrial and trading co-operatives.
[2] E.g. collective farms, Agricultural Development Fund.
Source: GUS – *RSF 1945–1967*, p. 236.

was shortened. The IB acted as a filter against 'hooking on' to the investment plan.[1] However, little information is available to support the optimistic evaluation of the Minister of Finance.

[1] It refused (presumably in 1966) to accept 7.5 bil. zł. of central investment and 13 bil. zł. of investment by associations. J. Albrecht, 'Pierwsze Doświadczenia i Wnioski', *ŻG* 26 (1967) p. 5.

The effectiveness of the 1965 financial reforms

The financial changes of 1965, like those of the 1956–8 period, were designed to sharpen the incentive effect of finance and to shape financial instruments, such as credit and interest rates, into effective weapons of economic control, which could be used instead of administrative regulations and discretionary commands of superior organs. Once again the reform built up a structure of financial stimuli, hoping that enterprises would become sensitive to them and in consequence adopt more realistic costing methods and improve management in general. Once again, however, progress in the realm of financial reform outstripped progress in the realm of planning and general management of the economy. The proposed changes in the relations between associations and ministries did not in practice materialise. The enterprise failed to achieve more autonomy as a result of changes affecting the association. In controlling enterprises associations failed to replace arbitrary commands by 'economic methods' and to create a climate of greater financial certainty for the enterprises. The index of profitability, contrary to expectations, did not become a factor injecting profit motivation into management, but a cumbersome addition to a multitude of directive indices handed down to enterprises by their superior bodies. The profit motive, which was in theory embodied in the index, was in practice further eroded by its changeability and the instability of norms determining the distribution of profit and the DF. The lack of progress in these fields rendered the changes in the financial superstructure impotent. The lack of co-ordination, and indeed the lack of any strong causal relationship between financial processes and real processes, continued to be the root cause of the ineffectiveness of the financial system.

It was generally agreed that the interplay between stocks and investment, which was allegedly strengthened by the financial reforms of 1965, was weak.[1] First, it has already been noted that the formation and the distribution of the DF was not, in fact, dependent on the performance and initiative of enterprises and that there was considerable uncertainty surrounding the fund. Secondly, difficulties

[1] See e.g. Siemiątkowski, pp. 228–9; R. Napiórkowski, 'Samofinansowanie a Niektóre Problemy Kredytowania i Kontroli Przedsiębiorstw', *WNBP* 9 (1968) pp. 376–81; 'Kilka...', pp. 20–4; 'Gra Zapasy – Inwestycje', *ŻG* 31 (1969) p. 10.

were encountered in the classification of stocks. It must be remembered that different stocks were financed from different sources. The new classification proved to be unsatisfactory, largely due to a high degree of arbitrariness in grouping stocks into current, seasonal, reserves, unnecessary and superfluous.[1] As was anticipated (see pp. 301–2), disputes on the subject between banks and enterprises increased.[2] 'The division of stocks into the groups mentioned above is made on the basis of criteria which are not completely unambiguous and are often very foggy.'[3] The author of this quotation claimed that mistakes made by banks in classifying stocks were likely to be considerable. Thus the amount of money spent on working capital from the DF (and hence the demand for credit) depended to some extent on arbitrary decisions by banks concerning stock classification. Thirdly, the interplay of stocks and investment rested mainly on enterprises having a high propensity to invest which, it was thought, would make them economise on stocks in order to leave as much of the DF as possible for investment. In fact the interplay was ineffective, for two main reasons: (a) the ratio between investment and stocks of enterprises was very small,[4] so that a small increase in stocks or a small fault in classification often left very little money for investment purposes; (b) in spending investible funds enterprises did not in fact have unfettered choice between stocks and fixed assets. Investment depended in the main on the physical resources available for its fulfilment and not on the availability of funds. 'The availability of money is not the only nor the most important condition of investment by enterprises.'[5] Having commented on the 'lack of co-ordination between the financial system and other sectors of planning and management'

[1] M. Znaniecki, 'Niektóre Zagadnienia Funkcjonowania Nowego Systemu Finansowego', *WNBP* 11 (1966) pp. 435–40.

[2] Michejda, 'Pierwsze...', p. 394.

[3] Napiórkowski, 'Kilka...', p. 21.

[4] Various estimates of the ratio are given; see for example, R. Michejda, 'Pierwsze...', p. 397. Napiórkowski ('Kilka...', p. 21) suggested that in the majority of enterprises the ratio did not exceed 2–3%. Kargol ('Kilka Uwag o Systemie Finansowania Inwestycji', *WNBP* 11 (1968) p. 454) estimated the ratio of investment by enterprises to working capital as 1:17.

[5] Napiórkowski, 'Kilka...', p. 20. A similar observation was made by Siemiątkowski (p. 229): 'The possession of money does not constitute the permission to invest, and by the same token does not give the possessor of the funds any freedom of preference. In view of this we may claim that the interplay between stocks and investment is largely eliminated from the system.'

and on the fact that due to shortages of materials banks were ordered in the last quarter of 1967, not to accept any more investment projects by enterprises, Siemiątkowski (who in mid-1968 became the Chairman of the NBP) suggested that: 'The whole carefully constructed concept of advantages derived from the possession of own funds, accumulated thanks to the thriftiness and good management of a factory, crashed once the theory was first confronted with hard reality.'[1] A further manifestation of the lack of a relationship between investment and its finance was that enterprises faced with a general shortage of capital goods placed orders for them well ahead (at least a year) of the proposed commencement of investment, irrespective of whether own funds were available or not. After all, if they were not available credit could be obtained or, in some cases, investment could be reclassified (for example from investment by enterprise to investment by association). Finally, permission to carry out investment projects was not always granted on economic grounds. Often it was not so much the purposefulness of the project and its estimated effectiveness that mattered as much as 'the ability to argue' and the support of local political authorities.[2]

Thus the interplay between stocks and investment and the system of incentives based on the DF was found to be so ineffective and administratively cumbersome that some advocated the abolition of the DF as the primary source of investment finance. More specifically, it was proposed that investment should be financed from credit, and that funds accumulated in the DF should simply be used to repay the credit.[3] However, judging by past experience, one may doubt whether the extension of credit finance alone could result in a substantial improvement in economic efficiency.

Indeed, the extension of the scope of credit finance after 1965 and the use of interest rates on credit as the primary weapon of bank control failed to play the role expected of them at the time of the reform. The dominant role of quantitative directive indices in planning was a barrier constraining the effectiveness of credit by blunting

[1] Siemiątkowski, p. 222. Unlimited investment by enterprises was sometimes advocated as long as the criteria of purposefulness and effectiveness were satisfied, see e.g. B. Blass, 'W Sprawie Dalszej Decentralizacji Systemu Funkcjonowania Gospodarki', ND 10 (1966) p. 69.
[2] Napiórkowski, 'Kilka...', p. 22.
[3] Such a proposal was made by Napiórkowski, 'Kilka...', pp. 22-3. See also 'Samofinansowanie...', pp. 280-1.

the sensitivity of enterprises to all financial instruments of action (e.g. index of profitability, special funds, prices). Michejda concluded: 'the ambitions and enthusiastic attempts to enhance the role of credit and its influence on the economic life do not, it seems, find full support in structural changes and those aspects of management which are independent of credit.'[1] It should also be remembered that credit financing central non-priority investment was not really credit in the full sense of the word, but a curious hybrid of a budgetary handout and credit, whose chief *raison d'être* was the desire to incorporate a penalty for not fulfilling investment projects according to plans. Such a change in finance, without prior changes in the process of decision taking on investment and in the face of weak profit motivation, was destined to remain without noticeable success. Also it is difficult to understand why 'technical credit' and not normal or 'economic credit' was adopted to finance this type of investment.[2]

The main reason for expanding credit finance was that it gave rise to bank control. However, it was not at all clear whether further extension of bank control of the type previously exercised would yield a positive effect. As before, bank control continued to be widespread, embracing practically every aspect of the activity of enterprises. Its scope was often criticised for being too wide and the means at the disposal of banks for carrying it out were criticised for being inadequate. Thus bank decisions (for example on stocks), which were in practice binding on enterprises, were often based on a superficial knowledge of their business and insufficiently rigorous economic analysis. Banks were also short of staff of the right calibre.

The postulate of a universal creditor who possesses expertise in the sphere of a comprehensive economic analysis and in the tactics of operations and commands a wide knowledge of the economics of some industries as well as the knowledge of specialist regulations concerning investment, wages, export, financial and credit systems, is in many cases a fiction.[3]

Furthermore, in some cases (usually important industrial enterprises) bank control was mitigated by what Boruń called 'side issues', such as the intervention of the association or political authorities,

[1] Michejda, 'Warunki...', *WNBP* 3 (1969) p. 98.
[2] Indeed this move was criticised by bankers and economists, who expressed a preference for 'economic credit', viz. 'anticipating credit', returnable and subject to interest, e.g. Blass, 'W Sprawie...', p. 68.
[3] Boruń, pp. 30–1.

making banks reluctant to apply sanctions.[1] In such a situation, therefore, attempts to extend bank control further without first altering its whole philosophy of operation could not be regarded as economically significant.

[1] Michejda, 'Warunki...', pp. 102-3. On the practical difficulties experienced by credit inspectors faced with the tasks of control see R. Napiórkowski, 'W Dążeniu do Usprawnienia Działalności Kredytowej Oddziałów Operacyjnych', *WNBP* 8 (1967) pp. 344-7. A credit inspector usually serviced three enterprises in key industries and 4-5 in other branches of the economy. He had to grapple with problems of plan fulfilment, costing, stock control, investment, wage payments and other settlements.

11

The banking and credit reforms of 1969–70: a bolder step towards credit finance of investment

Introduction: yet another phase of reforms

The results of the reforms of the mid-sixties, discussed in the previous chapter, were generally recognised by the late sixties as disappointing and the authorities continued to look for a formula of transition from 'extensive' to 'intensive' growth. In the meantime growth was sustained mainly through increased inputs of labour and capital. In 1968 the gross investment ratio reached its highest level of 31.7%.[1] At the same time the average rate of growth of national income (and *per capita* income) in the 1966–70 plan was less than in the preceding plans. Investment efficiency was falling.[2]

In 1968 there were already clear signs that a new wave of economic changes was planned. Discussions on these started in earnest at about the time of the v Congress of the Party (11–16 November 1968) and have continued ever since. Some reforms have already been carried out, others are in the debating stage. The events which followed the December 1970 riots in coastal areas (Szczecin, Gdańsk) have checked some changes (especially those connected with the new remuneration schemes) and are likely to bring about the rethinking of others, plus a sprinkling of new ones.

The general aims of the reforms remained essentially the same: to increase economic efficiency, so that the growth of production becomes less a result of factor inputs and more a result of increased factor productivity. Similarly the general strategy for achieving this transition remained basically the same: more self-management for enterprises and associations, stronger material incentives, more efficient use of existing assets, better planning of new investment so as to select the most efficient projects, and quicker execution of investment plans.

[1] GUS – *RDN 1965–8*, p. 35.
[2] K. Secomski, 'Dynamika i Kierunki Wzrostu', *Ekonomista* 6 (1970) pp. 1059–60.

322

In this chapter attention is given mainly to the banking reform, which has now been implemented, and the proposed new ways of planning and financing investment. Before proceeding to these topics it may be noted that, as far as the finance of working capital and the strategy of the lenient credit control are concerned, no fundamental changes have been introduced. Some alterations were, however, made in the finance of working capital.[1] The DF was abolished and working capital was to be financed directly from profits[2] and credit, without any more attempts to implement the interplay between stocks and investment which had proved of little value in the past (see pp. 317–20). Credit, as hitherto, was to finance 100% of seasonal stocks and reserves. 60% of current and incorrect stocks (see p. 301) were to be covered by own funds and the rest by other funds, mainly credit. If the enterprise financed less than 60% of these by own funds, credit was to be given at higher rates of interest. If, on the other hand, it decided to finance more than 70% from own funds, then banks were to charge lower rates. Clearly the whole strategy of lenient monetary policy, discussed in chapter 8 and elaborated in Chapter 9, continued. Credit restrictions were not to be relied on as a method of control; more faith in this respect was still placed in interest rates. At the same time the classification of stocks for finance purposes remained a problem and the capacity of banks to influence stock management a problematical issue.

Credit as the chief source of investment finance

It may have been noticed that in the various waves of reforms after the mid-fifties financial changes were by far the most perceptible, though not always the most gratifying. In the late sixties financial changes again became conspicuous, especially in the realm of investment.

For many years a key weakness of the Polish economy has been the low efficiency of investment. One way of improving investment efficiency, strongly advocated for some time, is to switch from budget finance to credit finance of investment. The arguments for this have already been discussed and no new ones appeared in the late sixties.

[1] See proposals of the CM published in *ŻG* 50 (1969) pp. 5–6.
[2] Distribution of profits was to be governed by long-term 'norms' (compare pp. 290–1).

It has been noted that after 1955 credit finance of investment increased, but not very significantly. Even in the 1965-6 reforms, when the authorities professed a preference for this form of finance, the move to replace budget finance of investment by 'technical credit' was rather timid (see pp. 310-11, 320). At the V Party Congress it was decided, among other things, to extend further credit ('economic credit') finance of investment and to concentrate the finance in one bank, so as to improve the supervision of investment activity. The II Plenary Session of the CC (3-4 April 1969) was devoted mainly to more detailed discussions of these proposals. It became generally accepted (at least in publications) that investment processes must be closely co-ordinated with national economic administration and that it is important in the national interest to concentrate on investment yielding the highest rates of return.

Consequently it was resolved to abandon the existing classification of investment in the state sector (see pp. 277-9) and instead to distinguish between three types of investment: Branch (*branżowe*) investments, investments of enterprises and investments of budget units (viz. non-production institutions). The last mentioned investments, which are of little interest to us, were to be financed from 'credit' (in the case of buildings) which was not subject to interest and was refundable from the budget, and from own funds.

The most important investments were to be branch investments. These include non-agricultural projects subject to central (as opposed to local[1]) planning, comprising over 90% of investment in e.g. industry, building, transport. Branch investments thus constitute the bulk of national investment, incorporating projects of vital economic importance. In terms of the previous classification of investment, branch investments included central investments, investment by associations, and a part (mainly construction) of investment by enterprises. They were to be undertaken chiefly by the associations, which were thus given much greater scope to decide on the development of sections of industry (see p. 288).

Investments by enterprises were to be somewhat restricted (by the exclusion of construction) compared with the previous situation. It may thus be said that the scope of enterprises to decide on their own expansion has been limited.

---

[1] In the sphere of production subject to local authority planning (*plan terenowy*), branch investments are also distinguished; they are of major local importance and are the responsibility of the national councils.

The new law concerning the finance of investment was passed by the CM on 15 July 1969,[1] to become operative from the beginning of 1970. Its main effect was to make bank credit (returnable and subject to interest) the principal source of investment finance. It may be recalled that in the 'Polish economic model' credit played this role before being replaced, as part of the overall process of centralisation in national economic management, by budgetary finance in 1949. Twenty years later, and after some half-hearted attempts at decentralisation, it was felt that, as part of the decentralisation process, it had become necessary to utilise credit more widely, as the most flexible method of finance available in a socialist economy.

Chart 5 summarises the main sources of investible funds. It may be seen that branch investment in building was financed exclusively from credit, whereas the investment fund of associations (IFA) covered mainly non-construction investments. Credit could also, but exceptionally, be used to finance the latter. The main source of repayment of credit is the IFA, formed by the apportionment of depreciation funds and of profits of enterprises.

The principal source of funds for investment and capital repairs (now linked again) of enterprises became the investment and repairs fund (IRF). Credit could, however, exceptionally be used to bridge a temporary shortage of finance. The fund was formed from a part of depreciation charges roughly covering estimated capital repairs needs and from allocations from profit calculated to cover new capital requirements.

Interest rates on investment credit are to be used flexibly. For credit on branch investment the normal rate is 3% (1.5% on projects involving modernisation). However, higher interest charges are levied in cases where planned costs are exceeded or where projects are not completed within the estimated time. Similarly compliance with cost estimates or premature completion entitles credit recipients to lower interest rates. Thus basically the post-1965

[1] Resolution 124 'On the principles of financing investment and capital repairs of state units.' *MP* 32 (1969) item 237. Information on the reform is also taken from S. Majewski, 'Zmiany Zasad Finansowania Inwestycji', *GP* 8 (1969); J. Trendota, 'Kierunki Dalszego Doskonalenia Systemu Finansowego Przemysłu', *Finanse* 8 (1969) pp. 8–10; A. Wołowczyk, 'Kierunki Zmian Finansowania Inwestycji', *ŻG* 30 (1969) p. 5. 'Nowy System Finansowania Inwestycji', *ŻG* 38 (1969) p. 6, 'Nowe Zasady Finansowania Inwestycji', *Finanse* 7 (1969).

Chart 5

Sources of investment finance after the 1969 reform

I. Finance of branch investment

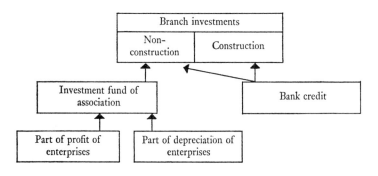

II. Finance of investment of enterprises

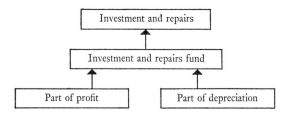

scheme of using interest rates as a financial incentive continues. Indeed in official pronouncements on the reform the possibility of linking credit finance with a system of 'incentives and sanctions' based on differentiated rates of interest was very strongly emphasised. Only the future will show whether enterprises in practice become sufficiently responsive to financial stimuli for the system to fulfil expectations.

Thus, after a long period of persevering with various schemes of investment finance, all of them giving priority to budgetary subsidies, the recent reform has returned to a system resembling that in operation before 1949, when the key source of investible funds was bank credit. It remains to be seen what effect the reform will have. The lesson of financial changes so far is quite clearly that the financial reform, which merely replaces one source of funds by another, is unable to exert much effect in isolation. Such a reform will prove useful only if the planning and realisation of investment are comprehensively improved and become responsive to financial impulses. Some form of 'market' reaction is needed before credit, an essentially market instrument, can exert controlling influence.

The banking reform

Ever since the NBP began to grant investment credit (in 1955), specialisation, whereby the bank granted short-term credit financing working capital and the IB financed investment, has become increasingly blurred. In general, the NBP financed mainly the investment of enterprises, whereas the IB granted credit for central and associations' investments. The problem of co-ordinating bank finance and control of investment, though it existed after the introduction in 1958 of decentralised (partly credit financed) investments, became more pressing after the 1965 reforms, which further extended credit finance. Co-ordination of operations between the NBP and the IB became necessary. In an interview in 1967 the Minister of Finance spoke of the two banks reaching 'a special understanding, determining the principles of co-operation',[1] but there was little evidence that a satisfactory *modus operandi* at the branch level was ever worked out. There was thus a need for institutional changes, which became inevitable after decisions were taken to reform the finance of investment once again.

Changes in the banking system had already been discussed by the v Party Congress and the II Plenary Session of the CC, which proposed the creation of a single bank financing all non-agricultural investment. Though both the Minister of Finance and the Chairman of the NBP claimed in their pronouncements on the bank reform that a number of variants of banking systems had been carefully considered,[2] there was little public debate on the issue. The main act

[1] 'Założenia Polityki Finansowej na Lata 1966–1970', *WNBP* 1 (1967) p. 3.
[2] The account given by the Minister of the variants considered (which apparently included a banking system with a 'bankers' bank' type of central bank) did not correspond exactly with that of the Chairman, but it is unlikely that there was serious disagreement on the version actually chosen.

changing the banking system was passed by the CM on 23 October 1969, the reform becoming operative from January 1970.[1]

The key provision of the reform was the amalgamation of the NBP with the IB. Thus the bank of issue was at the same time to meet both the short and long-term credit needs of the whole non-agricultural sector of the economy. The main reason for the amalgamation was the need to set up an institution capable of improving the efficiency of investment by supervising investment processes in industry more effectively and, in particular, by making certain that the new policy of selecting the most profitable investment projects was properly implemented. To this end the NBP was enlarged to become the principal institution executing the policy of transition from extensive to intensive growth. Before further discussing its impact on the NBP, some other important provision of the reform may be noted.

The AB became the central financial institution of the agricultural sector of the economy. There has taken place an exchange of customers between the NBP and the bank. For instance, the NBP took over from the AB the finance of the furniture industry and match making; the AB took over from the NBP the finance of saw mills and dairies. As a result of the reform the AB, together with SLCs, became the key source of external finance for agriculture, forestry and industries directly based on them. The TB remained the bank financing all requirements (including investment) of international trade enterprises. The CSB, which was mainly the bank for mobilising small savings, but which after 1960 started to extend a small amount of consumer credit (see table 60a), was turned into a full-blooded bank catering for the public at large. It remained the savings bank for the people, but now acquired the competence and capacity to extend credit to individuals. It took over the finance of private urban housing from the IB and consumer finance from the Hire Purchase Bank 'ORS', which ceased to exist.

The immediate impact of the 1969 reform on the structure of

[1] Resolution 195 'On some tasks and the change in the statute of NBP.' A number of separate enactments and orders of the Minister of Finance based on the resolution were subsequently passed; see *Przegląd Ustawodawstwa Gospodarczego* 1 (1970) pp. 16-17, 2 (1970) p. 46. See also S. Majewski (the Minister of Finance), 'Reforma Bankowości', *Finanse* 8 (1969); L. Siemiątkowski (Chairman of NBP), 'Przesłanki, Cele i Zadania Obecnej Reformy Bankowej', *WNBP* 11 (1969) 'Zadania Banku w Zakresie Opiniowania Planu Inwestycyjnego', *BiK* 11 (1970) 'Reforma Bankowa', *Rocznik Polityczny i Gospodarczy 1970*, pp. 468-76.

Table 69

Credit by the banking system 1969 and 1970

(*Balances at the end of the year ; a, bil. zł. ; b, percentages of total in each year*)

	1969		1970	
	a	*b*	*a*	*b*
Total credit	512.8	100.0	598.0	100.0
NBP	239.4	46.7	482.0	80.6
BI	165.3	32.2	amalgamated with NBP	
AB	60.5	11.8	65.2	10.9
SLCs	16.4	3.2	17.2	2.9
TB	14.6	2.8	15.0	2.5
CSB	9.1	1.8	18.6	3.1
'ORS'[1]	7.5	1.5	amalgamated with CSB	

Note:
[1] Hire Purchase Bank 'ORS'.
Sources: See table 60a; *NBP – Rocznik Informacyjny*, 1971, p. 21.

the banking system is illustrated by tables 69, 70a and 70b, and tables B1b and E1a in Appendices B and E respectively. Table 69 shows the relative importance of credit institutions after the reform. The NBP's dominance of the credit system has been strengthened, and the bank was responsible for extending 81% of all credit in 1970. The NBP and AB together extended 91.5% of all credit. The provisions of the reform affected the structure of liabilities of the banking system (table B1b), where budgetary deposits with banks (chiefly the NBP) increased in importance (being 25% of total liabilities in 1970) relative to all other sources of credit. Thus budgetary finance still plays a vital part in capital accumulation, but it is no longer granted directly to investors.

The nature of the credit reform is also strongly reflected in the NBP's balance sheet. First the bank's level of activity, as measured by the balance sheet total, increased between 1969 and 1970 by nearly 50%. The structure of its liabilities has changed (see table 70a). Budgetary deposits with the bank rose from 16% of total deposits in 1969 to 27% in 1970. Deposits allocated by enterprises for investment purposes increased between the two years from 5% to 17% of total liabilities. Bankers' deposits, on the other hand, fell from 28% to 19% of the total.

Table 70b shows the effect of the 1969 reform on the NBP's credit activity. Three points may be emphasised. First, the ratio of investment credit to the total credit issued by the bank rose from 6% in 1969 to 35% in 1970. In 1970 the bank extended 94.4% of all investment credit given to the socialised sector (compare with table 61c). Secondly, the ratio of the short-term credit granted by the bank to the bank's total credit issue fell, between 1969 and 1970, from 62% to 58%. On the other hand, the ratio of the short-term credit granted by the bank to the socialised sector to the short-term credit extended by the banking system to the sector rose, between the two years, from 69% to 87%[1] (compare with table 61b). Thirdly, with the relative growth of the bank and the reduction in the number of credit institutions, refinance of other banks decreased substantially, from 31% to 7% of total deposits. Thus the 1969 reform is a definite step towards a monobanking system. Indeed, as far as the non-agricultural sector of the economy is concerned, the NBP is for all practical purposes a monobank, not only as regards short-term credit (as was the case in the early and mid-fifties) but also as regards long-term credit.

As already stated, the chief provision of the reform was the enlarging of the NBP by amalgamation with the IB. It may be noted that the fusion of the central bank with the investment bank is not without precedent in socialist banking. Such a development had already taken place in Czechoslovakia in 1959 (see p. 191). A somewhat different solution to the institutional problems of banking has recently (1971) been proposed in Hungary. One of the intended measures is for the Hungarian National Bank to take over from the Hungarian Investment Bank the finance of investment in enterprises and other economic units. Thus one bank is to finance both fixed and working capital in the socialised sector. The investment bank is to be reformed as a Development Bank, whose function would be to advise on the control and finance (mostly from budget funds) of new investment projects of national importance.

Compared with Western central banks the newly constituted NBP has a unique characteristic of combining central banking functions (e.g. issue, of being the government's bank) with those concerned with short-term credit and the accumulation and distribution of long-term funds, which in the West are usually performed by the commercial banking system and the capital market. It still retains

[1] NBP – *Rocznik Informacyjny* (1971) pp. 42, 44.

Table 70a

Liabilities of the NBP before and after the 1969 reform

(*Balances at the end of the year : a, mil. zl.; b, percentages of total*)

Year	Total a	Current and deposit a/cs[1] a	b	Deposits for inv. purposes a	b	Budgetary deposits a	b	Bank deposits[2] a	b	Currency in circulation a	b	Settlements in progress a	b	Own funds a	b	Other a	b
1969	348,425	83,412	23.9	17,752	5.1	56,826	16.3	97,987	28.1	57,425	16.5	18,894	5.4	12,214	3.5	3,915	1.1
1970	518,484	91,468	17.6	89,743	17.3	140,250	27.1	98,240	19.0	58,644	11.3	21,095	4.1	16,287	3.1	2,753	0.5

Notes:

[1] Current accounts and accounts of special funds (e.g. factory fund) of enterprises.

[2] Mainly deposits of the CSB placed directly with the NBP.

Sources: *NBP – Information Bulletin*, 1970, p. 44; *NBP – Rocznik Informacyjny*, 1971, p. 45.

Table 70b

Credit activity of the NBP before and after the 1969 reform
(Balances at the end of the year: a, mil. zł.; b, percentages of total)

Year	Total	Direct credit									Refinance[1]	
		Socialised enterprises						Private sector				
		Total		Short-term		Investment						
	a	a	b	a	b	a	b	a	b	a	b
1969	348,425	237,355	68.1	216,409	62.1	20.946	6.0	1,927	0.5	109,142	31.3
1970	518,473	479,513	92.5	299,905	57.8	179,608	34.6	2,541	0.5	36,419	7.0

Note:
[1] Refinance of other banks.
Sources: Table 61a, NBP – *Rocznik Informacyjny*, 1971, p. 44.

the function of being the 'bankers' bank', though, as has already been mentioned, its refinance of other banks has declined drastically since the reform. This is of little practical consequence for a socialist central bank, which does not utilise open market operations as a method of monetary control. It is on its statutory rights and not on refinance that the bank's supervision over the whole banking system is based. The bank has thus become what may be called the central-universal bank of the economy.

In fulfilling its new key function of investment finance the bank has received some tasks additional to those which it already had. It is to become the centre of information concerning all aspects of investment. It is to analyse this information and utilise it in controlling investment processes and in advising the authorities on investment policy and on the feasibility and implications of new capital projects. Thus it becomes a key informational, advisory, financial and executive institution in the realm of capital accumulation. Its new duties thus assume a macroeconomic character and are additional to its more traditional functions of microeconomic control, which are based on checking on the purposefulness and effectiveness (see pp. 238, 284) of individual investment projects.

So that it could carry out these tasks efficiently, some changes were made in the bank's organisation. As may be seen from table E1a, after the amalgamation with the IB the number of the bank's branches rose from 422 in 1969 to 448 in 1970. This means that the amalgamation led to some rationalisation in branching. The operational branches were divided into two broad groups: general and specialist. Following the reform more specialist branches were created, but few details on this are available. The servicing of enterprises in key industries and building takes place mainly in specialist branches, or branches having specialist cells catering specifically for the clients' requirements. Thus about 2700 enterprises included in the central plan are credited in specialist branches (the rest, about 1100, being serviced by other branches), which are usually directly responsible to the headquarters of the NBP. Some specialist branches were also set up for servicing important enterprises subject to local government planning, but in this respect the typical procedure is for enterprises to be financed in ordinary branches subordinated to the voivodship headquarters, which are in turn subordinated to the central headquarters.

It is at the moment impossible to forecast how successful the reform will be. Doubtless, as before, the banking system will adapt its operations to the new requirements. However, reforms affecting only the sources of finance and their administration cannot be expected to exert a decisive influence on economic efficiency in general. Much must depend on changes in the management of real variables. At the time of writing, it seems that financial changes are again much more perceptible than changes in planning and in administration of production units. This has become a familiar pattern of economic changes in socialist states. But the latest reforms in Poland are not yet completed.

12

Some concluding observations

The structure and functions of the banking system

(a) The development of the financial structure

It may be useful to try to summarise our most interesting findings about socialist banking, finance and control. In doing so it must be remembered that these findings are based mainly on the experience of the Polish economy. This experience was quite typical of East European economies up to the sixties, but during the sixties greater diversification occurred in the national management of the economies. By and large, however, Poland's experience, even during the sixties, was not fundamentally different from that of her socialist neighbours.

Quite striking differences may be noted in the development of Western and socialist financial structures. In the West the questions of whether the development of financial institutions stimulates real development or whether real development largely dictates the development of financial superstructure continue to be debated. What is clear, however, is that there has been a close relationship between real and financial developments. Expansion of economic activity has usually been accompanied by accelerated growth of financial institutions and of financial instruments. Growth in the scale of production units has been matched by growth in the scale of financial units. In addition there has been a marked diversification in terms of new financial institutions and new financial instruments, with the result that developed countries are characterised by extremely complex financial structures and practices.

The development of socialist banks has perhaps matched the development of capitalist banks as regards the scale of operations. Socialist state banks are large institutions, but then they represent a large fraction of the whole financial system. Large capitalist banks

335

are, on the other hand, usually small parts of a highly complex financial structure. Indeed, the growing simplicity of the financial structure accompanying economic development has become the most striking characteristic of socialist financial development. This relative simplicity of the socialist banking structure can only be understood with reference to the role assigned to banks in the course of national economic management.

Banks and banking practices in socialist economies have been deliberately adapted by the authorities to the requirements of socialist planning. In Poland, and this is typical of other socialist economies, banking has been affected by every major reform in economic management.

The pre-war banking system in Poland, described in chapter 3, was dominated by the central bank, the Bank of Poland, and two state banks, the NEB and SAB, both of which were mainly long-term credit institutions. The strength of state banking at that time was chiefly the result of general economic underdevelopment. Poland has never reached a stage of developed capitalism. Inter-war crises caused a relative decline of native private banking and discouraged foreign banking. The government, anxious to develop the economy (especially after 1935) and to strengthen its defence, fostered the growth of state banking, using it principally to promote and finance expenditure envisaged in government economic programmes. Thus, in the pre-war etatism, state banking played a key role in economic development.

After the war, during the creation of the socialist system, there was no question of abandoning the institutions of money and banking. Indeed the currency reforms and the revival of the banking system received priority and proceeded smoothly, due largely to the initiative of the staff of the pre-war banks. The banking system had some interesting features. (*a*) It was, in essence, the pre-war system, but without the many private (usually small) and foreign banks, which were not permitted to reopen. The NBP became the central bank, replacing the Bank of Poland. For a time it functioned like its predecessor, mainly rediscounting bills and exercising monetary control over other banks. (*b*) The banking system was adapted to the tri-sectoral model of economic management, which was a salient feature of the 'Polish road to socialism' described in chapter 4. Each economic sector was serviced by a designated bank or banks and, in addition, the SAB serviced agriculture. (*c*) The system functioned (until the reforms of October 1948) without promulgating new laws, using the pre-war legal framework and banking practices and continuing the tradition of co-operation with the state. However, some Soviet banking principles (for example one client – one bank), whose evolution was briefly reviewed in chapter 2, were also adopted. (*d*) Banks, apart from the NBP, were universal, supplying short as well as long-term credit, though the NEB specialised in long-term finance. (*e*) The banking system played a key role in planning and financing investment. The state sector, embracing all large and medium sized industry, had its investment financed mainly by credit granted by the NEB.

Between 1949 and 1950 the economic system was drastically changed. The Polish road to socialism was abandoned and the Soviet model of planning was adopted speedily and mechanically, though there was no clear economic justification for this. The tri-sectoral approach was manifestly not a failure; the Three Year Plan (1947–9) achieved a rapid rate of economic recovery; there were no obvious reasons for thinking that the replica of the Soviet model of economic management and policy would perform well in Polish conditions. The reforms must be seen mainly in the light of contemporary international tension and the doctrine accepting the Soviet 'model' as a universal prescription for every socialist society. The reforms of 1948–53, described in chapter 5, resulted in a highly concentrated credit system (called the monobank) where, as in the Soviet Union, there was one dominant short-term credit bank, namely the NBP. The Budget represented the instrument of accumulation of investible funds and banks other than the NBP (viz. chiefly the IB and AB) were mainly institutions distributing budgetary funds. Such a financial system survived up to 1956, after which it was gradually modified.

Attempts at decentralisation after 1955 had a significant impact on the banking system. Two phases of development may be distinguished. During the first, lasting till the 1969 reform, the strict division of function between financial institutions, which was the salient feature of the Soviet model of banking, began to wane. Credit for investment began to be issued by the NBP, so that, although its amount was quite small, the bank moved towards becoming a universal bank. The IB continued to expand as a predominantly investment bank. There was a revival of the AB which, broadly speaking, recovered the competence it had lost in the 1948–53 reforms.

There was also a revival of the SLCs, which began to play an important part in the accumulation of savings and the granting of credit to the co-operative and private sectors. Thus, the first attempts to decentralise national economic management were reflected in changes in the relative importance of credit institutions. There was a move away from the monobanking system (though in the late sixties the NBP was still the dominant bank) towards the system which functioned in the late forties. But the attempts at decentralisation have not proved successful, in the sense that they failed to lead to 'intensive growth' characterised by increasing efficiency of capital.

In 1969, largely to improve control by banks over investment and thereby to raise investment efficiency, the two largest banks, the NBP and IB, were amalgamated, so that one bank became the sole source of external non-budgetary finance (both short and long-term) of state non-agricultural enterprises, enabling it to exercise effective financial control over the enterprises. Thus the present banking system is once again highly centralised, with the NBP extending 81% of the total credit of the banking system in 1970. In the socialised sector the monopoly position of the bank was even more striking; it granted over 94% of long-term and nearly 87% of short-term credit received by the sector.

(b) *Bank control as the key element in the financial structure*

The most important single factor which affected the structure of socialist banking was the desire to use banks for purposes of control over the activity of enterprises. The Soviet financial reforms of the late twenties and early thirties, which resulted in the establishment of banking institutions and financial practices accepted later (after the second world war) by all socialist countries, reshaped the banking system of the NEP period, which was influenced by the banking practices of pre-revolutionary days, into a banking system capable of exercising 'planning' and 'management' control (see pp. 47–8) over enterprises. It is what might be called 'control motivation' which has been the driving force behind all major adjustments in socialist banking. Just as in the West the fulfilment of the intermediation function by financial institutions resulted in a highly complex financial system, in socialist economies control motivation resulted in a remarkably simple financial system. Driven largely by the profit motive the Western financial entrepreneur has continuously resorted to financial innovations calculated to attract new savers and to develop new channels of investment, with the result that the saver has at his disposal a variety of savings media (and hence a variety of means of holding his wealth) and the firm has a variety of sources of finance. Driven by control motivation, the socialist authorities sought to centralise, to standardise and to simplify the financial system. One corollary of these developments is that while some banks in capitalist states (especially in Germany and Japan, and even the state-owned NEB in pre-war Poland) promoted industrial development by supplying enterprise and initiative in addition to finance, socialist banks are largely economically passive institutions, engaged mainly in supervisory, analytical, executive and coercive activities.

To exercise effective control socialist countries found it necessary to make enterprises directly dependent on bank finance, by abolishing non-bank external finance (bills of exchange, other commercial credit) and by forcing them to resort to bank loans (mainly by requirements that part of working capital should be covered by credit). Competition between banks has been completely eliminated and a strict demarcation of banking custom applies, so that neither banks nor enterprises are free to exercise any choice in this respect. Enterprises must open a current account with a bank, keep their financial resources in that bank, obtain credit only from that bank and use the other banking services provided by that bank. Such arrangements were conducive to centralisation in banking structure and to the development of a central banking system quite different from that in the West. It may be noted that control aspects in banking are by no means alien to Western economies. In general, however, problems of monetary control, largely in terms of stabilisation policies, are relatively new problems associated with central banking, which itself is a relatively new institution. Indeed Western monetary authorities have, in comparatively recent times, often utilised for control purposes practices previously voluntarily adopted by banks in order to restrain competition (e.g. by interest rates) or regulate behaviour (e.g. as regards the liquidity structure of bank assets). The intermediation function, on the other hand, has been continuously performed by Western financial intermediaries.

The NBP, like its counterparts in socialist economies, performs some functions usually regarded in the West as central banking

12

functions. It is the bank of issue and the government's bank, keeping the accounts of government departments, advising the government on monetary matters and carrying out its monetary policy. However, whereas the key function of the Western central bank is to be the 'bankers' bank', by maintaining the accounts of other banks, participating in clearing operations, refinancing (usually by rediscounting eligible paper) and acting as the lender of last resort, the key function of the NBP has been to act as the 'enterprises' bank', engaged directly in financing and controlling enterprises. It is true that NBP has also been engaged in refinancing other banks, but this has never played a vital part in its operations. Equally it is true that some Western central banks sometimes extend credit directly to firms, but this has never been their primary function. Thus, to reiterate, the main contrast between the central banks in Western and socialist economies stems from the fact that while the former are basically 'bankers' banks' the latter are the 'enterprises' banks'.

Credit finance

In contrast to the situation facing a capitalist firm, few sources of finance are open to a socialist enterprise. It cannot resort to a new issue market or the complex of institutions which comprise the money market in the West. Its finance comes mainly from the budget, its bank, its internal accumulation and, to a much lesser extent, from trade credit. Even with this limited choice of alternatives the enterprise has seldom been free to choose its sources of finance, because some assets had to be financed from strictly defined sources.

In Poland bank credit was of key importance, especially as regards investment finance, both before the war (pp. 64–71) and in the immediate post-war period, up to 1949 (pp. 88–92). In the centralised and detailed directive planning of the Soviet type adopted in the early fifties its role diminished in favour of budgetary finance. The budget became the chief instrument for the accumulation and distribution, in the form of grants, of investment funds. The credit system became basically a short-term credit system. In the state sector credit finance was mainly confined to 'above-normative', viz. basically seasonal or temporary, working capital requirements, strictly defined by regulations. Arguments for retaining credit in the state sector, based on 'the objective necessity' of short-term credit in socialist planning, were not found convincing (pp. 42–3). The *raison d'être* of credit was the authorities' desire to use it as a key weapon of bank control over enterprises, finance being organised in such a way as to force enterprises to borrow from banks (ch. 2).

Every attempt to depart from centralised planning was accompanied by financial reforms and is strongly reflected in the financial statistics given in successive chapters of part III. Basically, reforms aimed at decentralisation involved the gradual replacement of non-returnable, interest-free, budgetary finance, which encouraged wasteful use of resources, by self-finance and bank credit which, it was thought, could incorporate incentives to the more efficient allocation of resources. Credit especially, being returnable and interest-bearing finance granted after bank scrutiny of the creditworthiness of the applicant, was thought to offer a useful means, certainly superior to budgetary subsidies, of financing the expenditure of enterprises and, after 1965, of associations.

Both short and long-term credit finance has now been extended. During the sixties a larger proportion of working capital was financed by credit, largely in order to make enterprises more sensitive to changes in credit conditions, viz. to improve the efficacy of monetary control.

The desirability of financing investment by credit, as opposed to budget handouts, has been widely emphasised since the mid-fifties. Indeed, with every attempt at decentralisation credit finance of investment increased. Up to 1966 its expansion was associated mainly with investment undertaken by enterprises, viz. 'quick-yield investment' (ch. 7), 'decentralised investment' before 1961 (ch. 8) and 'investment by enterprises' after 1961 (chs. 9, 10). However, its importance in financing investment expenditure in the economy as a whole remained small, even after the 1965 reforms, which favoured this form of finance, had extended it to 'investment by associations' and 'centralised investment' (ch. 10). In 1967 credit financed only 7.4% of gross investment expenditure in the state sector (10.3% in the socialised sector). It was not until the reforms of 1969, discussed in chapter 11, that a decisive step was taken to make credit the key source of investment finance. Credit finance of investment has now been linked with financial incentives and penalties (p. 326), which are calculated to lead to a more efficient distribution of resources and ultimately to result in the 'intensive growth' which has so far eluded the authorities.

Bank control

(a) Aims and methods

'Control by money' is considered to be an integral part of the socialist planning mechanism. Its basic principles emerged in the Soviet Union after the 1927–33 financial reforms, discussed in chapter 2. Its economic foundation rests on two propositions: (a) the use of money in exchange makes money flows reflect real economic changes and hence the study of financial flows is helpful in analysing real magnitudes; and (b) the control of the purse strings affords a means of controlling the behaviour of enterprises.

Control by money, narrowly defined (see pp. 45–6), has been exercised in the course of fiscal transactions involving revenue collection and budgetary expenditure and in the course of banking operations. Bank control has been considered to be the most effective form, largely because of the close relationship between the enterprise and its bank, which, in serving as the 'enterprise's bank', is in continuous contact with the enterprise and is thus well placed to exercise control.

The object of bank control is to make certain that enterprises fulfil their plans ('planning control') and manage their affairs efficiently and in accordance with regulations ('management control'). In practice the scope of bank control has been very wide. The banker (usually the 'credit inspector') controlling the enterprise has to place himself in the position of its owner, but at the same time must not allow it to pursue a course contrary to the national interest. He has been a watchdog, seeing that plans and regulations are observed; a servant carrying out its orders (for example, in making credit transfers); a co-manager, empowered to take decisions (for example, in the sphere of settlements and credit) on its behalf and co-operating in the preparation of its financial plans; a mentor in financial matters; a disciplinarian coercing it to improve its management. In the realm of investment he has been the final arbiter of the correctness of costing and of the estimates of the efficiency of investment projects.

Banks exercised their control through monetary control (viz. through control by credit), through settlements and through control of wage funds. Two points of interest may be noted in connection with settlements. First, banks tend to carry out settlements on behalf of enterprises. Perhaps a vivid illustration of their direct involvement in settlements is the fact that when enterprises find themselves in payments difficulties this is often of greater concern to the banks than to them and that banks have shown greater anxiety than enterprises to remedy the difficulties. The comparative lack of involvement of enterprises in settlements came out clearly after 1958, when, being free to choose methods of settlement, few abandoned the customary '*inkaso method*' or showed any interest in other methods, such as cheques or credit transfers (ch. 8).

Secondly, credit on settlements has usually been granted for the duration of the transit of documents (for example, the invoice) involved in the settlement. There is otherwise a separation between settlements and the mainstream of credit financing mainly stocks. This has existed since the abolition of the bill of exchange, which has been widely used in the pre-socialist and early socialist stages of development of East European economies. The bill was at the same time a means of payment and, on discounting, a basis for bank credit. The elimination of bill finance, the separation of settlements from credit and the determination of the duration of bank credit by the transit of documents produced considerable difficulties, especially during periods of stringent monetary control.

Control of wage payments has been an important form of control, incorporating an incomes policy. The efficacy of wage control is not specifically discussed here, but it is noted that chronic over-payment of wages has been a regular feature, despite bank control. It is problematical whether wage control is a function appropriate to banks and whether it can exert a significant effect, considering that bank action occurs only at the point where wages earned are to be paid, viz. it tries to hit at the symptoms rather than causes of over-payment of wages, and this in a situation where, in practice, wages have always been paid because their payment takes precedence over other settlements. At first wage control was not linked with monetary control (pp. 49, 152–3), but after 1955 attempts were made to connect the two (pp. 170, 211), though at the same time a tendency developed to shift the control of wage funds of enterprises from banks to

12*

associations (pp. 251–2). However, it has never been fully integrated with monetary control.

(b) *Monetary control*

Though doubts were expressed from time to time about whether it was appropriate for a bank to engage in control through settlements and wage payments it was firmly agreed, even in the period of the highest degree of centralisation of economic management (e.g. in the early fifties in Poland), that monetary control, viz. control based on short-term credit, was the key, and the most appropriate, weapon of bank control.

Monetary control is practised in both Western and socialist economic management. In the West it forms one of the instruments of macroeconomic control used to stabilise the economy ('leaning against the wind'). Variations in credit conditions are considered, following the postulates found in Keynesian or Quantity theories, to be capable of affecting aggregate expenditure in a predictable direction. Socialist monetary control has a primarily microeconomic character. It is applied to individual enterprises and is designed, through changes in credit conditions, to affect their management and plan fulfilment. Indirectly it is expected to have macroeconomic implications, in particular to prevent issues of credit having no justification in terms of real flows, and to prevent an excessive share of stocks in the national product.

It has been argued that the 'real bills' theory, which in the eyes of many Western economists encourages practices contrary to the national economic interest, provided an acceptable philosophical basis for the socialist credit system. It is interesting to note that the United States and the Soviet Union were both searching for a formula of credit regulation at roughly the same time in history. Whereas it was perhaps appropriate that the idea of 'productive credit' (see p. 15), at first accepted by the Federal Reserve System and confirmed in 1923, was ultimately discarded in the United States, the same idea was successfully employed in the conditions of a Soviet economy, especially in the period up to the mid-fifties.

Basically, the 'real bills' doctrine is one of the theories reflecting the 'Banking School' view on monetary matters (see pp. 7 and 13–14), which denies the power of monetary variables to affect real variables. It held that credit could not be over-issued as long as it facilitated the movement of goods, representing its security. As far as banking practice was concerned, banks were to extend credit without restriction, as long as credit was requested for legitimate business needs.

In a socialist economy which is not subject to the influences of international trade experienced by more open capitalist economies, where aggregate spending is directly controlled by national economic plans and where many capital goods are rationed, where banks do not have to observe minimum reserve ratios and do not compete for custom, and where enterprises are not sensitive to financial impulses, the passive adjustment of credit to legitimate business needs implicit in the 'real bills' theory is a reasonable proposition. Active monetary control, in the sense of using credit conditions to affect real relationships, is destined to be unsuccessful, and this indeed has been borne out by experience.

In implementing monetary control the socialist authorities did not always act in accordance with the 'real bills' theory. Attempts to define legitimate business needs rigidly in terms of the principles of socialist credit (which, borrowing an American expression, we have called the *qualitative tests* of credit) geared to planned targets, and attempts to use credit as a coercive weapon during periods of stringent credit control were not consistent with the theory and proved ultimately unsuccessful. Some 'tests', especially that of specific purpose, were narrowly interpreted in terms of excessive fragmentation of credits. The banks' judgement in crediting was further inhibited by excessive regulations, which were often symptomatic of a general approach to national planning, notably that the efficiency and co-ordination necessary for rapid industrialisation could best be achieved by a mechanical adherence to detailed plans, rules and regulations governing every aspect of management. Planned productivity targets and stock building targets, which were of key importance in granting credit, being unrealistic (and never attained in practice) could not adequately reflect genuine business needs. Credit restrictions, used to rectify mismanagements, presupposed the ability of monetary variables to affect real variables.

This study of the implementation and experience of socialist monetary control has revealed some interesting features of socialist finance. Throughout the period of the study the strategy of monetary control remained unaltered – banks were to use credit to control plan fulfilment and the general management of the enterprises banking with them. The tactics of monetary control, however, changed in a slow trial-and-error way.

Broadly speaking two tactics were distinguished: stringent monetary control and lenient monetary control. They were analysed and evaluated mainly on the basis of the experience of Poland, where a decade (1951–61) of stringent credit, interrupted only by a brief (1957) hiatus of economic reforms, was both preceded and followed by more liberal credit periods.

The first period of liberal credit control (1946–51) was, in its initial stages, largely a matter of expediency. The basic economic aim at the time was economic recovery. As credit was the chief source of finance, monetary authorities were reluctant to refuse it lest they might impede economic recovery. At first, monetary control was based on direct co-operation between banks and enterprises and on the use of accounting methods. However, after a coherent financial system emerged following the financial legislation of August 1947, a policy of 'credit automatism' superseded the control based on accounting documents (chs. 4, 5).

Banks automatically settled all correct obligations (e.g. accepted invoices), giving overdrafts, called 'overdue credit', when enterprises had insufficient current account balances to meet obligations. Thus banks behaved very much in accordance with the tenets of the 'real bills' doctrine. Although overdue credit bore a penalty interest charge, it was not otherwise directly connected with incentives to improve financial management. There was, however, little confidence in Poland at the time in the potency of credit restrictions as stimuli to more efficient management.

Liberal credit, apart from being consistent with the 'real bills' theory, had an additional interesting rationale. The emphasis was on the 'signal role' of credit, where by overdue credit indicated shortcomings in the management of enterprises. In the financial system which operated at the time the credit was not a mere general indicator, but could pinpoint specific areas of mismanagement. On discovering these, banks could prescribe remedial measures not necessarily based on financial action.

In the early fifties the copying of Soviet economic methods applied to monetary control as well. It was then that Poland adopted outright principles of credit control, which incorporated the stringent *qualitative tests* elaborated in the Soviet Union immediately after the brief experience of credit automatism following the 1930 credit reform. Accordingly the emphasis shifted from credit as a diagnostic device to credit as a corrective device. Noncompliance with the *qualitative tests* was to lead to restrictions on the supply of credit until an improvement in the management of the recalcitrant client occurred. The stringent credit control was applied in two phases, the first being 1949–56 and the second 1958–60. Between the two phases came a short period of credit relaxation, accompanying the general economic reforms of 1956–7. Though there were some differences between the two phases of stringent credit control in terms of the underlying economic conditions and philosophy (see pp. 204–7), there was one crucial factor common to both phases, namely the reliance on restrictions of credit supply, to the neglect of interest rates, as the key method of action.

Banks did not fully utilise credit sanctions against badly administered enterprises, largely because the routine application of credit principles (viz. the *qualitative tests*) resulted in stringent credit conditions, leaving enterprises short of funds. Contrary to theoretical postulates, shortages of funds failed to exert sufficient pressure on enterprises to improve their management. Indeed enterprises paid little attention to financial management, priority being overwhelmingly given to the fulfilment of output targets. Such an attitude was made possible by the absence of causal links between the availability of legitimate finance and the production of output and the absence of a danger of bankruptcy.

Stringent credit control was frustrated by an unplanned creation of new financial claims, mainly in the form of trade credit, which financed the continuing production of insolvent enterprises, viz. enterprises short of legitimate funds to cover their current commitments.

Trade credit developed spontaneously when buyers failed to pay their invoices within a prescribed term. Suppliers did not react to bad debtors by stopping deliveries, often because they had no alternative markets and because such a stoppage would jeopardise plan fulfilment throughout a chain of interdependent firms. At the same time suppliers did not have the financial resources to extend credit, as all their money had to be kept in the bank and used only with the bank's permission for purposes consistent with correct plan fulfilment; financial planning did not allow enterprises to carry financial reserves, because bank credit was relied on to fulfil this function. Thus suppliers often became short of funds themselves, failing ultimately to pay their own debts. Trade credit, and not bank credit, provided the financial slack in the economy.

Doubtless some socialist enterprises were mismanaged compared with others. It is contended, however, that the accumulation of illicit finance was mainly the product of the planning system and the policy of speedy industrialisation. It occurred not only in Poland but in every socialist economy implementing the Soviet system. In the Soviet Union payments difficulties had been a problem ever since the elimination of 'credit automatism' in 1931.

These difficulties were bound to occur in a system which encouraged output while neglecting the cost of its production, where the *qualitative tests* were geared to planned targets, chiefly of stockbuilding, which were unrealistically low, and where the tenets of stringent credit control prevented the banks from discharging the function of the 'lender of last resort' to enterprises (which, as the final reserve of funds, they should *a priori* have fulfilled). Instead, the function had to be fulfilled in an unplanned way by trade credit.

The experience of the stringent credit control suggests that in a given situation (viz. given plans of production, the price level, the rate of change in labour productivity) the finance of a socialist enterprise is mainly demand-determined. The possession of finance or the possibility of securing finance was, in the period covered by the study, neither a sufficient nor a necessary condition for undertaking expenditure. The level of output of enterprises was dictated by directive targets. Their preoccupation with physical targets, and in particular with total output, made them neglect their financial targets and their financial management in general. Thus, on the whole, the availability of finance was not demand-determining but demand-determined and the authorities had little success in planning it. In cases where planned finance, in the sense of finance to which enterprises could legitimately resort, was not adequate, enterprises preferred to finance output from unplanned sources rather than reduce it. In this situation using bank credit as a coercive device was futile.

Stringent monetary control was modified in both periods, because of the alarming accumulation of illicit trade credit due to the failure of enterprises to settle promptly. The burden of eliminating payments difficulties fell not on enterprises but on the banking system, confronting banks with conflicting objectives of credit stringency and of dismantling the blockages in payments which resulted mainly from that stringency. In Poland (unlike the Soviet Union, where the BMS were allegedly effective) the various clearings of overdue debts arranged by the NBP (pp. 141–2) were not found adequate and the reduction of overdue indebtedness, and the consequent improvement in the payments situation, followed from more liberal bank lending and, in the first phase of stringent credit, a modified order of settlements (pp. 172–4). More generous credit on settlements (settlements credit or payments credit) in particular appeared to be a solution to the divorce of settlements from the main flow of short-term credit. Thus payments difficulties were alleviated only when the banking system began to assume the function of lender of last resort. Indeed in the first phase of the stringent credit control (1946–56) the banks' endeavour to unblock payments led paradoxically to 'credit liberalism', (ch. 6) which, however, must not be confused with unlimited credit supply ('credit automatism'). In the second phase (1958–60), credit was gradually liberalised (pp. 212–13) and ultimately credit restrictions were abandoned as key control measures.

Socialist experience of tight credit policy supports those propositions in Western monetary economics which claim that, provided business expectations are favourable, plans for expansion of production are not likely to be scaled down by a restrictive monetary policy which attempts to decrease the supply of specific financial claims, like the supply of money. Frustrated borrowers tend to replace bank finance by finance generated outside the banking system subject to the credit squeeze, despite the often higher cost of alternative finance.

The lack of success with stringent control led to a change in monetary tactics. Throughout East Europe the supply of credit as a means of monetary action began to be abandoned. In Poland this led to the second period of lenient credit control, which started after 1961. The *qualitative tests* were modified to allow credit even for purposes previously considered 'incorrect'. Payments credit (pp. 253–6) gradually developed into a credit of last resort, linking settlements with the mainstream of credit. Banks, whose discretion in controlling enterprises increased, were empowered to use the control measures which they thought most likely to exert the desired effect on their clients. It may be said that the new policy represented a more rational application of the 'real bills' theory, in so far as the rigid and detailed linkage of the *qualitative tests* to planned targets was abandoned and the banks were given greater discretion to ascertain legitimate business needs for purposes of crediting.

The new monetary policy, though it did not amount to the new credit automatism advocated by some (ch. 9), had a rapid impact by reducing overdue trade credit to a tolerable level. The ratio of overdue trade credit to short-term bank credit extended to industry, which was 13.4%, 17.5% and 16.9% respectively in the three years (1958–60) of stringent credit, fell after the transition to lenient credit control to 4.7% in 1963, 1.2% in 1966 and 0.6% in 1968.

The lenient credit control has now become a new orthodoxy. It may be said that by its adoption the authorities signify their recognition that, in the type of national economic management which actually exists, a financial squeeze is not capable of affecting real economic processes, that the divorce between settlements and credit, which had been a part of credit stringency, leads to an escalation of payments difficulties and that the discharge of the function of lender of last resort must, in the interest of orderly payments, be performed by the banking system.

The rejection of the use of credit supply as a method of control did not mean that monetary control was completely abandoned. With attempts to decentralise, credit finance increased relative to budget finance. The authorities continued to rely on monetary control, but this time by acting through interest rates, viz. through the cost of credit. Enterprises which had 'incorrect' assets or were recognised as 'badly-run' obtained credit at higher interest rates. The high cost of credit was intended to stimulate more efficient management in enterprises by acting on their profit and hence on the remuneration of employees through the factory fund and on the accumulation of money for self-finance.

During our discussion of the lenient credit approach, it was reflected that in conditions where the restriction of finance cannot check real processes the effect of a credit squeeze, such as that applied during the stringent credit period, can be primarily on cost or profit, because the squeeze leads to the accumulation of illicit finance subject to penalty interest charges. The weakness of the profit motive during the stringent monetary control was a further factor rendering control by the supply of credit ineffective. The success of the policy of acting through interest rates during the lenient credit period was not conclusively evaluated, but no evidence was found to suggest that it was effective. Higher interest rates were not widely applied, they were often not high enough to be of significance, their impact was frequently blunted by the use of interest rebates, and the profit motivation of enterprises was weak. Even when attempts were made to strengthen profit motivation the inertia of old planning methods was of decisive importance.

Thus, in practice, monetary control was weak. The relative neglect of the financial aspects of management associated with low profit motivation, and the weakness of market forces in general in affecting the decisions of enterprises, made the enterprises insufficiently responsive to financial stimuli.

(c) Non-monetary means of control

In view of the continuous weakness of monetary control, bank control was in fact exercised by non-monetary means such as inspections, checking the costing and the estimated efficiency of investment projects. Banks were thus primarily control organs, their control being, in the main, negative. As guardians of public property and the public interest, they checked the activity of enterprises, objecting to some actions and imposing sanctions to enforce their objections (we called this 'coercive control'). They were there mainly to prevent enterprises from pursuing a course of action and their criteria for decision-taking were not always objective. There was a presumption that the enterprise was inclined to pursue some narrowly conceived self-interest which often conflicted with the good of the economy; the bank, on the other hand, was presumed to be well aware of the wider public interest and was entrusted with the mission of redirecting the operations of its customers along the path of public interest. Though bank decisions were often arbitrary, they were in practice binding on enterprises. This was inconsistent with the autonomy of the enterprise, and sometimes led to bitter resentment on the part of enterprises.

It proved singularly difficult to estimate the effectiveness of bank control, largely because bank control was only one of a number of 'controls' to which enterprises were subjected and one of a number of forces acting simultaneously on them. In general, no strong and definite indications of its success were found. The main reasons were: (a) financial management was neglected, because of the emphasis on centralised directive planning coupled with the policy of industrialisation; (b) There was insufficient co-ordination between various forms of 'control' over enterprises; (c) sanctions imposed by banks were often waived by the superior organs of enterprises; (d) important enterprises which could muster the support of their superior bodies or Party organs were more leniently treated by banks than other less important enterprises; (e) bank control was basically management control, embracing every aspect of the management of enterprises and hence demanding from the banker the same expertise in the management of enterprises as that possessed by the director of the enterprise, in addition to expertise in financial matters and in the interpretation of the public interest; (f) in connection with the last point, it is doubtful whether, on the average, the banker possessed the necessary qualities and expertise to discharge his duty.

The scope of bank control was thus too wide and the capacity of banks to carry it out correspondingly too small. Often bank control resulted in routine operations and a superficial analysis of the problems of enterprises. Furthermore the preoccupation with microeconomic control and its routine execution made banks lose their macroeconomic perspective. This was especially true in the early fifties, when control became mechanical (ch. 6). With decentralisation banks gained more autonomy in dealing with enterprises, but some degree of routine or technical control (e.g. the checking of documents) persisted throughout the period of study.

The cost of bank control was probably high. Some aspects of bank control (e.g. over the normative) were very labour consuming. Although some rationalisation of control did occur after 1956, the cost in relation to its effectiveness was still probably high. This criticism was especially evident in the realm of stock control in enterprises.

Stocks were of special interest to banks. Being charged with the responsibility of making certain that enterprises did not accumulate excessive stocks and/or unwanted stocks, banks often engaged directly in stock management. Such control was intended to lead to a reduction in the ratio of the increase in stocks to the national income. Little clear evidence on the effectiveness of stock control was found. This was the case in different periods, when different methods of control operated. In any economy stock control is a notoriously difficult problem, because stock building can be a function of many variables. Some evidence was found to suggest that in socialised enterprises the accumulation of 'incorrect stocks' could be explained very largely by factors independent of the management of enterprises and outside the scope of bank action (e.g. frequent changes in plans, technological changes, shortages of supplies), so that the devices used by banks for controlling stocks (the normative, stringent credit, higher interest rates) often struck at symptoms without being able to get at the root cause of the problem.

It is difficult to agree with the rationale of direct bank participation with enterprises in the management of stocks. Naturally, in extending credit banks should pay attention to stocks. However, especially as more self-management for enterprises is advocated, it is hard to justify a situation where banks and not enterprises make binding decisions concerning the finance of stocks.

Possible future developments

The study has revealed that reforms in the credit system and other financial changes outstripped the adjustment in other spheres of economic activity. To be an effective control weapon credit must operate in an environment where there is a close link between financial and real processes. So far attempts at decentralisation have failed to produce such a link, making financial impulses ineffective as substitutes for directives. Moreover, the continuing reliance on detailed directive commands weakens the whole superstructure of financial incentives. The next step must be to try to make the management of enterprises more sensitive to financial stimuli and disincentives, to make real expenditure more dependent on the availability of finance from planned sources and to grant enterprises greater de facto autonomy, by relying more on financial instruments and less on detailed directives.

Perhaps the next stage in the development of socialist banking will be to pay more attention to the fulfilment of the intermediation function by banks. The whole system of capital accumulation based on the budget has now outlived its usefulness. With the rise in the real incomes of the population and the development of more self-management in enterprises, the accumulation of funds from savings and current account balances is likely to assume key importance. Indeed, savings and current accounts of individuals already account for a fifth of bank liabilities (table B1b). The savings propensity and the banking habit of the people may be increased by offering a wider range of savings media. Enterprises may also utilise their investible funds more rationally if a wider range of financial instruments is available as an alternative to real investment. Socialist authorities may be wise to consider the creation of 'marketable' national debt instruments, managed by banks, as an alternative to savings accounts. The structure of banking in Poland after the 1969 reforms, with the NBP acting as the central universal bank, financing and controlling industrial investment, among its other activities, seems to be well suited to link financial innovation with real industrial development.

It is possible that in the more distant future the socialist economies, which have recently made some progress in integrating their international trading activity with domestic production, will consider opening their economies to multilateral trade. So far, even within Comecon, trading is on the basis of bilateral agreements and conducted without currency convertibility. Moves towards convertibility, and in particular towards participation in Western international agreements on trade and currencies, must ultimately force socialist economies to review more fundamentally their financial and monetary systems, which still reflect many features of their Soviet predecessor in the thirties, created to serve the policy of 'industrialisation in one country'.

Appendix A: Credit finance and the control of the private sector, including private agriculture

This study has been concerned mainly with the impact of banking and monetary control on the socialised sector of the economy, because this constituted the essence and, in quantitative terms, the most important area of national monetary management. As may be seen from table A1, in the early fifties under 3% of total credit was given to the private sector; the proportion rose steadily after the mid-fifties, although it reached only about 12% in the late sixties. Considering that in the credit to the private sector we have included credit to private agriculture, consumer credit and the finance of private urban housing, and that credit is the major form of external finance of private ventures, the relative underdevelopment of this type of credit, and by the same token the low priority allocated to the activities which it helped to finance, are clearly shown.

The development of the private sector, which is based on often scattered, small-scale units, with a great variety of characteristics, is very difficult to plan. This applies particularly to private agricultural households. It is thus necessary to exercise some degree of control over the sector without reference to specific planned targets. This is a complex issue, which cannot be elaborated comprehensively here. As regards credit control of private production and consumption, it must be emphasised again that on the macroeconomic scale such control has not been of much significance to date. Credit has been used as a weapon of control of private business activity, but on the whole it has not been used, as it often is in the West, as a major control mechanism. In the West changes in credit conditions alone are sometimes expected to bring about a desired distribution of resources through market forces. In socialist countries credit has been used as one of many means of influence, including fiscal policy, laws and regulations, licencing, changes in plans (e.g. allowing more private housing). In most cases it represented an adjunct of a particular policy, designed to make that policy effective – for instance, a

355

Table A1

Credit to the private sector 1950–70

(*Balances at the end of the year: mil. zł. and percentages of total credit granted by the banking system*)

Year	Total credit mil. zł.	Credit[1] to private sector					
		Total		Production units[2]		Private individuals[3]	
		mil. zł.	%	mil. zł.	%	mil. zł.	%
1950	29,921	681	2.3	681	2.3	–	–
1951	37,205	806	2.2	806	2.2	–	–
1952	47,596	1,219	2.6	821	1.7	398	0.8
1953	62,867	1,769	2.8	927	1.5	842	1.3
1954	66,401	2,198	3.3	1,272	1.9	924	1.4
1955	67,109	2,457	3.7	1,626	2.4	831	1.2
1956	80,288	3,501	4.3	2,375	3.0	1,126	1.4
1957	98,546	5,657	5.7	4,075	4.1	1,582	1.6
1958	112,715	8,153	7.2	5,531	4.9	2,622	2.3
1959	128,418	11,785	9.2	7,035	5.5	4,754	3.7
1960	154,257	15,500	10.0	8,849	5.7	6,651	4.3
1961	168,785	17,683	10.5	9,793	5.8	7,890	4.7
1962	184,027	20,046	10.9	10,994	6.0	9,052	4.9
1963	229,079	23,477	10.2	13,413	5.9	10,064	4.4
1964	249,924	28,501	11.4	17,437	7.0	11,064	4.4
1965	277,159	34,652	12.5	22,151	8.0	12,501	4.5
1966	320,585	41,262	12.9	26,235	8.2	15,027	4.7
1967	369,971	46,295	12.5	30,749	8.3	15,546	4.2
1968	422,899	50,677	12.0	34,964	8.3	15,713	3.7
1969	511,873	57,519	11.2	38,638	7.5	18,881	3.7
1970[4]	598,044	62,732	10.5	44,217	7.4	18,518	3.1

Notes:

[1] Total credit includes small amounts of credit (see table A3), granted by, e.g. co-operative trading enterprises, which may have been refinanced by banks.

[2] Mainly in agriculture, industry, handicrafts, trade.

[3] For urban private housing and hire purchase.

[4] Data for 1970 may not be strictly comparable with the rest of the data in the table.

Sources: GUS – *RSF 1945–1967*, pp. 230–1, NBP – *Information Bulletin* 1970, p. 41; NBP – *Rocznik Informacyjny*, 1971, p. 42.

rise in the output of a consumer durable product may be planned side by side with provisions for easier finance for buyers. Credit conditions are then adjusted to the availability of and the demand for the product.

Table A2

Credit to private agriculture 1950–69
(*Balances at the end of the year*)

Year	Total mil. zl.	As percentage of all credit[1]	As percentage of all credit to private sector[2]	Share of investment credit in total[3]
1950	669	2.2	98.2	47.6
1951	801	2.1	100.0	41.4
1952	816	1.7	66.9	44.1
1953	917	1.5	51.8	43.2
1954	1,261	1.9	57.4	53.3
1955	1,617	2.4	65.8	58.9
1956	2,309	2.9	65.8	64.5
1957	3,785	3.8	66.9	68.6
1958	5,318	4.7	65.2	73.5
1959	6,865	5.3	58.2	74.8
1960	8,686	5.6	56.0	70.3
1961	9,619	5.7	54.4	70.8
1962	10,811	5.9	53.9	68.7
1963	13,218	5.8	56.3	65.0
1964	17,166	6.9	60.2	61.4
1965	21,631	7.8	62.4	60.9
1966	25,541	8.0	61.9	63.4
1967	29,863	8.1	64.5	65.1
1968	33,938	8.0	67.0	66.7
1969	37,540	7.3	65.3	69.0

Notes:
[1] Total credit extended by the banking system (see column 2 of table A1).
[2] See column 3 of table A1.
[3] I.e. in total credit given to private agriculture (column 1).
Sources: GUS – *RSF 1945–1967*, pp. 230–1; NBP – *Information Bulletin* 1950, p. 41.

A large proportion (see table A2) of credit to the private sector has been credit granted to private agriculture which, quite uniquely for Eastern Europe, is of major importance in the Polish economy. It may thus be appropriate to devote some attention to its crediting.

In every socialist country agricultural development has presented a difficult problem, partly because of a comparative neglect of agriculture, especially compared with heavy industry, and partly because socialist methods of production have not been as readily acceptable by those engaged in agriculture as they have in industry

Table A3

Banks financing private agriculture 1956–67

(*Credit at the end of the year*)

Year	Total mil. zł.	AB mil. zł.	%	SLCs mil. zł.	%	Others[1] mil. zł	%
1956	2,309	1,506	65.2	803	34.8		
1957	3,785	2,621	69.2	1,160	30.6	4	0.1
1958	5,318	3,401	63.9	1,912	35.9	5	0.1
1959	6,865	4,153	60.5	2,607	38.0	105	1.5
1960	8,686	4,883	56.2	3,597	41.4	206	2.4
1961	9,619	5,462	56.8	3,847	40.0	310	3.2
1962	10,811	5,889	54.5	4,518	41.8	404	3.7
1963	13,218	6,894	52.2	5,720	43.3	604	4.6
1964	17,166	8,450	49.2	8,116	47.3	600	3.5
1965	21,631	10,357	47.9	10,533	48.7	741	3.4
1966	25,541	12,788	50.1	12,043	47.1	710	2.8
1967	29,863	15,325	51.3	13,012	43.6	1,526	5.1

Note:

[1] Including advances from milk co-operatives and trade credit from some co-operative agricultural trading organisations.

Source: GUS – *RSF 1945–1967*, p. 245.

and have not always proved successful. At the same time, especially bearing in mind that a socialist economy is practically a closed economy, general economic development, in particular starting from a low level of *per capita* income, made the growth of agricultural output a *conditio sine qua non* of rising living standards.

Polish agricultural problems were basically similar to those of her neighbours. However, there has been no piecemeal socialisation of agriculture, which has remained predominantly privately owned. It presents, as indeed it often does in other developing economies, a web of political, social, ideological, religious and technological problems, so that whatever is said about it here must be either a broad generalisation or an isolated detail.

Though agriculture has remained mostly privately owned, it has always been the aim of the authorities to reconstruct it along socialist lines. Thus there has always been some discrimination against private households, even in the period of the 'Polish road to socialism' (see ch. 4). Discrimination was most severe between 1949 and 1954 (reflected in data on credit in table A2) and eased after 1955. It made the expansion of agricultural output, the introduction of technological improvements and the growth of the production unit very difficult, often impossible.

Data on credit to private agriculture given in tables A2 and A3 may become more meaningful if supplemented by additional information. First the contribution of agriculture to national product has remained high, in spite of industrial progress, ranging from 40.1% in 1950 to 28.2% in 1955, 23.3% in 1960 and 17.3% in 1968. Private agriculture has contributed a large part of total agrarian output: 92.0% in 1950, 80.7% in 1955, 89.2% in 1960 and 86.7% in 1968. Of the total cultivable area about 85% is privately owned. Food is a major item of expenditure (on the average 45% in 1966) in family budgets.[1]

The finance of state farms has, broadly speaking, been analogous to the finance of other state enterprises discussed in this book. This means that state farms could, in addition to credit, resort to budgetary funds, often generous, because of chronic losses made by the farms. Private agriculture relied on two sources of finance: savings (covering usually more than half of total expenditure) and bank credit. The latter was the only external means of finance.[2] On the other hand, it must be remembered that private households may often derive external economies from projects carried out by the socialised sector and financed from the budget or the Agricultural Development Fund (set up in 1959).

Bearing in mind the above observations it may be concluded that credit finance of private agriculture has been rather modest. This was especially so during the SYP when, in spite of food shortages and general agrarian backwardness, credit restrictions were one of many discriminatory measures (compare pp. 106–7), which resulted in capital consumption in agriculture, especially between 1951 and 1954.[3]

[1] GUS – *RDN 1965–1968*, p. 13; *RS 1969*, pp. 217–22; *CSYB 1968* pp. 125, 265.
[2] There is evidence of the existence of a third source, namely credit granted privately. Little is known about this form of finance, although a study has revealed that it is of some importance. 27% of surveyed farms used private credit, which in 1965–6 accounted for about 10% of total farm indebtedness. T. Wyszomirski, 'Problemy Kredytowania Indywidualnych Gospodarstw Rolnych', *WNBP* 5 (1968) p. 192. The existence of such credit must be interpreted as demonstrating the inadequacy of the supply of credit by the banking system.
[3] For a brief account of agricultural finance see J. Jankowski, 'Finansowanie Rolnictwa' in *FPL 1944–1960*.

Improvement in this respect started as early as 1955, when the
Party became anxious to raise falling living standards by encouraging
agrarian production. After 1956 there was much less discrimination
against private agriculture, which, however, has never had good
conditions for expansion, largely because of the policy of 'linking
expansion with socialist reconstruction', favouring investment by
collective organisations (like the 'agricultural circles') at the expense
of individual households. Nevertheless, by the late sixties about 8%
of total credit in the economy was given to private agriculture (four
times the percentage in the early fifties) and after 1954 an increasing
proportion was extended for investment purposes (see table A2).
Thus credit has become an important source of investment finance.
In the late sixties it covered a little over 40% of the total investment
expenditure of private farms.[1]

Distribution of credit and other banking facilities have also
improved considerably since 1956. The key bank has become the
AB and in spite of the fact that, especially between 1958 and 1965,
SLCs expanded their lending more rapidly than the AB (see table
A3), it has remained the chief financial executor of the government's
agricultural policy. At the same time the more numerous (see
tables E1a and E1b) and widespread rural SLCs helped to bring
credit and other banking facilities within easier reach of peasant
households.

As the planning of agricultural production based on numerous
small private units is practically impossible, the state controls it
indirectly by various methods, including credit. Credit as a control
tool is discussed below. It must be stressed that at no time has it
been solely relied on to influence production, nor has it been the
most important control method. In most cases it merely supplemented other measures or was calculated to make them effective.
The most important measures influencing private agriculture have
been: the sytsem of delivieries, including compulsory deliveries
(abolished in 1971) and deliveries on contract, price fixing,[2] fiscal

[1] In the 1966–70 plan, on the average, 41% of investment was to be financed from long-
term credit; the corresponding figure for working capital was 38–9%. S. Cieślak,
'Kredytowanie Gospodarki Chłopskiej', *BiK* 9 (1970) p. 343.
[2] This is of great importance. The state generally fixes the prices of compulsory deliveries
and influences the prices of goods delivered under contract. The state also fixes the
prices of fuel, fodder, other raw materials and agricultural machines and tools. The
state can thus, through prices, affect both the revenue and the costs of farmers.

policy, control of supplies to the country, plans involving, e.g. changes in output of fertilisers or agrarian machinery, and credit.

Several aspects of credit as a control weapon may be distinguished. First it is used as an economic weapon promoting development. In most cases its expansion follows decisions to raise the supply of agricultural inputs (fertilisers, seeds, machinery). It injects purchasing power into the hands of peasants, enabling them to avail themselves of these inputs. Quite often it is given as part of 'actions' designed to promote, e.g. the use of better seeds, electrification, use of fertilisers when these have been allocated to the country by the planners. Thus, in the main, credit follows real flows of supplies to private agriculture, rather than acting on economic activity as an autonomous lever.

Secondly, credit may serve as a political instrument. In injecting purchasing power banks may be directed to discriminate between certain types of claimants, or between different regions on (at least mainly) political grounds. Credit is also used to offer an inducement for farmers to behave in a way favoured by the state. Preferential treatment (easier and cheaper credit) is, for instance, given to those who enter into contracts with the state for agricultural deliveries. There are also instances of discrimination on economic and social grounds, when, for instance, households receive credit to help them recover from a disaster (pest, flooding).

Thirdly, credit is increasingly used to maintain an equilibrium between income and expenditure at a given level of prices. When, for example, harvests resulted in increased income for farmers, but the flow of goods and services in the country does not change commensurably (as in 1960-1), credit is restricted (so that own funds become a relatively greater source of investment, replacing credit). In subsequent years the supply of credit may be adjusted upwards. Thus credit helps to regulate aggregate demand in the country.

Finally, the availability of credit may be differentiated by its end use. For instance, it is easier to obtain long-term credit to finance investment in 'productive' building than in housing.

Interest rates on credit are, in general, low and are not relied on to control the demand for credit. As is the general case in socialist economies, short-term credit bears higher interest charges (3–6%) than investment credit (1–3%). State and collective organisations obtain credit at lower rates than private households. Also credit in some parts of the country bears higher rates than elsewhere. On the whole, however, interest rates are low (especially compared with Western countries) and exert little effect.[1]

[1] For more details see W. Machowski, 'Stopa Procentowa od Kredytów w Rolnictwie', *WNBP* 11 (1968) pp. 460–2.

Appendix B: Bank Liabilities

Table B1a

Liabilities of the entire banking system 1945–50
(*In percentages of total*)

End of year	Total mil. zł.[1]	Current deposits	Savings accounts	Government accounts	Investment accounts[2]	Foreign transactions[3]	Currency in circulation	Others
1945	1,141	27.9	0.2	–	1.4	–	69.2	1.3
1946	3,539	38.5	0.5	–	5.2	–	50.9	4.8
1947	7,552	37.6	0.5	2.1	14.7	5.0	36.3	3.8
1948	15,187	34.8	0.4	–	28.6	3.9	25.8	6.4
1949	28,827	23.4	0.2	17.2	34.5	2.9	17.9	3.9
1950	30,105	32.1	0.2	32.3	4.8	0.5	15.4	14.5

Notes:
[1] Values in 1950 currency.
[2] Special deposits by the government, mainly for financing investment.
[3] Liabilities arising from foreign trade transactions.
Source: GUS – *RSF 1945–1967*, p. 231.

Table B1b

Liabilities of the entire banking system, 1950–69[1]

(*In percentages of total*)

End of year	Total mil. zl.	Deposits of socialised sector[2]	Budget deposits	Banks' own funds	Savings and deposits of population	Currency in circulation	Others
1950	30,105	37.1	32.3	2.3	0.6	15.4	12.2[3]
1951	37,547	31.3	46.2	6.1	1.0	14.9	0.6
1952	47,980	26.3	51.9	7.0	1.0	13.0	0.7
1953	63,412	26.0	48.8	10.1	1.1	13.3	0.7
1954	67,152	27.6	44.8	10.8	1.5	15.0	0.2
1955	67,296	27.7	41.3	11.3	2.3	17.2	0.2
1956	80,520	28.0	37.0	10.0	3.3	21.6	0.1
1957	99,286	33.0	31.8	8.8	6.2	19.8	0.3
1958	113,383	38.0	25.4	9.1	7.3	19.9	0.2
1959	129,027	39.8	22.5	9.7	9.8	18.0	0.1
1960	155,062	39.2	24.8	7.8	10.9	17.0	0.3
1961	169,810	40.8	21.7	7.6	11.7	18.0	0.2
1962	185,230	39.2	21.4	7.3	14.2	17.6	0.3
1963	230,621	43.1	20.3	6.5	15.3	14.4	0.3
1964	251,748	35.0	26.7	6.2	17.2	14.6	0.3
1965	279,411	36.8	24.2	5.8	18.8	14.1	0.3
1966	323,489	43.7	16.6	5.7	20.1	13.6	0.2
1967	370,952	44.5	15.9	5.2	21.3	13.0	0.2
1968	424,241	46.3	15.0	4.3	21.5	12.6	0.2
1969	514,033	46.0	17.2	4.8	20.6	11.2	0.2
1970[4]	599,702	41.4	24.6	4.6	19.6	9.8	0.0

Notes:

[1] After 1950 a different classification of liabilities was adopted, hence two tables are needed to represent liabilities between 1945 and 1969.

[2] Of enterprises and other units of the socialised sector, including current account deposits and deposits in special accounts (e.g. for investment purposes).

[3] Much of this item consists of a windfall gain which resulted from the currency reform (see pp. 109–10).

[4] Data for 1970 may not be strictly comparable with the rest of the data in the table.

Sources: GUS – *RSF 1945–1967*, pp. 232–3; NBP – *Information Bulletin, 1970*, p. 42; NBP – *Rocznik Informacyjny, 1971* pp. 26, 43.

Appendix C: Types of external 'controls' over state enterprises in Poland

Chart C1

(Early and mid-1950s)

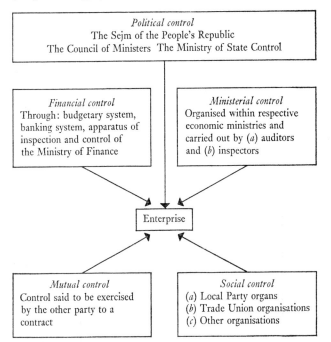

Appendix D: Working capital and credit in the USSR

Table D1

Some indicators of changes in working capital and short-term credit in the USSR

(Based on balances outstanding at the end of the year at market prices; units: percentages)

	1940–50[2]	1950–52[3]	1952–58[4]	1959	1960	1961	1962	1963	1964	1965	1966	1967	1968
Increase in total working capital[1]	–	6.5	7.7	14.8	7.1	9.2	8.1	8.7	10.4	5.3	9.6	10.4	8.9
Increase in stocks	–	10.1	8.3	15.8	7.1	10.4	9.1	8.3	10.9	4.8	8.8	11.6	8.4
Ratio of stocks to total working capital	–	69.5 in 1950	76.6 in 1958[5]	77.2	77.2	78.1	78.8	78.5	78.9	78.5	78.0	78.7	78.4
Increase in total short-term credit	12.0	11.2	7.5	19.3	8.1	11.0	7.2	10.1	12.9	7.6	13.7	13.5	10.3
Increase in credit on stocks	12.2	13.4	10.0	22.7	4.6	8.5	8.8	9.0	15.8	8.1	13.2	15.1	9.6
Increase in credit on settlements	10.2	9.1	2.4	10.7	9.1	15.5	2.2	15.2	5.3	2.3	9.7	1.9	4.6
Ratio of credit on stocks to total credit	61.4 in 1940	62.5 in 1950	74.4 in 1958	76.5	74.1	72.4	73.6	72.8	74.7	75.1	74.8	75.8	75.4

Notes:

[1] Excluding collective farms.

[2] Average annual rate of growth between 1940 and 1950.

[3] Average annual rate of growth between 1950 and 1952.

[4] Average annual rate of growth between 1952 and 1958. The rise in total short-term credit in 1953 was 2.3%, the average annual rise between 1953 and 1956 was 5.4%; in 1957 it was 8.3% and 20.1% in 1958.

[5] 74.3 in 1952.

Sources: TsSU – *N. Kh. SSSR v 1959*, p. 807; *N. Kh. SSSR v 1962*, pp. 56 and 640; *N. Kh. SSSR v 1964*, pp. 751 and 774–5; *N. Kh. SSSR v 1968*, pp. 749 and 779–80.

366

Table D2

Sources of finance of working capital in the USSR

(Balances at the end of the year: percentages of total)

	1950	1958	1959	1960	1961	1962	1963	1964	1965	1966	1967	1968
Own funds	38.0	39.3	38.0	38.8	38.2	38.9	39.9	37.9	38.3	36.6	35.8	33.8
Bank credit	40.5	42.2	43.9	44.3	44.6	43.9	44.7	45.9	47.1	47.9	48.5	48.3
Creditors[1]	20.0	16.1	15.8	14.0	15.0	15.1	14.5	13.7	11.5	11.6	11.2	12.3
Others	1.5	2.4	2.3	2.9	2.2	2.1	1.9	2.5	3.1	3.9	4.5	5.6

Note:

[1] Most of this item consists of unplanned trade credit.

Sources: TsSU – *N. Kh. SSSR v 1964*, p. 572; *N. Kh. SSSR v 1968*, p. 750; M. Pessel', 'O Funktsiyakh Kredita', *DiK* 4 (1964) p. 3.

Appendix E: Credit institutions

Table E1a

Network of credit institutions 1960–9 (end of December)
(*Number of banks and main branches*)[1]

	1960	1965	1966	1967	1968	1969	1970
NBP	1	1	1	1	1	1	1
branches	423	421	421	421	421	422	448
IB	1	1	1	1	1	1	–
branches	43	48	50	53	55	55	–
AB	1	1	1	1	1	1	1
branches	111	235	245	249	252	258	260
SLCs[2]	1	1	1	1	1	1	1
branches[3]	1,376	1,655	1,650	1,662	1,663	1,663	1,662
TB	1	1	1	1	1	1	1
branches	–	–	4	4	5	5	5
CSB	1	1	1	1	1	1	1
branches	196	225	238	242	241	242	242
Hire Purchase Bank	1	1	1	1	1	1	–
branches	64	40	38	37	36	36	–

Notes:
[1] Usually including 17 regional headquarters, one in each Voivodship.
[2] The Union of SLCs (see p. 191).
[3] Viz. SLCs, members of the Union of SLCs.
Source: *NBP – Information Bulletin*, 1970, p. 40; *NBP – Rocznik Informacyjny*, 1971, p. 41.

Table E1b

Branches and agencies of principal credit institutions (end of December)

	1967	1968	1969
NBP			
Voivodship headquarters	17	17	17
Operational branches	404	404	405
IB			
Voivodship branches	19	19	19
Branches	34	36	36
AB			
Voivodship branches	17	17	17
Local[1] branches	94	94	94
Credit[2] branches	138	141	147
Agencies at NBP branches	40	38	33
SLCs	1,645	1,646	1,646
Branches[3]	316	557	631
Permanent 'encashment points'[4]	1,858	1,724	1,729
Seasonal 'encashment points'[4]	591	494	551

Notes:
[1] Powiatowe.
[2] Kredytowe.
[3] Known as '*filie*'.
[4] '*punkty kasowe*'.
Sources: GUS – *RS 1968*, p. 575; *RS 1969*, p. 565; *RS 1970*, p. 548.

Table E2

Employment in credit institutions

	1960	1965	1966	1967	1968	1969
Total[1]	53,313	64,401	67,660	69,772	71,232	72,087
NBP	21,171	23,112	23,844	24,195	24,374	24,373
IB	2,987	3,398	3,693	3,825	3,836	3,837
AB	3,671	4,080	4,158	4,206	4,218	4,259
SLCs	9,568	13,651	14,128	14,723	15,308	15,796
TB	364	747	818	1,018	1,024	1,043
CSB	4,814	5,582	6,042	6,376	6,494	6,642

Note:
[1] Total employment in all financial intermediaries, including hire purchase and national insurance institutions.
Sources: GUS – *RS 1968*, p. 575; *RS 1969*, p. 566; *RS 1970*, p. 549.

Appendix F: Finance and changes in sources of investment funds

Table F1

Finance of investment and capital repairs in the socialised sector 1961–9

(mil. zl.)

	1961	1962	1963	1964	1965	1966	1967	1968	1969
Total	139,705	155,476	163,284	174,019	193,262	199,299	224,020	246,624	295,769
Balance at the beginning of the year	16,347	19,211	23,713	25,685	28,573	16,360	29,105	39,772	45,948
Funds accumulated[1]	123,358	136,265	139,571	148,334	164,689	182,939	194,915	206,852	249,821
Funds expended									
a. total	120,267	131,895	137,590	145,446	161,061	168,542	184,248	200,676	235,650
b. on investment	93,241	103,253	106,969	111,036	121,449	127,130	136,150	147,295	166,300
c. on repairs	20,091	21,994	22,945	25,251	28,544	31,438	34,945	38,804	41,893
d. repayment of credit	3,595	3,420	3,733	3,245	4,393	4,026	6,791	7,701	16,815
e. others	3,340	3,228	3,931	5,914	6,675	5,948	6,362	6,876	10,642
Balance at the end of the year	19,438	23,581	25,694	28,573	32,201	30,757	39,772	45,948	60,119

Note:

[1] Analysed in the next table.

Source: GUS – *RS 1970*, p. 108.

Table F2

Changes in the sources of investment funds 1961–9
(percentages of total)

	1961	1962	1963	1964	1965	1966	1967	1968	1969
Sources of investment funds[1]	100.0	100.0	100.0	100.0	100.0	100.0	100.0	100.0	100.0
Budgetary allocations	51.6	48.1	49.0	46.5	45.4	38.7	35.5	28.9	21.9
Depreciation	21.9	26.7	27.4	28.4	32.1	31.3	32.7	32.7	27.3
DF or profit	5.2	3.8	3.5	3.1	3.2	8.1	7.7	6.4	6.3
Bank credit	3.9	4.1	4.1	4.9	4.5	7.4	10.4	17.7	29.4
Others[2]	17.4	17.2	16.0	17.2	14.7	14.5	13.9	14.4	15.2

Notes:
[1] For the total see line 'Funds accumulated' in table F1.
[2] Including sales of fixed assets and working capital spent on capital repairs.
Source as in table F1.

Bibliography

I. Books

Published in the West

Alton, T. P. *Polish Post War Economy*, New York, 1955.

Arnold, A. Z. *Banks, Credit and Money in Soviet Russia*, New York, 1937.

Bain, A. D. *The Control of Money Supply*, London, 1970.

Currie, L. *The Supply and Control of Money in the United States (1934)*, New York, 1968.

Davies, R. W. *The Development of the Soviet Budgetary System*, Cambridge, 1958.

Degras J., and Nove A. (Eds.), *Soviet Planning*, Oxford, 1964.

Dziewanowski, M. K. *The Communist Party of Poland*, Harvard, 1959.

Feiwel, R. G. *The Economics of a Socialist Enterprise*, New York, 1965.

Fetter, F. W. *Development of British Monetary Orthodoxy*, Cambridge, Mass., 1965.

Garvy, G. *Money, Banking and Credit in Eastern Europe*, New York, 1966.

Gerschenkron, A. *Europe in the Russian Mirror*, Cambridge, Mass., 1970.

Goldsmith, R. W. *Financial Structure and Development*, Yale, 1969.

Górecki, R. *Poland and Her Economic Development*, London, 1935.

    Gospodarzzy Dorobek Polski w Latach 1918–1948 (Economic Achievement of Poland 1918–1938), London, 1946.

Grossman, G. (Ed.), *Value and Plan*, Berkeley, 1960.

    Money and Plan, Berkeley, 1969.

Harris, S. E. *Economic Planning*, New York, 1949.

Hicks, J. R. *Critical Essays in Monetary Theory*, Oxford, 1967.

Hicks, U. S. *Development Finance*, Oxford, 1965.

Hiscocks, R. *Bridge for the Abyss?* London, 1963.

Holzman, F. D. *Soviet Taxation*, Harvard, 1955.

Hubbard, L. E. *Soviet Money and Finance*, London, 1936.

Katzenellenbaum, S. S. *Russian Currency and Banking 1914–1924*, London, 1925.

Kisch, C. H. and Elkin, W. A. *Central Banks*, London, 1932.

Marx, K. *A Contribution to the Critique of Political Economy (1859)*, London, 1971.

Mints, L. W. *A History of Banking Theory*, Chicago, 1945.

Montias, J. M. *Central Planning in Poland*, Yale, 1962.

Nevin, E. *Capital Funds in Underdeveloped Countries*, London, 1961.

Robertson, D. H. *Money (1922)*, Cambridge, 1946.

    Essays in Money and Interest, Manchester, 1966.

Smith, A. *The Wealth of Nations (1776)*, London, 1965.

Thornton, H. *Paper Credit of Great Britain (1802)*, London, 1962.

Trescott, P. B. *Financing American Enterprise*, New York, 1963.

Wicker, E. R. *Federal Reserve Monetary Policy 1917–1933*, New York, 1966.

Zweig, F. *Poland Between the Two Wars*, London, 1944.

Collective work, *Capital Formation and Economic Growth*, Princeton, 1955.

Canadian Royal Commission on Banking and Finance, Report, 1964.

Committee on the Working of the Monetary System (Radcliffe Committee), Report, London, 1959.

Published in Poland

Boguszewski, J. *System Finansowy Przedsiębiorstw i Zjednoczeń* (Financial System of Enterprises and Associations), 1966.

Bolland, S. and Wierzbicki, J. *Finanse* (Finance), 1965.

Brus, W. *Ogólne Problemy Funkcjonowania Gospodarki Socjalistycznej* (General Problems of Socialist Economic Management), 1961.

Czyżniewski, K. *Efektywność Form Finansowania i Reprodukcji Środków Trwałych* (The Effectiveness of Finance and Production of Fixed Capital), 1966.

Dietrych, T. *Zasady Systemu Finansowego Polski Ludowej* (Principles of the Financial System of People's Poland), 1947.

    Elementy Polityki Finansowej Polski Współczesnej (Elements of Financial Policy in Contemporary Poland), 1947.

Drozdowski, M. *Polityka Gospodarcza Rządu Polskiego 1936–1938* (Economic Policy of the Polish Government 1936–1938), 1963.

Fedorowicz, Z. *Finanse w Gospodarce Socjalistycznej* (Finance in a Socialist Economy), 1962.

Fiszel, H. *Zagadnienia Cen i Rachunku Ekonomicznego* (Problems of Prices and Economic Calculus), 1958.

Gliński, B. *Teorie i Praktyka Zarządzania Przedsiębiorstwami Przemysłowymi* (Theory and Practice of Managing Industrial Enterprises), 1966.

Górecki, R. *The Activity of the National Bank of Poland*, 1928.

    Rola Banku Gospodarstwa Krajowego, 1928.

Grabowski, T. *Rola Państwa w Gospodarce Polski 1918–1928* (The Role of the State in the Polish Economy 1918–1928), 1967.

Ivanka, A. *Kontrola Finansowa w Państwach Socjalistycznych* (Financial Control in Socialist Countries), 1966.

Jaśkiewicz, J. and Z. *Polski System Finansów Publicznych* (Public Finance in Poland), 1966.

Jaworski, W. *Bankowość w Gospodarce Socjalistycznej* (Banking in a Socialist Economy), 1967.

    Obieg Pieniężny i Kredyt (Money Circulation and Credit), 1963.

    Zarys Rozwoju Systemu Kredytowego w Polsce Ludowej (An Outline of the Developments of the Credit System in People's Poland), 1958.

Jędrychowski, S. *The Fundamental Principles of Economic Policy in Industry*, 1957.

Karpiński, Z. *Bank Polski*, 1958.

Karpiński, Z. and Lindner, J. *Organizacja Bankowości w Polsce Ludowej* (The Organisation of Banking in People's Poland), 1954.

Kierczyński, T. *Przedsiębiorstwa Deficytowe w Gospodarce Socjalistycznej* (Deficit Enterprises in a Socialist Economy), 1962.

Kierczyński, T. and Wojciechowska, U. *Finanse Przedsiębiorstw Socjalistycznych* (The Finance of Socialist Enterprises), 1965.

Komar, A. *Struktura Budżetu PRL* (The Structure of the Budget of PPR), 1966.

Kucharski, M. *Kredyt Krótkoterminowy i Planowanie Kredytowe* (Short-term Credit and Credit Planning), 1955.

Pieniądz Dochód Proporcje Wzrostu (Money, Income and the Proportions of Growth), 1964.

Kurowski, L. and Sochacka, H. *Kontrola Finansowa w Polsce Ludowej* (Financial Control in People's Poland), 1965.

Kwiatkowski, E. *Obraz Gospodarstwa Polski w Roku 1937* (The Picture of the Polish Economy in 1937), 1937.

Landau, Z. *Polityka Finansowa PKWN* (Financial Policy of PCNL), 1965.

Lange, O. *Some Problems Relating to the Polish Road to Socialism*, 1957.

Pisma Ekonomiczne i Społeczne (*PES*) *1930–1960* (Economic and Social Essays), 1961.

Minc, B. *O Planie Trzyletnim* (On the Three Year Plan), 1948.

(Ed.), *Zarys Rozwoju Metodologii Planowania w Polsce Ludowej* (*ZRMPPL*) *1944–1954* (Outline of the Development of Planning Methodology in People's Poland 1944–1954), 1956.

Młynarski, F. *Genoa Resolutions and the Currency Reform in Poland*, 1925.

Pirożyński, Z. and Winter, E. *BudżetPaństwowy Polski Ludowej* (The State Budget of People's Poland), 1961.

Płocica, A. *Inwestycje w Polsce* (Investment in Poland), 1967.

Popkiewicz, J. *Stopa Zysku w Gospodarce Socjalistycznej* (The Rate of Profit in a Socialist Economy), 1968.

Samecki, W. *Ryzyko i Niepewność w Działalności Przedsiębiorstwa Przemysłowego* (Risk and Uncertainty in the Activity of an Industrial Enterprise), 1967.

Szczepański, J. *Finansowanie Środków Obrotowych* (Finance of Working Capital), 1965.

Szeliga, Z. *Kierunki i Założenia Reformy* (The Direction and Foundation of the Reform), 1966.

Szyr, E. *Nowe Elementy w Planowaniu i Zarządzaniu* (New Elements in Planning and Management), 1958.

Szyrocki, J. *Samofinansowanie Przedsiębiorstw* (Self-Finance of Enterprises), 1967.

Tennenbaum, H. *Struktura Gospodarstwa Polskiego* Vol. 2 *Kredyt* (The Structure of the Polish Economy Vol. 2 Credit), 1935.

Wierzbicki, J. *Zagadnienia Akumulacji Pieniężnej w Gospodarce Socjalistycznej* (Problems of Monetary Accumulation in a Socialist Economy), 1964.

Collective works, *Finanse Polski Ludowej* (*FPL*) *1944–1960* (Finance of the People's Poland 1944–1960), 1964.

Polityka Gospodarcza Polski Ludowej (Economic Policy of People's Poland), 1963 Vol. 2; 1965 Vol. 3.

Rozliczenia Pieniężne w Gospodarce Socjalistycznej (RPGS) (Monetary Settlements in a Socialist Economy), 1966.

Published in the USSR

Atlas, M. *Razvitie Gosudarstvennogo Banka SSSR* (Growth of the State Bank of the USSR), 1958.

Atlas, Z. V. *Denezhnoe Obrashchenie i Kredit SSSR* (Money Circulation and Credit of the USSR), 1947 and 1957 eds.

Bachurin, A. V. *Finansy i Kredit SSSR* (Finance and Credit of the USSR), 1958.

Barkovskii, H. D. *Organizatsiya i Planirovanie Kredita* (Organisation and Planning of Credit), 1968.

Batyrev, U. M., and Usoskin, M. M. *Kratkosrochnyi Kredit i Organizatsiya Denezhnogo Obrashcheniya v SSSR* (Short-term Credit and the Organisation of Money Circulation in the USSR), 1957.

Gosudarstvennyi Bank SSSR (The State Bank of the USSR), 1957.

Bogachevskii, M. B. *Finansy i Kredit v SSSR* (Finance and Credit in the USSR), 1969.

Gusakov, A. et al., *Denezhnoe Obrashchenie i Kredit SSSR* (Money Circulation and Credit of the USSR), 1960.

Ikonnikov, V. V. *Denezhnoe Obrashchenie i Kredit SSSR* (Money Circulation and Credit of the USSR), 1952.

Kronrod, Ya. A. *Den'gi v Sotsialisticheskom Obshchestve* (Money in a Socialist Society), 2nd Ed. 1960.

Lenin, V. I. *On Socialist Economic Organisation, Moscow* (no date given).

Collected Works, vol. 27, Progress Publishers (no date given).

Imperialism, the Highest Stage of Capitalism (1916), Foreign Language Publishing House (no date given).

Marx, K. *Capital* (1894), Moscow, 1962.

Marx, K. and Engels, F. *Manifesto of the Communist Party* (1848). Progress Publishers. No date given.

Parfanyak, P. *Voprosy Bankovskogo Kontrola Rublem v Promyshlennosti* (Problems of Control by the Rouble in Industry), 1954.

Rubinstein, Ya. *Ocherki Razvitiya Sovetskogo Kredita* (Essays on the Development of Soviet Credit), 1958.

Shenger, V. E. *Ocherki Sovetskogo Kredita* (Essays on Soviet Credit), 1961.

Shvarts, G. *Beznalichnyi oborot i Kredit v SSSR* (Cashless Turnover and credit in the USSR), 1963.

Vorob'ev, V. A. *Denezhnoe Obrashchenie i Kredit SSSR* (Money Circulation and Credit of the USSR), 1965.

II. Periodicals

Polish

Abbreviation	*Title*
BiK	*Bank i Kredyt*
	Ekonomista (The Economist)
	Finanse (Finance)
GP	*Gospodarka Planowa* (Planned Economy)
	Information Bulletin (NBP)
MG	*Myśl Gospodarcza* (Economic Thought)
ND	*Nowe Drogi* (New Ways).
	Rocznik Ekonomiczny (Economic Yearbook) Poznań University
RPiE	*Ruch Prawniczy i Ekonomiczny* (Legal and Economic Movement) Poznań
RPEiS	*Ruch Prawniczy, Ekonomiczny i Socjologiczny* (Legal, Economic and Sociological Movement) Poznań
SPB	*Spółdzielczy Przegląd Bankowy* (Co-operative Banking Review)
TL	*Trybuna Ludu* (People's Tribune)

Abbreviation	Title
WNBP	*Wiadomości Narodowego Banku Polskiego* (National Bank of Poland Review)
Zeszyty Naukowe SGPiS	*Zeszyty Naukowe Szkoły Głównej Planowania i Statystyki* (Scientific Papers of the Central School of Planning and Statistics) Warsaw
ŻG	*Życie Gospodarcze* (Economic Life)

Russian

DiK	*Den'gi i Kredit* (Money and Credit)
	Vestnik Finansov (Financial Herald)
	Voprosy Ekonomiki (Economic Problems)

III. Government publications, reports, etc.

Annual Report of the Bank of Poland 1937, 1938.

Bank Gospodarstwa Krajowego (National Economic Bank) Report of Directors for Financial Years 1936, 1937, 1938.

DURP Dziennik Ustaw Rzeczypospolitej Polski (Law Gazette of the Polish Republic).

The Fulfilment of the Three Year Plan of Economic Reconstruction in Poland, Warsaw, 1950.

MP Monitor Polski (Polish Law Gazette).

Plan Sześcioletni (The Six Year Plan), 1951.

IV Plenum KC PZPR Podstawowe Dokumenty (IV Plenary Session of CC PUWP Basic Documents), 1965.

Rada Ekonomiczna – Sytuacja Gospodarcza Kraju w Roku 1958 (Economic Council – Economic Conditions of the Country in 1958), 1959.

Rocznik Polityczny i Gospodarczy (Political and Economic Yearbook).

Russian

Direktivy KPSS i Sovietskogo Pravitielstva po Khozyaistvennym Voprosam (Directives of the Communist Party of the USSR on Economic Matters), 1957.

SUiR Sobranie Uzakonenii i Rasporyazheni (Collected Statutes and Enactments).

SZ Sobranie Zakonov i Rasporyazheni SSSR (Collected Laws and Enactments of the USSR).

British

BEQB Bank of England Quarterly Bulletin.

Economic Journal.

Committee on the Working of the Monetary System (Radcliffe Committee), Report, London, 1959.

USA

Federal Reserve Board Annual Report, 1923.

Statistical publications

GUS	*Główny Urząd Statystyczny* (Central Statistical Office, Poland) published all items listed below.
CSYP	*Concise Statistical Yearbook of Poland.*
RS	*Rocznik Statystyczny* (Statistical Yearbook).

Abbreviation   Title

RDN 1965–1968   *Rocznik Dochodu Narodowego 1965–1968* (Yearbook of National Income).

RSF 1945–1967   *Rocznik Statystyczny Finansów 1945–1967* (Statistical Yearbook of Finance).

RSIiST   *Rocznik Statystyczny Inwestycji i Środków Trwałych 1946–1966* (Statistical Yearbook of Investment and Fixed Capital).

TsSU   *Tsentralnoe Statisticheskoe Upravlenie* (Central Statistical Office, USSR).

N. Kh. SSSR   *Narodnoe Khoziyaistvo SSSR* (National Economy of the USSR – Statistical Yearbooks).

Articles

Albrecht, J. 'Niektóre problemy pracy aparatu bankowego w roku 1964' (Some problems facing the banking apparatus in 1964), *WNBP* 1 (1964).

'Pierwsze doświadczenia i wnioski' (First experiences and conclusions), *ŻG* 26 (1967).

Batyriev, V. 'Niekotorye voprosy dal'neishego razvitya kreditnykh otnoshenii' (Some problems of further development of the credit system), *DiK* 12 (1964).

Bautro, E. 'Niedociągnięcia w organizacji działalności kredytowej oddziałow operacyjnych' (Shortcomings in the organisation of crediting by operational branches), *WNBP* 12 (1967).

Blass, B. 'Nowy system finansowy' (The new financial system), *GP* 21 (1947).

'Problemy krztałtowania i kontroli funduszu płac' (Problems of the formation and control of wage funds), *Finanse* 3 (1964).

'Rozwój systemu finansowego przedsiębiorstw państwowych w PRL' (The development of the financial system of state enterprises in People's Poland), *Finanse* 9 (1961).

'W sprawie dalszej decentralizacji systemu funkcjonowania gospodarki' (On further decentralisation of economic administration), *ND* 10 (1966).

'Zadania banku w roku 1961' (The tasks of the bank in 1961), *WNBP* 3 (1961).

'Zasady systemu finansowego' (The principles of the financial system), *WNBP* 10 (1947).

'Znaczenie i drogi walki o obniżenie kosztów własnych produkcji w przemyśle' (The meaning and methods of the drive to lower industrial production costs), *Finanse* 4 (1954).

Błaszak, H. 'Oprocentowanie kredytu jako środek oddziaływania na gospodarkę przedsiębiorstw' (Interest rate as a means of control over enterprises), *WNBP* 4 (1968).

Bober, A. 'Samodzielność a inicjatywa' (Autonomy and initiative), *ŻG* 27 (1964).

Bobrowski, C. 'Początki planowania w Polsce Ludowej' (The initial stages of planning in People's Poland), *GP* 11 (1966).

'Rozwój planowania w Polsce Ludowej' (The development of planning in People's Poland), *Ekonomista* 5 (1964).

Boguszewski, J. 'Inwestycje zdecentralizowane a bank finansujący' (Financing decentralised investment by the bank), *ŻG* 24 (1959).

'Kilka uwag o kredycie inwestycyjnym' (Some comments on investment credit), *WNBP* 5 (1961).

Boruń M. 'Oddziaływanie banku na jednostki gospodarki narodowej' (Bank control over units of the national economy), *WNBP* 1 (1967).

'Odformalizować przepisy' (Simplify regulations), *ŻG* 38 (1963).

Bożyczko, E. 'Nadrzędna jednostka czy równorzędny partner' (Superior unit or equal partner), *ŻG* 15 (1963).

Choliński, T. 'Aktualne problemy upłynnienia zapasów zbędnych i nadmiernych' (Present problems of reduction of unnecessary and excessive stocks), *WNBP* 8 (1965).

'O ekonomicznym oddziaływaniu banku na gospodarkę przedsiębiorstwa' (Economic action of the bank on the management of the enterprise), *Finanse* 5 (1958).

'O nowe formy finansowania przedsiębiorstw' (The need for new methods of financing enterprises), *Finanse* 1 (1957).

'Próba oceny przebiegu realizacji postanowień uchwały Nr. 151 KERN' (An attempt to assess the way in which the resolution 151 of ECCM is being fulfilled), *WNBP* 3 (1961).

'Przyrost zapasów w bieżącej pięciolatce' (The rise in stocks in the current five year plan), *BiK* 9 (1970).

'Środki obrotowe przedsiębiorstw' (The working capital of enterprises), *Finanse* 7 (1958).

'Zagospodarowanie zapasów nieprawidłowych – problem nadal istotny' (Clearance of incorrect stocks – still a problem), *WNBP* 4 (1968).

Cramp, A. B. 'Two views of money', *Lloyds Bank Review* (July 1962).

Czernichowski, F. 'Zadania banków na tle zasad systemu finansowego' (The tasks of the banks in the light of the principles of the financial system), *WNBP* 12 (1947) and *SBP* (Dec. 1947).

Czyżniewski, K. 'Przyczynek do dyskusji na temat systemu rozliczeń' (A contribution to the discussion on the system of settlements), *WNBP* 3 (1963).

'Realizacja inwestycji zdecentralizowanych w pierwszym półroczu' (Decentralised investment in practice in the first half of 1960), *WNBP* 10 (1960).

Diachenko, V. 'Khozraschet kak sotsialisticheskii metod khozyaistvovaniya' (Economic accounting as a socialist method of management), *Voprosy Ekonomiki* 2 (1951).

Dietrych T. 'Elementy polityki finansowej Polski współczesnej' (Elements of the financial policy of the contemporary Poland), *WNBP* 10 (1946).

Dudziński, W. 'Inwestycje zdecentralizowane – rozdział zamknięty' (Decentralised investment – a closed issue), *ŻG* 18 (1960).

'Zjednoczenie czyli rozdzielnia niedoskonała' (The association - the imperfect distributor), *ŻG* 45 (1961).

Eshag, E. 'The relative efficacy of monetary policy', *Economic Journal* (June 1971).

Fedorowicz, Z. 'Kredyt a rozliczenia pieniężne przedsiębiorstw' (Credit and settlements of enterprises), *WNBP* 8 (1965).

'Normatywy, zapasy, inwestycje przedsiębiorstw' (Normatives, stocks, investment by enterprises), *Finanse* 3 (1965).

'System kredytowy a budżet państwa' (The relationship between the credit system and the budget), *WNBP* 3 (1957).

Fick, B. 'Nowy system kontroli funduszu płac' (The new system of control of wage funds), *ŻG* 2 (1965).

'System kontroli funduszu płac' (The system of control of wage funds), *ŻG* 18 (1969).

Ficowski, S. 'O nowy system finansowania przedsiębiorstw' (The need for a new way of financing enterprises) *ŻG* 12 (1956).

'O rewizję zasad finansowania przedsiębiorstw' (The need to revise the principles of financing enterprises), *WNBP* 11 (1956).

'Struktura zapasów w gospodarce narodowej w latach 1950–1955' (The structure of stocks in the national economy in 1950–1955), *WNBP* 1 (1957).

Fiszel H. 'O prawdziwy rachunek gospodarczy' (The need for realistic costing), *ND* 5 (1956).

'W sprawie oddziaływania prawa wartości na produkcję' (On the effect of the law of value on production), *Ekonomista* 1–2 (1954).

Florczak, M. 'Aby kontrola była kontrolą' (The need for an effective control), *ŻG* 20 (1956).

Frankel, S. 'Niedoskonała kontrola' (Imperfect control), *ŻG* 34 (1959).

Głowacki, W. 'Gorzkie żale dyrektorów (Bitter grievances of directors), *ŻG* 46 (1961).

Gluck, L. 'Działalność NBP w dwudziestoleciu Polski Ludowej' (The activity of NBP in the 20 years of People's Poland), *Finanse* 7 (1964).

'Nowe kierunki systemu kredytowego' (Changes in the credit system), *ŻG* 19 (1957).

'O środkach i sposobach realizacji zadań banku w dziedzinie pieniężno-kredytowej' (On ways and means of discharging the tasks of the bank in the realm of monetary policy), *WNBP* 3 (1959).

'Węzłowe zagadnienia w pracy NBP w roku 1960' (Key issues in the activity of the bank in 1960), *WNBP* 3 (1960).

'Zagadnienie zapasów w gospodarce narodowej' (The problem of stocks in national management), *WNBP* 2 (1959).

Golinowski, K. 'Wskaźniki dyrektywne w zarządzaniu przedsiębiorstwami' (Directive tasks in the management of enterprises), *GP* 3 (1969).

Gomułka, W. 'Od frontu jednolitego ku jedności ograniczonej' (From unified front to limited unity), *ND* 3 (1947).

'Węzłowe problemy polityki partii' (Key problems of the party), *ND* 6 (1957).

Gradowski, T. and Kiernożycki, A. 'Wskaźniki dyrektywne planu a samodzielność przedsiębiorstwa' (Directive targets and the self-management of the enterprise), *GP* 10 (1959).

Gruba, M. 'Problem funkcji kontrolnej kredytu' (The problem of the control function of credit), *WNBP* 7 (1967).

Grzybowski Z. 'Współpraca oddziału NBP z przedsiębiorstwem przemysłowym' (The co-operation between a branch of the NBP and the industrial enterprise), *WNBP* 3 (1962).

Gutowski, A. 'Wskaźnik rentowności czyli kłopoty nieprzygotowanego' (The index of profitability or the confusion of the unprepared), *ŻG* 21 (1967).

Hauvonen, J. J. 'Post war developments in money and banking in Yugoslavia', *IMF Staff Papers* vol. XVII 3 (1970).

Hermanowicz, J. 'Uwagi o kontroli finansowej przedsiębiorstw państwowych' (Some observations on the financial control of state enterprises), *WNBP* 1 (1949).

Hołdys, H. 'Zasady bankowej kontroli funduszu płac' (The principles of bank control of wage funds), *Finanse* 1 (1961).

Horowitz, L. 'Zarządzenia czy umowy' (Orders or contracts), *GP* 4 (1956).

Iwanicki, W. 'Wykonanie finansowe państwowych planów inwestycyjnych' (Financial fulfilment of state investment plans), *SPB* 3 (1948).

Jankowiak, L. 'Kontrola finansowa przedsiębiorstw gospodarki uspołecznionej' (Financial control of socialised enterprises), *RPiE* 1 (1958).

'Przerosty kontroli finansowej' (Excessive financial control), *ŻG* 25 (1956).

'W sprawie przerostów w kontroli finansowej' (On the excesses of financial control), *WNBP* 2 (1957).

Jaslar, M. 'Bankowa notyfikacja umów a legalność działalności inwestycyjnej' (Notification of contracts to banks and the legality of investment), *Finanse* 6 (1961).

'Bodźce w inwestycjach' (Incentives to invest), *Finanse* 9 (1964).

Jaworski, W. 'Automatyzm kredytowy i rozliczeniowy' (Automatism in credit and settlements), *WNBP* 2 (1966).

'Funkcja rozdzielcza kredytu' (The distributive function of credit), *Zeszyty Naukowe SGPiS* 45 (1963).

'Kredytowanie nieprawidłowych potrzeb przedsiębiorstw' (Crediting of incorrect requirements of enterprises), *Finanse* 8 (1961).

'Kryterium płynności a oddziaływanie banku na przedsiębiorstwo' (The test of liquidity as a means of bank control of enterprises), *WNBP* 7 (1967).

'Przyczynek do zagadnienia kontroli bankowej' (A contribution to the debate on bank control), *Finanse* 9 (1958).

'Rola kredytu bankowego w procesie rozliczeń bezgotówkowych' (The role of bank credit in the process of cashless settlements), *Finanse* 5 (1963).

'Rola kredytu krótkoterminowego w finansowaniu drobnych inwestycji' (The role of short-term credit in financing investment), *Finanse* 6 (1955).

'System kredytowy w 15-leciu Polski Ludowej' (The credit system in the 15 years of People's Poland), *Finanse* 7 (1959).

Jaworski, W. and Przywecki, S. 'Bank a samodzielność przedsiębiorstwa' (The bank and the autonomy of the enterprise), *ŻG* 25 (1956).

Jędrychowski, S. 'Bieżąca sytuacja gospodarcza' (The current economic position), *GP* 7 (1961).

Kaczmarek, E. 'Rozwój rozliczeń pieniężnych' (The development of monetary settlements), *WNBP* 2 (1965).

'Rozliczenia między jednostkami gospodarki uspołecznionej' (Settlements between socialist enterprises), *WNBP* 5 (1966).

Kaldor, N. 'The new monetarism', *Lloyds Bank Review* (July 1970).

Karczmar, M. 'O isotocie i funkcjach kredytu socjalistycznego' (The nature and functions of socialist credit), *WNBP* 2 (1955).

'O umocnienie roli kredytu' (The need to strengthen the role of credit), *Finanse* 4 (1954).

'O usprawnienie rozliczeń między przedsiębiorstwami' (The need to improve settlements between enterprises), *Finanse* 1 (1954).

'Problemy reformy systemu kredytowego' (The problems of reforming the credit system), *WNBP* 3 (1957) also in *Finanse* 3 (1957).

Karpiński, Z. 'Organizacja systemu pieniężnego w latach 1945–1950' (The organisation of the monetary system in 1945–1950), *WNBP* 1 (1965).

'Zmiany ustroju pieniężnego w Polsce w okresie miedzy rokiem 1918 a 1950' (Changes in the monetary system of Poland 1918–1950), *WNBP* 12 (1958).

Kazantsev, A. 'O chem govorit praktika postoyanno deistvuyushchikh zachtov' (The implications of the contemporary practice of settlements), *DiK* 4 (1956).

'Voprosy effektivnosti vzaimykh raschotov' (Problems of the efficiency of mutual settlements), *DiK* 10 (1955).

Kieżuń, W. 'Oddziaływanie banku na sytuację gospodarczą i finansową przedsiębiorstw' (On the way the bank influences the economic and financial management of enterprises), *WNBP* 5 (1965).

Kostowski, M. L. 'Aktualne zagadnienia systemu kredytowego' (The current problems of the credit system), *WNBP* 1 (1957).

'NBP w latach organizacji systemu bankowego' (The NBP during the period of the organisation of the banking system), *WNBP* 1 (1965).

'Nowe zasady kredytowe' (The new credit principles), *Finanse* 1 (1952).

'Zagadnienie przeterminowanych zobowiązań i należności fakturowych' (The problem of overdue trade debts and credits), *WNBP* 12 (1952).

'Założenia nowej instrukcji kredytowej' (Provisions of the new credit instruction), *WNBP* 1 (1951).

'Zasady systemu kredytowego' (The principles of the credit system), *ŻG* 2 (1951).

'Znaczenie nowej kolejności regulowania zobowiązań płatniczych' (The implications of the new order of settling debts), *WNBP* 6 (1956).

Krzak, M. and Zaczek, T. 'Jak usprawnić finansowanie inwestycji' (How to improve the finance of investment), *ŻG* 8 (1965).

Kucharski, M. 'Czy zapasy hamują rozwój' (Do stocks impede growth), *ŻG* 16 (1960).

'Ku czemu zmierza reforma systemu kredytowego' (The aim of the reform of the credit system), *WNBP* 9 (1957).

Kunicki, M. 'Rozwój inwestycji szybkorentujących się' (The development of quick-yield investments), *WNBP* 2 (1962).

Kurowski, S. J. 'Demokracja i prawo wartości' (Democracy and the law of value), *Kierunki* 14 (1956).

'Rynek i plan' (The market and the plan), *TL* (6 Feb. 1957).

'Model a cele gospodarki narodowej' (The model and the objectives of national management), *ŻG* 7, 12 (1957).

Landau, Z. 'Banki i kredyt Polski Ludowej w roku 1944' (Banking and credit in People's Poland in 1944), *WNBP* 10 (1964).

Lange, O. 'Rozwój gospodarczy Polski Ludowej w latach 1945–1954' (Economic development of People's Poland 1945–1954), *Ekonomista* 3 (1954).

Laskowski, L. 'Program polityki kadrowej w NBP' (NBP staffing policy), *WNBP* 1 (1959).

'Zagadnienie kadr w pietnastoletnim rozwoju NBP' (Staff problems in the fifteen years of the NBP's development) *WNBP* 6 (1960).

Lenczewski, J. 'Kredytowanie przedsiębiorstw w rachunku bieżącym' (Current account crediting of enterprises), *WNBP* 5 (1962).

Lipiński, E. 'O przedmiocie ekonomii i prawach ekonomicznych' (Economics and economic laws), *Ekonomista* 5 (1956).

Lissowski, W. 'Problem inwestycyjnej samodzielności przedsiębiorstwa przemysłowego' (The problem of the investment autonomy of the industrial enterprise), *GP* 4 (1959).

Lissowski, W. and Baran, S. 'O szybką i gruntowną zmianę systemu planowania i finansowania inwestycji i remontów' (The need for a quick change in planning and finance of investment), *GP* 12 (1956).

Machowski, W. 'Stopa procentowa od kredytów w rolnictwie' (Interest charges on agricultural credit), *WNBP* 11 (1968).

Madej, Z. 'Hierarchia kryteriów' (The hierarchy of criteria), *ŻG* 26 (1963).

Majewski, S. 'Reforma Bankowości' (The reform of banking), *Finanse* 8 (1969).

'Zadania NBP w roku 1966' (NBP's tasks in 1966), *WNBP* 1 (1966).

'Zmiany zasad finansowania inwestycji' (Changes in the principles of investment finance), *GP* 8 (1969).

Malesa, R. 'Bankowa kontrola funduszu płac' (Bank control of wage funds), *WNBP* 12 (1957).

'Krztaltowanie się należności i zobowiązań inkasowych w okresie lat 1954–1956' (Changes in the structure of trade debts and credits in 1954–1956), *WNBP* 7 (1957).

'Rozwój działalności kredytowej NBP w ostatnich dwóch latach' (The development of the NBP in the last two years), *WNBP* 8 (1957).

Malesa, R. and Sikora, S. 'Zmiany w bankowej kontroli funduszu płac' (Changes in bank control of wage funds), *WNBP* 9 (1958).

Mazur J. 'Jak usprawnić system bankowej obsługi rozliczeń pieniężnych' (How to improve bank servicing of settlements), *WNBP* 8 (1960).

Michejda, R. 'O ewolucji organizacji i kontrolnej funkcji kredytu' (The evolution of organisation and control function of credit), *WNBP* 8 (1963).

'Uwagi na temat obecnego systemu finansowania inwestycji' (A comment on the present system of financing investment), *WNBP* 6 (1969).

'Warunki skutecznego działania kredytu bankowego w praktyce' (Prerequisites of effective credit action in practice), *Rocznik Ekonomiczny* 1961 (1962).

'Warunki zwiększenia roli kredytu' (Conditions for enhancing the role of credit), *WNBP* 3 (1969).

Miłkowski, W. 'Bankowa obsługa budżetu państwa i ministestw w latach 1945–1951' (Bank servicing of the budget and ministries in 1945–1951), *WNBP* 3 (1965).

'Współudział NBP w kontroli wykonania budżetu państwa' (The share of NBP in the control of the fulfilment of budgetary targets), *WNBP* 2 (1953).

Minc, H. 'Sześcioletni plan rozwoju gospodarczego i budowy podstaw socjalizmu w Polsce' (SYP of economic development and the building of socialist foundations in Poland), *ND* 4 (1950).

'Zadania gospodarcze na 1951 rok' (Economic targets for 1951), *ND* 1 (1951).

Misiak, M. 'Aktualne problemy reformy metod planowania i zarządzania' (Current problems of the reform of the methods of planning and management), *ND* 9 (1966).

'Bankowcy o analizie kosztów' (Bankers on the analysis of costs), *ŻG* 50 (1964).

'Dyrektywne fikcje' (The fiction of directives), *ŻG* 38 (1959).

'Naczynia niepołączone' (Unconnected vessels), *ŻG* 38 (1964).

'Sprzeczności bodźców' (Conflicting incentives), *ŻG* 12 (1961).

'600 miliardow czeka na oprocentowanie' (600 billion awaits the imposition of interest rates), *ŻG* 41 (1964).

Mitel'man, E. 'Razvitie printsipov pryamogo bankovskogo kreditovaniya' (The development of the principles of direct bank credit), *DiK* 5 (1970).

Nagler, G. 'Rekonstruktsiya kredita i kreditnoi sistemy' (The reform of credit and the credit system), *Vestnik Finansov* 1 (1930).

Napiórkowski, R. 'Gra zapasy-inwestycje' (The interplay between stocks and investment), *ŻG* 31 (1969).

'Kilka uwag na temat funkcjonowania aktualnego systemu finansowania przedsiębiorstw' (Comments on the functioning of the present system of financing enterprises), *GP* 11 (1968).

'Niektóre aspekty kredytowego oddziaływania banku' (Some aspects of credit policy of the bank), *WNBP* 9 (1966).

'Pozaekonomiczne srodki oddziaływania NBP' (Non-economic means of action by NBP), *WNBP* 1 (1968).

'Samofinansowanie a niektóre problemy kredytowania i kontroli przedsiębiorstw' (Self-finance and problems of crediting and control of enterprises), *WNBP* 9 (1968).

'W sprawie syntetycznych mierników ekonomicznych' (On synthetic economic indicators), *Finanse* 2 (1969).

Niemski, K. 'Bank Rolny w swietle bilansów rocznych' (The AB in the light of the annual balance sheet), *WNBP* 7 (1962).

Nowakowski, L. 'O właściwe ustawienie bankowej kontroli płac' (The need to restructure bank control of wages), *WNBP* 9 (1957).

Orłowski, M. 'Bank i kontrola finansowa' (The bank and its financial control), *WNBP* 5 (1946).

'Gospodarka planowa a sektor prywatno-gospodarczy' (The private sector in a planned economy), *WNBP* 11 (1946).

Osiecki, M. 'Proporcje między przyrostem zapasów a składnikami dochodu narodowego' (Ratios of the rise in stocks and the components of national income), *WNBP* 12 (1964).

'Przyrost zapasów a dochód narodowy w Polsce' (Increases in stocks and the national income in Poland), *GP* 6 (1967).

'Zapasy gospodarczo nieuzasadnione' (Economically unjustified stockbuilding), *WNBP* 9 (1965).

'Zapasy gospodarczo nieuzasadnione w latach 1962–1964' (Economically unjustified stocks in 1962–1964), *WNBP* 9 (1965).

Paszynski, A. 'Odwrócony porządek' (Reverse order), *Polityka* 43 (1963).

Pawlak, M. 'System kredytowy a rozliczenia' (The credit system and settlements), *Finanse* 3 (1964).

Pessel', M. 'O funktsiyakh kredita' (On the functions of credit), *DiK* 4 (1964).

Pessel', M. and Shraiber, I. 'Nazrevshie voprosy kreditovaniya i raschotov' (The most pressing problems of credit and settlements), *DiK* 5 (1963).

Pirożyński, 'Budżet państwa podstawowym planem finansowym PRL' (The state budget as the basic financial plan of the People's Poland), *Finanse* 4 (1954).

Płocica, A. 'Jeden czy dwa poziomy cen' (One or two price levels), *Finanse* 1 (1965).

'Na co czekają zjednoczenia' (What are the associations waiting for), *ŻG* 21 (1959).

Popkiewicz, J. 'Biurokracja czy rynek' (Bureaucracy or the market), *ŻG* 16 (1957).

'Prawdziwa rentowność' (True profitability) *TL* (5 Jan. 1957).

Pruss, W. 'Nowa instrukcja kredytowania działalności przedsiębiorstw uspołecznionych' (The new regulation on crediting socialised enterprises), *WNBP* 1 (1962).

'Organ władzy czy pomocy' (Unit of power or service), *ŻG* 21 (1963).

'Kredyt i rozliczenia pieniężne przedsiębiorstw uspołecznionych' (Credit and settlements of socialised enterprises), *WNBP* 7 (1965).

'Rozliczenia między przedsiębiorstwami uspołecznionymu i ich kredytowanie' (Settlements between socialist enterprises and their crediting), *WNBP* 1 (1961).

'Zmiany w systemie kredytowania działalności eksploatacyjnej przedsiębiorstw uspołecznionych' (Changes in crediting of working capital of socialist enterprises), *Finanse* 2 (1958).

'Zmienność potrzeb kredytowych przedsiębiorstwa' (Fluctuations in the demand for credit in an enterprise), *WNBP* 5 (1965).

Przyborowska, K. and Zachwieja, F. 'Problemy funkcjonowania nowego systemu finansowego przedsiębiorstw' (Problems of the working of the new financial system of enterprises), *WNBP* 10 (1967).

Przywecki, S. 'Niektóre problemy dotyczące finansowania inwestycji' (Some problems of investment finance), *WNBP* 4 (1959).

'Niektóre problemy inwestycji przedsiębiorstw na przełomie roku 1960/1961' (Some problems of investment finance 1960/1961), *WNBP* 1 (1961).

Radecki, J. 'Zapasy w przedsiębiorstwach uspołecznionych' (Stockbuilding in socialised enterprises), *Wiadomości Statystyczne* 8 (1971).

Radetskii, F. 'Bankovskii kontrol' i ego zadachi v protsesie rekonstruktsii kredita' (Bank control and its tasks during the reform of credit), *Vestnik Finansov* 2 (1930).

Rajczyk, M. 'Kredyt płatniczy' (Payments credit), *WNBP* 8 (1966).

'Wysokość kredytów przyznanych przedsiębiorstwu jako element kredytowej działalnosci banku' (Amount of credit as an element in bank control of enterprises), *WNBP* 3 (1967).

'Propozycje uelastycznienia techniki kredytowania przedsiębiorstw' (Proposals to make crediting of enterprises more flexible), *WNBP* 7 (1967).

Rejman, F. 'W sprawie branżowego banku rolnego' (On the specialised agricultural bank), *ŻG* 4 (1957).

Saidak, Z. 'Inwestycyjny półmetek' (Halfway mark in investment), *ŻG* 33 (1963).

'Kredytować czy usprawniać' (To credit or to improve), *ŻG* 15 (1965).

'Rola banków w realizacji inwestycji' (The role of banks in carrying out of investment), *ŻG* 41 (1960).

'Zalety i wady inwestycji zdecentralizowanych' (Pros and cons of decentralised investment), *ŻG* 21 (1959).

'Zamrożone miliardy' (Frozen billions), *ŻG* 1 (1962).

Sawicz, T. 'O oddziaływaniu bankowym' (On bank action), *WNBP* 5 (1967).

Sayers, R. S. 'Monetary thought and monetary policy in England', *Economic Journal* (December 1960).

Secomski, K. 'Dynamika i kierunki wzrostu' (The dynamics and the course of growth), *Ekonomista* 6 (1970).

'Na przełomie dwóch planów pięcioletnich' (On the eve of the next five year plan), *WNBP* 7 (1965).

Shvarts, G. 'Ekonomicheskaya osnova vzaimykh raschotov' (The economic foundation of mutual settlements), *DiK* 4 (1956).

Siemiątkowski, L. 'Czy normatyw jest przydatny' (Is the normative useful), *ŻG* 40 (1964).

'Ekonomiczne problemy bankowej klasyfikacji zapasów' (Economic problems of bank classification of stocks), *WNBP* 9 (1965).

'O systemie finansowym zjednoczeń i przedsiębiorstw przemysłu kluczowego' (On the financial system of associations and enterprises in key industries), *WNBP* 6 (1968).

'Przesłanki, cele, i zadania obecnej reformy bankowej' (Reasons, objectives, and tasks of the present bank reform), *WNBP* 11 (1969).

'Reforma bankowa' (Bank reform), *Rocznik Polityczny i Gospodarczy* (1969).

'Zadania banku w zakresie opiniowania planu inwestycyjnego' (The bank's duties in giving counsel on the investment plan), *BiK* 11 (1970).

Slipko, W. 'Zbędna i kosztowna praca' (Superfluous and costly effort), *ŻG* 15 (1963).

Szarota, R. 'Rozwój systemu finansowania inwestycji' (The development of the system of financing investment), *Finanse* 7 (1964).

Szczepański, J. 'Próba oceny efektywności polityki finansowania' (An attempt to assess the effectiveness of financial policy), *Zeszyty Naukowe SGPiS* 45 (1963).

Sztajer, K. 'Z polskich zagadnień walutowych okresu odbudowy gospodarczej 1944–1949' (Polish monetary problems in the period of economic reconstruction 1944–1949), *Finanse* 5 (1957).

Sztyber, W. 'Funkcjonowanie nowego systemu cen' (The functioning of the new price system), *Ekonomista* 3 (1969).

Szymczak, Z. 'W sprawie finansowania inwestycji z zakresu modernizacji i mechanizacji' (On financing of investment leading to modernisation and mechanisation), *MG* 8 (1957).

Szymot, B. 'Podstawowe założenia wykonania budżetu państwa przez bank centralny' (Basic principles of budget servicing by the central bank), *RPEiS* 1 (1962).

Szyndler-Głowacki, W. 'Inwestycje' (Investment), *ND* 3 (1966).

Szyr, E. 'Niektóre zagadnienia walki o realizację planu gospodarczego na 1950 rok' (Some problems of the struggle for fulfilment of the economic plan for 1950), *ND* 4 (1950).

'O roli zjednoczenia i przedsiębiorstwa' (The role of the association and the enterprise), *ND* 6 (1964).

Szyrocki, J. 'O Biurach Wzajemnych Rozliczeń' (On BMS), *Finanse* 1 (1954).

'System kredytowy może być prosty' (The credit system can be simple), *ŻG* 21 (1957).

Szyszko, L. 'Cele i metody polityki kredytowania' (Aims and methods of credit policy), *Finanse* 12 (1965).

'Kilka uwag na temat dyskusji w sprawie reformy polskiego systemu kredytowego' (Some observations on the reform of the Polish credit system), *Zeszyty Naukowe SGPiS* 35 (1961).

Toeplitz, J. 'Co z tą samodzielnością?' (What about this self-management?) *ŻG* 18 (1959).

'Na co czekają przedsiębiorstwa?' (What are enterprises waiting for?), *ŻG* 20 (1959).

'Narada plus skargi' (Consultations plus complaints), *ŻG* 47 (1960).

Trendota, J. 'Jak usprawnić system finansowy przedsiębiorstw' (How to improve the financial system of enterprises), *ŻG* 51 (1964).

'Kierunki dalszego doskonalenia systemu finansowego przemysłu' (The direction of further improvement of the financial system of industry), *Finanse* 8 (1969).

'Warunki sprawności systemu finansowego' (Requisites of an efficient financial system), *ND* 6 (1964).

'IV Plenum KC PZPR i zadania aparatu finansowego' (IV Plenary session of CC PUWP and the tasks of the financial apparatus), *Finanse* 10 (1965).

Tymowski, A. 'Znaczenie kontroli bankowej w gospodarce socjalistycznej' (The importance of bank control in a socialist economy), *ŻG* 24 (1951).

Wierzbicki, J. 'Finansowanie inwestycji zdecentralizowanych' (Financing decentralised investment), *Finanse* 9 (1965).

'Zagadnienia samodzielności finansowej przedsiębiorstw państwowych' (Problem of the financial autonomy of state enterprises), *RPiE* 1 (1960).

'Zapasy w gospodarce polskiej w latach ostatnich' (Stocks in the Polish economy in recent years), *WNBP* 1 (1963).

Wierzbicki, K. 'Bank a przedsiębiorstwo' (The bank and the enterprise), *ŻG* 11 (1963).

Winter, E. 'Akumulacja finansowa w latach 1955–1960' (Financial accumulation in 1955–1960), *Finanse* 7 (1964).

'W jakim kierunku zreformować system finansowy przedsiębiorstw' (How to reform the financial system of enterprises), *Finanse* 1 (1960).

Wojciechowska, U. 'Czynniki określające fundusz rozwoju' (Determinants of the development fund), *Finanse* 8 (1961).

'Fundusz rozwoju przedsiębiorstwa przemysłowego' (The development fund of the industrial enterprise), *ND* 9 (1966).

Wołowczyk, A. 'Bankowa kontrola inwestycji' (Bank control of investment), *Finanse* 9 (1961).

'Czy i jak kredytować inwestycje' (Whether and how to credit investment), *Finanse* 6 (1965).

'Kierunki zmian finansowania inwestycji' (The course of changes in investment financing), *ŻG* 30 (1969).

'Nowy system finansowania inwestycji' (New system of investment finance), *ŻG* 38 (1969).

'Nowe zasady finansowania inwestycji' (New principles of investment finance), *Finanse* 7 (1969).

'Realia i utopie finansowania inwestycji' (Fact and fiction in the finance of investment), *ŻG* 7 (1964).

Wołowczyk, A. and Zaczek, T. 'Kierunki usprawnień działalności inwestycyjnej' (Ways of improving investment activity), *Finanse* 8 (1964).

Wyczałkowski, M. R. 'Polityka pieniężna i kontrola finansowa w gospodarce planowej' (Monetary policy and financial control in a planned economy), *WNBP* 3 (1946).

Wyszomirski, T. 'Problemy kredytowania indywidualnych gospodarstw rolnych' (Problems of crediting peasant farms), *WNBP* 5 (1968).

Zakharov, V. 'O beznalichnykh raschotakh' (On cashless settlements), *DiK* 5 (1970).

Zamoyski, F. 'Niekonsekwentne sankcje' (Unfair sanctions), *ŻG* 20 (1963).

Ząbkowicz, L. 'Przedsiębiorstwo a zjednoczenie w ramach systemu zarządzania przemysłem' (The enterprise and the association in the framework of industrial management), *GP* 10 (1968).

Żebrowski, A. 'Dwadzieścia lat działalności NBP' (Twenty years of NBP's activity), *WNBP* 7 (1964).

'Nasze zadania w roku 1962' (Our tasks in 1962), *WNBP* 1 (1962).

'Zadania NBP w roku 1964' (NBP's tasks in 1964), *WNBP* 2 (1964).

'Bank a przedsiębiorstwo' (The bank and the enterprise), *ŻG* 8 (1964).

Znaniecki, M. 'Funkcjonowanie kredytu płatniczego' (The functioning of payments credit), *WNBP* 1 (1964).

'Krytyczne uwagi o inkasowej formie rozliczeń' (Critical comments on the inkaso method of settlements), *WNBP* 4 (1967).

'Niektóre zagadnienia funkcjonowania nowego systemu finansowego' (Some problems of the working of the new financial system), *WNBP* 11 (1966).

Zwass, A. 'Ewolucja kierunkow kontroli bankowej' (The evolution of the aims of bank control), *WNBP* 10 (1963).

'Propozycje usprawnienia systemu rozliczeń' (Proposals for improving the system of settlements), *WNBP* 8 (1962).

Zweig, F. 'Nowe drogi przemysłu polskiego' (New ways of Polish industry), *Ekonomista Polski* (London) 3 (1943).

Index

functions of (1948–54), 115–18
functions of (1955–68), 190, 237, 280, 310, 316, 327
amalgamation with NBP (1969), 328, 330, 333, 338
IRF, *see* Investment and repairs fund

Jankowiak, L., 158, 159
Jaworski, W., 148, 198, 260, 274

Karczmar, M., 130, 147
Kostowski, L., 140, 208
Kronrod, Ya. A., 43
Kucharski, M., 102, 126, 163
Kwiatkowski, E., 59, 70, 71

Lange, O., 105n, 167, 168, 169n
Lenient monetary (credit) control (policy), 241, 248–71, 303–6, 323, 346, 350
Lenin, V. I., 18, 19–20, 38, 46–7, 113
Letters of credit (*akredytywa*), 36n, 132, 171
Liberal credit policy, 127, 129, 132, 145, 151, 274, *see also* Credit automatism
Liabilities (of banks), 81, 125, 192, 298–9, 329, 331, 363–4

Majewski, S., 287, 301, 303
Marx, K., 18, 19
Michejda, R., 272, 320
Ministry of Industry and Trade (MIT), 95, 96, 97, 98, 115
Misiak, M., 266, 268
MIT, *see* Ministry of Industry and Trade
Monetary control,
concept of, 3–12 *passim*, 50
and 'real bills' theory, 12–17
in the West, 6–8, 8–12 *passim*, 224–5, 226, 252
Soviet (or Soviet-type), 50–7, 222–6, 343, 344–51
and inflation, 32, 54–5, 149, 207, 222–4, 225, 275
in Poland, 69–71, 104, 149, 152, 153, 156–63 *passim*, 222–6 *passim*, 343, 344–51, *see also* Lenient monetary control *and* Stringent monetary control
Monetary theory,
'real bills' theory, *see* 'Real bills' theory
Socialist, 42–3, 156, 271–7, *see also* Monetary control
Western, 6–8, 222, 224–6, 275, 344
Mono-bank, 118–19, 330
Municipal banks, 68, 83, 86, 115–18 *passim*

Napiórkowski, R., 267, 271, 293n
National Bank of Poland (NBP),
branches of, table 9, p. 84, 124, 192, 333, 368–9

creation of, 80–1, 336
functions of (1945–8), 81–4 *passim*, 92, 93–4, 96, 97, 100–4
functions of (1949–54), 109, 115–35, 141, 142, 143, 146, 153, 160, 162, 337
functions of (1955–68), 175, 176, 177, 189, 190, 191, 192, 205, 228, 231, 235, 238, 280, 282, 294–9
functions of (after 1969 reform), 327–34, 338, 339–40, 354
National Economic Bank (NEB),
abolition of, 115
and credit policy, 66, 71
and finance of investment, 64–6
functions (1930s), 62–7, 336, 339
functions (1946–8), 83, 84, 85, 102
origin of, 61–2
NBP, *see* National Bank of Poland,
NEB, *see* National Economic Bank,
NEP, *see* New Economic Policy,
New Economic Policy (NEP), 20–3, 25, 28, 35, 338
Normative (of working capital), 33, 41–2, 86, 95, 96, 104, 122, 151, 160, 198–203, 204, 208, 270, 290, 299–300, 301, 305
compulsory partial coverage by credit of, 200, 201–2, 246–7, 253
finance of, 42, 96, 122, 160, 199–203, 208

Order of payments (settlements), 131–2, 138, 172–3, 196
Overdue bank credit, 125, 126–7, 129, 130–1, 148, 151, 171, 193, 219, 220, 253, 255, 259, 262, 304, 305
Overdue (illicit) trade credit, 137–45, 149, 151, 157, 162, 171, 172, 173, 194, 196, 197, 198, 209, 213, 216–21, 225, 226, 257–60, 264, 267, 271–7 *passim*, 304–6, 348–51
Overdue trade indebtedness, *see* Overdue trade credit *above*

Payments blockages, 141–3, 146, 151, 223, 262, 349, *see also* payments difficulties,
Payments (financial) difficulties, 145, 150, 151, 198, 205, 209, 218, 221, 250, 254–6, 275–6, 349, *see also* Payments blockages *and* Overdue trade credit
PC, *see* Planning Commission
PCNL, *see* Polish Committee for National Liberation
Planning Commission (PC), 180, 184, 216, 236, 242, 243, 283, 287, 292
Polish Committee for National Liberation (PCNL), 76, 80, 82
Postal Savings Bank, 67, 71, 86, 116
Principle of differentiation, 170–1, 194, 210, 256